RISING FROM GROUND ZERO

GREGORY P. SHEA, PAUL BROWN, ANDRÉ KOTZÉ
with LAUREN STARKEY

RISING FROM GROUND ZERO

9/11 and the FDNY's Path through Crisis to Transformation

GREGORY P. SHEA, PAUL BROWN, ANDRÉ KOTZÉ
with LAUREN STARKEY

DE GRUYTER

ISBN 978-3-11-224720-4
e-ISBN 978-3-11-224721-1 (PDF)
e-ISBN 978-3-11-224722-8 (E-PUB)
DOI https://doi.org/10.1515/9783112247211

Library of Congress Control Number: 2026940652

Bibliographic information published by the Deutsche Nationalbibliothek
The Deutsche Nationalbibliothek lists this publication in the Deutsche Nationalbibliografie; detailed bibliographic data are available on the internet at http://dnb.dnb.de.

De Gruyter and Walter de Gruyter GmbH are part of De Gruyter Brill.
www.degruyterbrill.com

Questions about General Product Safety Regulation:
productsafety@degruyterbrill.com

Original Photograph: Ozgur Donmaz
Cover Image & Design: Lara Andrea Taber
Book Design & Typesetting: Lara Andrea Taber

“To the fallen, those who continue to fall, and those who live with the memories.

—Greg, Paul, and André

“To Iris, my wife, and to Emmy and Meredith, our daughters, for lovingly helping me to rise from the ground zero of cancer ... and to newly arrived courageous Colton.

—Greg

“To my family, my wife Rita Marie, children Adeline, Matthew and Margaret, for loving and inspiring me always. To Ray Brown Sr., a great role model and the inspiration behind my becoming a firefighter.

—Paul

“To Joyce Hartpence for helping and incubating something eight years in the making. I love you.

—André

Advance Praise for *Rising from Ground Zero*

Rising from Ground Zero is a masterful account of the response of New York firefighters to the calamitous events of 9/11 and the later rebuilding of their decimated ranks. Drawing on depth interviews with those who rushed to the World Trade Center on that fateful day, Greg Shea, Paul Brown, André Kotzé, and Lauren Starkey provide a graphic and compelling account of the firefighters' "lived experience" and the enduring lessons for crisis leadership at its best.

—***Michael Useem****, Professor of Management Emeritus, Wharton School, University of Pennsylvania, and author of* The Leadership Moment

Rising from Ground Zero: 9/11 and the FDNY's Path through Crisis to Transformation belongs on every leader's bookshelf. It presents FDNY responder, on the ground, personal stories of 9/11 and what followed. Moving and inspiring, it is a story of crisis, endurance, and healing. It is also a story of transformation, of how to transform even the most elite of organizations. Any leader navigating stormy seas or facing the daunting task of organizational renewal should read *Rising from Ground Zero* - carefully.

—***Admiral James Stavridis****, 16th Supreme Allied Commander of NATO and author of* 2084: A Novel of Future War

Rising from Ground Zero preserves what must never be lost: the lived truth of those who answered the call on September 11 and in the long decades since then. Some books inform. *Rising from Ground Zero* transforms. The unvarnished words of the 9/11 FDNY responders show us what leadership looks like when the ground itself gives way. This book is honest, humane, and quietly devastating. Read it slowly. Listen to the people's voices, their pain, their grief, their strength and their hope. If you lead anyone – a team, a company, a family – open this book, let these firefighters speak, and take to heart what only they can teach us.

—***Annie Mckee**, bestselling author and leadership expert; co-author of* Primal Leadership

A deeply human account of 9/11 and its aftermath, told by those who lived it. *Rising from Ground Zero* is as much about leadership, trust, and resilience as it is about tragedy – and offers enduring lessons for anyone leading through crisis.

—***Laura Kavanagh**, 34th FDNY Commissioner (Ret.), Distinguished Visiting Urbanist, New York University*

A powerful and fully immersive narrative, *Rising From Ground Zero* chronicles the most tragic event in the storied history of the FDNY. Through a gripping reconstruction of that fateful day – and the critical decisions that followed – the book offers a rare window into leadership under extreme pressure.

Drawing on firsthand accounts and rigorous analysis, the authors illuminate the sacrifice, bravery, and resilience of one of the world's premier first responder organizations. Both a tribute and a study in crisis management, *Rising From Ground Zero* is essential reading for leaders and aspiring professionals across public safety, government, the military, and beyond.

—***John Sudnik**, FDNY Chief of Department (2018–2021)*

This is the go-to book for firefighters and leaders – the definitive FDNY 9/11 book. This is the story of the survivors and leaders who brought the FDNY though unfathomable disaster and led the department into the future. Everyone who is or wants to be a leader should read this book, put themselves into an FDNY leader's shoes, and answer the authors' "whisper in your ear" question. It's the book every firefighter coming on the job over the next hundred years should read.

—***Vincent Dunn***, *FDNY Deputy Chief (ret.), author of* Collapse of Burning Buildings

This book brings it home: the horror, the camaraderie, the heroism, and the lessons of that fateful day and after. From interviews and quotes of those involved, the intensity, heartbreak and courage are palpable. From the leadership reflections on the events, the wisdom and learnings we all can take from the FDNY are pivotal.

—***Mark Turner***, *Former CEO and Executive Chair, WSFS Bank, author of* The Path to Sustained Excellence

Rising from Ground Zero is multi-layered and each layer has critical elements that contribute to the whole. First is the emotional first-person account of that seminal day in American history September 11, 2001 when America changed forever. As you hear the firefighters and other first responders relate their story, you weep and feel their pain, and you also remember every moment of that day. The next layer is a realization of the training and command structure that allows large organizations like the New York City Fire Department, the military and others to function, even when they have been decapitated of leadership. Next, comes the leadership lessons and what we see is how well-trained women and men respond, adapt, and prevail in the most difficult situations imaginable. This is a book to be read, meditated upon and experienced. Well done.

—***Thomas E. Beeman***, *PhD, LHD (hon), LFACHE, FCPP Rear Admiral (U), US Navy*

Most books about 9/11 ask us to remember. *Rising from Ground Zero* asks us to learn, and that is much harder. Shea, Brown, and Kotze have made the FDNY's story useful without making it smaller or less personal. The firefighters speak in their own words, and what emerges is not a monument but a manual for any leader who has ever had to rebuild something while it was still on fire. But the lessons cut deeper than crisis leadership. After 9/11, a fantastic fire department transformed itself into a modernemergency management agency. That is exactly the challenge facing healthcare: to transform from smart, caring providers of care into a modern health assurance system. This book shows us the way.

—***Stephen K. Klasko****, MD, MBA, Executive in Residence, General Catalyst; former President & CEO, Jefferson Health*

What an incredible book! It transports you back to 9/11 and into the hearts and minds of the firefighters. Truly a page-turning read. I hope that every management PhD student reads this book to see what top of class research looks like. *Rising from Ground Zero* deftly presents a multiple decade, carefully researched case study in the words of the people who lived the case. The lessons matter in their own right, but the depth of research centers and grounds the book. It is a case study of how to construct a case study. The book lays out poignant, concrete advice for any leader facing acute crisis, prolonged hard times, or organizational change. Leaders will find many invaluable, to-the-point takeaways here.

—***R. Edward Freeman****, Bachand University Professor, The Darden School, University of Virginia*

9/11 devastated the FDNY. Starting with the events of that day, this work delivers a truly unique account of how the FDNY reacted, adapted, and implemented sustainable change in the years following. Telling the story through first-person accounts and ample documentary evidence, the book reveals the closeness of connections between personal lives and organization and offers insights applicable to more ordinary days.

Abstract concepts like organizational commitment, trust in leadership, and collaboration so often get measured with a few survey items. Understandably so. But constructs like those are nowhere more real and vivid than in this book.

—***R.A. Guzzo****, Workforce Sciences Institute (co-president); co-editor,* Psychology and Economics of Work: Interdisciplinarity for Theory and Practice

Rising from Ground Zero will matter to the FDNY community, to leadership scholars, and to anyone who has ever wondered what it looks like when ordinary people find extraordinary reserves of purpose in the worst moments of their lives. It ascribes meaning to the leadership lessons distilled from lived experience.

—***Mukul Pandya****, founding editor-in-chief of* Knowledge@Wharton

Drawing on personal vignettes from New York firefighters, the authors capture both heroism and humanity on a day that redefined a generation of first responders. While poignant and heart-rending, this book also offers powerful lessons for how high-performing organizations confront unimaginable circumstances and emerge stronger.

—***Michele L. Malvesti****, PhD, former senior counterterrorism official on the National Security Council staff at the White House*

An inspiring and informative read for anyone interested in leadership under uncertainty, crisis management, and the power of continuous learning to create sustained change. This compelling book traces the FDNY's journey through crisis and renewal, honoring the voices of the leaders that built a stronger, more resilient department while preserving its heart and soul.

—***Todd Henshaw****, LTC US Army (R), former Academy Professor and Director of Leadership at United States Military Academy (West Point); Senior Fellow Wharton Center for Leadership and Change Management*

Rising from Ground Zero presents one of the most important stories of our generation. The legacy of the book and the way the authors constructed it will live on long past its authors. This is a masterclass in letting the firefighters of 9/11 tell their story, in their own words, while also helping the rest of us glean learnings from their lived experiences. The book treats the firefighters of the FDNY not merely as subjects but as teachers who found a way to keep learning in the aftermath of the worst days in the department's history. Through nearly ninety hours of interviews with the men and women who were there, Shea, Brown, and Kotze have done what the best instructor cadres do: they have surfaced the tacit knowledge that would otherwise die with the operators who hold it. That is not a small thing. That is the whole thing. Read this book. Then go tell someone the story.

—***Preston B. Cline, Ed.D.***, *Co-Founder, Mission Critical Team Institute; Senior Fellow, Center for Leadership and Change Management, The Wharton School, University of Pennsylvania*

Rising from Ground Zero is a rare, inside look at how a world class, purpose driven organization chose to evolve its culture and improve rather than rest on its reputation. Through the FDNY's own voices, you see an accomplished, proud, tradition bound department confront unimaginable loss and rethink how it leads, learns, and cares for its people – guided always by its mission to save lives and protect one another. For leaders facing culture change, this is an unflinching, practical study in aligning structures and behaviors with a clear sense of purpose under the most demanding conditions imaginable.

—***Colonel Russell Williford***, *USAF (Ret), leader of multiple successful Air Force-wide organizational culture change transformations*

From an operational and leadership perspective, this book is a fantastic debrief of the incident and post-incident organizational change that any leader in an emergency services organization should read. As a first responder, I found the personal stories and vignettes from the responders especially impactful. A team of first responders without a strong organizational culture and ethos is just a collection of trained individuals who share a location during a shift. There are plenty of lessons to be learned from what went well and not-so-well during the massive 9/11 response, but this book is an inspirational testament to the first responders out there that when an organization's leaders instill a sense of duty, team belonging, and shared mission and purpose, those responders will rise to the occasion as a team and navigate the unthinkable with courage.

—***Michael Carunchio****, NRP (Paramedic), host of* The World's Okayest Medic Podcast

The lessons learned from the FDNY's response on and after 9/11/01 are universally applicable, demonstrating that the strength of an organization in crisis is forged in the values it establishes long before the event. Nowhere is this more evident than in the raw and resolute voices of the FDNY personnel who lived it. Shea, Brown, and Kotze offer an unprecedented look at how the FDNY's storied history, paramilitary structure, and deep-rooted brotherhood created a foundation that held when everything else gave way. The narrative reveals how culture and character take over when even the most rigorous planning is eclipsed by the unthinkable. It is a necessary piece of our national history that captures the heart of public service and the extraordinary lengths to which our first responders go to protect their fellow countrymen. I encourage you to read this slowly – it will undoubtedly touch you. You should therefore proceed with the care and attention that the book deserves. *Rising from Ground Zero* is essential reading for everyone, especially every American.

—***Guy Barber****, MPH, FACHE, NREMT-P, Air Medical Executive & EMS Educator, Strategic Specialist in Healthcare Operations & Emergency Systems*

Even though many of us believe we already know the story of 9/11, *Rising From Ground Zero: 9/11 and the FDNY's Path through Crisis to Transformation* offers a vivid and compelling account drawn from the firsthand experiences of brave individuals who lived through the attacks on New York City and the difficult days that followed. The authors do far more than preserve an important oral history. They reconstruct the timeline of events with remarkable detail and, just as importantly, distill the critical lessons learned from one of the most consequential tragedies in modern American history.

This is a must-read for first responders, emergency managers, and public officials, as well as military, intelligence, and government leaders charged with leading large, complex organizations through crisis, uncertainty, and transformational change. While 9/11 may seem like distant history to some, the lessons of that day – leadership, resilience, preparedness, and unity in crisis – are as timely and relevant today as ever.

—***W.R. Gade****, U.S. Army (retired) and Intelligence Community senior leader*

What makes *Rising from Ground Zero* especially compelling is its authenticity. The result is a powerful and deeply personal account of one of the most challenging periods in the history of the FDNY. The book demonstrates how initiative, experience, and problem-solving at every level of the organization combined with strategic direction and vision from leadership.

One of the book's greatest strengths is that it does more than recount history. The authors thoughtfully draw leadership and organizational lessons from each chapter, helping readers connect these experiences to challenges they may face in their own professions and lives.

Rising from Ground Zero is a story of tragedy, recovery, leadership, and resilience. Most importantly, it is a story about people, ordinary people who faced extraordinary circumstances and stepped up. I am grateful that their stories have been captured so thoughtfully and preserved for future generations.

—***Frank Leeb****, retired FDNY Deputy Assistant Chief, firefighter in FDNY Squad 270 on 9/11/2001*

I'm a retired San Diego firefighter who competed for 17 years in the ultra-endurance sport of Adventure Racing in the most challenging terrain on earth – so I know a little something about professional challenge and risk. I'm also the Founder of the 501c3 Project Athena Foundation (CNN Heroes 2014), which helps survivors live their adventurous dreams as part of their recovery; so healing and building an organization dedicated to others is near and dear to my heart. *Rising from Ground Zero* is about all of that and more. The book lays it out clearly and impactfully: It's not about the setback... It's about the comeback. It's about how we build those deep connections to one another that help all of us rise through times of incredible adversity and challenge. Important book. Great read.

—***Robyn Benincasa**, Founder/Minister of Dreams Project Athena Foundation*

Acknowledgments

First and last, thank you to every responder who accepted our invitation to interview and who all then generously shared their experiences – heartfelt and sometimes outright painful – revisited 20 plus years on. Thank you for sharing so much and for entrusting us with presenting and with preserving it. Nothing related to this project would have happened without your experience, service, and generosity. You are the stuff of this book. Thank you for your sacrifices on and after 9/11. Thank you for granting us the privilege of passing on word of it.

All three authors, and especially Paul, would like to acknowledge all of those who made Paul's career in the FDNY possible and, thereby, this book. Or, as Paul says, "Thanks to everyone on the FDNY who led the way, set an example, taught me anything, had my back, lent support and friendship or broke my balls."

In the Afterword, each of the authors speaks to the effect of this project on them. Paul, like the FDNY responders on 9/11 we interviewed, willingly opened aging files from difficult times. Thanks to Felicia Cambi of the FDNY Counseling Services Unit for helping Paul maintain his mental wellness while immersed in the material that became this book.

Other FDNY helpmates not interviewed include: Battalion Chief (retired) Tom Martin, Captain Stephen Rhine FDNY Press Office, 1st Deputy Commissioner (retired) Robert Turner, Assistant Chief Al Turi (retired), Assistant Chief Mike Butler (retired), Deputy Chief Nick Visconti (deceased from 9/11 illness), Chaplain Chris Keenan, Lieutenant Jeffrey Warner, Chris Schulte PNW-IMT, Robbie Vorhaus. Each of you helped to advance our understanding and thereby advanced the quality of this book.

A special thanks to Mukul Pandya who generously shared his great skill as an editor in developing the final version of the text (especially its overall structure) and in validating the effectiveness of its unique combination of voices. Mukul also led us to Jaya Dalal and through her to De Gruyter Brill. We could not have asked for better partners in bringing this book to readers. Jaya, as promised by Mukul, "got it." She understood our mission and respected our intent. She then successfully brought De Gruyter Brill to the same place.

Thanks to the Wharton School of the University of Pennsylvania which in several ways precipitated the authors' collaboration. The authors met in the course of delivering executive education programming with Professor Michael Useem at Wharton's Aresty Institute. Wharton also contains the Center for Leadership and Change Management, which Mike led. The Center developed programming with the FDNY to advance its leadership following 9/11. That effort helped to connect Greg, a Senior Fellow at the Center, with the FDNY, its leadership, and its terrorism center. Thank you, Mike.

We thank everyone who attended to our work, who took time to proffer comment and, often, encouragement. Among them, we specifically thank Arjun Rao for helping us visualize content and navigate the media environment. You all made it better.

We also thank Wharton (*Knowledge@Wharton*), *Harvard Business Review, Firehouse Magazine,* and *World Financial Review* for publishing articles based on our interviews. Doing so helped to validate the project for others and, frankly, also for the authors.

Thanks to writers whose writing helped our writing by showing the way. In particular, Studs Terkel helped by showing the world the power of contemporary oral history well done, i.e., a carefully gathered and respectfully rendered description of life as experienced by interviewees and with limited authorial interruption.

Thanks also to the best of war and disaster correspondents ever and everywhere. They demonstrate how to narrate the searingly important, namely sparsely, and to exit quickly in order to let events and participants speak for themselves. In the American version of that tradition, thank you to Stephen Crane and especially to Ernest Hemingway who, at his best, showed how to say less to communicate more.

Finally, thank you to each reader of this book, especially to those who pass it on.

The authors welcome contact with readers. For those so inclined, please write to contact@risingfromgroundzero.com.

Table of Contents

“

I think knowing that things will get better and that you can find happiness and some joy as time goes on; when that event first happened, I didn’t know that I would ever be able to feel that again.

—Dr. Kerry Kelly MD, then FDNY Chief Medical Officer, Bureau of Health Services, Headquarters Downtown Brooklyn

Introduction

Thank you for choosing to spend time with this book.

It rests on nearly 90 hours of interviews from 40 interviewees, 32 of whom were FDNY first responders. All had close experience with the FDNY response to the burning and collapse of the two World Trade Center Towers on September 11, 2001 and afterward. We conducted these interviews over eight years, and often, they lasted for more than two hours each.

Prior to the pandemic, the interviews regularly occurred in interviewees' dining or living rooms. The pandemic drove us to Zoom and, as with so many tasks, we tended to stay there post pandemic.

The interviews covered the events of 9/11 and the ways that the FDNY and its firefighters dealt with them. We also devoted considerable attention to what has come in its wake.

We aimed to capture the lived experience of those we interviewed. In aggregate, the interviewees' words form a collective account of a defining moment for the department – personal and unfiltered. The book samples broadly from those interviews. They constitute the core of the book and the center of our work.

The Opening Chapters

We begin with some context about the world you will enter in these pages. Most importantly, we include interviewees' quotes about why they became firefighters, including words from Paul Brown, Capt. (retired), FDNY, Ground Zero veteran, and co-author of this book. Paul recounts what it was like for firefighters to be on the FDNY at that time. In Chapter Two, interviewees reflect on September 10 – a day that unfolded as usual before September 11 pulverized the usual.

The Central Chapters

The next six chapters comprise about 70 percent of the book and constitute its core. Each chapter has two parts: Part A, a sparsely narrated oral history built from selected interviewees' experiences, and Part B, a distillation of key lessons derived from that history. Read together, these elements offer both a record of events and a framework for considering what they reveal. Readers may choose to focus on one part, the other, or both, depending on their interests.

Each of these six chapters follows a consistent structure built around the voices of FDNY first responders: brief excerpts from the interviews offer personal accounts of what unfolded, without a tactical focus. The chapters span moments as brief as a few hours and as extended as months, but in every case the firefighters' own words form the center of the narrative.

Chapters Three through Five focus on the two airplane strikes, the towers' collapse, and the immediate few hours that followed. In these chapters, we provide minimal narrative, ordering and clarifying the accounts while allowing the story to unfold through the voices of those directly involved.

The second part of each chapter reflects our work to distill insights and lessons from the lived experiences just shared. It offers a summary of the events, lessons for leaders, and commentary that connects those experiences to leadership research and established frameworks – perspectives some readers may find helpful in considering what unfolded.

Chapters Six through Eight turn to a less examined part of the FDNY story: the longer-term adjustment to loss and the organizational change that followed. These chapters show how individuals and the department as a whole confronted trauma while attempting to adapt and move forward. Our commentary includes explicit leadership lessons embedded in that experience.

The Conclusion

Two chapters end the book. Chapter Nine examines the legacy of the FDNY experience of and with 9/11. It focuses on how interviewees and their organization responded to profound loss and rebuilt in its aftermath. It highlights a range of legacies – personal, institutional, and national – that emerged from the rubble and carnage of that day.

Chapter Ten centers on interviewee responses to a single reflective question: *"If you could return to 9/10 and have the chance to whisper into the ear of your then self, what would you whisper?"* The book proper ends with the voices of FDNY responders, thereby acknowledging again the centrality of their stories to the book and the generosity with which they shared them.

An Afterword presents a distilled list of Lessons for Leaders along with a statement from each author regarding the impact of this project on them.

Lastly, the Honor Roll of all firefighters killed on 9/11 followed by the Honor Roll of firefighters who succumbed to 9/11 related illness from service at the site on the day or days that followed.

Appendix A introduces the interviewee voices heard throughout the book through short biographies. Appendix B presents the interview protocol used to gather these accounts. Appendix C provides a responders' lexicon to help readers navigate the language of the event. Appendix D outlines the FDNY command structure as it stood on the morning of September 11, 2001. Appendix E presents the FDNY WTC Task Force structure as of 0700 on September 15, 2001, and Appendix F provides a map of the World Trade Center complex. The evolution of the recovery effort is documented in Appendices G and H through the WTC Incident Action Plan for September 27–28 and planned actions and operating instructions for the period September 22 to September 30, 2001. Appendix I logs subsequent activations of the FDNY Incident Management Team. Appendix J provides a Manhattan Dispatch transcript from 9/11, and Appendix K offers additional resources for further study. These supplementary materials are followed by the Endnotes and a concluding About the Authors section, completing the organization of the book's final pages.

The Interviews

Participation in the interviews was entirely voluntary. One individual declined, explaining that it was still too difficult to speak about the events of 9/11. Typically, we recorded audio and video, with interviewees free to pause or stop recording at any time for any reason (breaks to collect themselves were common, and brief suspensions did occur rarely).[1] At the conclusion of each interview, we invited participants to revise, edit, or add additional comments.

We determined who to speak with by following our noses (Paul's in particular), speaking with those who were central to the FDNY story on and after 9/11.[2] Many were firefighters, company officers or junior chiefs on duty that day. In the years that followed, a significant number rose to senior positions: fire commissioner (two), first deputy commissioner (one), chief of department (six), and other staff chief positions (six). In short, interviewees were both on the ground on 9/11 and central to FDNY's recovery and reconstruction.

In addition to contributing as field recorder, André, an executive coach, veteran and long-time mountain rescuer, served as a management thought partner and organizing force for the interview work throughout the project, overseeing the organization of 90 hours of interviews and thousands of pages of interview transcripts. His efforts as phenomenological advocate, AI explorer, technical guide, writer, and librarian prevented us from getting lost in the sheer volume of material we collected. He contributed input throughout the book and took the lead in writing chapters Two and Ten. André also, importantly, enforced a norm of "no combat porn," avoiding the pursuit of or dwelling on the sensational.

Greg led the interview process to obtain a long look back from those who were there on the day and often played prominent roles in what came after. He approached each interview as a partnership, listening at the pace set by the interviewees and remaining attentive to their terms of involvement, spoken and unspoken. Throughout the project, he consistently reinforced a core principle: that all writing should remain grounded in, and derived from, the interviewees' own words. He wrote significant parts of the book including the Lessons for Leaders and Commentary sections. He developed and maintained the voice of the interview narrator and guided the overall development of the book.

Paul contributed directly to the manuscript, writing significant sections of the book, including Chapter One, the chapter summaries, and multiple appendices. He also served as primary and relentless fact checker. Together, Paul and André selected and curated interviewee quotations, built the timeline and compiled images. Paul, most importantly, served as the project's sponsor within the FDNY community. Paul initially approached each potential interviewee about participating in an interview. As testimony to his reputation, as noted, precious few declined.

At the outset, colleagues told Paul that pursuing this project would end his participation in the FDNY community. At the time, the department still largely resisted any discussion about the actions of commanders and firefighters on and after 9/11, seeing such conversations as sacrilege. That resistance underscored the difficulty in revisiting 9/11 – and why this project required an essential trust in order to succeed.

More recently, firefighters have grown eager to speak about their experiences. One interviewee reported that fewer than 600 firefighters remain in the department (of over 11,000) who were at the WTC: "They need to learn what we went through." When Paul arranged later interviews, he had to request they hold off their recounting of events until the recorded interview, in order to preserve their conversations accurately. Some FDNY veterans told him, "It's about time someone got these stories before we're all gone," and one said, "You are doing God's work." The breadth and fullness of participation speaks loudly to the perception of the project.

We record several narratives involving the fallen. Paul contacted their loved ones regarding use of their loved one's name. We offered to refrain from using names absent their blessing. Conversations, expected to be tense, proved anything but. Each family made the same request, "please use their name, please tell their story, help us preserve their legacy."

Lauren joined the project to help shape a years-long interview archive into a book. She worked with the authors to evaluate publication options, brokered meetings with agents and publishers, and provided editorial guidance throughout the process, including a final line edit of the manuscript. She also contributed notably to developing approaches to taking the book to the reading public.

The authors[3] have self-funded the research and writing of this book. We chose this path to preserve the independence and control that we felt necessary in order to honor the commitments we made to the interviewees. Additionally, we have incorporated and formally committed to contribute 51 percent of any net profits of the book to FDNY charities that support members killed or injured in the line of duty, and their families. The toll never abates for New York City's firefighters. Since

September 11, 2001, the FDNY has suffered 39 line-of-duty deaths and over 400 WTC-related-illness deaths.

Obviously, the authors believe that the stories presented here matter. We also recognize that, all of our work notwithstanding, that they capture but a part of the story of the FDNY and the impact of 9/11 which captures but a part of the story of New York City and the impact of 9/11 on it which comprises but a part of the total story of 9/11, a story that includes flight crews and passengers on hijacked planes, people at the Pentagon, those in and near the World Trade Center and people around the world impacted by the day – what it took and what it yielded. We have tried to faithfully present a piece of a piece of a piece...as key participants in that piece remember it.

We hope this book captures and honors the experiences of those who so generously shared their stories, and through them, the experiences of their FDNY colleagues on 9/11 and on the many days that followed. We also hope that our restraint as authors allows the reader to hear those voices clearly. We have intended from the start of this project not only to provide a platform for those voices, but also to offer enduring lessons based on their experiences and insights – for the benefit of leaders and followers – in moments that most test both.

Section One: Before

“

I have no ambition in this world but one, and that is to be a fireman. The position may in the eyes of some appear to be a lowly one, but we who know the work which the fireman has to do believe that his is a noble calling.... [O]ur proudest endeavor is to save...lives.... Under the impulse of such thoughts, the nobility of the occupation thrills us and stimulates us to deeds of daring, even at the supreme sacrifice.

—Edward F. Croker, Chief of Department FDNY (1899–1911)[4]

“

Lord, take me where You want me to go;
Let me meet who You want me to meet;
Tell me what You want me to say;
And keep me out of Your way.

—Father Mychal Judge, Chaplain FDNY (1992–2001)[5]

Chapter One

FDNY: "The Job, The Work, The People"

> Very proud, very confident, best job in the world. It really is. The mood in the firehouse was extreme confidence. The guys in my firehouse were very professional and I could count on them to go to anything, anything. The mood then was fun. It was a real fun time, a lot of laughter, a lot of joking around.
>
> *—Captain Glenn Rohan, then Lieutenant in Ladder 43, Spanish Harlem, Manhattan*[6]

> My brother was a firefighter. 'You have to see this way of life. You have to see the second family that I have.'
>
> *—Fire Commissioner (2010–2014) Sal Cassano, then Assistant Chief at Headquarters, Downtown Brooklyn (served as Chief of Department 2006–2010)*

> My father was very happy being in the fire department as were all the friends of his that I knew. Pete Ganci used to say, 'The only friend of his father that was happy, he said was a firefighter.'
>
> *—Fire Commissioner (2014–2022) Dan Nigro, then Chief of Operations Headquarters, Downtown Brooklyn (served as Chief of Department 2001–2002)*

> We love the job. We all do. What a blessing that is. A difficult, difficult job and God calls you to it. And then he gives you a love for it so that a difficult job will be done well.[7]
>
> —*Father Mychal Judge, Chaplain FDNY (1992–2001); his last homily delivered on 9/10*

Firefighter Dom Delio with Jake
Firefighter sharing his meal with the firehouse dog Jake in a typically well-equipped firehouse kitchen.
With permission from the private collection of Jeffrey Warner

Part A: Responder Voices

Why become a firefighter?

Roughly 40 percent of New York City firefighters have firefighter relatives, and countless others have friends or neighbors on the job. Many of those share similar motivations for joining the FDNY.

> My father was a New York City firefighter, as was his father. Both of my older brothers preceded me onto the FDNY. My father and brothers were unique among people I knew; they went to work happy, they came home happy but tired, a good tired. They spoke with glowing praise for 'the job' and the people they worked with.
>
> —*Captain Paul Brown, then Lieutenant covering in Division 15, Brownsville, Brooklyn; FDNY IMT*

Chief Downey
An Incident Commander monitors a high-volume fire.
Photo by Todd Maisel

“ My dad was a firefighter for 32 years. My Uncle Joe was a firefighter for 30 years. My Uncle John was a firefighter for 42 years. My older brother did 23 years and I have seven cousins who have done 20 [years] or better in their careers. It produces a pride and a dedication and a continuing of a family legacy to a job that we all love.

—Battalion Chief Fred LaFemina, Chief of Rescue Services, then Captain of Squad 270, South Jamaica, Queens; FDNY USAR

“ It was inbred from my father in the firehouse. I got a great feeling and just being able to help. It was inbred. The heart to do it, the want to do it. It's not a job, it's a calling. You get somebody that's totally qualified in the test, if they're not really into being a fireman and if they treat it as a job, they're not going to fit in.

—Battalion Chief Bill Moore, then in Battalion 10, Yorkville, Manhattan

“ A lot of the guys that I had grown up with had taken the fire department test. At the time, they were getting hired, and they all came back with these great stories about how fabulous the New York City Fire

Department was and I was like, 'You know what? If I'm going to work for the city of New York, I'm going on the fire department.'

—Firefighter Louis Giaconelli, then in Engine 53, Spanish Harlem, Manhattan; FDNY IMT

Attacking the seat of the fire FDNY firefighters moving in through heavy smoke and debris at an active scene. *Photo by Todd Maisel*

" A friend whose father was a lieutenant said, 'Do you want to take the fire department test?' He got me the application. I didn't grow up necessarily really wanting to be a firefighter as much as it was a great option to have. I was thrilled when it came along. Once I got a taste, there's no going back. It was just a wonderful group of people. The thrill of it, the excitement, the camaraderie, there was an awful lot to like. I sort of found a home from what I was doing prior to that. I went to a very special firehouse initially that treated me very well. I wanted to be as good as I could be. I just wanted to be the best because that's what they brought out in you.

—Chief of Department (2010–2014) Ed Kilduff, then Deputy Chief in Division 3, Midtown, Manhattan and past IMT Incident Commander

" My brother was a firefighter. When I came home from Vietnam...my brother took me under his wing: 'You have to see what's going on here. You have to see this way of life. You have to see the second family that I have.' When he took me around and I saw the camaraderie amongst the members and their families and if somebody was in trouble they were going to be helped, I said, 'This is for me.'

—Fire Commissioner (2010–2014) Sal Cassano, then Assistant Chief at Headquarters, Downtown Brooklyn (served as Chief of Department 2006-2010)

Why remain a firefighter?

There is an adage: "No one goes to their grave wishing they spent more time at work...except firefighters." What is it about firefighting? What is it about the New York City Fire Department? Some say the people, the camaraderie. Others say the work itself.

“Oh, I just loved it. I loved it. I was lucky enough to go to a busy fire house, so that kept most of them either too busy or too tired to bust my chops as a probie. When they found out that I was going to do my job... and I wasn't going to leave them in the hallway. That was it, I just loved it and I stayed, and the rest is history. I liked the guys, I liked the schedule, I liked the excitement. Probably most of all is no two days are the same, there was nothing monotonous about this job. You didn't know what to expect every day you walked through the door, and that's what I liked.

—Firefighter Lois Mungay, then in Engine 235, Bedford Stuyvesant, Brooklyn

Casualty evacuation
Working efficiently in heavy bunker gear and breathing apparatus to evacuate a patient with the help of Emergency Medical Services.
Photo by Todd Maisel

“ This is my passion and you know, it was a blessing of a lifetime. So you love the work itself in addition to the service component. The excitement, the camaraderie, the understanding that it's you and me, we have to trust one another. We have to have a mutual trust and we're all about the team because firefighting it's all team. We do individual deeds, we do individual jobs at fires; [but] when it all comes together, it's a team, and I enjoyed that.

—Chief of Department (2020–2022) Tom Richardson, then Battalion Chief in Battalion 53, Bayside, Queens

“ I can't tell you it's completely altruistic. I enjoy serving the public, I enjoy being a benefit to people, I enjoy helping people. I think the primary motivating factor is maybe a little bit of the adrenaline. I like the diversity of the activity. I think that's probably the biggest factor. I like the fact that you're not really sure what's coming down the road. If you're in a busier area, and a more complex area, there's more likelihood of that kind of diversity of incidence.

—Battalion Chief Tom Winship, then a District of Columbia FD firefighter; responded to the Pentagon on 9/11; appointed to FDNY 2003; FDNY Pipes and Drums; IMT

“ The fire service is a special breed of people. Everybody is in it to help somebody else. If everybody's on the same page helping others, then you're amongst good company. Nobody is doing it to get a medal, nobody is doing it for a pat on the back. There's no ulterior motive except to go out and help people. If you're in a firehouse that everybody is on the same page, it's a win-win-win. The reason you stay in a job is because you like what you do and you get also satisfaction out of it. It's a good thing, right. Everybody supports each other regardless of what someone's shortcomings are. You take your strengths, their strengths, and help each other towards the end goal, a better organization.

—Lieutenant Joe Minogue, Commanding Officer of Ceremonial Unit; Department Bugler; then a firefighter in Engine 289, Corona, Queens

“ The opportunity to get a job where you are not in business to make money. You come to work every day, and your job is to help people. I would say that liking the nature of the work in terms of the tasks, what the work produced ultimately, was a benefit to society. Our department

has high morale in terms of its members' camaraderie.
You eat together, work out together, go to responses together, go to wakes and funerals together. Everybody will say they like their job, it's like a family. But the fire department's another step, another level above that, because you are getting on a firetruck together, you're putting your life on the line together. There's tremendous morale.

—Deputy Chief Jim DiDomenico, then in Division 13, South Jamaica, Queens

“ Firefighters are involved in each other's lives to the degree that I often felt as if I had dozens of uncles growing up. All the firehouse families knew each other from picnics, Christmas parties, fishing trips, and family get-togethers. When work was done on our house, ten firefighters showed up to help. They got paid with pizza and beer and camaraderie.

—Captain Paul Brown, then Lieutenant covering in Division 15, Brownsville, Brooklyn; FDNY IMT

Not always good days

Hardships and tragedy within the department are a certainty and reverberate throughout the department.

“ The relationship you have with the people in the fire department, it just can't compare to anywhere. I remember when I first got in, there was an old timer and he says, 'Kid, this is the greatest job, but just remember, when we have a bad day, we have a bad day.' And that's unfortunate, that's the downside, but you also know if that day comes, that there's so many people out there, they're going to help your family, they're gonna have a lot of support. So that camaraderie, that doing, that public service is just.... You can't beat it, you can't beat it.

—Assistant Chief Tom Galvin, Chief of Training (2004–2015), then Deputy Chief in Division 3, Midtown, Manhattan

“ You find yourself again in an emergency room having to tell his wife that he's not coming home. It's by far the worst part of the job. Certainly for our members, sometimes when someone's in a hospital, and they're facing serious medical problems, it's not too big a surprise, but when a young person goes off to work in the morning and three o'clock in the afternoon, they're suddenly not with us, it's a terrible shock to the families. The funerals, the wakes.

—Fire Commissioner (2014–2022) Dan Nigro, then Chief of Operations Headquarters, Downtown Brooklyn (served as Chief of Department 2001–2002)

Dignified transfer of firefighter Jonathan Pollard
FDNY brothers salute as the deceased Firefighter Pollard is carried by the members of his firehouse, Ladder 170, Engine 257 Canarsie's Bravest.
Photo by Todd Maisel

" My dad was a firefighter 28 years and loved the job, worked always in the same firehouse and, although he suffered, like all firefighters do, the line of duty death of his colleagues, we had that model as a family and knew how to respond. In fact, in his good grace, he had the children of one of his colleagues who died spend the summer with us when we were youngsters.... Didn't really understand at the time what the future would be, but understood in a moment we acquired new cousins.

—Malachy Corrigan NP, then Clinical Director, Counseling Services Unit SoHo, Manhattan

" I think we had five or six buildings on fire. You think that's the biggest fire. Then the Father's Day Fire, we lost three firefighters. I was a lieutenant in that unit. I lost my driver Harry Ford and Brian Fahey. You accept it. You really do. It can't get worse than this. That was

June of 2001. It's just honestly another incident. There's going to be another big one whether I'm around for it or not. There'll be another big one that they'll have to go to.

—Battalion Chief Fred LaFemina, Chief of Rescue Services, then Captain of Squad 270, South Jamaica, Queens; member FDNY USAR

Part B: FDNY: The Department

A culture of confident readiness

FDNY routines rest on a culture marked by high morale and strong bonds. Firefighters describe a place where you advanced based on tests rather than connections, where you could move around the city, and where you worked with people you trusted. That trust includes the belief that fellow firefighters would take it upon themselves to look after your family should anything happen to you. Readiness had come to include developing psychological services centered on substance abuse.

“ It provides tremendous opportunity to advance because advancement is 99.9% predicated on you studying hard, and doing well on a test, not on who you know. You have opportunities to advance. You also have opportunities to move around in the organization. You want to work in Manhattan and experience high-rise firefighting? If you want to go to places that have a lot more fires, you build a good reputation. You put in a paper to transfer.

—Deputy Chief Jim DiDomenico, then in Division 13, South Jamaica, Queens

“ My first boss was a very hands-on guy. He had just come out of the field, and he was very interested in taking care of the firefighters in the firehouse. He was very aware of how emotions were post line-of-duty death or critical injury, and very aware of the families who had lost someone. Our thinking kind of matched up. His school was the school of a firefighter, mine was a little more theoretical, but we certainly matched up on the emotional level, and he brought me to many firehouses and introduced me and made it possible [to] operat[e] inside the firehouse itself, certainly in times of loss.

—Malachy Corrigan NP, then Clinical Director, Counseling Services Unit SoHo, Manhattan

The firefighter through others' eyes

Two quotes from non-firefighters capture much of why people chose to serve as New York City firefighters.

First, the legendary chef and media personality Anthony Bourdain[8] put it best: "No matter how badly led, ridiculously under-equipped, underappreciated, no matter how doomed their mission, they take a bizarre and quite beautiful pride in at least being screwed more than everybody else and doing it with style...it's not a job; it's a calling."

Second, following a dark day for the department, when three firefighters were killed in two separate fires, including one from Paul's company, the editor of the *New York Post* asked: "Here is an enduring mystery: what is it that draws young New Yorkers into the uniformed service of their city when the work is so fundamentally dangerous and the temporal rewards so modest by comparison? What is the attraction? Why do they do it? It's a decent job, with a fair wage and a good pension. But there is more...there is the challenge, physical and mental. It's a tough job, and not everyone can measure up. There is danger and lots of it, which always has attracted brave [people] and which, thank god, always will. These men are a breed apart. [W]hen it matters the most and when everything is on the line, they go where few others would dare...and they do it with studied professionalism and great personal courage. Every now and again, NYC is reminded anew that it has in its service [people] routinely capable of sacrifices that cannot ever be repaid."[9]

Why be a firefighter? For many, the answer begins with belonging – being a part of something larger than oneself, rooted in shared and noble purpose. The work brings exposure to tragedy, loss, and adversity, bearing witness to the consequences of the worst of humanity. It also brings pride, meaning, and a deep sense of accomplishment, both as individuals and as members of the New York City Fire Department.

The New York City Fire Department as It Was, and in Many Ways as It Remains

Organizational structure and operational traditions

The FDNY is organized as a paramilitary institution, mirroring the command hierarchy of the U.S. military. The department's 11,400 uniformed firefighters are assigned to 357 fire companies, each typically comprised of up to 30 firefighters and three lieutenants led by a captain. These companies are grouped administratively into battalions and divisions across the city's five boroughs, with each level reporting up a defined chain of command. The Chief of Department – the highest-ranking uniformed officer – reports to the Fire Commissioner, a civilian appointee serving under the Mayor of New York City.[10]

Entry into the FDNY is extremely competitive. Entrance exams are given on average every four years. One recent exam had over 47,000 applicants competing for around 2,400 positions over the four years between exams – an applicant-to-hire ratio of almost 20:1.

Once on the job, assignment to a "good" firehouse is extremely competitive. Contrary to what one might expect, busy firehouses have waiting lists. Many firefighters with family ties to the department seek assignments to the same units where relatives served, and it is not uncommon to see several firefighters working together whose fathers worked side by side years earlier. These generational traditions run deep and instill a strong sense of dedication.

Seniority is respected as a marker of experience and knowledge. Many of the department's senior firefighters, officers, and chiefs gained that experience during a period known as the "War Years," spanning the 1960s

Firehouse drill
Firefighters L to R, Godwin Chery, Zavannie Walters, Ryan Hilgendorf, Chris Lyons. Firefighters Drilling at the firehouse.
With Permission from the private collection of Jeff Warner

Firefighter Dom Delio Ladder 158 in the kitchen
Firehouse meal being prepared by the chef of the day.
With permission from the private collection of Jeff Warner

through the early 1980s, and punctuated by intense fire activity, civil unrest, and urban blight.

The department operates on a principle similar to mission command. Namely, firefighters of every rank are expected to understand their role, their unit's responsibilities, and the overarching goals of every operation. This culture of shared purpose and situational awareness enables rapid, autonomous decision-making in high-stakes environments. Firefighters take great pride in knowing their job and their ability to act without

Firefighters Tom Hanley, Kevin McGoldrick, Andy Savage drilling on an abandoned vehicle
Firefighters drilling (training) on an abandoned vehicle.
With permission from the private collection of Jeff Warner

waiting for direct orders, using their judgment to apply proven best practices in dynamic and dangerous conditions.

Personal pride and company pride are central to the department's operational doctrine of aggressive interior attack. Rather than containing fires from the outside, FDNY companies prioritize entering a structure to locate and extinguish the fire at its source, a critical approach in New York City's vertical environment. This tactic reduces the production of toxic smoke—responsible for the majority of fire-related deaths—and increases the chances of rescuing trapped occupants. Though inherently hazardous, this proactive strategy reflects the department's fundamental mission: to protect life first, even at great personal risk.

Training and culture

The FDNY operates within a results-driven culture that values adaptability, judgment, and teamwork over rote procedures. Recognizing that no two emergencies are alike, firefighters are trained to rely on experience, initiative, and collaboration in dynamic, high-risk situations. A deep tradition of mentorship and continuous learning-both formal and informal-reinforced this culture.

All new firefighters – known as "probies" – begin their careers at Probationary Firefighters School (Probie School) at the FDNY Training Academy on Randall's Island. There, they receive foundational instruction

Tower Ladder 114 moving in
In a scene reminiscent of the "War Years" Firefighters from 114 on a tower ladder confront intense flames erupting from building windows.
Photo by Todd Maisel

in fire behavior, equipment use, building construction, forcible entry, ventilation, and emergency medical care. The probies are introduced to the department's tradition of generational teaching and learning here. All of the instructors are veteran firefighters with decades of practical, real-world firefighting experience. Captain Paul Brown gave an example of this depth of generational and institutional knowledge: "One of my instructors at Probie School in 1989 was Seymore Schenker. He was a "War Years" firefighter with 40+ years of experience fighting fires in Brownsville, Brooklyn. Prior to the FDNY, he served in the U.S. Navy. During WWII, he was a firefighter on an Aircraft Carrier in the Pacific. Seymore spoke, we listened. This was our introduction to the department's extraordinary depth of tradition and generational learning."

Following the Fire Academy, a new firefighter's true education begins informally in the firehouse, where the unwritten rules of trust, reputation, and operational excellence encourage continuous learning. The firehouse kitchen sits at the center of this life. Every shift begins and ends with a stop in the kitchen, where the unofficial exchange of information occurs: Who caught a job [fire]? What went well, and what didn't? What tools or equipment are in need of service? Who got stitches last night? Who's out with the flu? Who had a baby? Firehouses function as second homes, and the camaraderie forged through shared risk and sacrifice creates what many members describe as family.

This family-like structure lies at the core of the FDNY's enduring strength. It is reinforced through shared challenges faced and daily rituals, especially meal preparation, which is followed by dining at large communal tables, much like family holiday dinners with lively conversation. Everyone participates. If you're not a good cook, then you're a good pot scrubber. Turnover is remarkably low, and barring injury, many companies retain core members for decades. All uniformed leadership roles are filled from within the ranks, reinforcing a culture rooted in experience and continuity. Knowledge is passed down through generations, often through stories, drills, and the example set by senior firefighters, helping prepare each new generation of firefighters for the unexpected.

From the "War Years" to 9/11: growth and leadership

Seasoned FDNY leaders in 2001 were forged in the crucible of the "War Years," embodying the department's long-standing commitment to readiness, resilience, and internal leadership development. This period was characterized by unrelenting fire duty, much intentionally. Entire neighborhoods – particularly in the South Bronx, Harlem, and parts of Brooklyn – were devastated by arson and abandonment. Firefighters routinely responded to multiple structural fires in a single shift, honing their skills under extreme conditions.

This era not only produced some of the most battle-tested firefighters in FDNY history, but also strengthened the department's culture, fostering deep camaraderie, resilience, and tactical innovation. All senior leaders on 9/11, from 1st Deputy Commissioner Bill Feehan (who held every rank during his 42-year career) and Chief of Department Pete Ganci (33 years) through Deputy Chief Pete Hayden (33 years), rose through the ranks during "War Years."

A history of going it alone

FDNY's tightly knit, family-like structure was paired with a commitment to organizational autonomy and self-reliance. The department's size and depth of resources meant it rarely, if ever, needed outside assistance. With 357 firefighting units, FDNY could rotate personnel without exhausting its ranks. 1st Deputy Commissioner Frank Cruthers recalled: "At that time, I would say, we had a reputation not just for size but effectiveness. Operationally, there really wasn't any experience that required outside, never mind federal and state assistance."

By 2001, department leaders – who had been forged in the "War Years" – were among the most seasoned firefighters in the world, and they knew it. Looking outward for new approaches or learning from other departments simply didn't occur to them. Retired Chief of Department (2010–2014) Ed Kilduff put it bluntly, "To say that we were narrow and provincial before September 11th is an understatement. We were a mom-and-pop organization. There's no question about it."

While firefighters from around the world traveled to New York to study FDNY operations, the department itself seldom ventured beyond city limits to learn from others. Thirty-nine-year veteran Captain Jeff Simms commented, "We thought we were so big that we couldn't learn a thing from these people." Tactics, training, and procedures were developed in-house, informed almost solely by the FDNY's own experience. This closed-loop culture led former Fire Commissioner Sal Cassano to relate an oft heard quip describing the the department as having "150 years of tradition unimpeded by progress."

Chapter Two

September 10 – A Moment in Time

> “We were in a firehouse where the division [Deputy Chief’s office] was.... [W]e all ate dinner that night.... It was just a great kitchen table. We were kidding around, we were all laughing.
>
> *—Lieutenant Artie Riccio, then a firefighter in Ladder 119 South Williamsburg, Brooklyn, working in Ladder 110*

> “One of the last stops was 22 Engine and 13 Truck and before I left, they invited me back to have lunch the next day. I told them...I’ll be back for lunch.
>
> *—Assistant Chief Tom Galvin, Chief of Training (2004–2015), then Deputy Chief in Division 3, Midtown, Manhattan*

September 10, 2001 dawns clear and unremarkable in New York – a late summer Monday. The forecast calls for a high near 80 degrees, lows in the low 60s, light winds, and more of the same tomorrow.

Around the world, the Second Intifada is in full swing, its cycle of violence dominating the headlines. U.S. Secretary of State Colin Powell engages in shuttle diplomacy, speaking with Israeli Foreign Minister Shimon Peres and Palestinian leader Yasser Arafat in an effort to advance the Mitchell Report recommendations.

At home, the news is routine. Washington, D.C. marks the 50th anniversary of the ANZUS Treaty as Australian Prime Minister John Howard visits the capital. That evening, President George W. Bush travels to Florida to discuss education reform. Mayor Rudy Giuliani has reached his term limit; voters would choose his successor in November.

Fashion designers from all over the world descend on Manhattan for Fashion Week at Bryant Park. Hip Hop fans await tomorrow's release of Jay Z's album *The Blueprint,* including tracks orchestrated by a rising, little-known producer named Kanye West.

Financial markets reflect uncertainty in the long shadow of the dot-com bubble. On September 10, the Dow Jones Industrial Average closes at 9,605.51 – virtually unchanged for the day but down significantly from its highs earlier in the year. Investors are nervous. The unemployment rate has reached 4.9 percent, signaling growing strain in the labor market.

In sports news, Michael Jordan is hinting at another comeback. On *Monday Night Football,* the Giants lose to the Denver Broncos. Barry Bonds hits his 63rd home run in his pursuit of Mark McGwire's record.

At the National Fire Academy in Emmitsburg, Maryland, firefighters from around the country settle into 420 dorm rooms as a new session of classes begins. As he often does, the superintendent walks through the classrooms and common areas, checking that rooms are clean, the food is decent, and repairs are addressed. Leadership is taught in the curriculum and practiced in the hallways.

In firehouses across New York City's five boroughs, the six-by-nine tour begins: 6:00 p.m. to 9:00 a.m. Though it may be 24 hours on duty for many of the department's 11,400 uniformed firefighters, spread across 203 engine companies, 143 ladder companies, five rescue companies, and seven squad companies. On an average day, the FDNY answers about 6,300 calls – roughly 2.3 million a year – making it the busiest fire department in the world.

On the morning of the 10th, the work is familiar; coffee percolates, apparatus checked, hoses tested, air bottles filled, radios charged, tools cleaned. The same checklist that has anchored thousands of previous shifts unfolds again.

For many firefighters, though, a shadow crosses the day. Eight days earlier, they buried Firefighter Michael Garumba of Engine 163. He died of an apparent heart attack while battling a fire in an auto body shop on Staten Island, leaving behind a pregnant wife and a two-year-old son. Garumba had graduated from the fire academy just one month earlier.

Across the city, a class of 252 probies is out on field training, assigned to firehouses in all five boroughs. In a week, they will return to the fire academy for additional classwork. They are scheduled to graduate on November 1st.

Downtown, about 50,000 people ride the elevators to offices in the sky at the World Trade Center. For nearly three decades, the Twin Towers have anchored the lower Manhattan skyline, evolving from controversial newcomers into accepted landmarks. They rise 1,368 and 1,362 feet, a combined 220 stories above a 16-acre complex, 43,600 windows, 40,000 door frames, and 198 elevators.[11] Morgan Stanley, Cantor Fitzgerald, Marsh & McLennan, and Windows on the World are familiar tenants – businesses and lunch destinations.

The FDNY of September 10 operates with confidence built over 136 years of tradition and hard-won expertise. The department's firefighters can, in Denis Onieal's phrase, "stomp any fire out." They rarely need

New York City skyline remembered
A wide-angle, daylight view of the Lower Manhattan skyline in New York City, dominated by the original World Trade Center's Twin Towers.
Carol M. Highsmith, Public domain, via Wikimedia Commons

help, rarely ask for it, and seldom look beyond their own borders for new ideas. Why would they?

Firefighters shaped by the "War Years" – the brutal stretch of arson and urban decay in the late 1960s through early 1980s – pass their knowledge on to younger members. Promotion comes entirely from within. Every chief, captain, and lieutenant has climbed the same ladder, studied for the same exams, and learned the same lessons. People know their jobs and trust that the people around them know theirs.

Gotham, the city the FDNY serves, contains many parts and pieces. Midtown's Division 3 encompasses some of the busiest companies in the department. In Spanish Harlem, Engine 53 and Ladder 43 face a different set of challenges. Downtown, Engine 10 and Ladder 10 literally sit in the shadow of the towers. Each firehouse functions as a small universe, held together by tradition, pride, and the intimacy forged through shared meals, shared quarters, and shared history.

On September 10, 2001, the FDNY feels, and is widely seen as, ready – ready to fight any fire imaginable, rescue anyone trapped in the city's five

Twin Towers from the Brooklyn Bridge
The Twin Towers of the World Trade Center as photographed through the Brooklyn Bridge.
Carol M. Highsmith, Public domain, via Wikimedia Commons

boroughs, and respond to an almost countless set of emergencies. Its firefighters carry well-honed and well-practiced tools and tactics.

Morning routines

For some members of the department, the rhythms of administrative leadership and support shape the day – teaching, overseeing training, and tending to the equipment.

> [It] was a normal day [for me] as superintendent of the National Fire Academy. It was the beginning of a new session. I made it a practice to visit every class while I was on campus; everything was okay, rooms clean, food's okay, any problems, let me know. It was, because, first of all, we taught leadership. You need to, if you're the superintendent, you need to demonstrate leadership.
>
> *—Denis Onieal, then Senior FEMA Rep., Superintendent, National Fire Academy*

> On September 10th, I was working to get a radio that we put in service, and we had some problems with it. It wasn't working as well as we liked....September 10th that's what I was doing, I was working on this project. I can distinctly remember that the night of September 10th, I was very distraught because my Giants got destroyed by the Denver Broncos, and I stayed up late watching the game. I went to work on September 11th pretty tired from the night before.
>
> *–Fire Commissioner (2010–2014) Sal Cassano, then Assistant Chief at Headquarters, Downtown Brooklyn (served as Chief of Department 2006–2010)*

> Monday. My day was typically a mix of seeing individual clients, typically in terms of the substance abuse day treatment program. I would have one educational class a week and one group a week so that I was familiar with the gentlemen in the program, and the ladies. I wanted to always have that, so I stayed in touch with the issues as they present[ed]. My day would be focused about half the day on individual cases.
>
> *—Malachy Corrigan NP, then Clinical Director Counseling Services Unit SoHo, Manhattan*

> “On September 10th, there was a lieutenant's test six weeks away. Guys studied for these tests for 18 months, two years, sometimes longer. I was teaching [a test prep class] that day, and each week you have an assignment. You would teach once every six weeks. I left home heading to Staten Island to get there early.
>
> *—Deputy Chief Jim DiDomenico, then in Division 13, South Jamaica, Queens*

Normal shifts

Operationally, the day feels like a typical tour. Chiefs move through their battalions and divisions, visiting companies, checking in, and answering questions. Lieutenants and firefighters do what they always do: show up, take the rig out, handle whatever comes in.

Some firefighters remember the day less for a particular call than for the feel of the job – the tempo of runs, sense of camaraderie, and confidence residing within the firehouses.

Battery Park
Aerial view of Lower Manhattan, dominated by the Twin Towers of the original World Trade Center rising above the skyline. *Carol M. Highsmith, Public domain, via Wikimedia Commons*

Best job in the world
A firefighter rescues a cat from a fire escape ladder.
Photo by Todd Maisel

" September 10, 2001, if I can go back to that day.... We were doing work, pretty steady work, and we're getting hammered every day. With the fire department, it was tight. It was a tight job, guys looked out for one another, they cared about one another. The bosses cared about the troops. The troops cared about the bosses. It was like you take care of me; I take care of you.

—Captain Kerry Hollywood, then in Engine 53, Spanish Harlem, Manhattan; Commanding Officer Family Assistance Unit

" Very proud, very confident, best job in the world. It really is. Placards came out after the 11th [that] said, 'FDNY still the greatest job on Earth.' The mood in the firehouse was extreme confidence. The guys in my firehouse were very professional and I could count on them to go to anything, anything. I liked working there and they liked that I was there. It was a very hard house to get assigned to. There were some heavy hitters who wanted to get that position that I got. I owe it to the captain. He went to Peter Ganci, Chief of Department in uniform Class-A saying, 'This is the guy I want. Here's his paper.' That's the reason I got 43 truck. The mood then, like I said, was fun. It was a real fun time, a lot of laughter, a lot of joking around.

—Captain Glenn Rohan, then a Lieutenant in Ladder 43, Spanish Harlem, Manhattan

Ladder 131
Firefighters from Ladder 131 "the Happy Hookers" direct their tower ladder's high caliber stream.
Photo by Todd Maisel

“ The FDNY is probably the pinnacle of a results-based organization. We always like to say, 'Every fire we've ever responded to went out.' You don't leave until the situation's been mitigated, and that's drilled into your head. When the rulebook doesn't work, you use something else. You re-evaluate over and over again until you find something that works, and you get it out or you call in more people, or you [call] more equipment. Everything we do is based on the result that we don't leave until that particular emergency is mitigated.

—Captain Paul Brown, then a Lieutenant covering in Division 15, Brownsville, Brooklyn; FDNY IMT

“ The department always has multiple irons in the fire, so to speak, projects going on. One of the key issues then was our communications, our handie-talkie radios. We had made a switch to digital and that did not work out quite well and had to put all of our old equipment back in service. We were trying to figure out how we would make this transition and how that would go on. That was a big topic of conversation.

—Fire Commissioner (2014–2022) Dan Nigro, then Chief of Operations Headquarters, Downtown Brooklyn (served as Chief of Department 2001–2002)

Tradition and discipline

“We go on orders. My first captain, Artie Paranello, taught me the job. He was a very difficult man to work for, but he taught me how to take orders, how to do the right thing, and how to always take pride. That's the way it was, it's all about pride, it's all about doing your job, doing a good job, helping people. That's what he taught me from the beginning, and I carried that through for the rest of my career. I taught other guys the same thing. I wasn't as harsh as he was, but that's what I taught with and that's in my heart.

—Lieutenant Artie Riccio, then a firefighter in Ladder 119 South Williamsburg, Brooklyn working in Ladder 110

“The absolute, the strength of the fire department is that officer and those...guys in the firehouse. You just can't break it up. That goes back to the Civil War. We came into existence in the Civil War as a result of the draft riots.... The fire department was founded on those tight-knit relationships, just like the military. Military units and fire department units had an awful lot in common in terms of their unit cohesion and things like that, and traditions that are passed on.”

—2nd Deputy Commissioner Tom Fitzpatrick, then in Headquarters, Downtown Brooklyn

Venting
Firefighters Botti and Bergin opening the roof as flames erupt at close range.
Photo by Todd Maisel

Commercial fire
Anthony "Tony" Edwards and a fellow firefighter survey the damaged interior of a laundromat following a destructive fire.
Photo by Todd Maisel

> “ My attitude is, never forget the fear. There is a fear factor. You have to override it, but never forget it. Put yourself in that spot. If you know it's dangerous or something, you're going to have to do it, but do it as safely as possible. Other times, you can't.
>
> *—Battalion Chief Bill Moore, then in Battalion 10, Yorkville, Manhattan*

Personal moments

Beyond the firehouse, life continues in familiar ways: children's sports, family businesses, Alcoholics Anonymous meetings, late-summer pool days – each carrying its own meaning.

> “ September 10th is actually a day that I remember very, very vividly. I was going to be working overtime on September 11th. What I used to do a lot when I was working two-night shifts, because I lived two hours away, on a perfect day...I would go into the city and I would go to an

AA meeting, watch a movie, and I'll always stop by and park at this firehouse, Ladder 3.

—Lieutenant Ray Brown, then in Ladder 113, Crown Heights, Brooklyn

“ That period of time in my life, actually, I was very, very busy coaching my son in baseball. My son was coming up on 10 years old. On his way to become a professional ballplayer, of course.

—Chief of Department (2020–2022) Tom Richardson, then a Battalion Chief in Battalion 53, Bayside, Queens

“ That Sunday...was the closing day of our swim club. I belonged to a swim club on Staten Island, which has many firefighters and police. I was talking to several other people who would not be with us after 9/11. I remember thinking there's some senior people here and this might be the last time we see them, because in a year's time when the pool opens, they may no longer be with us.... Yet ironically when the pool opened, many of them were still with us and many of the people who you least expected to die were no longer.

—Dr. Kerry Kelly MD, then FDNY Chief Medical Officer, Bureau of Health Services, Headquarters Downtown Brooklyn

“ My son graduated from probie school the Saturday before [September 8, 2001]. Technically, it wasn't a graduation. He had started a new program where you go through probie school and they would assign you to a firehouse for 14 weeks.

—Battalion Chief Bill Moore, then in Battalion 10, Yorkville, Manhattan

Evening

As the day moved toward evening, the work of the department and the life of the city kept unfolding on parallel tracks.

“ That Probie class, Monday night and Tuesday night, they were being trained in their CFR [Certified First Responder] program to New York City protocols. My son got home, I guess, about midnight.

—Battalion Chief Bill Moore, then in Battalion 10, Yorkville, Manhattan

" September 10th, I went to work that night, I was the on-duty deputy chief in Division 3, which is Midtown Manhattan. Early that night [I]started visiting people, going by firehouses, just stop by to see what's going on, answering any questions. One of the last stops was 22 Engine and 13 Truck and before I left, they invited me back to have lunch the next day. I told them I'll see – I'll be back.

—Assistant Chief Tom Galvin, Chief of Training (2004–2015), then a Deputy Chief in Division 3, Midtown, Manhattan

" September 10th was great. It was a night tour. I had Johnny Colon driving me for the 24 hours. Johnny Colon is a Marine Vietnam veteran. Johnny Colon, to me, was the greatest firefighter I ever worked with. Totally professional, would always be properly dressed, big medal [many department commendations] guy, roof rope rescues, real, never talk about it. Sometimes he talked about 'Nam.

—Captain Glenn Rohan, then a Lieutenant in Ladder 43, Spanish Harlem, Manhattan

" Well, I got off on the night of the 10th. Everybody in that firehouse that night when I left there, were all murdered the next day. I was home and my family had a plumbing business in town and that was what I did on my days off, and that's where I was, I was working for my father, my uncle, my cousin.

—Battalion Chief George Maier, then in Battalion 9, Hell's Kitchen, Manhattan; FDNY IMT

" The 10th, we had this mass, the 11th, there was a golf outing for two friends of mine who had passed away prematurely. Pete Ganci, I think was scheduled for jury duty on the 11th. I can't have both of us out on the same day. I skipped that. It would've been a beautiful day for golf, but it ended up being a dreadful day.

—Fire Commissioner (2014–2022) Dan Nigro, then Chief of Operations Headquarters, Downtown Brooklyn (served as Chief of Department 2001–2002)

" More than a few firefighters parted company saying, 'See you at the big one.'

—Lieutenant Ray Brown, then in Ladder 113, Crown Heights, Brooklyn

Another day, another night

By Monday night, New York City has settled into its usual patterns. In firehouses, crews finish evening rituals. Dinner dishes are washed. Apparatus is backed into quarters. Tools are returned to their brackets.

On Randall's Island, Bill Moore's son finishes his CFR training and gets home near midnight. In Midtown, Deputy Chief Tom Galvin completes his rounds – one more stop, one more kitchen table – then leaves Engine 22 and Ladder 13 with a promise: I'll be back for lunch.

In Spanish Harlem, Glenn Rohan rides out the night with Ladder 43, Johnny Colon driving. The calls are the usual mix – stuck elevators, car accidents, gas leaks – busy but familiar, the kind of tour you forget as soon as it ends. Except for two young firefighters covering from Engine 22 and Ladder 13. Rohan clocks the way they move: squared away, reliable, the kind you'd steal for your own firehouse if you could.

In Hell's Kitchen, George Maier finishes his tour and heads home to the family plumbing business. Ray Brown, staying in the city between shifts, parks by Ladder 3 the way he often does – planning an AA meeting in the morning before working overtime.

At 7:11 p.m., the sun sets behind the Manhattan skyline. The Twin Towers' aircraft warning lights blink, as they do every night. The forecast calls for another clear morning, with a high near 80: good flying weather.

And the small unfinished things remain exactly where they were. The radios still aren't right. The lieutenant's exam is still six weeks away. The Giants still lost. Pete Ganci still has jury duty on Tuesday.

The city keeps its rhythms. Sirens sound in the distance. Garbage trucks begin their rounds. The subway rumbles. Inside firehouses, firefighters check the riding list for the morning tour, testing equipment one more time. The next shift would, as usual, have what it needed. Across the city, 343 firefighters pass their final hours – finishing shifts, beginning new ones. Some rest waiting for the next alarm. Another Monday passes into Tuesday. Another busy, tiring, and yet ordinary Monday.

> “September 10th, I had two kids with me from 22 Engine and 13 Truck. I remember we ran a lot that night, a lot of runs. No fires. We ran a lot. We had elevators, we had car accidents, gas [leaks]. I like these two kids, I said, 'Man, I'd love to see these kids at 43' (his company). These kids struck me. They died the next day. These two kids.
>
> *—Captain Glenn Rohan, then a Lieutenant in Ladder 43, Spanish Harlem, Manhattan*

Franciscan Friar[12] and FDNY Chaplain Father Mychal Judge is known as "The Firemen's Friar." Smiling and beloved, he has boundless energy. On September 10 he delivers the Homily in his soft Irish lilt at the rededication of the firehouse of Engine 73 and Ladder 42 after being renovated.

"That's the way it is. Good days. And bad days. Up days. Down days. Sad days. Happy days. But never a boring day on this job. You do what God has called you to do. You show up. You put one foot in front of another. You get on the rig and you go out and you do the job – which is a mystery. And a surprise. You have no idea when you get on that rig. No matter how big the call. No matter how small. You have no idea what God is calling you to. But he needs you. He needs me. He needs all of us."[13]

Section Two: The Day

“

The sky is dark’ning like a stain.
Something is going to fall like rain.
And it won’t be flowers.

—W.H. Auden

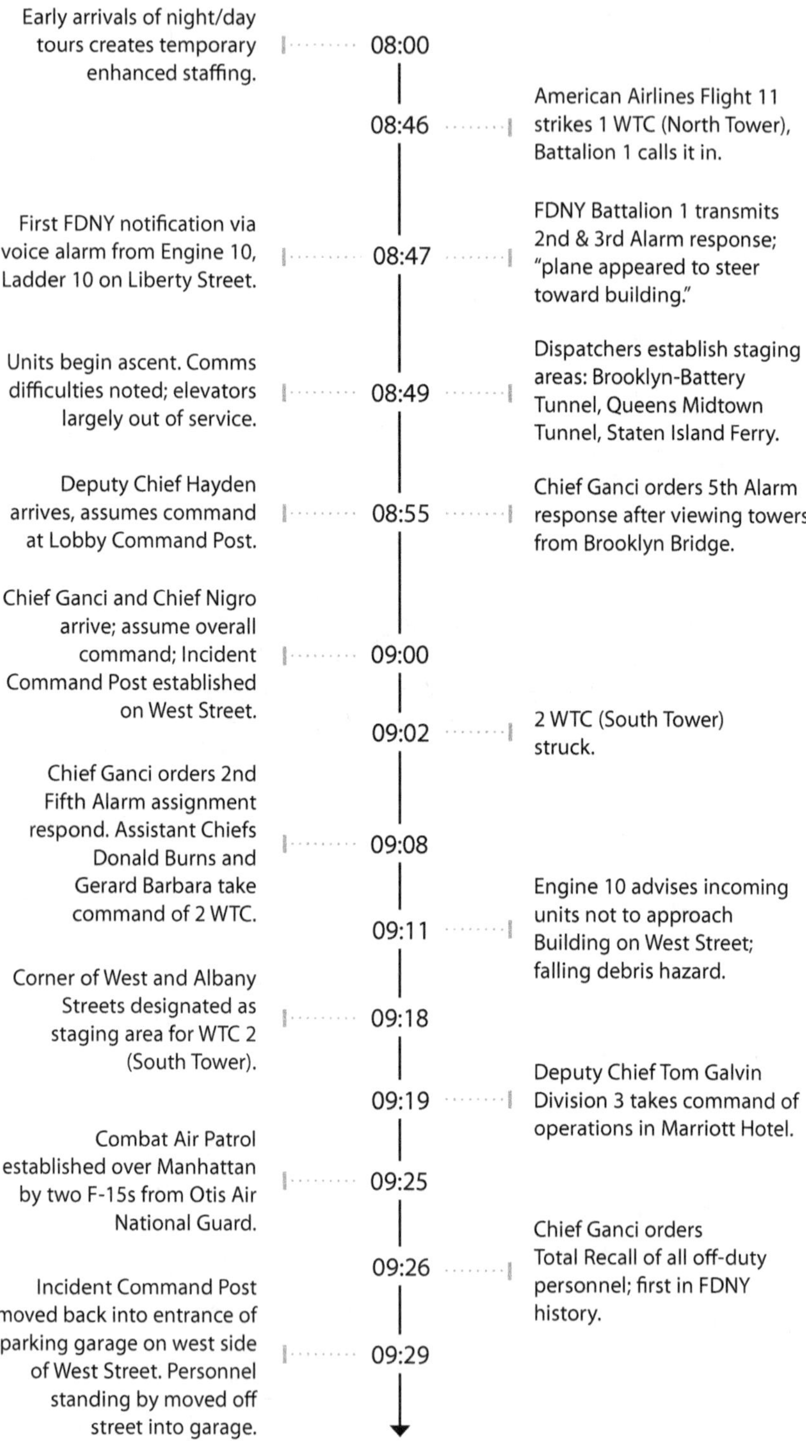
Early arrivals of night/day tours creates temporary enhanced staffing.
08:00
08:46
American Airlines Flight 11 strikes 1 WTC (North Tower), Battalion 1 calls it in.
First FDNY notification via voice alarm from Engine 10, Ladder 10 on Liberty Street.
08:47
FDNY Battalion 1 transmits 2nd & 3rd Alarm response; "plane appeared to steer toward building."
Units begin ascent. Comms difficulties noted; elevators largely out of service.
08:49
Dispatchers establish staging areas: Brooklyn-Battery Tunnel, Queens Midtown Tunnel, Staten Island Ferry.
Deputy Chief Hayden arrives, assumes command at Lobby Command Post.
08:55
Chief Ganci orders 5th Alarm response after viewing towers from Brooklyn Bridge.
Chief Ganci and Chief Nigro arrive; assume overall command; Incident Command Post established on West Street.
09:00
09:02
2 WTC (South Tower) struck.
Chief Ganci orders 2nd Fifth Alarm assignment respond. Assistant Chiefs Donald Burns and Gerard Barbara take command of 2 WTC.
09:08
09:11
Engine 10 advises incoming units not to approach Building on West Street; falling debris hazard.
Corner of West and Albany Streets designated as staging area for WTC 2 (South Tower).
09:18
09:19
Deputy Chief Tom Galvin Division 3 takes command of operations in Marriott Hotel.
Combat Air Patrol established over Manhattan by two F-15s from Otis Air National Guard.
09:25
09:26
Chief Ganci orders Total Recall of all off-duty personnel; first in FDNY history.
Incident Command Post moved back into entrance of parking garage on west side of West Street. Personnel standing by moved off street into garage.
09:29

Chapter Three

The Strikes

“I remember just looking out at the sky and just saying, ‘What a gorgeous day.’

—Assistant Chief Tom Galvin, Chief of Training (2004–2015), then a Deputy Chief in Division 3, Midtown, Manhattan

“When I got a...view of the exterior of the tower, I had a very deep sense within me there were going to be firefighters that were going to get killed in addition to all the civilians who already were killed. I knew that this was going to be a dark day for the fire department.

—Chief of Department (2004–2006) Pete Hayden, then a Deputy Chief in Division 1, SoHo, Manhattan

“We go around front, now people are still jumping, and they are cutting themselves in half on the atrium right in front of us. It was heartbreaking.

—Lieutenant Artie Riccio, then firefighter in Ladder 119 South Williamsburg, Brooklyn working in Ladder 110

> “ I remember I called my wife at work and I said, ‘They’re back. They came back’...I watched the second plane hit. Then I said, ‘Well, now we’re all going to work.’
>
> *—Assistant Chief Bob Maynes, Queens Boro Commander then a Battalion Chief in Battalion 41, East Flatbush, Brooklyn, and past IMT Incident Commander*

> “ They [French filmmakers] showed the faces of the firefighters in the lobby of the tower waiting for an assignment that they well knew they might not be getting home from.
>
> *1st Deputy Commissioner (2004–2010) Frank Cruthers, then an Assistant Chief at Headquarters, Downtown Brooklyn (served as Chief of Department 1996–1997, 2002–2004)*

> “ I’d see things in the corner of my eye and I knew that was the bodies that were falling.
>
> *—Lieutenant Ray Brown, then in Ladder 113, Crown Heights, Brooklyn*

> “ A plane, hit that building.... [I]t happened so fast. I think what–what was already unimaginable doubled. It just doubled instantly.
>
> *—Fire Commissioner (2014–2022) Dan Nigro, then Chief of Operations Headquarters, Downtown Brooklyn (served as Chief of Department 2001–2002)*

A new day

A beautiful Tuesday. 65 degrees. A deep blue cloudless sky, cloudless and borderline blindingly crisp. The day enables a clear view of the stunning architectural profile of a great modern city. New York City’s expansiveness with skyscraper fingers reaching into the sky. Scanning the city, the Twin Towers in Lower Manhattan command at least a moment of special attention.

The day shift begins for the busiest fire department in the world.

9:00 a.m. Time for change of shifts within the FDNY. The change, by custom and practice, begins about an hour earlier. 0800 marks the expected time for arrival at firehouses across the city.

Firefighters pull personal gear off racks. They remove helmets, boots, bunker coats, and pants and place them neatly by firefighting apparatus – in anticipation of the next call. Each firefighter on the incoming shift replaces a firefighter on the outgoing shift. One for one.

Next stop: the kitchen, the warm and ever-beating heart of the fire house. Companionship and food – both served up in the fire house by the firefighters. Food preparation occurs in a near commercial grade kitchen. Outgoing and incoming firefighters mingle. Coffee and conversation. Doesn't anyone need to leave? What's on the calendar for today? Which tools are going in or out of service? Any details to pass along?

Firefighters inspect or test every piece of equipment. Mask cylinders, nozzles, hoses, medical equipment, and SCBA (self-contained breathing apparatus).[14] Firefighters swap out batteries and inspect all tools. Ladder companies start and test all power equipment. Engine companies inspect and test all nozzles, hoses and medical equipment.

Any firefighters sent to work in another firehouse to equalize staffing? Shift swaps get arranged. Did the outgoing crew go to the "Big One" last night?

9:00 a.m. Some companies hold a formal roll call on the apparatus floor. Most companies conduct roll call informally.

More coffee as required. A frequent quip: firefighting is the only job that begins and ends with a coffee break.

Part A: Responder Voices

September 11, 2001. Firefighters living lives...at home and at work, moving through the ordinary start of a day.

> “6 o'clock at night on the 10th I went to work, supposed to go off duty at 9 o'clock in the morning. 9/11 is my wedding anniversary, that happened to be my 25th wedding anniversary. I still can't believe this. I had arranged to take the second part of it off. My relief was in.
>
> *—Chief of Operations Pat McNally, then a Deputy Chief in Division 14, Flushing, Queens*

> “Pete Ganci was hands-on. Everybody wanted to be around Pete. The day usually started in his office for the staff chiefs. It would be

somewhat similar to the kitchen table in the firehouse. Discussions of whether it was sports, families, anything else besides the projects we were working on and coffee and whatever. Pete was usually the first person in, for some reason, the last person to go. It broke up 8:40-ish, just before the first plane hit the North Tower. Everybody went their separate ways as we did every other day, and then the day changed.

—Fire Commissioner (2014–2022) Dan Nigro,
then Chief of Operations Headquarters, Downtown Brooklyn
(served as Chief of Department 2001–2002)

“ We knew each other from work and we had a lot of mutual friends. He said, ‘I got to go upstairs,’ and he came downstairs and he had a yoga mat in his hand. As he’s walking away, I said, ‘Hey, Paddy, [Captain Paddy Brown Ladder 3] are you going to yoga?’ He goes, ‘Yes.’ I said to him, ‘Yoga? You used to go to Gleason’s gym and beat people up.’ He turns around and he looks at me and he says, ‘There’s no girls at Gleason’s,’ and he trots off, and that’s the last time that I saw him.

—Lieutenant Ray Brown, then in Ladder 113,
Crown Heights, Brooklyn

“ I’m supposed to work overtime in Engine 214. I had called up 214, I spoke to [Lieutenant] Chris Sullivan, he was coming to 113 [Ray’s company]. He said, ‘I’ll go to 214.’ Chris Sullivan and Engine 214, they went to the Trade Center and they all passed away. That was my first God moment or the universe. Things aligned at that point for me.

—Lieutenant Ray Brown, then in Ladder 113,
Crown Heights, Brooklyn

The first strike

At 8:46 a.m., American Airlines Flight 11, a jumbo jet loaded with fuel for a transcontinental flight, slammed into the North Tower. Fire erupted in floors 93 through 99. FDNY began dispatching units at 8:47. The first to arrive established a Lobby Command Post inside the North Tower. Dispatchers designated multiple staging areas at 8:49. Later arriving chiefs established the overall Incident Command Post [ICP] on West Street (it would move twice by 9:30 a.m. due to debris falling).[15]

The first strike drew attention – from both on and off duty firefighters and from the media.

Timelapse of strike
Timelapse of Flight 11 striking the north face of the North Tower at 8:46 a.m. and fire erupting from the south side of the tower.
Wolfgang Staehle, Public domain, via Wikimedia Commons

“ My office was about maybe three miles north of the Trade Center, and I actually heard the plane crash…I knew that this was going to be a dark day for the fire department and this was not good.

—Chief of Department (2004–2006) Pete Hayden,
then a Deputy Chief in Division 1, SoHo, Manhattan

“ The chief of department was on the 7th floor in the corner, direct view of the Twin Towers. My office was two doors down. I went back to my office after our little meeting broke up, and sat at the desk and heard – the building shook. I said, ‘What the heck was that?’ As soon as that happened, Pete [Ganci] yelled out, ‘Dan, look out the window. A plane just hit the World Trade Center.’ Of course I look out. We didn’t have a bird’s eye view of the north face of the tower, but the black smoke and the flames were clearly visible, that this was a sizable event.

—Fire Commissioner (2014–2022) Dan Nigro,
then Chief of Operations Headquarters, Downtown Brooklyn
(served as Chief of Department 2001–2002)

“ I came down for coffee around eight o’clock and over the voice alarm comes a second alarm for a fire in the World Trade Center. Then we started getting the word, it’s a plane, so we are thinking a small plane and then we turned on the TV. I had detailed one of my members [to] Squad 252 in Brooklyn. He called and said, ‘Cap, I’m at the firehouse [Squad 252]. The rig just pulled away. Should I follow them, go to the fire? I said, ‘No, no, come back to quarters and eventually, we are going to go. You’ll just go with us.’ He came back to quarters. [All six members of Squad 252 were killed.] We started getting bomb threats in the subways in Queens, so we were running around and trying to keep track of the fire, listen on the radio.

—Battalion Chief Fred LaFemina, Chief of Rescue Services,
then Captain of Squad 270, South Jamaica, Queens;
member FDNY USAR

“ As I walked back in, there was the picture on the television screen of the North Tower burning. I was at the 1993 bombing and I always thought they would be back. As they zeroed in, I said, ‘That’s 15 floors of fire. That’s not a small plane.’ I said immediately, ‘They’re back.’

I remember I called my wife at work and I said, 'They're back. They came back.'

—Assistant Chief Bob Maynes, Queens Boro Commander, then a Battalion Chief in Battalion 41, East Flatbush, Brooklyn, and past IMT Incident Commander

“ I'm working in 113 [Ladder 113]. I go down to the kitchen and the guys are watching this plane which is crashing through the Trade Center and they're all thinking like everybody, it was a Cessna. You can see the fire and some of the guys were asking me, 'Hey, Ray, you've been to high-rise fires working in rescue [Rescue 1].' They asked me, 'What do you do?'

—Lieutenant Ray Brown, then in Ladder 113, Crown Heights, Brooklyn

“ I was in the hospital [Staten Island University Hospital] making rounds and I got on my beeper that a plane had hit the World Trade Center. In my mind, I always think of the years ago when a plane hit the Empire State Building. That was my image. Then I was talking to a patient and I looked up and I saw on the TV, that explosion. I said to myself, 'This is going to be a big response with the fire department. I should be there because some of our members may get hurt and I better be there.'

—Dr. Kerry Kelly MD, then FDNY Chief Medical Officer, Bureau of Health Services, Headquarters Downtown Brooklyn

“ We [Chief of Department Pete Ganci and Nigro] decided we would go together so we could talk a little strategy on the way. Flew over to [the] Brooklyn Bridge, looked up. I said to Pete two things of note: 'We can't put out this much fire,' and 'this'll be the worst day of our lives.' Because he [Ganci] just knew this was above and beyond anything else we had ever seen. He immediately transmitted a fifth alarm [45 units, 200 firefighters] to bring the extra units in.

—Fire Commissioner (2014–2022) Dan Nigro, then Chief of Operations Headquarters, Downtown Brooklyn (served as Chief of Department 2001–2002)

“ Everybody's in their mode. Chief Ganci is responding, Chief Nigro is responding, Chief Burns, Barbara, we're all doing our job as chief.

I look out the window before I leave, I had a great view of the Trade Center from one of our offices. I turned around to a battalion chief behind me and he says, 'This is no accident. Look at the sky, it's beautiful and all you can do is see this big plume of black smoke.'

—Fire Commissioner (2010–2014) Sal Cassano,
then Assistant Chief at Headquarters, Downtown Brooklyn
(served as Chief of Department 2006–2010)

“ We're 10-8, meaning we're available. I said [via radio to Manhattan], 'Do you want us to proceed downtown?' And he says, 'No, 43 return home.' I'm going, 'What?' Johnny Colon, again, the greatest, he goes, 'Boss, what do you want to do?' I say, 'John, we've got to go back [to their firehouse]. I've been given an order and I'm going back, that's it.' You can't just assign yourself. It's just everything falls apart from the rest of the city.

—Captain Glenn Rohan, then a Lieutenant in Ladder 43,
Spanish Harlem, Manhattan

“ I paid an insurance bill in town, [and a] young lady is pointing to the TV about the plane hitting the tower. Well, I got to work. I went home, picked up my bag, called my wife said, 'I'm taking the cell phone, the only flip phone that we had. I'll see you when I see you.' I was probably at the firehouse in 45 minutes. That was the easiest 60 miles I've ever driven, the quickest 60 miles I've ever driven.

—Captain Kerry Hollywood, then in Engine 53,
Spanish Harlem, Manhattan; Commanding Officer
Family Assistance Unit

“ I was not aware that the tower had gotten hit at that time. I thought it was just a large fire. I got to the class location. There were several hundred firefighters there waiting for the [promotional exam prep] class, but they were all out in the street. I asked them what was going on. They all told me there were two fifth alarms. Two buildings were hit by planes. I knew at that point that this was terrorism. The fire department had issued a recall; recall is members coming in from home. Even without that, at my rank, I had to go to work. The [Verrazzano] bridge was closed, I showed them my ID. They let me cross. I reported to my firehouse in Queens. They said there was a staging area in Cunningham Park, which is somewhere in Queens. Went to the staging area, got on a bus immediately with 30, 40 other members. We went to the site. I got to the site around noon.

—Deputy Chief Jim DiDomenico, then in Division 13, South Jamaica, Queens

“ I went to the fire house and I just missed them by 10 minutes. I had hung a U-turn trying to get some pork chops, because I figured they're going to be hungry that night. That took 10 minutes, a U-turn, got the food and went to the fire house, they were already gone. [4 firefighters from Engine 235 were killed.]

—Firefighter Lois Mungay, then in Engine 235, Bedford Stuyvesant, Brooklyn

“ As I'm driving in, I had a few cell phone conversations with my wife, my mom, my sister [NYPD]. My dad worked for the Port Authority [WTC landlord] and he was in the building earlier that morning, but he wasn't there when it happened. My mom informed me that they didn't know if my brother Ray [Lieutenant, Ladder 113] was working, but he's not answering his phone.

—Captain Paul Brown, then a Lieutenant covering in Division 15, Brownsville, Brooklyn; FDNY IMT

“ I knew it wasn't an accident and then I get my car, I'm responding over.... [E]verybody wanted to come with us, and I actually held some people back to say, ‘You got to stay here. We need some people in headquarters in case.’

—Fire Commissioner (2010–2014) Sal Cassano, then Assistant Chief at Headquarters, Downtown Brooklyn (served as Chief of Department 2006–2010)

“ As we attempted to cross the street, there were bodies coming down off the building so everyone said, ‘Be careful, you can't go that way.’ We walked around and as we walked around, there was more debris from the fallen plane and there were body parts. It was just a terrible scene.... We went into 10 and 10 [Engine 10, Ladder 10 on Liberty St. across from the WTC]. When I went into the 10 and 10 the firehouse, the television was on and they showed the Pentagon being hit. Then I think it really struck me that this was a wartime situation.

—Dr. Kerry Kelly MD, FDNY, then Chief Medical Officer, Bureau of Health Services, Headquarters Downtown Brooklyn

“ The whole time we're looking up and we can see the Towers. We see the ash coming over. So we get to the Brooklyn Battery Tunnel [a staging area]. Tom Manley [Union official and Ladder 113 firefighter] hops on the rig and he tells us, ‘They bombed the Pentagon, they bombed the White House, and we hear there's other targets.’ Dennis [Dowdican], the Vietnam veteran, says, ‘This is war.’...We're going through the tunnel, I remember saying ‘Willie [Roberts, Ladder 113 chauffeur], just get us through.

—Lieutenant Ray Brown, then in Ladder 113, Crown Heights, Brooklyn

“ When we got there I saw something weird coming off the building, and I looked up and I didn't know what it was, and I was trying to get a sense of what was happening.... [I]t turned out they were bodies, they were people jumping off the top of the buildings, so then I realized how bad it was up there.... The reason they jump is because they're relieved, and this is a hard concept to understand. They are burned or they can't breathe, so when they jump, they actually feel better. It's a realization that's harsh. In our case, it was like you put your head down and you say, ‘Well, this is it. This is what I'm here for.’ That's what you do.

—Firefighter Louis Giaconelli, then in Engine 53, Spanish Harlem, Manhattan; FDNY IMT

“ We set up [Incident Command Post, ICP] initially in the middle of West Street, but things were coming out of the building. It didn't seem like a good location, so we moved just across the street by the World Financial Center, still having a good view of the North Tower. Chief Hayden was the 1st division chief on duty. He went into the North Tower and the staff chief on duty was [Assistant Chief] Joe Callan and he was put in command of the North Tower. Companies would report into the lobby and they would be given their assignments by those chiefs.

—Fire Commissioner (2014–2022) Dan Nigro, then Chief of Operations Headquarters, Downtown Brooklyn (served as Chief of Department 2001–2002)

> "The lobby there was chaotic and you could see some of the devastation that had already occurred. The first order of business was to establish the command posts, and to get some communications going. Communications traditionally are not good in high-rise buildings and they weren't working, then the elevators were out of service. We were at a distinct disadvantage.... The key was that we stayed calm. We knew we were in a lot of trouble, we knew what our procedures were, even though some of the procedures had failed such as the communications and certainly the use of the elevators. Basically, all the building systems, the systems had been running ineffectively. The sprinkler systems, the communication system, that's due to the plane crash.
>
> —*Chief of Department (2004–2006) Pete Hayden, then a Deputy Chief in Division 1, SoHo, Manhattan*

Street view of the burning WTC towers
Smoke billows from the North Tower (on the left) as photographed from Battery Park City Marina.
rds323, 2001, Public Domain, via Wikimedia Commons

"People are still jumping, and they are cutting themselves in half on the atrium right in front of us. It was heartbreaking. A friend of mine, Danny Suhr, was in [Engine] 216. He was hooking up to a hydrant and somebody landed on him and killed him. He was probably the first person to die at the Trade Center.

—Lieutenant Artie Riccio, then a firefighter in Ladder 119 South Williamsburg, Brooklyn, working in Ladder 110

"The [call takers] would be getting phone calls reporting, 'A plane hit the building, building's on fire, what floor people were trapped on.' You would be directing [the fire companies] which way to go, informing them that, 'Command posts will be set up here and you're going to respond over to this area.' Basically, we would be making decisions about where they would be assigned and what companies. I felt extremely overwhelmed and not even sure exactly how we would handle this.

—Fire Alarm Dispatcher John Lightsey, then in Manhattan Communications Office, Central Park, Manhattan

UA Flight 175 hits 2 WTC
Fire erupting from the north side of the South Tower immediately after Flight 175 strikes the South face of the South Tower.
Robert J. Fisch, CC BY-SA 2.0, via Wikimedia Commons

“ We get to the Trade Center and now we're in the middle of the road there. It's just like madness, there's cars and sirens and you can smell it. You could smell the burning rubber which we later learned was the tires from the jet. [I] had a little chat with the guys, 'Listen, guys, get ready, this is going to be a long day.'

—Lieutenant Ray Brown, then in Ladder 113, Crown Heights, Brooklyn

The second strike

At 9:02 a.m., United Airlines flight 175 slammed into the South Tower, all but cutting through the building. Fire erupted in floors 77 through 85. Firefighters continued flooding into the area. Organizing efforts continued even as difficulties mounted. Desperate civilians in the building hurled themselves to certain death to escape the flames engulfing them. Solemn firefighters trudged the seemingly endless stairs of another tower.

Firefighters poured in. On duty. Off duty. They had seen. They had heard. They were responding. The Call for all off-duty FDNY members to report went out at 9:29 a.m. across radio frequencies, voice alarms, firehouse teleprinters, and all broadcast media outlets. Many FDNY members, perhaps several thousand, had not waited for the call. They were already on site or en route.

“ I get to Broadway, you can see stuff coming off the building. We thought it was just debris coming out, but it was actually people jumping out of the building. I turned down Liberty, there's thousands of people watching, thousands. Now I'm maneuvering around them and all of a sudden the second plane hits over our head right in front of us into the building. Now I have those thousands of people running at the rig.

—Lieutenant Artie Riccio, then a firefighter in Ladder 119 South Williamsburg, Brooklyn, working in Ladder 110

“ As I'm pulling up on West Broadway, adjacent the 7 World Trade Center I had a great look [at] where the plane had crashed into the building and a smoking huge hole, and you know it's not a small plane from the cloud of smoke and the plume of smoke, and then all of a sudden

I hear another explosion, which I thought in my mind was a secondary explosion. We're under attack.

—Fire Commissioner (2010–2014) Sal Cassano, then Assistant Chief at Headquarters, Downtown Brooklyn (served as Chief of Department 2006–2010)

“ Pete [Ganci] and I were organizing whatever else was going on and we heard this extremely loud noise that made you look up. I looked up just in time to see – and I could tell it was a United Airlines plane but traveling, over 500 miles an hour, hit that building. It was seriously damaged. That plane traveling so fast just came right through and you saw the plane parts and engine over by the Post Office building. Of course, Pete transmitted a second fifth alarm. Eventually, there would be a third fifth alarm assignment. [Assistant Chief] Donald Burns just got off duty, and [Assistant Chief] Jerry Barbara were there with us. We assigned them to run the operations now in the South Tower.

—Fire Commissioner Dan Nigro (2014–2022), then Chief of Operations Headquarters, Downtown Brooklyn (served as Chief of Department 2001–2002)

“ When we get reports of people calling for help on certain floors, we pass it to the command post. The floors above the fire, we stopped telling everybody because we knew they weren't coming out. You could basically see that on the TV. You're supposed to pass it along. We didn't pass it along because we realized that those people aren't going to survive.

—Fire Alarm Dispatcher John Lightsey, then in Manhattan Communications Office, Central Park, Manhattan

“ Despite what was going on, I did see in some people, more the senior people than the others, really a look of dread when they left the command post and we're going to go into [the] building. We always take risks, but some are worse than others. Boy, I could see that in a few people. They just had the look like they wouldn't see you again, but they did it anyway. We say that all the time, that no one that I know of or no one ever said to me, one of the units that responded refused an order, either to enter the building or to go up the stairs.

—Fire Commissioner (2014–2022) Dan Nigro, then Chief of Operations Headquarters, Downtown Brooklyn (served as Chief of Department 2001–2002)

“ I went over to talk to the Chief, ‘If you could send us in as soon as possible.’ Your thought as a firefighter is you want to get there. The guys are there and they’re all ready and we start hearing the bodies. I remember looking over and then – we could see them jumping. I’m still piecing it together after almost 20 years. It’s mind-boggling.

—Lieutenant Ray Brown, then in Ladder 113, Crown Heights, Brooklyn

“ There was one elevator in the South Tower that for some amount of time was able to get up maybe the 43rd floor, something like that. We could have ferried some more people close. [Battalion Chief] Orio Palmer and [Fire Marshal] Ron Bucca and Ladder 15, they made it to the impact area. [Battalion Chief] Eddie Geraghty was up there. They were just about to make their move. When they got there to that sky lobby, it was a gruesome scene of victims. Most of them were dead, but not all. They were going to get into that stairwell and try to get anybody out that may have been trapped above. That was the strategy.

—Fire Commissioner (2014–2022) Dan Nigro, then Chief of Operations Headquarters, Downtown Brooklyn (served as Chief of Department 2001–2002)

“ It’s a simple format, you’re really just working with another firefighter at the command post [LCP inside 3 WTC, Marriott Hotel] recording this stuff. So, it’s just pencils and paper. But what happened that day, you had the back-to-back fifth alarms, and we just had too many units coming – when you transmit alarms too fast and it’s uncoordinated, that’s what led to some of the confusion on where they were going. Because most of these people coming in have probably never been in Manhattan – [or] which is the North Tower, which is the South Tower.

—Assistant Chief Tom Galvin, Chief of Training (2004–2015), then a Deputy Chief in Division 3, Midtown, Manhattan

> “Once we had everyone assigned and in motion, I told Pete [Ganci], ‘I’m going to walk around the building and see what it looks like from the other sides.’ Especially the South Tower, which was hit second. When I got on Vessey Street and looked up, I could see that the parts of the plane actually flew through the building, took out the northeast corner of the South Tower and a large piece of it. We had thought about localized collapse on the floors. Everybody said people knew the buildings could collapse.
>
> *—Fire Commissioner (2014–2022) Dan Nigro,*
> *then Chief of Operations Headquarters, Downtown Brooklyn*
> *(served as Chief of Department 2001–2002)*

> “Along the way I see Father Mychal Judge [FDNY Chaplain]. He was just a wonderful, wonderful person, besides our chaplain, and we looked at each other and I can see this very nervous look on his face, and he gave me a nod and I said, ‘Father Mike, we’re in for a bad day, We’re going to need more chaplains here.’
>
> *—Fire Commissioner (2010–2014) Sal Cassano,*
> *then Assistant Chief at Headquarters, Downtown Brooklyn*
> *(served as Chief of Department 2006–2010)*

Part B: Summary, Lessons, and Commentary

Summary

Many people remember where they were when they learned of a historic event. What most FDNY firefighters remember about 9/11 is that it was a perfect, beautiful day – then it wasn’t.

As Chief Tom Galvin told us, “The first thing I remember when we were responding down to the Trade Center. I remember just looking at the sky and just saying, ‘What a gorgeous day.’”

1 WTC, the North Tower, was struck by an airplane at 8:46 a.m., fully engulfing floors 93 through 99 in fire. Battalion 1 reported: “We just had a plane crash into upper floors of the World Trade Center. Transmit a second alarm [approximately 25 units and 100 firefighters] and start relocating companies into the area.”

Seconds later from inside Engine 10’s firehouse on Liberty Street opposite the WTC, Lieutenant Greg Atlas transmitted, "World Trade Center 10-60 [major emergency] send every available ambulance, everything you've got to the World Trade Center now."[16] Engine 10 and Ladder 10 headed toward the building's entrance, avoiding debris in the roadway as they drove – airplane, building, and human.

Inside the North Tower, fire companies reported to the Lobby Command Post for assignment. Some immediately assisted civilians who were critically burned when aviation fuel flashed down the elevator shafts and then barreled out into the lobby. Others rescued people trapped in multiple elevators stalled throughout the building. As firefighters climbed higher, they encountered civilians trapped behind stairway doors jammed shut when the building swayed from the airplane's impact. Floor by floor, firefighters forced doors open and breached holes in walls to free terrified civilians. Many who had attempted to self-evacuate needed help due to injury, disability, or exhaustion.

At headquarters, Chief Cassano attempted to limit excess responders: "Everybody wanted to come with us, and I actually held some people back: 'You got to stay here. We need some people in headquarters in case.'"

As Division 1 Commander responsible for lower Manhattan, Deputy Chief Hayden knew the department's procedures for high-rise fires: establish a Lobby Command Post and get communications started. Inside the Towers, the buildings' hard-wired systems were inoperable from the crash, and radio communications – historically unreliable in high-rise buildings – were poor. As Hayden, an experienced 33-year veteran firefighter, later recalled, "The key was that we stayed calm. We knew we were in a lot of trouble." Firefighters continued working with what they had.

Chiefs Ganci and Nigro responded together, gathering information and strategizing en route. Once they viewed the North Tower, Ganci transmitted a fifth alarm which would bring an additional 45 units and over 200 firefighters to the scene. Earlier arriving chiefs had set up the Incident Command Post [ICP] in the middle of West Street in front of the tower. As debris began falling, the Command Post was moved across West Street, and then farther back onto the ramp of a parking garage. Firefighters were sent inside the garage while awaiting orders – a decision that would later save lives.

Chief Nigro later recalled that he and Chief Ganci had just arrived and were being briefed at the Incident Command Post when the South Tower was struck between the 75th and 78th floors. What had been the biggest fire in FDNY history suddenly became the two biggest fires, multiplying the scale and complexity of the operation. Chief Ganci immediately transmitted a separate fifth alarm for the South Tower.

A third alarm [approximately 30 units and 150 firefighters] was transmitted for the 22-story Marriott Hotel, located between the towers. Struck by flaming debris, the hotel required a separate response assignment to fight fires and evacuate its 825 rooms. Deputy Chief Tom Galvin was given command. Additional alarms followed for fires in surrounding buildings throughout the WTC complex. The busiest fire department in the world did what it always did in the face of adversity: stayed calm and called more units to the scene.

The command structure was in place to meet the challenges, with two senior chiefs assigned to each tower. Every one of them was a War Years veteran, likely the most experienced and knowledgeable staff in department history. Chief of Department Pete Ganci and Chief of Operations Dan Nigro had overall command, at the Incident Command Post, of over

The two largest fires in FDNY history burning side by side
The Twin Towers smoking, the North Tower with the thicker, darker smoke.
English: Kenneth Gross (released into public domain by NIST, via FOIA), Public domain, via Wikimedia Commons

220 fire companies and more than 750 firefighters. Assistant Chief Joe Callan and Deputy Chief Pete Hayden commanded fire and rescue operations inside the North Tower at the Lobby Command Post [LCP], while inside the South Tower, Assistant Chiefs Donald Burns and Jerry Barbara were in charge at the LCP.

At the LCP inside the South Tower, firefighters got their orders and began climbing. Once again, they encountered injured civilians as they made their way up. Artie Riccio remembered, "Going upstairs it was civilians to the left, firefighters to the right.... [W]e had to get them to the left-hand side so we could walk up." Flight 175 hit the South Tower with such force that it caused firefighters to encounter jammed doors and trapped occupants on much lower floors. Elevators needed to be located and occupants rescued. A contingent of firefighters, led by Battalion Chief Orio Palmer and Fire Marshal Ron Bucca, reached the 75th floor. Here, they reported on fire conditions and a large number of deceased civilians.

Chief Nigro, after conferring with Chief Ganci, decided to walk the perimeter for a personal assessment of the scene. Both towers would collapse before Nigro's return.

Chief Hayden recalled being questioned later regarding ordering firefighters into harm's way. "I said, 'That's what they signed on for.' Nobody backed away, they went up those stairs and they took their assignments and God bless them."

In firehouses across the city, firefighters who just got off duty were realizing the magnitude of the event. A significant number remained in their firehouses while those at home headed in. One off-duty firefighter with Ladder 43 asked if he should remain on duty. Glenn Rohan replied, "There's going to be a recall. The whole job has got to come to work today."

Minutes later, the order came. Transmitted over the FDNY Voice Alarm System, every FDNY frequency and teleprinter [response computer] in all five boroughs, as well as the Emergency Broadcast System via all broadcast media. The fire department had issued the first total recall in its history, though many off-duty firefighters were already on their way.

TO ALL UNITS AT THE PRESENT TIME THERE IS A TOTAL RECALL
OF ALL FIREFIGHTERS AND COMPANY OFFICERS.
By Orders of Chief of Department
Peter J. Ganci, Jr.

MESSAGE FROM RCT5
......................TO ALL UNITS..............
AT THE PRESENT TIME THERE IS A TOTAL RECALL OF FIREFIGHTER
AND COMPANY OFFICERS.

.SIGNED PETER J. GANCI JR.
CHIEF OF DEPARTMENT

09/11/01 092739

Total Recall Notification
FDNY teleprinter printout of "TOTAL RECALL" of all off duty firefighters. The only such recall in the FDNY's over 150 years of existence.
With permission from the private collection of Paul Brown

Lessons for Leaders

1. **Know.** Any day. Any time. Maybe today. Maybe tomorrow. Maybe never. The unthought, the unimagined, can appear in a New York minute.

2. **Act accordingly.** Do not turn your back on the ocean. Rogue waves arise when they arise. Stay alert but not obsessed. When off duty, enjoy the beach, the water, family, friends...a golf outing, a day off. Enjoy all of it. Stay informed, be aware. Don't turn your back. Not ever.

3. **Take in reality.** As unreal, as incredible as it may be – commercial jetliners aimed at buildings or people hurling themselves from 100 stories up. Register it as it is. Look up. Adjust.

4. **Ride to the sound of the guns.** Send out the call and trust that others ride too and will meet you there...summoned or not.

5. **Get to work.** Do what you can do as fast as you can do it. Help others do the same. Organize as much, as well, and as fast as possible.

6. **Fight the chaos.** Create pockets of order by doing what you know how to do. Impose order where you can. Strike back. Stride to alter the reality faced, the reality recognized.

7 **Accept that what comes next comes next.** Eyes peeled. Hands at work. Resolve to address whatever unfolds.

Commentary

On September 11, 2001, the United States experienced a coordinated terrorist attack carried out through the hijacking of commercial airliners. Two planes were flown into the World Trade Center Towers in New York City, triggering massive fires, catastrophic structural failure, and the eventual collapse of both buildings. A third plane struck the Pentagon; a fourth crashed in Pennsylvania after passengers revolted. In New York, this attack was the second international attack on the WTC, the first being the explosion of a van bomb at the North Tower on February 2, 1993, an attack that killed six people and injured over a thousand.

On 9/11, the reality in the WTC complex and in the surrounding area literally changed minute by minute. Responders worked with limited verified information and persistent uncertainty, including about additional threats. Responders faced an unprecedented mass-casualty environment requiring rapid coordination under extreme risk and ambiguity. The FDNY did not operate in a vacuum, yet much of what shaped the day sat outside the department's line of sight – before the first alarm and in the hours that followed.

Much of even the best management literature addressing leading amidst crisis concentrates on prevention or anticipation of calamity and post calamity learning. All fair enough. For the FDNY, indeed for most people anywhere, the strikes on the towers trivialized much of even the most imaginative scenario planning and what most organizations term a crisis. On 9/11, the FDNY issued the first total recall of firefighters in its history.

Additionally, much of even the best management literature does not address leadership in the midst of such a piercingly acute crisis. Nothing even roughly equivalent to two massive buildings collapsing in and amidst flames within about an hour of impact from two jumbo jets. The colossal scale and extreme time compression of 9/11 pushed conditions far beyond the reach of standard guidance or commonly cited best practices. Yet, those frameworks still matter – not as instructions for the extraordinary, but as tools for distilling lessons from the extraordinary into more familiar leadership challenges under more common situations. The acuity of the chaos and catastrophe of 9/11 heightens several key aspects of preparing for and addressing the unexpectedly trying, even horrific. These aspects merit special attention in preparing for the "merely" challenging events that many leaders actually do encounter.

In *The Prepared Leader: Emerge from any Crisis More Resilient than Before*, Erica H. James and Lynn Perry Wooten argue that crisis management has five distinct phases.[17] The FDNY's experience on 9/11 and beyond both aligns with – and strains – this framework.

> **I: Early Warning and Signal Detection.** The FDNY didn't monitor airplane flight paths, deviation from those paths, or flight training schools in Florida. These signals lay well outside the department's domain and responsibility. (Later, the FDNY came to reconsider its purpose and operation in this regard.)
> **II: Preparation and Prevention.** The FDNY knew how to fight fires, including large and complex ones. Yet, scale and complexity can overpower scenario planning and overwhelm conventional approaches. Then, the ability to adapt becomes key, including adoption of new or altered practices in the moment and after.
> **III: Containment.** Traditionally, the FDNY attacks fires. Its firefighters do not seek to contain fires. They seek to defeat them. On 9/11, they gave ground. They adapted to the vastness of the challenge faced and of the damage done. They moved back to move forward, to contain and then to defeat.
> **IV: Recovery.** In the months and years that followed, the FDNY would learn and apply many lessons. Some of those lessons pertained to its own recovery and healing – recovery on a scale far beyond anything in its prior experience: physical recovery at the site, individual, and organizational recovery.
> **V: Learning and Reflection.** In retrospect, drawing a clean line between where adaptation ended and learning began may prove of little value. What matters is that the behaviors stemming from adaptation and reflection reshaped the FDNY in lasting ways, with effects that continue to this day.

James and Wooten go on to delineate four key steps to build a team to lead in crisis: compose your crisis team, establish purpose and accountability, create the culture, and empower your team to respond and adapt.

And the FDNY? It selected and trained a small fraction of applicants to join a storied organization with 150 years of history. That history embodied a simple, lived mission to serve the community by saving lives and protecting property. The explicit motto: “New York’s Bravest,” a motto echoed by individual units such as the EMS, “New York’s Best” and FDNY’s Squad Company 1, “No fire too difficult, no rescue too great.” Strong words and high standards in a famously tough city accustomed to competition and superlatives.

Firefighters trained together. They worked together. They even ate together. Typically, when they showed up at a fire scene, they determined then and there how best to apply shared training and acquired experience. Frequent rotation of personnel over decades of service created extensive and richly dense networks of personal connections, relationships forged in the field and in training and strengthened over many, perhaps countless, shared meals. Such is the stuff of trust, which James and Wooten counsel developing before crisis.

In that sense, the FDNY prepared for 9/11 without knowing it, by doing what it did the way that it did, day after day.

How might leaders assess whether an organization has prepared for crisis? Murphy and Murphy offer a method to assess preparedness.[18] Questions 5–9 and 19–20 in their Volatility Leadership Assessment (found in Leading on the Edge of Chaos) seem particularly relevant in determining preparedness for turbulent, volatile, and uncertain conditions. Among them:

- “The employees at your organization are loyal, fulfilled, hard-working, passionate, and do not experience conflicts between their own self-interest and the interests of the company.”
- “You personally ensure that while employees may have different skills and perspectives, they understand, agree with, and have passion for the organization’s core values.”
- “Your organization consistently fills key positions with the right people for the job, based on talent, previous success, ability to innovate, and commitment to the organization’s values, rather than on political pressures or outdated hiring practices.”
- “When you hire employees for your team or department (even if they’re an internal hire), you personally perform a thorough reference check to carefully evaluate whether the candidate has the necessary skills and abilities to accomplish what you need.”

- "Your organization effectively manages its knowledge assets and ensures that people in the organization have the appropriate information they need to excel at their jobs."
- "When faced with complex and seemingly overwhelming problems, your organization is able to quickly and smoothly get things under control by focusing on key areas of importance and following a disciplined and orderly plan of action."
- "When faced with complex and seemingly overwhelming problems, you are personally able to quickly and smoothly get things under control by focusing on key areas of importance and by following a disciplined and ordered plan of action."

Yet, in the moment, before after-action reviews and long before considered reflection, how should a leader proceed?

Initially, the FDNY poured into what Snowden and Boone would likely classify as an ordered environment, namely a large building on fire.[19] Thousands of firefighters brought with them thousands of accumulated years of practice, procedures, and experience. They went to work.

Psychologist and Nobel laureate Daniel Kahneman examines how people think and decide under pressure.[20] He would likely term this as "System 1" thinking (fast, intuitive, and emotional) and in this context, rightly so. "System 2" thinking (slow, logical, and deliberate) would emerge later and characterize so much of the FDNY's recovery and transformation. Emotion, however, would remain present throughout – acknowledged, not suppressed.

James and Wooten[21] also write that crisis-ready leaders should:

- "Make space for other people to stand up, speak up, and contribute as the situation dictates." (In other words, leave room for and even expect initiative, both during key events and in adjusting to as well as in learning in their aftermath.)
- "Let go of your ego and be humble enough to allow others to take the lead as the situation dictates." (This will occur in more and less dramatic ways as events and their aftermath unfold.)
- "Let these things happen spontaneously and without obstacles as the situation changes." (That includes the massive obstacles that resulted from the collapse of the towers both immediately and in the months and years that followed.)

Finally, as Snowden and Boone might term it, FDNY firefighters did what they knew how to do.[22] Questions emerged about what made this fire possibly very different – the height of the buildings, the massiveness and intensity of the fires, the integrity of the towers, and the number (in the tens of thousands) who needed evacuating. Command established itself and guided the work. In Snowden and Boone's words, FDNY firefighters sensed, categorized, and responded. Like always, except more so.

Then, the battle changed.

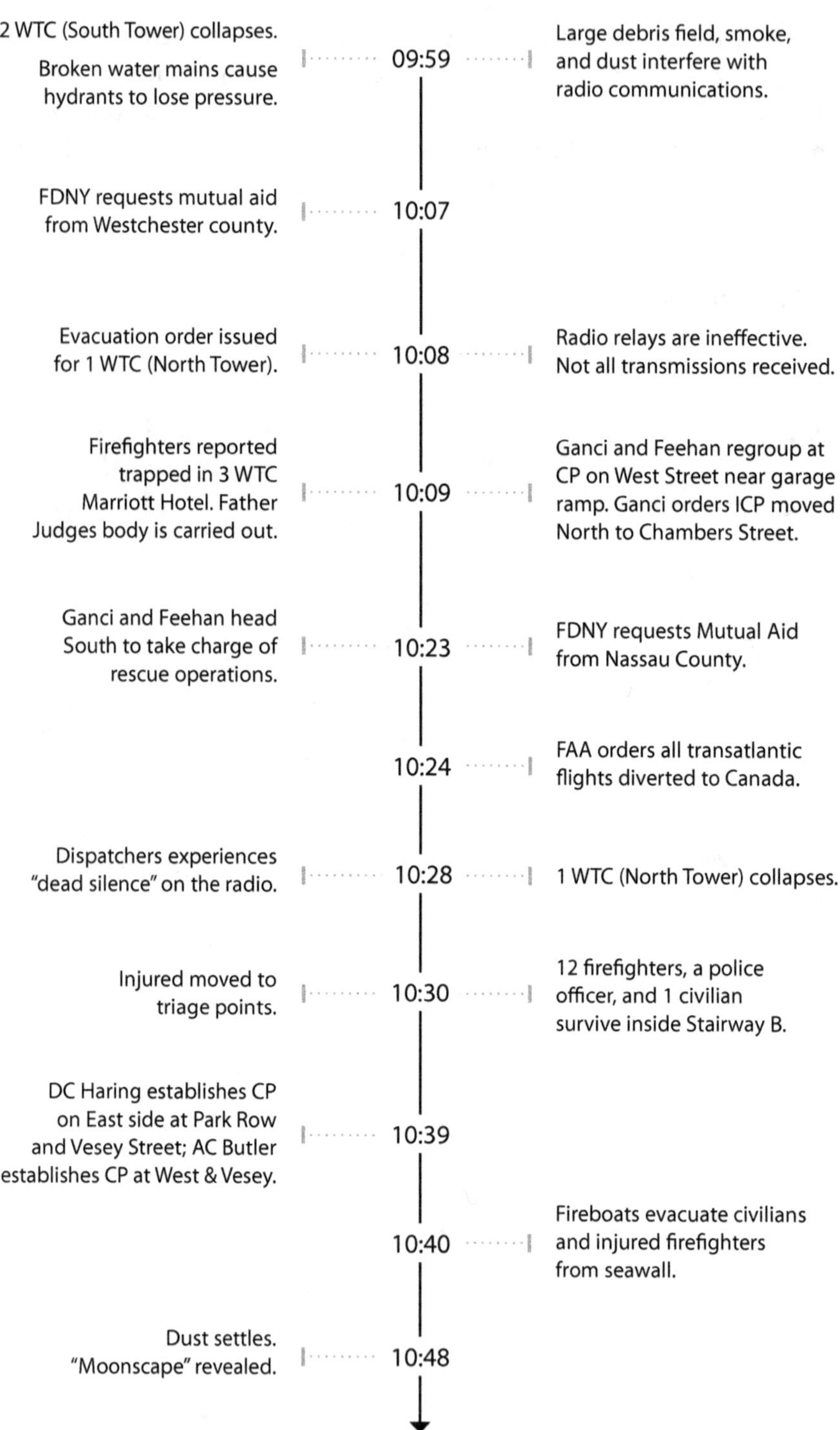

2 WTC (South Tower) collapses.
Broken water mains cause hydrants to lose pressure.
09:59
Large debris field, smoke, and dust interfere with radio communications.
FDNY requests mutual aid from Westchester county.
10:07
Evacuation order issued for 1 WTC (North Tower).
10:08
Radio relays are ineffective. Not all transmissions received.
Firefighters reported trapped in 3 WTC Marriott Hotel. Father Judges body is carried out.
10:09
Ganci and Feehan regroup at CP on West Street near garage ramp. Ganci orders ICP moved North to Chambers Street.
Ganci and Feehan head South to take charge of rescue operations.
10:23
FDNY requests Mutual Aid from Nassau County.
10:24
FAA orders all transatlantic flights diverted to Canada.
Dispatchers experiences "dead silence" on the radio.
10:28
1 WTC (North Tower) collapses.
Injured moved to triage points.
10:30
12 firefighters, a police officer, and 1 civilian survive inside Stairway B.
DC Haring establishes CP on East side at Park Row and Vesey Street; AC Butler establishes CP at West & Vesey.
10:39
10:40
Fireboats evacuate civilians and injured firefighters from seawall.
Dust settles. "Moonscape" revealed.
10:48

Chapter Four

The Towers Collapse... and Then, the End of the Beginning

> “Usually it's 'Mayday, mayday, mayday.' It wasn't. It was 'Get the fuck out now.' He said it about five times.
>
> *—Lieutenant Artie Riccio, then a firefighter in Ladder 119 South Williamsburg, Brooklyn working in Ladder 110*

> “There's a lot of dead people here. This isn't like a fire with two people dead. No, you know this is going to be multiple.... There's hundreds of people going to be dead.
>
> *—Captain Glenn Rohan, then a Lieutenant in Ladder 43, Spanish Harlem, Manhattan*

> “The command post was completely gone.
>
> *—Chief of Operations Pat McNally, then a Deputy Chief in Division 14, Flushing, Queens*

> “[I]t was dead silence...trying to get somebody on the radio.... It was an eerie feeling. That never happens on the radio.... All of a sudden, the phone stopped ringing. There was nothing there.
>
> *—Fire Alarm Dispatcher John Lightsey FDNY, then in Manhattan communications Office Central Park*

> “When we got outside, like I said, I thought that the command post was at West & Vesey, so I worked my way over to West & Vesey and it turns out that the command post was not there.
>
> And things started to lift, everybody was in a state of shock, looking around, people, guys just walking around like that. It was eerie, it was really quite eerie.
>
> *—Chief of Department (2004–2006) Pete Hayden, then a Deputy Chief in Division 1, SoHo, Manhattan*

> “We had nothing but our will power, our human spirit.
>
> *—Captain Jeff Simms, then a Lieutenant in Engine 58, Harlem, Manhattan; FDNY IMT*

The unimaginable

Before 9/11, firefighters often “signed off” in conversations with “see you at the big one.” By mid-day, 9/11 became something else, something very different, crushingly different. It became “the big one.” The valediction went out of use.

The South Tower, the second tower struck, collapsed first, at 9:59 a.m. The North Tower collapsed 29 minutes later, at 10:28. Excerpts below from the Manhattan Dispatcher Transcripts trace the chronology: pulverizing, thunderous, suffocating, blinding, entrapping, death dispensing collapses.

Both collapses had their own stories, both similar and different from each other. The collapses shaped the day and everything that followed. The recollections that appear below describe cyclones of destruction and the initial shared and yet so personal clawing out, the effort to regroup and to pursue a mission of rescue, then recovery...and eventually an altered future.

Before each collapse, thousands of firefighters labored to evacuate building occupants. Firefighters, loaded with gear, trudged upstairs – floor after floor. They broke through inoperative exit doors sprung by twisting towers. They escorted people to safety. Some people could walk. Others needed carrying.

At the same time, the FDNY toiled to establish command and control at the site. To begin, the FDNY positioned a command post. Conditions deteriorated. The situation changed quickly and the FDNY repositioned its command post, moving it further from the towers. The collapse of the South Tower forced an immediate reorganization and another command post relocation. The second collapse brought further devastation and more loss of senior FDNY leaders – three of the department's five most senior officers had perished. In all, 23 chiefs died that day. Their white helmets, once rallying points amid flames and smoke, had vanished.[23] The radios stopped crackling. They went silent.

Nearly a thousand firefighters on site. 343 dead. Their remains mixed in with hundreds of thousands of tons of debris from over 200 skyscraper stories.

An estimated 25,000 people evacuated the two towers in just under 90 minutes from the time a plane slammed into the North Tower. Ash covered many of those who escaped, including the firefighters. The evacuated worked their way away from the site, searching for a way home.

The firefighters stayed. Their work didn't end; it changed. More firefighters arrived – first from across the FDNY, then from surrounding areas, and eventually from as far away as France.

Part A: Responder Voices

First collapse: South Tower, 9:59 a.m.

Below are excerpts from radio traffic between the FDNY Manhattan Fire Alarm Dispatcher John Lightsey and field units at the World Trade Center.

"Manhattan calling Field Comm............"
"Manhattan calling Field Comm............"
"Manhattan calling Field Comm............"

"[garbled]. to Manhattan, urgent."

"Go ahead, K"

"... One of the buildings... the entire building has collapsed...... Major collapse in one of the towers."

"Which tower?"

"Tower 2,... Tower 2... the entire tower, major collapse."

"Ten-four."

"...have them mobilize the Army... we need the Army in Manhattan."

"Manhattan to any unit operating at No 2 World Trade Center, urgent. I want you to go to the nearest chief, Fire Department chief and have him come to the radio forthwith. If you find anybody with a White [helmet], get him to the radio. I need a report to find out what else I can send to him."

"Also be advised in the area at the Marriott Hotel receiving reports of firefighters trapped and down."

"Be advised, Mobile Command Center is set up in front of Pier A [6 blocks south on the Hudson River]. I have no radio contact with anybody else at this time. As soon as I get something I'll let you know."[24]

“ I knew something bad was happening. I didn't know what, but I knew something bad was happening. You have to keep stuff calm.

—Lieutenant Artie Riccio, then a firefighter in Ladder 119 South Williamsburg, Brooklyn working in Ladder 110 [Inside North Tower when South Tower collapsed.]

“ The ambulance pulled away [she had just treated FF Daniel Suhr, Eng. 216, who had been fatally struck by a jumper] and I started to cross the street.... Somebody said, 'The tower is coming down!' I remember looking up and seeing it sort of coming down and rushing to the edge of the street where there was like a little bit of a protection and then everything just went dark because everything just started coming down. Then things got quiet and I thought, 'Well, I'm still alive.'

—Dr. Kerry Kelly, then FDNY Chief Medical Officer, Bureau of Health Services, Downtown Brooklyn [Liberty Street outside 2 WTC]

❝ We look up and didn't know the extent of the collapse, but we knew something was going on. We make our way, we duck into the garage where we had thought we might go if we needed to, and everything is pitch black. Pitch black, can't see a thing, smoke, dust, choking, and you can hear Pete [Ganci], he's chief of department, he's still in command.

—Fire Commissioner (2010–2014) Sal Cassano, then Assistant Chief in Headquarters, Downtown Brooklyn. (served as Chief of Department 2006–2010) [West & Vesey Streets]

❝ First we feel the ground rumble and then we hear, 'Pop, pop, pop, pop.' We look up and you can see the floors exploding and popping out. We probably all yelled, 'Run. I'm outta here,' so I started running. It took nine seconds for the Tower to come down. I don't know how far I actually got in nine seconds. I'm running and there's debris landing all over me, right and left of me, I can see it's hitting people. Pieces of the building, steel, concrete. 'Pop-pop-pop-pop-pop' and it's hitting people and it's killing them. Next thing I'm flying through the air. People were getting hit and they were getting killed and this isn't Hollywood. All of a sudden I'm engulfed in the dust and I can't see a thing and it's black and it hit us. It was so black I couldn't see anything. I-I'm trying to get up and I can't get up and I'm trying to crawl and I can't breathe. I can't breathe but there was a voice in me and a voice was saying, 'Keep moving, keep moving.'

—Lieutenant Ray Brown, then in Ladder 113, Crown Heights, Brooklyn [West & Liberty Streets]

❝ When the hotel [Marriott, 3 World Trade Center] started to rock, I didn't realize what was going on. I thought. [T]his building is possibly gonna collapse, and then the next thing I know is when just everything went dark and I just got knocked down to the floor. The next thing I remember is hearing somebody say, 'Can you hear my voice?' And I remember saying, 'yeah.' He says, 'well, that means we're alive.'

—Assistant Chief Tom Galvin, Chief of Training (2004–2015), then a Deputy Chief in Division 3, Midtown, Manhattan

" First of all, you heard it coming down. I didn't think at the time, that the whole building was coming down and did in fact come down. I thought that a piece of the building had come off. I didn't really realize. I actually didn't even know till later on that the whole building had come down. Of course, when it started coming down, you start to get – I guess you realized that things are not going so well and you better do something. You brace yourself. I wound up diving under one of the rigs.

—Firefighter Louis Giaconelli, then Engine 53 Spanish Harlem, Manhattan; FDNY IMT [On ramp of parking garage on West Street]

" Going upstairs it was civilians to the left, firefighters to the right, with screaming, the civilians because they're coming down the stairs, we had to get them to the left-hand side so we could walk up. We get to 21, light haze, not real smoke. We split up, we started searching. The next thing I know all the windows started breaking. [Moment of first collapse] I had fresh air hitting me in the face, and as one of the guys said, 'Let's go.' He was a probie. I said, 'Run, get out of here.' I didn't know it was the South Tower coming down. I laid on the floor, I put my feet on the door and I held it so the fire wouldn't come into the hallway where we were. Inside I knew something bad was happening. I didn't know what, but I knew something bad was happening. You have to keep stuff calm. Once it calmed down, we opened the door, it was black smoke. We went back in, no fire, just smoke.

—Lieutenant Artie Riccio, then a firefighter in Ladder 119 South Williamsburg, Brooklyn, working in Ladder 110 [Inside North Tower]

" At that point, I heard a noise, looked up, and said, 'I think we're too close to this building right now.' We weren't, and we were able to find a doorway, not get into the building, but at least get into a deep doorway where we were safe. The building came down. We were covered with all the dust and breathed in all the dust. I said, 'Now, let's try to get back to the command post.'

—Fire Commissioner (2014–2022) Dan Nigro, then Chief of Operations at Headquarters, Downtown Brooklyn (served as Chief of Department 2001–2002) [Near Church and Fulton Streets]

" I got to where I parked just off of Westside Highway, about a block south of the Trade Center Campus, about 10 minutes before the first collapse. I contacted Chief Ganci and asked where he wanted me. He told me where they had the command post and I should contact command post. The collapse occurred, took care of a few things at that corner before heading up there.

—1st Deputy Commissioner (2004–2010) Frank Cruthers, then an Assistant Chief at Headquarters, Downtown Brooklyn (served as Chief of Department 1996–1997, 2002–2004) [Near West and Liberty Streets]

Post-first tower collapse

Thunderous. Deafening. Percussive. Horrifying. A tsunami of dust and smoke.

Reorganization began before the dust began to clear. The site wasn't 'just' a fire anymore. Still, the mission – rescue – remained. Losses notwithstanding, much of the chain of command also remained intact.

Reset. Deploy. Divide the site. Work it. Employ protocols—and adapt. Civilian evacuation from the remaining tower became paramount. Firefighters rushed in. Evacuees streamed out. Reconnaissance followed.

Assessment, individual and collective. With communications crippled, FDNY runners became essential.

" When the South Tower collapsed, the debris from the South Tower pushed into the lobby of the North Tower and we were covered in soot and black and darkness. The elevator lobby protected us from getting a direct hit. Then one of the firefighters called over and said, 'I found somebody,' and I went over there and put a flashlight on him and it was Father Judge, and he was dead. He was somebody who the firefighters loved.

The EMTs took Father Judge to a Catholic church, just maybe a quarter of a mile up the road. They laid him on the altar up there and they called the Franciscans to come and get him.

—Chief of Department (2004–2006) Pete Hayden,
then a Deputy Chief in Division 1, SoHo, Manhattan
[Lobby Command Post, North Tower]

WTC collapse before and after
The collapse of the South Tower of the WTC at 9:59 a.m., as seen from Williamsburg, Brooklyn. *Pauljoffe at English Wikipedia, CC BY-SA 3.0, via Wikimedia Commons*

“ Pete [Ganci, Chief of Department] says to me, ‘Sal, get me...’ and he asked for a number of companies, ‘and tell them meet me south.’ He’s going to take charge of the rescue – We knew we had tons of civilians there, but he knew we had tons of firefighters there who were trapped. He knew. He starts to make his way south. He tells me, ‘we got to move the command post north.’ With that, I just gather my thoughts a bit and say, ‘Okay.’ I start to turn and lo and behold in front of me is Chief Pfeiffer and Chief Hayden, who were at the lobby command post in the North Tower [when the South Tower collapsed]. They were in command with Chief Callan. I didn’t see Chief Callan at the time. He tells me right away, ‘Father Judge is dead.’

—Fire Commissioner (2010–2014) Sal Cassano, then Assistant Chief at Headquarters, Downtown Brooklyn (served as Chief of Department 2006–2010) [West and Liberty Streets]

“ I just remember thinking, this is like the end, and then a minute or probably it was just seconds, but thinking, ‘I’m still alive, I’m still alive.’ Then things got quiet and I thought, Well, I’m still alive.’ Then I came out and it was just all, everything, was black and you literally couldn’t see in front of you very well, but there was so many pieces of paper just floating around. It was so amazing to me that all these pieces of paper were all there, but it was like, it went from day to night, instantly. It was just so dark. Then, we started looking for people and that’s when I saw Kevin Shea, who was injured and we got him to a protected area in a basement.

—Dr. Kerry Kelly, then FDNY Chief Medical Officer, Bureau of Health Services, Downtown Brooklyn [Near West and Liberty Streets]

“ I had kind of reached a point where I was safe and everything was okay for me, but I decided, don’t ask me why, I have no idea. Later on after it was all over, for some reason, I went back...I wound up working my way back through the building and I came out in the front, and I came out right where we had been when we first got the command post.

—Firefighter Louis Giaconelli, then in Engine 53, Spanish Harlem, Manhattan; FDNY IMT [Brookfield Place, opposite North Tower]

“There were other chiefs who were trapped in a car or other firefighters who were calling in for help. We tried to coordinate where they were and tried to get companies to get over there. There was one chief or a captain, I believe, that was trapped on the West Side Highway in his car. There was companies saying he was giving landmarks about where he was.... I remember a Marine Company, [Marine 1 Fireboat John D. McKean], came on the air and said, ‘We got firefighters there and we can see where he’s talking about. We’ll go in and take care of that.’ I believe that they sent crews from their boat and walked in there and some other companies walked in there, too, to try to rescue him. They would set up water relays from the rivers to get the water flowing. It would just turn into a rescue effort after that.

—Fire Alarm Dispatcher John Lightsey,
then in Manhattan Communications Office,
Central Park, Manhattan

“And then a chief got on the radio and told us to get out, but.... Usually it’s, ‘Mayday, mayday, mayday!’ It wasn’t. It was ‘Get the fuck out now!’ He said that about five times. Our lieutenant who was with us, Wayne Meara, we were about the B staircase now, and – the probie was going back to C [stair]. The lieutenant says, ‘No, let’s go down here, right here.’ We went down the B staircase and that’s the only reason why we lived. Every other staircase is blocked with rubble from the South Tower coming down, the B staircase came to the middle of the lobby.... At about the 18th floor, I found a woman crying in a corner on the stairwell. ‘Come on, let’s go.’ I got a chair, I put her on the chair, me and another guy we carried her down 18 flights; the woman who was the angel, they called her. We passed her, she was in B staircase on the fourth floor when we got there, we went – other guys are helping already, a civilian was with her. I said, ‘Get out, we’re just taking a break, it’s okay.’ We kept on going. I got down to the lobby, in my head right now is a black and white picture. All dust and everything.... Now I carry the woman by myself across the street and put her in an ambulance and my arms are shaking, my legs – I’m done. I sit down on West Street highway divider.

—Lieutenant Artie Riccio, then a firefighter
in Ladder 119 South Williamsburg,
Brooklyn, working in Ladder 110

“ Right after the collapse, we gave the order to evacuate the building and we gave that over the handy-talkie radios to get everybody out. Once again, we were not sure that everybody heard that. A lot of the post interviews with the firefighters that survived, when they were questioned, whether they heard that, many of them said they heard it up to maybe about the 35th, 40th floor, or whatever it was that they heard it. At least we were able to get some of the firefighters out.

—Chief of Department (2004–2006) Pete Hayden, then a Deputy Chief in Division 1, SoHo, Manhattan [Lobby Command Post, North Tower]

“ A couple of minutes went by and the smoke was coming in, the dust really, not even smoke. The dust was coming in, but that had subsided. We both went back out into the street. We were able to see now something devastating had happened. But again, still I was not convinced that the whole building had come down. I thought maybe the top 10 floors, whatever.

—Chief of Operations Pat McNally, then a Deputy Chief in Division 14, Flushing, Queens [Parking garage on West Street, opposite North Tower]

“ There were a couple of firefighters around where I was [staging area near West and Liberty Streets] who were killed. The chief who gave me the orders, Chief Barbara [Assistant Chief Jerry Barbara] was killed, jeez. Sometimes, I think there's so many, 343 guys and I don't remember all their names. I can tell you the names of every firefighter that died from 1979 when I got on, till that day [there were 59] but September 11th is just too many to remember.

—Lieutenant Ray Brown, then in Ladder 113, Crown Heights, Brooklyn

“ I'm separated from my guys and I kept moving and I heard some somebody say, 'Fireman, help me.' I couldn't breathe and I'm thinking to myself, 'Well, they can breathe.' Also now I was panicking, 'I think I'm going to die. This is it.' I could not breathe. They say I don't know if I had a white light experience but I experienced a tremendous amount of just peace and like, 'Okay, I'm dying.' Then all of a sudden, I realized and said, 'Wait a minute I'm in this dust, this cloud, they're talking.' I reached in my mouth and I took out a ball of the concrete dust and whatever it was that had solidified and that was why I couldn't breathe. And people were all coming to me, 'Fireman, help me, help me.' I just kept saying, 'Go to the river. Go to the river.' I get to my fire truck and I didn't know at the time, but I had had a mild concussion.... It's like being in the fog. We could not see it but you could see the fire in it. I guess it was the Deutsche Bank building, upper floors, cars, literally hundreds of them. One of my guys comes up and he goes, 'All right, Ray, what are we going to do?' I remember just for a second I stop and I said, 'Holy cow, this sense of pride in these guys.'

—Lieutenant Ray Brown, then in Ladder 113, Crown Heights, Brooklyn

“ The command post [West and Vesey Streets] was completely gone. Ray [Ray Downey, Chief of Rescues] decides that he wants to wait for Pete [Ganci, Chief of Department], thinking Pete's behind us, but he's not. A few more minutes go by and the Chief of Safety [Al Turi], and I guess one or two other chiefs came by and said, 'Okay, the command post is gone.' I was ordered to set up another command post further north [at West and Chambers Streets]. Said, 'Set it up as soon as you can in any place that looks like it's going to be okay.'

—Chief of Operations Pat McNally, then a Deputy Chief in Division 14, Flushing, Queens

“ The dispatcher says, 'Manhattan to division one.' No answer. 'Manhattan to division three.' No answer. 'Manhattan to field comm.' No answer. This is the fifth alarm fire now, so Field Comm there. Everybody's there. Hazmat's there, multiple rescues? He says, 'Manhattan to any unit operating at box 8087 come in.' Nothing. How many guys? There are hundreds of people there. No one could get to a radio. I said, 'Ladder 43 to Manhattan.' 'Go ahead, 43.' I said, 'I'm on 52nd and Third, let me take in the box (respond). I'll let you know what's going on.' He says, 'You got it. Take it in.' And that was it. Now we're assigned.

—Captain Glenn Rohan, then a Lieutenant in Ladder 43, Spanish Harlem, Manhattan

“ 'Where's the command post,' and they point down towards the middle of West Street, the financial building, in the ramp there. I remember walking down there, actually with Chief Cassano.

—Chief of Department (2004–2006) Pete Hayden, then a Deputy Chief in Division 1, SoHo, Manhattan

" I was supposed to go into the South Tower and we walked up the block, moved a couple rigs out of the way, then came back to the command post [at West and Vesey Streets]. The South Tower collapsed. I would have been in the South Tower which was the first building to come down. I would have been crushed, probably killed in the collapse. So that saved our lives. That saved our life the first time.

After the first tower comes down, now it's a lot of the bosses had been killed. I started walking towards the North Tower. It was all dusty and dirt, and the North Tower was still intact, believe it or not, I still heard bodies, people jumping and landing, hitting the canopy. If you ever watch the French film, that's the sound. When you hear the 'Boom, boom,' that's the sound of bodies hitting the canopy of the building, or the street, one or the other. Anyway, when I popped out, that was still going on, but there was nobody around. I was pretty much by myself, and it was desolate.

—Firefighter Louis Giaconelli, then in Engine 53, Spanish Harlem, Manhattan; FDNY IMT

" When I got to the firehouse the garage doors were up so I see, basically everybody just huddled around. So, I'm thinking, 'Okay, they're listening to the radio, they're trying to pick up whatever communications or information they have.' I park the car, I get out. I see one guy look over his shoulder at me, turn back to the group, then the entire group turned and looked at me. Then they leaned back and huddled, and then the senior guy slowly meandered out towards me.... I remember seeing him and going, 'Oh my God, he's about to give me the news.' He came out and he said, 'Ray [his brother, Lt. Ray Brown] was working today, and 113 [Ladder 113, Ray's unit] is there. The Manhattan dispatcher is on the radio calling every single unit that was at the scene, and no one's 'answering.' I remember thinking in that instant that, 'You know what? You don't know what you don't know. There is nothing I can do about it. There's a lot of business to take care of.' There was a chief in that firehouse, I went straight up to the chief's office, spoke with him about what to do.

—Captain Paul Brown, then Lieutenant covering in Division 15, Brownsville, Brooklyn; FDNY IMT [Arrived at the firehouse around 10:30 a.m.]

" [Deputy Chief] Tom Galvin comes up and he says, 'Ray, Engine 58 is trapped in the Marriott Hotel in the lobby between the Marriott and the North Tower. You've got to take charge.' I just said to him, 'Okay, Chief, I got it.' I was like, 'Holy cow. We just went through hell and they're asking me...?' I said, 'Okay guys, let's go.' One of my guys was helping a woman and he said, 'Ray, she needs help.' I said, 'Leave her alone. Come on.' I heard the firefighters were trapped and I did a mental triage and I said to myself if they're [civilians] breathing, then they don't need our help. Firefighters were trapped and that's where we were going. We were heading south.... We realize what we've got to do. We have a collapse. Guys were trapped. I was telling guys what to get and they knew what to get. As we're going in, people are flying out. Everybody's flying out. Everybody, not just civilians. They're heading out the door. Some guy says to me, 'There's firefighters trapped in there,' and I say, 'Okay, come with me. Just show me where they are.' All of a sudden we get to where they are and I turned to thank him and he's gone. That's what he had to do at that moment. I'm sure whoever he was, he was probably there for weeks and days and months afterwards but at that moment, like my father said, he knew it was time to get out. We were on a mission and we had a job to do. We get there and being it's Engine 58 so I knew some of the guys. [Ray's brother and father had both worked in that firehouse].... Boy, just wish we had another hour [before the 2nd tower came down]. If we'd had another hour, we would have got those guys. We were so close to Bob Nagel [Lt. Engine 58] and in true fashion he's telling us, 'Forget me, go get them.' They were right there. Just another hour, we would have been able to, I don't know. That's a regret that I always have. There's nothing I could do about it. It was their time.... We were cutting through pipes. There were a lot of pipes. It wasn't beams. We were just trying to figure out what we got. There was aluminum, there was ducts, ventilation ducts.... Normally, I wouldn't give one of our tools to another guy, but I knew him. It was his officer and my guys had plenty to do. We start going in and we're tunneling and he's cutting out debris. The best way to explain it is, if you have an accordion and then you go, 'Whoop,' and now you got to cut through that accordion. We were cutting and were cutting away and then...

—Lieutenant Ray Brown, then in Ladder 113, Crown Heights, Brooklyn

West Street showing the Marriott WTC Hotel following collapse of the South Tower
Marriott WTC Hotel on West Street showing center section destroyed by collapse of the South Tower.
Photo credit Bill Biggart, copyright estate of Bill Biggart

Second collapse: North Tower, 10:28 a.m.

The second collapse resembled the first collapse. It also differed. The second collapse brought even more carnage and debris. It also further depleted the FDNY command structure. A potentially immobilizing number of FDNY senior leaders lay dead under the rubble: three of the five most senior leaders and overall 93 ranking leaders.

Continued below are excerpts from radio traffic between the FDNY Manhattan Fire Alarm Dispatcher John Lightsey and field units at the World Trade Center.

"Urgent! Urgent!...we had a collapse of the second tower. Everybody's running from there."

"Ten-four.... Attention all units, we're receiving reports that No. 1 and No. 2 World Trade Center collapsed. All units at the scene receiving reports, No. 1 and No. 2 World Trade Center, both towers collapsed."

"Manhattan announcing, any division or any staff chief at the scene of the World Trade Center? Any division chief or any staff chief at the scene of any of the World Trade Centers?"

.... [Silence]

"Mobile Command Center, what chief do you have at your Mobile Command Center?"

"Negative on any chief. Right now we're all alone. The second building came down. I can't see. So we have no contact with anybody at this time."

"Ten-four."

"Division 6 acting to Manhattan [Deputy Chief Thomas Haring] The command post is going to be set up at Park Row, south of City Hall at Vesey Street. It's the only place where we can, [until] the dust cloud has relieved."

"Car 5 [AC Michael Butler] is on West and Vesey. We're trying to establish a command post up here. I've got E.M.S. and everybody at Vesey and West Street...and we've got plenty of help."[25]

“I don’t remember this but I was told I said, ‘Get out. It’s coming down!’ Apparently, Fitz, [firefighter Mike Fitzgerald, Eng. 58] he got out and he hurt his foot and I got knocked into the reinforced area [a section of the lower three floors had been reinforced following the 1993 bombing]. I was buried a little bit but they saw my flashlight. That’s when Richie [Nogan, Ladder 113] and the guys from 58 Engine, they carried me out, they had to carry me up and then down the rubble. I was five feet from Bob Nagle [Lt., Eng. 58]. They never found their bodies.

—Lieutenant Ray Brown, then in Ladder 113, Crown Heights, Brooklyn

Casualty evacuation of Ray Brown from the Marriott
Lieutenant Ray Brown Ladder 113 being assisted from the Marriott Hotel by Firefighters Todd Haney and Frank DiLeo Engine 209 following the collapse of the North Tower.
Todd Meisel/New York Daily News via Getty Images

“He’s within arm’s reach of Bobby Nagel. Mike [Fitzgerald] says that the rumbling starts again, and it’s like a freight train coming through a station. At the last minute, he jumps off the pile of rubble but he gets caught by some debris on his thigh. That was where the gusts came up to. Everyone on the left side of him gets killed, never to be seen again including Bobby Nagel. Everyone on the right side survived.

—Captain Jeff Simms, then a Lieutenant in Engine 58, Harlem, Manhattan; FDNY IMT

“I was looking up in the sky and I don’t know if you ever saw the shot of the-the tower, it-it sort of kicks out like about a little bit then drops.... I turned around and started sprinting south again. And the next thing I know, I just got caught in that, I didn’t get caught in the debris field, that pressure blast.

—Assistant Chief Tom Galvin,
Chief of Training (2004–2015), then a Deputy Chief
in Division 3, Midtown, Manhattan

“A chief comes over and says, ‘Go north, get out of here.’ I said, ‘Chief, I can’t walk, my legs are – I’m done, I need to, just give me a minute or so.’ He said, ‘Get out of here, go north.’ As I’m going up, the guy yells at me, ‘Run, Artie, run.’ I look up, there was a tidal wave, the North Tower is coming down on top of us. They always say I could do anything when I’m afraid, I’m going to run and I couldn’t. I took three steps, I rolled in the street, hit the divider because I knew the divider was in the middle of the street. I was hoping maybe that cement divider would save me and it did. I got buried in this cement dust.

—Lieutenant Artie Riccio, then a firefighter in Ladder 119
South Williamsburg, Brooklyn working in Ladder 110

“On the west side of the Westside Highway, there are several mostly financial buildings that I had somehow come to know were interconnected. Rather than try to make my way up through the debris field, while I was in passage through those buildings, I heard the second collapse.

—1st Deputy Commissioner (2004–2010) Frank Cruthers,
then an Assistant Chief at Headquarters, Downtown Brooklyn
(served as Chief of Department 1996–1997, 2002–2004)

“I hear this bang, bang, bang forcing you to look up and there’s pieces, it looks like they’re just blowing out from all over the place. I’m like, ‘This building’s coming down.’ I said, ‘Everybody, run. Turn around and run North.’ I’m saying if it’s leaning, we’re dead. It just went down like that. We were very, very lucky. Now I’m like, ‘Oh my God, we lost a lot of guys.’ You knew it right then and there. There’s a lot of dead people here, this isn’t like a fire with two people dead. No, you know this is going to be multiple. There’s not enough buses, ambulances, hospitals. There's hundreds of people going to be dead.

—Captain Glenn Rohan, then a Lieutenant in Ladder 43, Spanish Harlem, Manhattan

“ Coming through the tunnel, the midtown tunnel and the second building falls down. We were on route. So we get the word now and I'm still formulating what's going on and we pull the apparatus off. They [Chiefs] had moved to the command post way back down on West Street, a couple of blocks away, like three blocks, but you can see what's going on. There's fire in every building, there is smoke, there's total chaos.

—Battalion Chief Fred LaFemina, Chief of Rescue Services, then Captain of Squad 270, South Jamaica, Queens; member FDNY USAR

“ We turned into one of the schools just north and went into an alleyway. Everybody stopped going in right now because you could see the clouds coming in between streets and all-enveloping. Everybody on air [Scott air packs]. Being on air in the street, that's pretty unusual, and it just came at us like a locomotive, and we just bunker down. Then when it stopped, you can't see anything. It was like oatmeal, and we walk south. Because you can't really see anything, we're using the search rope in the street.

—Captain Glenn Rohan, then a Lieutenant in Ladder 43, Spanish Harlem, Manhattan

“ We were walking there [West and Vesey Streets] and that's when the North Tower came down.... We both started running, but you couldn't run far enough or fast enough, those buildings came down in 10 seconds. I actually curled under a truck, then after that for several minutes afterwards, it was a deadly silence. I was like swallowed in the dark, you couldn't see. Things started to lift, everybody was in a state of shock, looking around people, guys just walking around like that. It was eerie, it was really quite eerie.... I walked down towards West Street and Liberty, because I was told that there was a staging area there.

—Chief of Department (2004–2006) Pete Hayden, then a Deputy Chief in Division 1, SoHo, Manhattan

> "I started to walk towards the North Tower, and next thing I know I heard that same sound again. I knew what it was and I started to run and I ran back to the door. Now, meanwhile, the building is collapsing and I ran and I somehow make it to the doorway of this glass structure, which is not going to get me any protection whatsoever. Anyway, I get in there and just as I get in at the building, that concussion again and all hell breaks loose and I get blown down this entranceway. It was like a hallway basically and I'm tumbling and same thing all over again. The hot gases, the smoke, the dust, the debris, and everything's coming down all around me. My helmet gets blown off, obviously didn't have my chin strapped on. I believe that I'm the only guy between the two bridges [pedestrian bridges over West Street], between the Towers and the World Financial Center that lived. I think I'm the only guy that was on the street that made it out of there alive.
>
> —*Firefighter Louis Giaconelli, then in Engine 53, Spanish Harlem, Manhattan; FDNY IMT*

The towers collapse
An aerial view of the WTC moments after the collapse of the Twin Towers. 7 WTC remains standing to the left.
rds323, CC0, via Wikimedia Commons

“ Just around that time, the second time, the North Tower collapsed.... In front of it. We were not at a good spot. We both basically took off. Now, it's just the two of us. I don't have my aide with me anymore. He didn't have anybody with him. He was able to get under a truck on West Street, and I was able to make it to the corner of the World Financial building. Basically, at this point the visibility was completely socked, and the noise from that collapse was fairly obvious that it probably was the whole building coming down. There was a lot of debris flying. It's not a good situation.

—Chief of Operations Pat McNally, then a Deputy Chief in Division 14, Flushing, Queens

“ I turn around to go back and meet with Pete [Ganci, Chief of Department].... I turn to start to walk south and then I hear this huge roar, I said, ‘Oh my God,’ and when I look up, all I can see was the antenna from the North Tower imploding into the building as you saw on television.... I start to run north and I look back up and I realized I'm not outrunning this baby. There was a rig on the corner of West and Vesey. It was a rescue rig [FDNY rescue truck]. I dove under there and just waited it out. I didn't know if the rig was going to survive or I was going to survive, but I thought I didn't have any options.

—Fire Commissioner (2010–2014) Sal Cassano, then Assistant Chief at Headquarters, Downtown Brooklyn (served as Chief of Department 2006–2010)

Post-second tower collapse

For the fourth time in about 90 minutes, the FDNY attempted to organize itself, the site, and the firefighters on hand. Move the command post. Reset the command structure. Meanwhile, work on what's in front of you.

“ Both of the buildings came down, and it was dead silence, trying to get somebody on the radio. I don't know, it was an eerie feeling.... That never happens on a radio. If you ever listen to the fire radios... you never get dead silence. It was an eerie feeling. All of a sudden, the phone stopped ringing. There was nothing there for a little while. I couldn't even tell you how long...” “Eerie – you just couldn't understand that part. You'd be going on the radio and going through any Chiefs out there, or any officers, any companies, and you wouldn't get any response back. It'd be dead silence for a little while. How long? Not a clue.... We saw both towers come down, watching them on the TV. We realized that anybody in the buildings, they're gone, they're done. It was just silence...until we started getting companies coming from different boroughs. They'd come up on the radio. I'm really glad they did. It is just an eerie feeling.

—Fire Alarm Dispatcher John Lightsey, then in Manhattan Communications Office, Central Park, Manhattan

“ The cement started going back into my mouth, congealing back to cement. I couldn't breathe. Because I rolled in the streets, hit the divider and tucked, and my mask is wrapped around me. I was pulling cement out of my mouth to breathe and then it all stopped. It was a beautiful sunny day that day. You couldn't see the hand in front of your face when the building was coming down. From there I think we all said this to ourselves, ‘It's all right, God. If this is what you want, I'm okay with it. I hope I did a good job for you, and just take care of my family.’ That's what I was thinking about. Somebody came over to me and I started moving and someone started yelling, ‘I got someone.’ I said, ‘I'm all right, don't worry about me, keep on going, get somebody else.’ Right now I have cement dust on my right side of my lungs, and I have flying glass on my left side. They say it will never leave but I'm okay, and we stay there till five o'clock the next morning.

—Lieutenant Artie Riccio, then a firefighter in Ladder 119 South Williamsburg, Brooklyn working in Ladder 110

“ I tried to get up to walk and I just couldn't walk. I had got hit in my back. There was a couple of paramedics or EMTs with a stretcher.... They loaded me up and as they're wheeling me away, I just realized my helmet, I got to get my helmet.... They load me up in an ambulance, they take me to St Vincent's Hospital and all I could think in my mind was, ‘Oh my God, this place is going to be crazy.’ We back into the ambulance bay, they open the door and I can vividly remember all these medical people, the nurses, doctors, PA, whatever they were, standing there, waiting for people to come, and nobody was coming. There was nobody there.

—Fire Commissioner (2010–2014) Sal Cassano, then Assistant Chief at Headquarters, Downtown Brooklyn (served as Chief of Department 2006–2010)

“ You're looking for some kind of 'Who's running this?' you don't know who to report to, so you just say 'Let's start to do something.' There's fires going on all over the place with the trucks and the cars. I said, 'Get to the pumper, put it in pumps and use 500 gallons that we carry on the pumper and put that fire out.' I said, 'We're going to start searching in these trucks, fire department vehicles that are crushed.' We didn't find anybody in them. We had the combination of guys putting out fires with any water they could get out of the pumpers and the rest of them searching.

—Captain Glenn Rohan, then a Lieutenant in Ladder 43, Spanish Harlem, Manhattan

“ The North Tower came down and we turned around and retraced our steps back. I found one of our communications trucks was down south of the Towers, parked. We stopped there and I said to them, 'Who has survived? Have you talked to anyone? Where is the command post?' He gave me the name of a deputy chief [Thomas Haring, Division 6] that I hadn't even known was there. He said he was in charge and the command post was on Broadway. I was shocked really, because that would indicate to me that all of the higher-ranking chiefs had died in these two collapses. In actuality, they had already taken upon themselves, people that were there to take command of a sector because there were fires burning in different places. There was assumptions that people were trapped. That chief that he mentioned was not actually in charge of anything but a sector. We did make it back to West and Chambers and gathered whoever was around. Some chiefs had come in from home and began the follow-up. Pete [Ganci, Chief of Department] was missing, Chief Feehan [Ist Deputy Commissioner Bill Feehan] was missing, [Assistant Chief] Donald Burns.

A lot of people were still unaccounted for, some were accounted for. The chiefs...in the North Tower, all got out safely and survived.

Not so much in the South Tower. Tom Galvin [Deputy Chief Division 3] survived from that group in the hotel, but Ray Downey [Chief of Rescue Operating Battalion] did not.... Seven World Trade Center, which is a 50-story high-rise that caught on fire. 'It was already beyond what we could probably handle, and certainly beyond what we can handle because we didn't have the resources and the water right there. Structurally, it didn't even look real good, but it also had a pretty good fire going on many floors.

—Chief of Operations Pat McNally, then a Deputy Chief in Division 14, Flushing, Queens

" We just started gathering equipment from every corner of thefirehouse, anything we get our hands on. A couple of guys ran to hardware stores, bought more flashlights. Then at one point we were told that we're supposed to gather people together, and then buses would pick us up at the division chief's firehouse and they would drive us in, so that anybody off duty would go to the site.... But the guys didn't want to wait. I go back to the guys, we start talking about what we're going to do and how we're going to get there. Then one guy pulls me to the side and he goes, 'Hey, listen, we're going to go grab a city bus.' So, I said, 'How are you going to grab a city bus?' 'I don't know. We're going to find a city bus and we're going to take it.' I go, 'Can anybody drive it?' and one guy said, 'I used to be a city bus driver. Go do it.' It's hard to describe what they looked like, but they drove a pickup truck with six guys in the back of it.... They ran out to the first main road, and they basically ran a city bus off the road, threw the driver and the passengers off it and drove it back to the firehouse. Everybody piled in with what little gear we had, and we went to the chief's firehouse. Then from there, we went to the foot of the Manhattan Bridge, the police had a barricade set up. As we were getting closer and closer, we could just see the column of smoke, it was on a scale of nothing I'd ever experienced. Both towers are down. The police are stopping us. There were several buses with us, I'm not sure exactly how many, but there were several buses with us.... Completely filled, standing room only. The police stop us at a barricade, and they're not letting us go over. There were tens of thousands of people walking across the Bridge from Manhattan to Brooklyn. It was just almost unimaginable, that many people, and it never stopped. There is no ebb and flow to it, it was a continuous crowd of people coming over the bridge. A few people, including the chief, tried to go over and speak to the police officers, that you've got to let us get over. The police officers said, 'The bridge is closed, we can't let anybody over it,' and the chief said, 'Okay, we're not anybody, we're the fire department.'

—Captain Paul Brown, then a Lieutenant covering in Division 15, Brownsville, Brooklyn; FDNY IMT

" Chief Nigro said, 'I can't get anybody on the radio.... No one is responding at all.' We all trudge back up. I think we took Broadway up, and again, went back up into that area. We set up an emergency response place where people could come. I think we were in the Woolworth Building initially. Not many people came.... They also had a rounding up area right by City Hall, plus they called everyone in off duty. People started arriving. None of the radios are working. It felt like the Revolutionary War where someone would say, 'Go tell this person to do this,' and then he'd run back and then he'd say, 'He needs 10 more guys,' and they would take the guys and bring them over.

—Dr. Kerry Kelly, then FDNY Chief Medical Officer at Bureau of Health Services, Downtown Brooklyn

" Then I heard this more commotion and it was this group of people that had this woman on the stretcher that I had passed earlier in the day, earlier when I was trying to get out of the building. I came across them again and they were all disorientated and it was a complete disaster. I crawled and worked my way back out into the debris field again, and crawled along and followed along the walls. We're taught, crawl and follow the walls and I saw more light, and then I found the doorway that went out to the harbor side again. I popped out on the harbor side and then I knew the way out and then I went back and got them all, counted and got them all out.

—Firefighter Louis Giaconelli, then in Engine 53, Spanish Harlem, Manhattan; FDNY IMT

" Here's the leadership issue. Staff chiefs had been killed immediately. There was no strategy. There was no coordinated effort. It was individuals who stood up and took control.... Full bunker gear on, no masks...no radios. There was no way to communicate. You had to do it in person. There was no equipment. All the equipment was destroyed.

We had nothing but our willpower, our human spirit.

—Captain Jeff Simms, then a Lieutenant in Engine 58, Harlem, Manhattan; FDNY IMT

❝ At that point in time, there was no command structure. A couple of companies would come in from Brooklyn. We would direct them to, say, 'Be on the north side of the Trade Center and set up a command post. Gather anybody you can until you get relieved by a white helmet. Just to set something up and try to take command, until you get more guys coming in.' We did the same thing for other units for different sides at the Trade Center. Eventually, we told the engine companies or truck companies, whatever, whoever they were, they commanded this side and others commanded the other side. Eventually, I believe one of the Chiefs came on the radio. I think he said he's going to set up a command post where we already have one of the units on the west side. He requested units coming into that location. Everybody, we would just move people around best we could and instruct the officers and the engine stuff, start doing rescue and try to gather firefighters if you see anybody on the ground to help out and collect them. Yes, pretty much. I haven't listened to the tape. I'm going by what I was told that they tell me, 'Yes, you can hear us directing companies to set up command posts and take over, be in charge of that section until you get help, until somebody else higher comes in.'

—Fire Alarm Dispatcher John Lightsey, then in Manhattan Communications Office, Central Park, Manhattan

❝ Then we got our tools together from the storage rooms and we went down to Shea Stadium, now known as Citi Field [home of NY Mets]. We staged down there, getting ready to go on buses, Home Depot, in Flushing, brought a whole bunch of tools down for us to just grab and take. Kudos to Home Depot and their crew. We got on buses, then they said, 'All right, we're not going. Everybody off the buses.' They were afraid of a secondary device taking out the bridges and tunnels. We got off, and then we got back on the buses again, and they said, 'All right, we're not going. Everybody go back to the firehouse.'

—Lieutenant Joe Minogue, Commanding Officer of Ceremonial Unit; Department Bugler, then a firefighter in Engine 289, Corona, Queens

New Jersey National Guard Black Hawk helicopter over ground zero
Black Hawk helicopter with New Jersey Army National Guard, hovers over Lower Manhattan.
The National Guard, CC BY 2.0, via Wikimedia Commons (U.S. Air National Guard photo by Tech. Sgt. Mark Olsen)

> “ The damage was at the lower end of the list of considerations. The first thing is, going back to the collapse that occurred when I first got there [first tower], I'm looking at this building and thinking at first we could have lost 100 firefighters, and then, we could have lost 200 firefighters. Emotionally, I couldn't go beyond 200 estimate. It was tragically short.... First of all, you're trying to get a hold of who you have, where are they, and start, along with a basic collapse rescue plan by making an initial surface survey and search [and] of course, fight the fire.
>
> *—1st Deputy Commissioner (2004–2010) Frank Cruthers,*
> *then an Assistant Chief at Headquarters, Downtown Brooklyn*
> *(served as Chief of Department 1996–1997, 2002–2004)*

> “ Meanwhile, there were some serious fires burning one of them in 7 World Trade, which had appeared to suffer some serious structural damage when the North Tower came down.
>
> *—Fire Commissioner (2014–2022) Dan Nigro,*
> *then Chief of Operations Headquarters, Downtown Brooklyn*
> *(served as Chief of Department 2001–2002)*

Elsewhere

An attack on the Pentagon. Another attack thwarted...and mobilization of resources far from NYC had begun. Those resources would come to play a large role in the impact of September 11 on the FDNY.

> “ Yes, on our time out west. We were starting to move by about – I'm going to call it 8:00-8:30 in the morning, our time [MST] on the 11th. To me it was, this one's really different. Why? I'm going where? I'm going to New York. I'm going to Manhattan. It was this surreal aspect began to kick in pretty quick. Because all the aircraft are grounded. The teams scattered all over the western US. To get to where we needed to be in Albuquerque, New Mexico by the time which was 21:00 that night on the 11th for our ride back to New York.
>
> *—Dan Oltrogge, Commander National Area Command Team (2009–2011), then Incident Commander Trainee SW-IMT, Chief of Fire and Aviation Grand Canyon National Park (served as SW-IMT Incident Commander 2003–2007)*

> “ Anyway, my phone rings and it's Ken Burris [Chief Operating Officer for the United States Fire Administration]. He said, 'We're sending you up to New York City. You have a blank check from the federal government. I will not question any decision you make. Help them any way we can.' What was going on behind the scenes is the fact that at that moment, that was not a federal disaster. Only thing that made it a federal disaster was that there were plane crashes.
>
> *—Denis Onieal, then Senior FEMA Representative, Commandant of National Fire Academy*

Part B: Summary, Lessons, and Commentary

Summary

It had been the proverbial "Big One" – except it wasn't one. Two towers were on fire, as were several other buildings inside and adjacent to the WTC complex. Either one could have been counted as the Big One. Instead, one crisis became two, and then something far worse. The first collapse multiplied the horror, the death, the complexity, and the operational challenges. When the second tower collapsed, the scale of destruction was more than anyone on the scene could comprehend. Associated Press journalist Stephanie Gaskell later described the "thousand-yard stares" that followed.

More than 220 FDNY firefighting units were on scene, more units than the entire fire departments of Boston, Philadelphia and Washington D.C. combined. In an instant, their firefighting effectiveness was eliminated.

New York City firefighters held an abiding faith in their leaders, just as FDNY leaders felt steadfast confidence in the abilities of their firefighters. The challenges were many and significant. Anyone who has seen the Naudet Brothers footage taken inside the lobby of the North Tower remembers the faces of the firefighters as they prepared to climb the stairs to meet the fire. Chief Pete Hayden put it bluntly: "As a fire department, I firmly believe you don't get to choose your alarms. You're a firefighter, and when the bell goes off, you go out the door. You are never going to know what you're going to be faced with. You don't get to pick and choose your battles. That was just a losing battle for us that day."

Inside the North Tower, Deputy Chief Pete Hayden saw Fire Department Chaplain Father Mychal Judge moments before the South Tower collapsed: "He looked frightened, he looked like he was praying. When the South Tower collapsed, the debris pushed into the lobby of the North Tower, and we were covered in soot and black and darkness. One of the firefighters called over and said, 'I found somebody.' I put a flashlight on him. It was Father Judge, and he was dead." Chief Hayden immediately gave the evacuation order for the North Tower.

Dr. Kelly had just treated Firefighter Daniel Suhr, Engine 216, who had been fatally struck by a jumper. "The ambulance pulled away and somebody said, 'The tower is coming down.' I remember looking up and seeing it sort of coming down, and everything just went dark. Then things got quiet and I thought,' Well, I'm still alive.'"

Fire Alarm Dispatcher John Lightsey, at the Manhattan communications office in Central Park, saw the events unfold on live television. He desperately sought to reach commanders on site: "Manhattan to any unit operating at Number 2 World Trade Center, urgent. I want you to go to the nearest chief, Fire Department Chief, and have him come to the radio forthwith. If you find anybody with a white [helmet], get him to the radio. I need a report to find out what else I can send to him." No reply.

Chiefs, firefighters, and civilians were all traumatized survivors. Civilians were sent north while firefighters headed south individually and in groups. They paired with officers and chiefs as they moved. Near the now-destroyed command post, Assistant Chief Sal Cassano recounted, "Everything is pitch black, can't see a thing, smoke, dust, choking, but you can hear Pete [Ganci], he's chief of department, he's still in command. [He] says to me, 'Sal, get me...' and he asked for a number of companies, 'and tell them meet me south.' He's going to take charge of the rescue." Ganci then ordered the command post moved further north. The FDNY had begun its third attempt to establish command and control.

A desperate rescue attempt began inside the Marriott Hotel [3 WTC, located between the towers]. Following the collapse of the South Tower, Lieutenant Ray Brown and Ladder 113 joined Engine 58 to rescue trapped firefighters. Bob Nagle, Engine 58's Lieutenant, was trapped in a pocket [a narrow void in the debris] along with Battalion 12 Chiefs Fred Scheffold and Joe Marchbanks.

Ray recalled, "We start going in and we're tunneling and cutting out debris. We were cutting and cutting away and then...[the North Tower 1 WTC collapsed]. I got knocked into the reinforced area [a section of the hotel had been reinforced following the 1993 bombing]. I was five feet from Bob Nagle [Lieutenant Engine 58]. They never found their bodies."

Ladder 43, sent by the dispatcher to report on conditions, had just arrived as the North Tower collapsed. Glenn Rohan described: "You could see the clouds coming in between streets and all-enveloping, and it just came at us like a locomotive. When it stopped, you can't see anything. It was like oatmeal. [I] had a painful realization, 'Oh my God, we lost a lot of guys.' You knew it right then and there. There's a lot of dead people here."

Pete Hayden had just made his way to where the Incident Command Post had been: "You couldn't run far enough or fast enough; those buildings came down in 10 seconds. It was a deadly silence, swallowed in the dark."

While conducting a personal reconnaissance Dan Nigro had survived the collapse of the South Tower. Attempting to make his way back, he reasoned: "we could come back up north and get to the command post, we never made it. The North Tower came down, I didn't think our original route would work anymore, we turned around and retraced our steps. It took a while to get back to the command post."

Thousands of off duty firefighters were already headed toward their firehouses. Most had not waited for the official recall order. The first Mutual Aid request in FDNY history meant firefighters from suburban fire departments were on their way to help.

Smoke and piles of debris made radio communication nearly impossible. Commanders began using "runners" to deliver orders and receive reports. Dr. Kelly likened it to the Revolutionary war.

Elsewhere, everywhere, civilians headed north toward safety, firefighters headed south.

Lessons for Leaders

1 **Expect the random.** Expect it. Accept it. It's part of the chaos that creates crises and that crisis creates. "Why" or "How" don't matter in the midst of chaos or in the immediate aftermath of catastrophe.

2 **Authorize getting the f*** out.** Sometimes it's simply time to run away. The building is collapsing. Order flight because at such moments affording people, especially dedicated professionals, permission to flee can help save them as well as to prepare them for regrouping and rejoining the fight.

3 **Assess the basics but with urgency.** Check fundamentals. Assess quickly what is possible [and what is not].

4 **Model and direct taking action.** Considered action, but action. Breathe. Observe. Act locally. Create building blocks or pockets of order quickly, however small.

5 **Use the tactics you know.** Start there. Formulate a strategy as possible.

6 **Attrit the event.** Wear it down – as possible, where possible. Persist.

In the face of the catastrophic and the unfathomable, start your assessment immediately and start with the basics, the true basics, the personal fundamentals. Look around. Assess what's left, including the people.

You may even need to start with answering the question of how you are, including "Am I alive?" Take a moment, even two, to examine and to collect yourself. Then, with others, take the first steps of recovery – personal and organizational.

That recovery will require that you remain alert and do not wait for authorization. Improvise and reset with who and what is at hand. Connect the pockets of order as possible. Work from the bottom up as the top builds down. Act locally and quickly. Create building blocks. As possible, then connect those pockets of order and thereby form the sinews of the burgeoning organization.

Finally, regarding others: as a leader, there are moments when dissolving the unit is exactly the right thing to do. Let your command go. Let your people drop who they are, for the moment. Let them shed their professional skins and, literally, run for their lives. Doing so can prove essential – lifesaving – and, literally, afford them the chance later to return to the scene, to reclaim their professional selves, and to reengage with you as their leader.

Commentary

Devastation and death filled the moment. Doubt remained about the possibility of a follow-on attack. Nonetheless, the FDNY had begun to contain the site. The original plan included the location of the incident command post—adjusted, readjusted, and readjusted again in the face of on-the-ground exigencies. The FDNY's fourth attempt to organize its efforts on 9/11 took shape. More reorganizations would follow in the weeks and months ahead, eventually altering the FDNY itself.

Firefighters sprang into considered, focused action. They looked for a sprout of hope. The risk-reward calculations were shifting, intentionally and deliberately. So much destruction created extremely dangerous conditions and strained already diminished resources. Rescue efforts needed prioritizing and, eventually, a more systematic approach. Time would quickly show how few feasible rescue opportunities existed. Tenacity of purpose and flexibility of approach came to define the FDNY's approach to working the site, to responding to this massive environmental assault.

Eric Trist, sociotechnical scholar, offers a useful way to consider the environment confronted by the FDNY and the challenge of matching action to conditions.[26] His work provides a first step toward connecting the experiences described in this chapter with more frequently faced ones. Trist, building on his work with Fred Emery,[27] described a type of environment that they termed "turbulent" and explored what it feels like to attempt to operate in such an environment. They focused on a strategy of collaboration and not on leadership in crisis per se, but the language that they developed to describe turbulence maps closely onto the experience of 9/11. Their language also provides a bridge to the Snowden and Boone framework already introduced in Chapter Three and which will receive further attention in Chapter Five.[28]

Trist contended that turbulent environments produce "contextual commotion – as if the ground were moving.... Subjectively we experience it as a loss of the stable state."[29] He references Russell Ackoff's assertion that in such an environment, "no longer are there problems but systems of problems which constitute messes."[30] These messes dominate the environment and resist linear solutions.

Trist warns that people operating in such conditions face the risk of making dangerous psychological adjustments, becoming "dissociated from and unresponsive to others."[31] Doing so would cut them off from a highly valuable antidote: the value of personal networks. In later work with Perlmutter, Trist acknowledges "on the one hand, the fragility and vulnerability of...most of the systems in which we are embedded; and, on the other, [the need to] put some trust in the resilience of the individual, and his capacity to change these systems or invent alternatives at present not discernible."[32]

Trist claims that amid a dominating turbulence, the individual, "rather than any institution or system, would seem to become 'the leading part' and to be the agent of change in whom there is the most hope, if any hope there be."[33] Restated, Trist emphasized the importance of individuals maintaining connections with others precisely when environmental turbulence presses them to retreat from all connections with others and makes them relationally unresponsive. When surrounded by turbulence, organizations must turn to and rely upon the fortitude of individuals not only to endure disruption, but to repair the organization itself.

Another implication follows from this emphasis on the individual. Karl Weick would likely locate much of that fortitude in sense-making grounded in identity. Restated, firefighters retained their identity, their sense of self as firefighters. They entered the buildings as firefighters. They fled the buildings as firefighters. They climbed out of, and then over, the rubble as firefighters. Hence, they viewed the hell about them as firefighters. They had a place to stand psychologically and a commensurate way to act, a place from which to work, however the environment had pummeled them. They had a way to look at what they saw all about them, and they shared that view with the other dust-encrusted firefighters around them.

A third implication concerns organizational design. Organizations can help their members survive even shattering turbulence by consistently fostering personal connections. As noted, these connections facilitate not only individual survival, but also that of the organization itself.

Again, Trist's work addresses planning within the presence of four types of organizational environments, none acute crises. However, his concepts apply to the operational and tactical realities faced by the FDNY. One can bring Trist's language down to plaza level here. The ground-shifting turbulence of 9/11 created 'messes' that could easily have immobilized both the FDNY as an organization and the firefighters as individuals. Neither happened—not on that day nor in its aftermath.

Instead, FDNY leadership set about figuring out over and over how to approach the work on site, and then whether and how to re-form itself over time. On the day, firefighters focused on the work that they could see in front of them. They acted in pre-existing and long-established units and in newly self-forming units that reconfigured like liquid mercury from a broken thermometer.

These actions helped firefighters to retain a sufficient sense of personal agency and to avoid isolation and disassociation. So enabled, firefighters emerging from the collapse of the Towers acted. The actions, in turn, helped firefighters survive as individuals and the FDNY to survive as an organization.

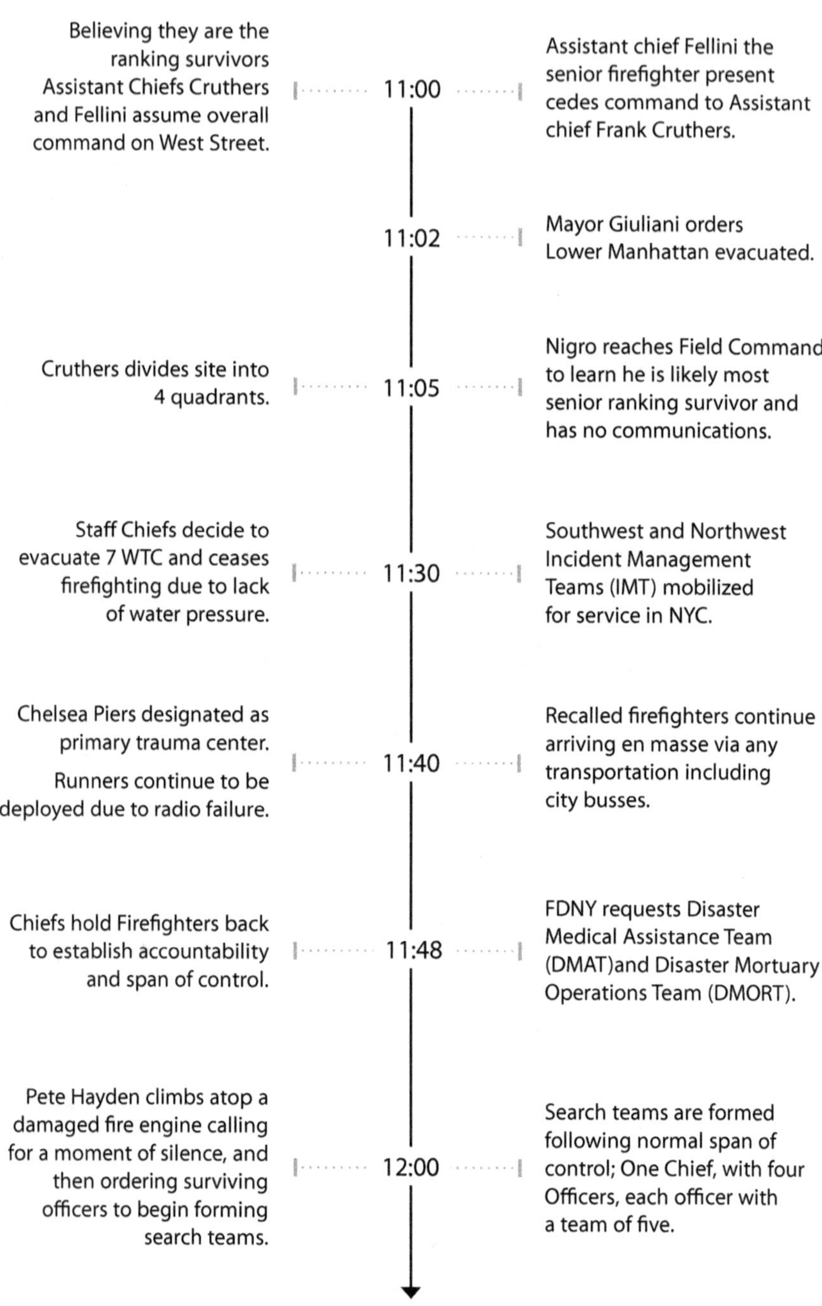

Believing they are the ranking survivors Assistant Chiefs Cruthers and Fellini assume overall command on West Street.
11:00
Assistant chief Fellini the senior firefighter present cedes command to Assistant chief Frank Cruthers.
11:02
Mayor Giuliani orders Lower Manhattan evacuated.
Cruthers divides site into 4 quadrants.
11:05
Nigro reaches Field Command to learn he is likely most senior ranking survivor and has no communications.
Staff Chiefs decide to evacuate 7 WTC and ceases firefighting due to lack of water pressure.
11:30
Southwest and Northwest Incident Management Teams (IMT) mobilized for service in NYC.
Chelsea Piers designated as primary trauma center.
Runners continue to be deployed due to radio failure.
11:40
Recalled firefighters continue arriving en masse via any transportation including city busses.
Chiefs hold Firefighters back to establish accountability and span of control.
11:48
FDNY requests Disaster Medical Assistance Team (DMAT)and Disaster Mortuary Operations Team (DMORT).
Pete Hayden climbs atop a damaged fire engine calling for a moment of silence, and then ordering surviving officers to begin forming search teams.
12:00
Search teams are formed following normal span of control; One Chief, with four Officers, each officer with a team of five.

Chapter Five

Regrouping...in One of Hell's Circles

> "[S]omebody said God help those poor people, all of them. One of the things that crossed my mind was God help the survivors. The people who were killed that day were in a better place, not the people who were left, because of the loss, because of the tragedy, because of the families and massive amounts of stuff that happened. I said, "I don't know how we're going to deal with the survivors, how we will help them get through this." We were very good as a department helping one family get through one incident, one loss, but on hundreds that we were talking about, and that time we didn't know if it was 300 or 500 or 1,500. Couldn't tell. How would we help them? That was beyond me.
>
> *—2nd Deputy Commissioner Thomas Fitzpatrick, then in Headquarters, Downtown Brooklyn*

“ Whatever your job was yesterday, it’s not your job today.

—2nd Deputy Commissioner Thomas Fitzpatrick, then in Headquarters, Downtown Brooklyn

“ As far as dedication, motivation, professionalism, the mentality of the firefighters to get the job done no matter what was confronted...of – of course the enormity of the incident was like nothing we’d ever seen before. There was no difference to me except for the loss of life and the change in leadership. As far as in my head I just had to go to work and do what I had to do.

—Battalion Chief Fred LaFemina, Chief of Rescue Services, then Captain of Squad 270, South Jamaica, Queens; member FDNY USAR

“ Then we started, there were little groups of us, and we started. If there was anybody injured or anybody needed help, pick them up, carry them, get them out of the way, [then] try to regroup.

—Firefighter Louis Giaconelli, then in Engine 53 Spanish Harlem, Manhattan; FDNY IMT

The Towers were down. The command structure shredded. A sandstorm of dust filled the air...and the lungs. Eyes caked and burned. Thousands of vehicles and pieces of equipment were destroyed. Piles of debris and carnage were stories high. Fire burned underfoot and ringed the plaza, in the car fires...of 7 WTC’s 47 floors, 10 were aflame. On another day, it would have been an historically large fire...but not today. Seemingly countless missing. The dead still untallied. A darkened sky snowed paper. The FDNY was in prolonged Response Mode.[34]

What needed doing...

The defining events had happened. The planes had struck the towers. The initial response had saved thousands of lives. The towers had collapsed. Human and physical wreckage filled the WTC complex...and the danger had not passed. Firefighters still fought fires, still searched for the trapped and injured, for the shockingly few still alive beneath the rubble, and for New Yorkers both near to and far from the site.

What response could the FDNY muster now, in the immediate aftermath, through the afternoon and evening, and over the next few days that followed, amid fears of further attacks?

Firefighters qualified as both rescuers and victims. Through it all – the need for care, for treatment – of victims, of others, of self and of those who provided it.

Part A: Responder Voices

Initial regrouping – from the bottom-up...and from the top-down

> “ I remember being struck by, even in the middle of this absolute devastation, they're [firefighters] still coming up and they're looking for rank and structure and organization, because that's how we operate and what we're comfortable in.
>
> —*Captain Paul Brown, then a Lieutenant covering in Division 15, Brownsville, Brooklyn; FDNY IMT*

Firefighter in the smoke
Firefighter Dan Connolly Engine 230 searching for the missing members of his company. Six of whom perished in the collapse.
Public Domain

"I kind of remember now that we were all kind of stunned, but there was nobody really barking out orders. A lot of times when you're operating, it's not really a rank thing, like no one's really barking out orders. Most of the time, the men pretty much know what they have to do.

—Firefighter Louis Giaconelli, then in Engine 53, Spanish Harlem, Manhattan; FDNY IMT

"[T]he chauffeur survived because he had to go quite a few blocks out of the way to find a working hydrant. He didn't know where they were, he goes, 'I dropped them off in the front, I don't think they're alive.' I said, 'What are you doing,' and he says, 'I'm cleaning the fire truck.' I said, 'what the fuck are you cleaning the fire truck for?' He goes, 'Well, I got a hydrant, supplied somebody with water, and I'm cleaning the truck.' He was in shock. He was just cleaning the truck because he didn't know what to do. He was by himself. All I wanted to do was make sure we got to that guy that was cleaning the fire truck.

—Unattributed out of respect for the privacy and sensitivities of those involved

"We had 25 guys went down there. Who was going to check these voids? Who's got a hose to direct into this fire, who's in this sector just sifting through stuff looking for remains? What did you see? People walking around looking for people in their company, looking for their brothers. I was looking for my brother. My brother was in one of the squads [FDNY Squad Company].... Construction guys, the ironworkers were cutting things, there were machines already on site to move debris. It was like organized chaos. It was an amazing thing to look at. Things were getting done without anybody telling anybody what had to be done, because the whole command structure and the thing was gone.

—Captain Kerry Hollywood, then in Engine 53, Spanish Harlem, Manhattan; Commanding Officer Family Assistance Unit

"Well, I think the most important thing is you got a grasp of yourself. It's like, 'Okay, I'm all right.' Then you get down to basics real fast. What do I have? What do I need and what am I going to do? What needs to be done? What am I going to do? How am I going do it? You work your way through those things. I would have to say that thinking back on it now that the fire department, no organization, except for maybe the incident management teams, were equipped at the time to handle something like that on that scale.

—Firefighter Louis Giaconelli, then in Engine 53, Spanish Harlem, Manhattan; FDNY IMT

“ The smoke actually helped psychologically, because you could only take in the little piece that you could see. You didn't have to take in the whole scene all at once. It prevented it from being too overwhelming, and that's how I approached it, in that I can only affect what is right here in front of me at this moment, so let me do something about what's here.

—Captain Paul Brown, then a Lieutenant covering in Division 15, Brownsville, Brooklyn; FDNY IMT

“ You have all these guys running around trying to do something, but really without direction, separated from their officers. Some just came without any officers, some just went, took a car, took a bus, hijacked the bus and went down there. Everybody's kind of scurrying around trying to do something to help people because we're here to help people.

—Captain Glenn Rohan, then a Lieutenant in Ladder 43, Spanish Harlem, Manhattan

“ We initially tried to search these voids and search areas and see what we could do to help folks if we could find anybody. There were different reports throughout the course of the day that we would find people here, find people there, there were no people there. I guess at the end of the day, it was very heroic, and people were operating under extremely dangerous conditions, but there was no structure to it at all. We were just doing things, what we thought we could do with the command structure that we had in place and with the skill set that we had at that time.

—Chief of Training Mike Meyers, then a Lieutenant covering in Division 15, Brownsville, Brooklyn; FDNY IMT

“ I had an off-duty deputy [Deputy Chief] come and say said to me, ‘Pete, what can we do?’ We had the equivalent of a third alarm burning up on 90 West Street. I said, ‘Bobby just take some guys up there and do what you can, put that fire out.'... There was a fire in Battery Park City. There was a young battalion chief there and I told him, 'Hey, John, just take some guys, go up there, and put that damn fire out.' I said, 'Don't even get on the radio or tell anybody, just put the damn fire out and come back.' That's the type of scenario we were dealing with. We were dealing with chaos, we're dealing with shock, we're dealing with anger and an extremely dangerous situation there. That went on like that for quite a while.

—Chief of Department (2004–2006) Pete Hayden, then a Deputy Chief in Division 1, SoHo, Manhattan

" Every single available space in these buildings had fire coming out of it [4 and 5 WTC]. There were vehicles on fire in the street, there were hoses laid everywhere, there were fire trucks with various states of damage.

—Captain Paul Brown, then a Lieutenant covering in Division 15, Brownsville, Brooklyn; FDNY IMT

Dust cloud seen from the water
U.S. Coast Guard evacuating civilians in the Hudson River; often called the "9/11 Boatlift."
Coast Guard News, Public domain, via Wikimedia Commons

The need for self-care—and for those who provide it. Firefighters as both rescuers and victims. Stoicism does not mean being self-destructive.

“ We were all over the pile. We were looking for people. When they first pulled me out, I had probably about two inches of cement come off my face and my eyes. I was going by E.M.S. Ambulance [FDNY, Emergency Medical Service] and they said to me, 'Come on, let me clean you up.' I said, 'No, there's people worse behind there. Don't worry about me.' They said, 'No.' It was a woman, she held a mirror to my face and said, 'Look at yourself.' I said, 'Holy shit.' I let them clean my eyes out, whatever. We got some water and we just went back in looking for people.

—Lieutenant Artie Riccio, then a firefighter in Ladder 119 South Williamsburg, Brooklyn working in Ladder 110

“ There were always EMT crews or paramedic crews around and they would be administering first aid. Of course, if you had a problem, you would go over to them and say, 'My eyes are bothering me.' They would wash them out for you but after a while, they would only do it so much and then at night, they told me I had to go to an aid station that they had set up. They said, 'Now you got to go to the hospital.'

—Firefighter Louis Giaconelli, then in Engine 53, Spanish Harlem, Manhattan; FDNY IMT

“ All of the hospitals will be filled with victims. Take me to a trauma [in] Queens, don't bother trying to go to a local hospital, they'll be full of people. We go to the hospital in Queens, nobody was there. They had nobody. 'You're the first person we've had to deal with. We waited for somebody all day to treat. It's just nobody's come to the hospital. Nobody came out in Manhattan and even the hospitals downtown.'

—Chief of Operations Pat McNally, then a Deputy Chief in Division 14, Flushing, Queens

“ Richie [FF Rich Nogan Ladder 113] and the guys from 58 Engine, they carried me out. If you look at the pictures, they had to carry me up and then down the rubble. I wake up in the hospital and the doctor's there and he looks at me and he says, 'Your men are okay. Your daughter knows you're alive.'

—Lieutenant Ray Brown, then in Ladder 113 Crown Heights, Brooklyn

“ Another thing that kind of worked in my favor was, I was on the west side of Manhattan. The wind was blowing west to east, so the smoke was going west to east which was blowing away from us. We caught a little bit of a break with inhaling all that. We inhaled plenty of it. I was swimming in the stuff at first when the two buildings had come down.

—Firefighter Louis Giaconelli, then in Engine 53, Spanish Harlem, Manhattan

Initial regrouping – stepping back

The place, the tragedy, and the people had a nearly gravitational pull. Yet, stepping back started quickly and grew in importance. How to organize in the moment, to do the work, to protect the living, to consider building 7, to handle other calls throughout the city, and to move toward an organization for tomorrow?

“ Somebody said 'God help those poor people, all of them.' One of the things that crossed my mind was God help the survivors. The people who were killed that day were in a better place, not the people who were left, because of the loss, because of the tragedy, because of the families I don't know how we're going to deal with the survivors, how we will help them get through this. We were very good as a department helping one family get through one incident, one loss, but on the hundreds that we were talking about, and that time we didn't know if it was 300 or 500 or 1,500. Couldn't tell. How would we help them? That was beyond me.

—Chief of Department Pete Hayden, then a Deputy Chief in Division 1, SoHo, Manhattan

“ It was pretty empty [St. Francis Hospital]. I was quickly triaged, cleaned up, X-rayed and released.... I went back to headquarters and started operating out of headquarters to try to gather who we had missing, what was going on as far as the fires. We had so many chiefs come from home to help set up commands for us there. We had lost the chief of department, we had lost Donald Burns who was unbelievable, Chief Jerry Barbara.

—Fire Commissioner (2010–2014) Sal Cassano, then Assistant Chief at Headquarters, Downtown Brooklyn (served as Chief of Department 2006–2010)

“ Within an hour, I forget the time but I'm pretty sure within an hour, after the collapse of the building, we had returned to normal response time throughout the city [though call volume was reduced]. Which is remarkable that we were able to commit that much resources to an event like that, suffer the loss that we incurred, both as far as human life and equipment and apparatus and everything and within an hour, the department was back up to normal response capabilities. Quite a statement, I was pretty impressed with that. Everybody forgets we lost 92 pieces of apparatus. All the tools, the equipment, the hoses.

—Chief of Department (2004–2006) Pete Hayden, then a Deputy Chief in Division 1, SoHo, Manhattan

“ Then there were just decisions, people just wanting to do something good, they had to make decisions like, 'No, we're not going to do that.' There was a lot of search and rescue during the daytime going on. The members that weren't buried were reachable. All efforts were being made to locate them as well as civilians. There were chiefs and companies that just did heroic things.

—Deputy Chief James DiDomenico, then in Division 13, South Jamaica, Queens

“ We were just doing rescue and recovery, and we really just dealt with surface victims and anybody that could tell us – we think somebody's in that doorway or there's an opening you can go in there. My biggest fear was to lose more people looking for people who were either not verified or unrecoverable. We were concerned.

—Chief of Operations Pat McNally, then a Deputy Chief in Division 14, Flushing, Queens

“ So many chiefs came from off duty and did a tremendous job in ad-hoc, setting up command posts and getting all the people that are coming in from home and try to get some semblance of order and command, and a plan of action on how we were going to handle what we had facing in front of us.

—Fire Commissioner (2010–2014) Sal Cassano,
then Assistant Chief at Headquarters, Downtown Brooklyn
(served as Chief of Department 2006–2010)

“ The youngest member of the company, the new kid, two weeks in the firehouse, his father was a big chief in the transit police. He had assigned two policemen to find what happened to Andy, his son. The cops walk up to us, we know he jumped on the rig. He was an extra guy and we were asked by the police, ‘Where’s Andy? His father is looking for him.’ That’s what we jokingly refer to as our ‘Saving Private Ryan’ moment. The cops stayed with us for a pretty good amount of time until finally the radio for the police crackled and they found Andy. We want to know where the rest of our guys are and if they’re okay. We walked around the whole thing, came up on the south end on the west side and that’s where we found the guys. Mooky [firefighter John Wilson, Engine 58] was the first guy I saw and he said, ‘Bobby is gone [Lt. Bob Nagle Engine 58].’

—Captain Jeff Simms, then a Lieutenant in Engine 58,
Harlem, Manhattan

“ That’s when it gets interesting from a leadership point of view. After the first tower came down, a lot of the bosses had been killed. Now, we’re in a situation where something we’ve never really been exposed to, but we have to figure out what to do, and that’s where the self-initiative, and your training, and well, we have to do it by steps. What’s the first thing we do? I guess the first thing we do is take account of ourselves, what do I got, what do I need? The first thing I did, I think I remember, because I was having such a hard time with the air, was I found our masks.

—Firefighter Louis Giaconelli, then in Engine 53,
Spanish Harlem, Manhattan; FDNY IMT

“ At that point in time, the goal was – we weren’t going to extinguish the fires, except the surrounding fires that we were able to handle, not underneath the buildings. Don’t get any more firefighters killed and getting organized a search and rescue strategy in place here, but that

Street level aftermath
Barclay Street to the north of 7 WTC following the Towers collapse.
Anonymous. Courtesy of the Prints and Photographs Division. Library of Congress, Public domain, via Wikimedia Commons

was at 12 o'clock, and the rest of the day and through the night, more and more companies came in like that. We slowly got some structure, we had four different sectors operating.... More supervision, less personnel, that's what we needed...just keep it really confined to these areas over here and make sure that we watch out and make sure that nobody gets hurt additionally. In the aftermath of everything, when all was said and done, we never lost a firefighter, we didn't lose construction workers, we didn't lose anything. At least we can say that.

—Chief of Department (2004–2006) Pete Hayden,
then a Deputy Chief in Division 1,
SoHo, Manhattan

“I was at Shea Stadium [now Citi Field; used as a staging area]. They gave me a megaphone. As you could imagine, the brothers and sisters in the fire department were very, very anxious. Many were angry that they couldn't go. So, at some point, people just got in their cars and left. They went to the site.

—Chief of Department (2020–2022) Tom Richardson,
then a Battalion Chief in Battalion 53, Bayside, Queens

" I saw leadership from the top. I saw it then transition while the search and rescue always continued. We had to start transitioning to make the search and rescue more efficient. There were people behind the scenes making decisions too, and probably other people besides FDNY, get what we needed there.

—Deputy Chief Jim DiDomenico, then in Division 13, South Jamaica, Queens

" Our command structure was shattered. The chief of department was lost. Two of the top assistant chiefs were lost, but the people below them picked up the pieces and started doing things because that's what we do as firefighters; we fix things. The initial operations were by ad hoc groups of firefighters with very little direction from above. They saw things that needed to be fixed. They saw areas that needed to be searched. That's what we do. People started doing them. As command structure started getting rebuilt, we started capturing the information that those people were telling us. They were doing their jobs, just by training and the nature of what their work is.

—Deputy Assistant Chief John Norman, Chief of Special Operations, then a Battalion Chief in Battalion 16, Harlem, Manhattan; FDNY USAR

" I got down there. It was surreal, it was like a movie set. It was like something you just couldn't believe. It was like a snowstorm, the dust was just blowing and the only thing you saw was steel. In the air was paper and dust and it was just swirling around.

—Battalion Chief Bill Moore, then in Battalion 10 Yorkville, Manhattan

" Now you could focus on something and focus the men on something. It was so huge, this huge elephant that I have to somehow eat. It's thousands of elephants and firemen just tell us what to do and we're going to do it.

—Captain Glenn Rohan, then a Lieutenant in Ladder 43, Spanish Harlem, Manhattan

" I just remember watching these grown men, National Guard, state police, NYPD, firefighters, all these big tough guys...walking around with thousand-yard stares, that normally is equated with serious combat, and it was just this major disbelief.

—Stephanie Gaskell, then a journalist, Associated Press, New York (covered WTC site for duration of FDNY operations)

“ I report there [Special Operations Command, Roosevelt Island]. From there I went down to the site. Special Operations was kind of putting together a little logistics center, tools and equipment, and trying to get enough equipment there. They were doing it in the back of the World Financial Center, across from the Trade Center. And they set up a little staging area in there. We were starting to put together a tool cache. So we had tools and equipment for the units to operate. And that's where I was that day.

—Chief of Department (2020–2022) Tom Richardson, then a Battalion Chief in Battalion 53, Bayside, Queens

“ We reported to the command post and a bunch of us were sent on West Street through to the World Financial Center buildings and we came out on the second floor window on top of the rubble and we were supervising – just trying to, there was guys digging, they had torches going already, there was a lot of construction workers there, and I was there over the whole night.

—Battalion Chief Bill Moore, then in Battalion 10, Yorkville, Manhattan

Initial regrouping – the grieving

Clarifying the extent of the loss came first. The extent and the particulars, the names, needed gathering and tabulating. It amounted to determining how bad the hurt was and therefore how extensive the effort to heal needed to be.

“ 'Well, we have 27 here.' I said, 'Well, that's incredible. That would be tremendous.' He says, 'Well, there's 10 pages' [names of missing firefighters who were on site before the collapse]. Now I knew we had taken a tremendous hit. That's the first time I realized what we had committed. It wasn't until even years later that I found out that we probably had maybe between 700 and 800 guys working at the time when the buildings collapsed. We lost almost half of them. I spent the rest of the afternoon and into the night, addressing people who were missing or if we found an opening that we could get into quickly. We didn't have any equipment to dig.

—Chief of Operations Pat McNally, then a Deputy Chief in Division 14, Flushing, Queens

“ I ran into people I knew. People I was with ran into someone they knew, and it seemed like every time you would cross paths with somebody and have a conversation, they would drop another name of someone who is confirmed to have died.

—Captain Paul Brown, then a Lieutenant covering in Division 15, Brownsville, Brooklyn; FDNY IMT

“ I knew the South Tower came down...I was on my way home listening to the radio. I said, ‘We just lost a couple hundred guys.’ I came home, grabbed as much of my equipment as I could, threw it in the car and drove into Manhattan.

—Chief of Department (2010–2014) Ed Kilduff, then a Deputy Chief in Division 3, Midtown, Manhattan and past IMT Incident Commander

Dust covered civilians leaving Ground Zero
Two survivors, covered in dust, help each other away from the collapse site.
Don Halasy, Public domain, via Wikimedia Commons

“ We go up, when we got to that veranda, there's this kid from 10 engine, dead, lying on the street. I don't know how he died, I don't know his name, but it's the first time I ever saw a firefighter killed in the line of duty. Where I was, we've seen plenty of guys injured, plenty of guys going to hospitals, but never a guy dead. That's when it really hit me that we're losing. We lost guys here, I don't know. There's going to be a lot more than him probably.

—Captain Glenn Rohan, then a Lieutenant in Ladder 43, Spanish Harlem, Manhattan

“ Early on, I went to headquarters. We identify people on the civilian workforce who could be taught in a hurry to use a template, how to take a phone call from a grieving family member, or a family member who didn't know if their person was alive. All these people were volunteers. Anybody who was overwhelmed was free to go home, they could have left. In each civilian unit, we asked each supervisor to identify a few people they felt they had these qualities. I didn't know the call takers. We trusted them.... I made templates. For example, spouse, child, parent, co-worker, boss, concerned neighbor. I made as many templates as I could think of and gave them that at their workstation. A person calls up and says, ‘I'm missing my husband.’ We turn to the spouse page, go from there and there's just a whole series of what the person might know, what they don't know, what they might want to know, what they might say. I made it as graphic as I could so the call taker could get focused on the kinds of things they would be hearing. There was a lot of camaraderie among all branches of the fire department, and a lot of help that way.

—Malachy Corrigan NP, then Clinical Director, Counseling Services Unit, SoHo, Manhattan

“ We lost so much of our staff, our leadership. One thing that saved the fire department was the retirees. Guys, retirees came. A lot of them went right down to headquarters, a lot of the retired chiefs, and they sat down and came up with plans, and took control. Meanwhile, the active guys were still in the field.

—Battalion Chief Bill Moore, then in Battalion 10, Yorkville, Manhattan

“I was in Chicago with a bunch of retired chiefs. We heard about the towers right away. We were glued to the TV; we were on the phones. We kept hearing more and more people killed who we knew, sons of guys we worked with. It was torture. We had to get back to New York to help. Flights were all cancelled, we couldn't find rental cars anywhere. So, we went to the Amtrak station to see if we could get on a train. It was crowded and the lines were really long. All the trains were sold out we were standing around talking about what to do. I saw a girl [Amtrak employee] come out of the ticket office. I went over and showed my fire department ID and told her we were all retired firemen and need to get to NY. She said, ‘They might be adding cars to the next train. Stay close by and I'll get you on it.’ About twenty minutes later, she popped her head out the side door and waved me over. She took my credit card and got all of us on the train.

—Battalion Chief Tom Martin, Retiree liaison to Chiefs Association

“After I went to the ambulance, they sat me down and they gave me some water. My wife thought-- thought I was dead. She sat in front of TV and cried. My niece saw me drinking a bottle of water on TV and she called my wife and said, ‘I saw Artie. He's alive.’

—Lieutenant Artie Riccio, then a firefighter in Ladder 119 South Williamsburg, Brooklyn, working in Ladder 110

“I heard the name of someone who died that I was familiar with but didn't know well. Five minutes later, I see this firefighter leaning up against a car, just staring forward, looking absolutely devastated. I started to head towards him to ask him if he was okay. I was wondering if he had a physical injury. As I got closer, I realized that it was the brother of the guy they just told me was confirmed to have died. I just stopped in my tracks. I had nothing to say. I could not come up with any words. I knew that nothing I could say to him would console him, and I just kept walking.

—Captain Paul Brown, then a Lieutenant covering in Division 15, Brownsville, Brooklyn; FDNY IMT

“Probably it wasn't until I got back to the third division...that's when I fully grasped the loss of life.... [T]he thought is like, you know, who's missing, who got killed? You know, uh, what apparatus got destroyed, the equipment, and now it was going into a mode of, uh, that's when I first realized it. These are the group that's missing. You know, we're not – we-we can't find them anywhere. They're not in hospitals.

—Assistant Chief Tom Galvin, Chief of Training (2004–2015), then a Deputy Chief in Division 3, Midtown, Manhattan

“ Bernie Kerik was the police commissioner at the time.... I remember he says, ‘You think you lost some people?’ I said, ‘We lost a couple hundred people.’ I'll never forget his face either. He's like, ‘Cops, lost 23.’

—Chief of Department (2010–2014) Ed Kilduff, then a Deputy Chief in Division 3, Midtown, Manhattan and past IMT Incident Commander

“ Phone calls, people checking in on you.... I didn't have a cell phone at the time. I had one of those recordings things...which was a horrible, horrible experience for me. It was probably one of the worst things that happened to me, was having to listen to that machine.... Because it was your family and your friends thinking you were dead. They'd say, ‘Louis, are you home?’... It was like a pause and they didn't know what to say. It was like, ‘Call me.’ It was horrible. I threw that tape away. I never wanted to listen to it again.

—Firefighter Louis Giaconelli, then in Engine 53, Spanish Harlem, Manhattan; FDNY IMT

“ The head of our union, Jack McDonald, who was UFOA [Uniformed Fire Officers Association] president, came up to me and said, ‘I think we lost about 340, 350 members today.’ I said, ‘How do we know that?’ He said, ‘We've called every firehouse.’ They had called every firehouse and said, ‘Who you got, who do you not got?’... It really hit you, the enormity. You were speculating all day. ‘I wonder how many people didn't make it,’ but now you had a number attached to that.

—Deputy Chief Jim DiDomenico, then in Division 13, South Jamaica, Queens

“ Now, our civilian people all stayed at work or came back to work, and they were already hard at work trying to figure out who we lost, which took a couple of days because it wasn't just the people that were assigned to work that day. We didn't really know for a couple of days exactly who we lost. That took a while.

—Fire Commissioner (2014–2022) Dan Nigro,
then Chief of Operations at Headquarters, Downtown Brooklyn
(served as Chief of Department 2001–2002)

Initial regrouping – as for the leaders themselves...

“ I must say that was a – there were times when I was not sure I could continue on.

—Fire Commissioner (2014–2022) Dan Nigro,
then Chief of Operations Headquarters, Downtown Brooklyn
(served as Chief of Department 2001–2002)

“ I saw Chief Nigro, who was the highest-ranking survivor. A guy said, 'Man he looks shot.' I said, 'Can you imagine the weight he's feeling right now?'

—Captain Paul Brown, then a Lieutenant covering in
Division 15, Brownsville, Brooklyn; FDNY IMT

Deputy Chief Pete Hayden directing firefighters
FDNY personnel and rescue squads coordinate efforts amidst the debris at Ground Zero, New York City, September 2001.
Bill Bennett @BillBennettPhoto

“Somebody said something to me the other day. We were talking, and I was thinking and putting it all in perspective: 9/11 was a day where I [as a firefighter in the Washington D.C. Fire department] went to one of the biggest instances of my life [Pentagon]. It paled in comparison to what was going on in New York.... There were incidents within the greater incident in New York City on all those activities that individually, would have been the largest incident the organization would have faced. It all just pales in comparison. It was a unique day.

—Battalion Chief Tom Winship, then a District of Columbia FD firefighter; responded to the Pentagon on 9/11; appointed to FDNY 2003; FDNY Pipes and Drums; IMT

Restoring command and control

“Whatever your job was yesterday, it's not your job today.

—Deputy Commissioner Thomas Fitzpatrick, then in Headquarters, Downtown Brooklyn

“I was making my way up to where the command post had been, and I meet Frank Fellini [Assistant Chief of Operations]. Frank gives me a quick rundown of what they were doing, and who had died, who was missing. Frank and I were the same rank, he was senior. And then he said, 'Frank, I'm turning command over to you.' My immediate response was, 'Okay, Frank, you're the operations chief.' Shortly after Frank turned over command, I grabbed an OEM rep and told him to initiate requests for USAR, DMAT [Disaster Medical Assistance Team] and DMORT [Disaster Mortuary Operational Team].

At that moment, you had to go in and manage initiative. People were taking initiative to try to fill in the gap that they perceived, and you had to intervene, step back a moment, or step down, or step over, or whatever for a moment. Those attitudes and commitments are what we deal with all the time. You more often have to give direction to try and limit people from taking unwarranted risks, even though they seem well warranted from their perspective. You have a somewhat broader, hopefully, more comprehensive view and supervise them for their safety when there was no real justification for that level of risk.

You're intervening, trying to create some order amidst a larger chaos. Then it [Command Post] was moved north, out onto the street. I wind up over there. [West and Chambers]

We've got, it seemed like, hundreds of off-duty guys waiting to be put to work. Some fully outfitted, some with nothing at all. We had to deal with that. I'm just trying to sort out communications. A couple of chiefs though who were at different locations, thought they might be the only or the senior surviving and started to act as and get through to dispatch that they were. We had to straighten out that there was only one command post, this was it. This is who you should contact and contact the field people some by radio, some by messenger. Where the command post was, who was in command, so on.

—1st Deputy Commissioner (2004–2010) Frank Cruthers, then an Assistant Chief at Headquarters, Downtown Brooklyn (served as Chief of Department 1996–1997, 2002–2004)

“ These off-duty guys starting to come in. There was no command structure, everybody shouldn't go on their own at that point in time. So, I'm in my own little corner over there on West and Liberty, so I try to get their attention. There was a couple of hundred firefighters at the time, there's anger, there's shock, there's sadness, every range of emotion just existed there for these men. ‘Where's this company, where's that company?’ ‘Have you seen my father?’ ‘Have you seen my son?’ In my heart, I knew what the answer was. I would just tell them, ‘No, I haven't seen them.’ Anyway, I got up on the pumper. A Lieutenant gave me a megaphone and I got their attention. I said, ‘Look, we just lost a lot of guys here today. We just lost a lot of guys, let's have a moment of silence for those we lost today.’ I took off my helmet and I held it; I just calmed everybody down. I just held it and then I said, ‘Okay, Chiefs and officers come over, we're going to form up the search teams, and we're going to give assignments out.’

—Chief of Department (2004–2006) Pete Hayden, then a Deputy Chief in Division 1, SoHo, Manhattan

Chief Hayden's actions are cited in the 9/11 Commission report as the moment command and control was restored by the FDNY.

Part B: Summary, Lessons, and Commentary

Summary

As the dust settled following the collapse of the second tower, survivors collected themselves, tried to wrap their heads around what happened, and then to work out what to do next. The line between victim and rescuer had blurred. Victims included numerous first responders, those normally responsible for assisting victims.

A deep loss and numbing trauma saturated over 11,000 remaining members of the FDNY – active firefighters, support personnel, and retirees. Still, firefighters, including survivors and new arrivals of all ranks, began to regroup in numerous locations within the site. Individually and in small groups, they headed back toward the carnage. Acting with personal initiative, without awaiting orders or direction – traits embedded in the culture of FDNY – they began the search for survivors.

A firefighter Louis Giaconelli recounted, "Then we started. There were little groups of us, and we started. If there was anybody injured or anybody needed help, pick them up, carry them, get them out of the way, [then] try to regroup."

Soon, off-duty firefighters arrived in great numbers. Lieutenant Glenn Rohan said, "Some took a car [or] hijacked the bus and went down there. Everybody's kind of scurrying around trying to do something...because we're here to help people." The department's strong hierarchical command structure would come into play as groups of firefighters aligned with lieutenants and captains to form ad-hoc units. These groups then coalesced under chiefs. One deputy chief recalled, "After the collapse, there was a natural flow towards chiefs, but we didn't know where the command post was supposed to be."

Under these extraordinary conditions, many difficult decisions were made. Chief Pat McNally related, "We were finding some victims that were deceased.... It always bothered me...directing the firefighters: '...you have to leave them. We just have too much work to do. Maybe we'll find some other people alive.'" Arriving soon after the collapse of the second tower, Captain Fred LaFemina surveyed the scene. "The thing that amazed me," he said, "I knew how big the incident was, but there were a thousand operations going on at the same time, and you're so focused on what you're doing that you kind of lose sight of that."

Captain Kerry Hollywood recalled that the scene "was like organized chaos. It was an amazing thing to look at. Things were getting done without anybody telling anybody what had to be done, because the whole command structure of the thing was gone."

Chief Nigro's personal reconnaissance of the towers from all sides was never accomplished. Soon after the second collapse, he found an FDNY communications truck staffed by a lone firefighter. Here, Nigro learned that the ranking commander heard on the radio was a deputy chief who had established a command post south of City Hall. Nigro was stunned by the implication. This meant all staff chiefs had been killed, including his friend Pete Ganci the chief of department. Nigro immediately felt the weight that implied; the realization that he was the ranking survivor. Responsibility for the entire incident was his to bear. However, he was in an isolated location, unable to communicate with other surviving chiefs. In other words, in that moment, Nigro was in no position to assume command.

Simultaneously, Chief Cruthers found Assistant Chief of Operations Frank Fellini, and the two briefly exchanged information. Commissioner Feehan and chief Ganci had been too close to the South Tower to have survived, there was no word from Nigro. Cruthers and Fellini believed they were the ranking survivors. Fellini outranked Cruthers and yet Frank Cruthers had previously served as Chief of Department. In light of that experience, Fellini said simply, "Frank, I want you to take command."

As hundreds of arriving off-duty firefighters streamed into the site, ranking commanders struggled with organization and accountability. Marshalling them effectively would be a monumental task. Chief Nigro said, "We were able to sector out like we usually do at large operations, give people command of an individual area." Each sector was commanded by a deputy chief or staff chief. Holding the firefighters back to maintain accountability and span of control would prove most difficult. Battalion Chief Bob Maynes recalled his efforts to "get in" with his group: "It was hard keeping the guys from mutiny trying to get in there.... We tried numerous times, [and] we were stopped."

Receiving orders at the Broadway Command Post, Lieutenant Paul Brown was directed with a team to operate on Church Street near 5 and 6 WTC, which were fully engulfed in fire. Throughout the day, he received little information regarding his brother Ray, also a Lieutenant. He knew

Ray was working and that his unit Ladder 113 had responded. They had not been heard from post-collapse. Surveying the scene, he realized it would take a very long time to make his way around to the West Street side of the pile where Ladder 113 had likely responded. Concluding that there were hundreds, if not thousands, of firefighters at other locations surrounding the site, Brown determined, "I needed to do what I could, where I was. I had faith that other firefighters would be doing their best at other locations. They would be searching for surviving firefighters, including my brother."

Within each sector, teams were sent in with a command structure reflecting the department's standard span of control. Each team consisted of one Battalion Chief with several [three–five] company officers [Lieutenants and Captains], each officer with five firefighters respectively. Teams were not sent in with any specific instruction or directive; the order was "go here, see what you can do." Because few radios were available on scene, commanders utilized runners to communicate with the command post.

Intermittent radio transmissions made their way through to Deputy Chief Nick Visconti on West Street. Ladder 6's "Mayday" transmission was received. Visconti ordered Battalion Chief Mark Ferran to lead the rescue effort. He quickly assembled a contingent from Ladder 43 and Engine 53 to rescue 12 firefighters, a police officer, and a civilian trapped in the remains of a stairway. The effort was later known as "The Miracle of Stairway B."

Firefighters, off-duty, on-duty massed by the hundreds eager for direction, Deputy Chief Pete Hayden climbed atop a damaged engine. A lieutenant handed him a megaphone. Hayden announced, "Look, we just lost a lot of guys. Let's have a moment of silence for those we lost today." He removed his white chief's helmet. He held it. Those with helmets removed them. Silence replaced the cacophony. Hayden had their attention. He then called company officers forward to form up search teams. The FDNY had regained command and control for the fifth time in three and a half hours. It would hold.

Lessons for Leaders

1 **Prepare for the day that changes everything.** Hire for grit and service. Train your people side by side – to improvise under

pressure, to act locally when cut off, to solve problems amid confusion and loss. Build bonds before you need them. When the structure shatters, the bonds hold.

2 **Do something.** Act. Hold the line or relinquish it, but act. Work with what you've got. Even cleaning the grime off a rig emptied forever of colleagues – if that's what reclaims your agency, start there. Staggering events need not remove the capacity to act.

3 **Encircle the wound.** Find the boundaries of the event. Contain its spread – physical and emotional. Fight back, but fight back smart. Identify what's approaching. Prioritize. Focus on the big ones: so many people without a chief, 7 WTC still standing. Let the rank and file dress the wound in front of them while senior leaders shape the perimeter.

4 **Guard against self-destructiveness.** You need these people tomorrow. Their families need them more. Sacrifice and heroism don't require charges of the light brigade. Crises are not for the foolhardy, the crazy brave, the phony tough. Balance pressing on with pulling back. Neither deadened defeat nor delusion serves.

5 **Stand close to the loss.** Tally the dead. Pause when a body is found. One person's death is a tragedy; hold tight to that truth before the numbers turn death into statistics. Moving on from tragedy will include standing still. Denial may help in the moment but serves no one well as a strategy. The pain will ground and connect you.

Leaders facing a world all but obliterated, a world needing the halting of further destruction, restoring, and rebuilding, such leaders would best push back in a shattered environment while learning from it. They need to adapt to reality without confusing bravery with foolhardiness. People do better if they can avoid becoming deadened to reality, either defeated by reality or delusional about their capabilities in the face of it.

Leadership in such moments requires grappling for understanding and control across the temporal, spatial, and human dimensions of the crisis. Leaders help people understand both what they can do and what they cannot. Ideally, that understanding arises long before catastrophe strikes – through shared practice, common purpose, interpersonal bonds, and the deliberate cultivation of collaborative instincts – instincts forged through shared training and ongoing reshuffling of assignments. People who learn, work, and struggle together bond and synchronize.

Leaders also need to act. They need to recognize the importance of any opportunities to do so. Seizing those opportunities demonstrates agency to oneself and to others. People need a sense of agency to begin the stupefying amount of work at hand, to move forward, to get about it, to try something. Leaders should therefore allow, model, and encourage local initiative. They likely need to shape more and direct less, letting efforts evolve and seeing what becomes possible as they do.

Additionally, leaders should accept that everything takes longer amidst catastrophe. It slows everything down. Catastrophe leaves behind debris and trauma, broken and wounded bits that need working around. It also necessitates not waiting, though, and getting on with repairing and transplanting the sinews of organization: making field promotions to repopulate the chain of command, gaining control of pace (beginning with your people), determining what needs doing beyond the exigencies of the moment, establishing perimeters, controlling the site, thinking and working in as many directions as seem feasible and potentially productive, identifying needed resources – fighting against both overload and scarcity. And, leaders must periodically lift their heads, look around, and consider what comes next.

The work at hand includes recovery of those who labor, including one's self. Recovery for self and for others begins with acknowledging reality, the agony and all. That individual and shared truth provides footing for regrouping and, eventually, healing. That's where Pete Hayden began–standing on the damaged hulk of a fire vehicle, an intervention in the moment and a metaphor of much that would follow.

For guidance, listen to yourself. Let what you hear guide you. Every life, living and ended, matters. Hold tight to that belief. Hold tight to the pain and the truth that comes with it. Fight Kurt Tucholsky's notion expressed by Joseph Stalin: "The death of one man is a tragedy; the death of millions is a statistic." In summary, use your mind and your heart to hone your understanding of the challenge your people face and, so, to guide your actions.

Commentary

Arguably, four events marked the end of the beginning of the FDNY and September 11, 2001. The first two occurred between about 11:00 a.m. and noon. Frank Cruthers and Frank Fellini created the first of those events. In effect, they reconstructed the most senior on-site command, remarkably and collaboratively, before the dust had begun to settle from the collapses. Around noon, Pete Hayden climbed atop a damaged fire vehicle and created the second event. He successfully initiated a rank-and-file level reorganization. (The second two events would come later that day, in the afternoon and concern how to approach building 7 and plan for the next day.)

Regrouping under the conditions described above requires a number of skills. One of those skills boils down to figuring out the environment faced. In this extreme case, in which circle of hell does one find one's self? Increasing one's capacity to do that can expedite dealing with even extreme crises, such as, in this case, the essential need to reestablish organization and the chain of command.

Organizational theorists Dave Snowden and Mary Boone offer a way to think about environments under pressure – one that complements Trist's work.[35] In a 2007 article, they introduce the Cynefin framework, a planning model designed to help leaders recognize what kind of environment they are operating in and adjust their actions accordingly. Cynefin distinguishes between ordered and unordered contexts, with further differentiations of *simple and complicated* on the ordered side, and *complex and chaotic* on the unordered side.

Like Trist, Snowden and Boone Cynefin developed their framework for large-scale planning rather than for acute crisis response.[36] Yet, again like Trist's work, its language travels well. It helps characterize how the environment faced by the FDNY on 9/11 shifted, what those shifts demanded of leaders, and how the department began the difficult work of containing and then climbing out of the chaos created by the collapse of two 100+ story buildings.

Snowdon and Boone would likely describe the initial post strike situation as an obvious or simple situation.[37] Leaders facing such situations should sense, categorize, and respond using established best practices. Just so, the FDNY initially attacked this huge version of what they did every day, namely fight building fires, evacuate people, and organize complex fire sites. Firefighters relied on practiced, honed routines for rescue and recovery. At the same time, the situation included a defining "known unknown" characteristic of complicated situations, so-called single morbidity problems. In this case, would the towers collapse, and if so, then when? Time did not permit the recommended assembly of panels of experts, only the recommended "sense, analyze, respond," albeit with limited analysis. Tens of thousands of people needed evacuating and time proved even more limited than anticipated, let alone than desired...or hoped for. The pancake collapse of floor upon floor of each tower came sooner and more completely than expected.

The first collapse radically altered conditions at the site, but not yet beyond recognition born of experience. The FDNY had handled collapsed buildings before and quickly moved to reorganize and to continue the work. The second collapse, however, catapulted the environment into what Snowden and Boone would likely describe as chaotic: an environment defined by extreme uncertainty, high tension, and an absence of reliable cause-and-effect relationships.[38] Leaders needed to act, sense, and respond. Command and control needed immediate restoration because of the extensive losses of formal leaders and the now overwhelming physical disaster and exceedingly difficult terrain as well as limited sight. Communication depended on that restoration. Meanwhile, individuals acted and teams formed spontaneously. Firefighters tackled the work laying directly in front of them, whatever work. That response served to move the situation, as Snowden and Boone would probably opine, from *chaotic,* down to *complex.*

The FDNY shifted accordingly. Its firefighters probed, sensed, and responded. It restrained the impulse to "accelerate resolution." Cruthers's acceptance of site command from Fellini, along with Hayden's message from the disabled truck, helped to create order and to attrit the crises. Later that afternoon, Nigro cleared the area and allowed Building 7 to collapse. This departure from established practice prevented additional loss of firefighters and enhanced the possibility of the FDNY effectively regrouping on site, in real time. In combination, these leadership actions slowed the action, reclaimed a workable pace, and thereby helped the coordination and focus of on site activity.

By the next day, conditions returned to the "merely" complicated. The next day also saw experimentation in how best to coordinate onsite work efforts. The path forward consisted largely of what Heifetz might classify as "adaptive challenges," distinct from technical problems solvable with existing know-how.[39] Moving forward required learning and adapting in real time. Pursuing learning precipitated experimentation, which would, in turn, lead to lasting organizational change. The FDNY came to embrace the use of outside experts. It would also formalize and expand initiatives for the treating of traumatized firefighters. Step by step, beginning on the afternoon of 9/11, that work began – the work the next chapter takes up.

Section Three: The Time Following

"

But man is not made for defeat.
A [person] can be destroyed but not defeated.

—Ernest Hemingway

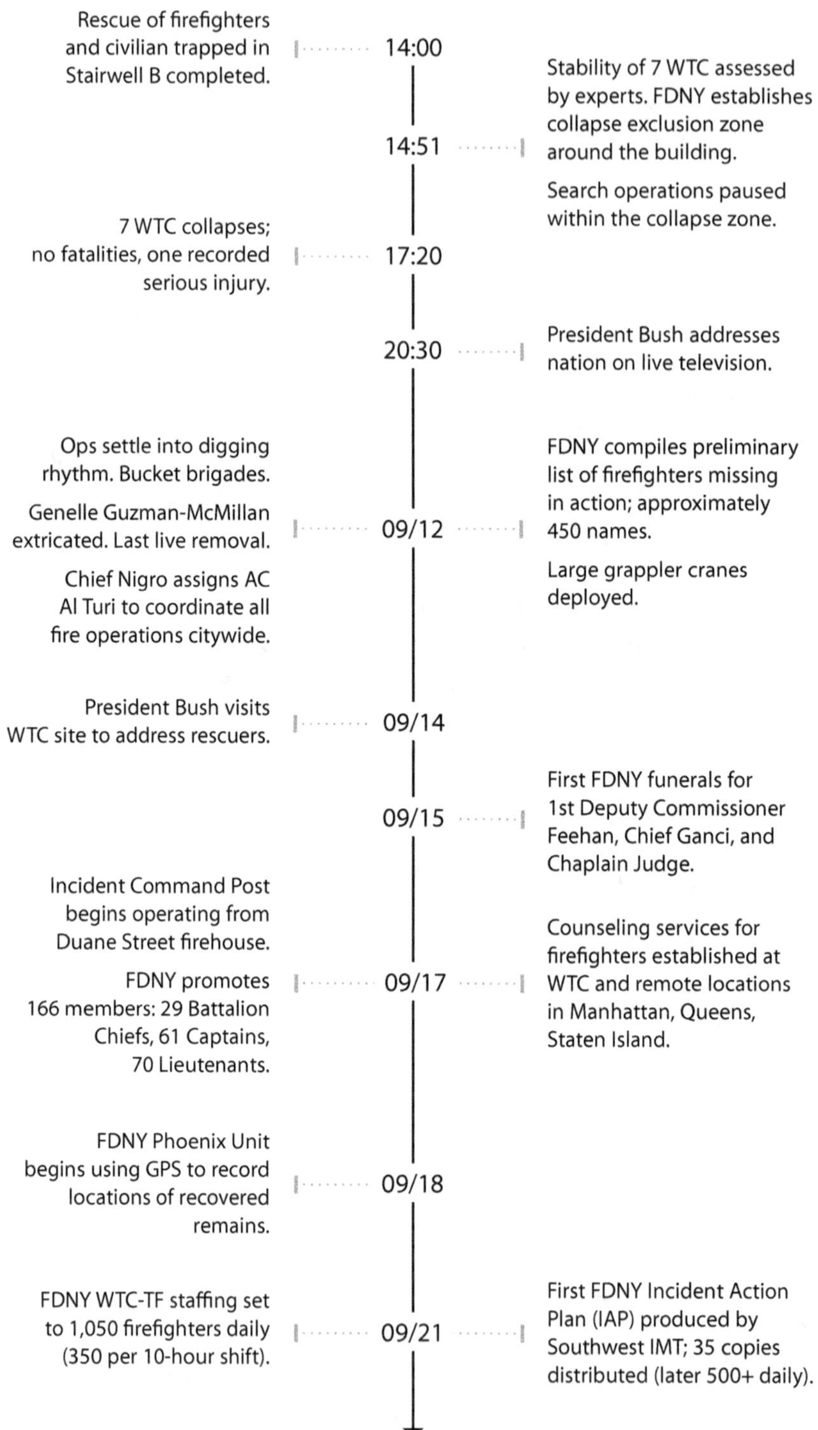

Rescue of firefighters and civilian trapped in Stairwell B completed.
14:00
14:51
Stability of 7 WTC assessed by experts. FDNY establishes collapse exclusion zone around the building.
Search operations paused within the collapse zone.
7 WTC collapses; no fatalities, one recorded serious injury.
17:20
20:30
President Bush addresses nation on live television.
Ops settle into digging rhythm. Bucket brigades.
Genelle Guzman-McMillan extricated. Last live removal.
Chief Nigro assigns AC Al Turi to coordinate all fire operations citywide.
09/12
FDNY compiles preliminary list of firefighters missing in action; approximately 450 names.
Large grappler cranes deployed.
President Bush visits WTC site to address rescuers.
09/14
09/15
First FDNY funerals for 1st Deputy Commissioner Feehan, Chief Ganci, and Chaplain Judge.
Incident Command Post begins operating from Duane Street firehouse.
FDNY promotes 166 members: 29 Battalion Chiefs, 61 Captains, 70 Lieutenants.
09/17
Counseling services for firefighters established at WTC and remote locations in Manhattan, Queens, Staten Island.
FDNY Phoenix Unit begins using GPS to record locations of recovered remains.
09/18
FDNY WTC-TF staffing set to 1,050 firefighters daily (350 per 10-hour shift).
09/21
First FDNY Incident Action Plan (IAP) produced by Southwest IMT; 35 copies distributed (later 500+ daily).

Chapter Six

From Rescue to Recovery: The First Two Weeks

“ The first two weeks were pretty much a blur to me.... All we were doing was searching. We still needed the discipline.... Everybody’s emotions were raw.

—Lieutenant Artie Riccio, then a firefighter in Ladder 119 South Williamsburg, Brooklyn, working in Ladder 110

“ I remember seeing people sitting in Central Park enjoying their day and then me just a few miles down. It was like night and day. They’re digging out. They’re still digging out bodies from the rubble. The thing was on fire for three months.

—Stephanie Gaskell, then a journalist, Associated Press, New York (covered WTC site for duration of FDNY operations)

“ [T]he dedication and commitment, that nobody flinched. I think it made a difference to the country.

—Chief of Operations Pat McNally, then a Deputy Chief in Division 14, Flushing, Queens

2,653 airplane passengers and crew, and office personnel from the Twin Towers. Most of the bodies missing. 343 firefighters, along with 60 police officers, dead. Most of the bodies missing. FDNY command structure decimated, all but decapitated: three of five ranking staff chiefs and 93 officers dead...and along with them approximately 4,400 years of FDNY experience...lost.

Over $4 billion (in constant dollars) of departmental losses incurred. Nearly 100 firefighting vehicles and thousands of tools destroyed. Seven buildings gone, nine others suffering major damage. 14.6 acres of debris from more than 3,400 vertical feet of building totaling 1.5 million tons. Fires burned in eight buildings. The fires under stories of debris turned steel beams cherry red and sent deadly, acrid smoke up into the plaza and into firefighter lungs. The ongoing fires meant the FDNY claimed the site as theirs. They were in charge. They insisted. Still, a massive and hugely complicated city had its voluminous ongoing needs. 8.5 million people called for assistance over 5,200 times a day and over 2.3 million times a year, a number that made the FDNY the busiest fire department on the planet.

Firefighters are first responders. Emergencies, especially fires, happen. Firefighters appear to fight the fire and to rescue people. They are

Firefighting continued for over 90 days
Firefighters operating a hoseline atop debris at Ground Zero on September 19, 2001.
Andrea Booher, Public domain, via Wikimedia Commons

organized to carry out their work for hours, perhaps one–two days. Occasionally, they carry on for three–four days. As Paul Summerfelt, Section Chief of the Southwest Incident Management Team from Flagstaff, Arizona, put it: “Fire departments are really good at three- to four-hour incidents. Once it exceeds that, struggles begin. And…that’s if everybody’s intact and everybody’s there.”

Clocks of all types were ticking. Time to find any survivors was running out. Victims’ families urgently wanted answers and needed support. Those still standing stood in shock. Some people worried about a possible second attack, many swelled with grief. Lives lost needed mourning. Families needed support.

And yet fallen firefighters, especially officers, needed replacing, however reluctantly and painfully. They needed replacing now. Additionally, those replacements needed immediate organizing to enable ongoing work at the site and to protect the city at large. The scale and scope of the work that lay ahead gradually came into focus. The FDNY had the lead for the near and foreseeable term. It regrouped and cobbled itself back together to fight its way through 9/11 and the first day after. The pieces began to reconnect, to reform like mercury from a broken thermometer on a kitchen floor.

The work at hand

In the shadow of horror, work on an unprecedented scale needed identifying, organizing, and doing: task upon task upon task. An image from 9/11 captured the challenge of this time as well: the image from the afternoon of Chief Hayden clamoring atop a damaged fire vehicle to lead both initial grieving and initial organization. The FDNY needed to continue to scramble atop its damaged self. It needed to organize as it performed the work at hand – the physical work as well as acknowledging and attending to its anguish. Just how would the FDNY approach all that needed doing, to move through rescue to recovery on its way to rebuilding and recreating itself? Specifically, how would the FDNY:

1. Reestablish a functioning command structure
2. Identify the missing
3. Rescue any survivors
4. Recover remains

5. Extinguish major fires in surrounding buildings (two among the largest in NYC history)
6. Battle the fires burning beneath the debris pile
7. Restore leadership capacity
8. Support families, friends, and fellow first responders
9. Coordinate with a devastated community
10. Protect and serve a still-functioning city
11. Tend to the physical and emotional well-being of those still standing

The FDNY pressed forward with the work as it pursued order. It accepted and reached out for help. It mobilized resources, at hand and out of sight, familiar and beyond experience. The resources would help to address immediate challenges and to provide future opportunities, require key decisions, and shape the future of the FDNY.

Part A: Responder Voices

> “I started orchestrating. I called OEM [NYC Office of Emergency Management], one of our lieutenants working over there. I said, ‘We’re going to need a lot of help. See if you can activate the Search and Rescue system, the federal system. We have 28 teams [USAR Teams].’[40] He said, ‘Well we’re going to ask for a number. How many teams?’ I said, ‘Whatever the Pentagon doesn’t need we’re going to need here,’ and that kind of started the ball rolling, and right away. We have to get to work now. [26 of the 28 USAR teams were activated for the 9/11 attacks. 20 teams operated at the WTC.]
>
> *—Battalion Chief Fred LaFemina, Chief of Rescue Services, then Captain of Squad 270, South Jamaica, Queens; member FDNY USAR*

> “Early afternoon, about 1:30–2:00, I started communicating with our operations center for information that they were seeking from the command post...[he was sent to 1 Police Plaza to act as liaison at NYPD headquarters]. We were very aware of how the hospitals were structuring themselves and then the idea that we were going

to be getting people out, transporting them to hospitals, how many newer members would we need down there just from a manpower perspective.

—Chief of Department (2010–2014) Ed Kilduff, then a Deputy Chief in Division 3, Midtown, Manhattan and past IMT Incident Commander

“ The guys waited for a while then really started to get frustrated. As more and more guys came off the bus, some of them started to taunt the cops, saying things like ‘You don’t have enough bullets for all of us. Let us in there.’ Finally, I think a Battalion Chief walked up to a police sergeant and said, ‘You need to let us over the bridge or you’re going to have a riot on your hands. Our guys are dying over there and you’re not letting us help them.’ The sergeant got on his cell phone, spoke to somebody, came back and told his guys to move the barricade and we went across the bridge.

—Captain Paul Brown, then a Lieutenant covering in Division 15, Brownsville, Brooklyn; FDNY IMT

“ They were keeping us away. It was hard keeping the guys from mutinying, getting in there. We tried numerous times, we were stopped. And then after 7 [WTC] came down then we all got put to work.

—Assistant Chief Bob Maynes, Queens Boro Commander, then a Battalion Chief in Battalion 41, East Flatbush, Brooklyn, and past IMT Incident Commander

“ At that point, it started to get dark now, and what are you going to do? We’re going to keep working. We worked and worked and worked. I got home, finally. I got off the pile Friday afternoon late.

—Battalion Chief Fred LaFemina, Chief of Rescue Services, then Captain of Squad 270, South Jamaica, Queens; member FDNY USAR

“ I was taken to do other stuff and really didn’t make any headway. I started thinking, ‘How long will this take to clean this up?’ I think it was sometime around ten o’clock or so. Tom Galvin was a deputy chief who had survived both collapses. He told me, ‘Bob, why don’t you just go back to the firehouse. Everybody's here now, why don't you go back now and change, get a little more rest and come back early in the morning because everybody's going to burn out tonight. If we can get some of you guys to go back and come back in the morning, we can distribute the work better, instead of everybody being exhausted together the next day.'

—Assistant Chief Bob Maynes, Queens Boro Commander then a Battalion Chief in Battalion 41, East Flatbush, Brooklyn, and past IMT Incident Commander

WTC NOAA citation 3,300 ft

Remains of the World Trade Center complex in downtown Manhattan, United States, after the September 11 attacks. Image taken by NOAA's Cessna CitationJet on September 23, 2001, from an altitude of 3,300 ft (1,005 m).

National Oceanic and Atmospheric Administration (NOAA), Public domain, via Wikimedia Commons

“ I didn’t get out of the Police Plaza [NYPD HQ] until about 11 o’clock in the evening. Somebody came over to relieve me.... I went over to the Trade Center. I met up with some folks that had a command center pretty well established. I was assigned to assist another deputy chief in an area, and basically they were still fighting fires.

—Chief of Department (2010–2014) Ed Kilduff, then a Deputy Chief in Division 3, Midtown, Manhattan, and past IMT Incident Commander

“ They started their bucket brigade, we were digging by hand. You really needed a bulldozer and a Hi-Lo. You really needed a tractor, but we did the best we could. I don’t think anyone else was – since early that afternoon – had actually been rescued. It was total devastation. Anyway, around midnight, I decide I am going to head back to the firehouse. We finally did get to the firehouse. They saw us pull up, the doors were open. John Newell, the captain of the company at the time, he comes out and says, ‘Jeff, you got to work tomorrow at nine o’clock.’ They had begun 24 hours on, 24 hours off. It was an extreme. Never before in my career had we gone to shifts. Anyway, it’s very difficult now that you’re wide awake to rest and I had to be back at nine o’clock in the morning.

—Captain Jeff Simms, then a Lieutenant in Engine 58, Harlem, Manhattan; FDNY IMT

“ Now, believe me, at 3:00 a.m., it wasn’t all in place, but it’s fascinating how much was in place by 3:00 a.m. There were already the steelworkers cutting the steel and the trucks there taking the steel out of there. It was beginning to get somewhat organized.

—Deputy Chief Jim DiDomenico, then in Division 13, South Jamaica, Queens

“ We had a meeting on the 12th in the morning with uniformed people and civilians as to what the next steps were going to be. I think we lost 91 pieces of equipment, numerous tools, masks, radios. Taking inventory of what we need to get back in service. Start working on a schedule – we can’t have everyone in the department at the World Trade Center 24/7. A checklist of things. High on the list was the families, what are we going to do about the families?

—Fire Commissioner (2014–2022) Dan Nigro, then Chief of Operations Headquarters, Downtown Brooklyn (served as Chief of Department 2001–2002)

“I think the first funerals, four of them, Father Judge too, on Saturday. Pete Ganci's funeral, I think, Bill Feehan's funeral was that day. A member from 21 Engine. This was going to be a major, major issue with dealing with the families. We had a meeting, I don't know what, if it was the night of the 12th, perhaps it was at a hotel in the evening with family members. It was very emotional. Very emotional from their point of view. What are we doing? It ended up a priority list of what the department needed to do. A, top of the list, take care of the families of those we lost, and we did that. B, maintain a presence at the World Trade Center.

—Fire Commissioner (2014–2022) Dan Nigro, then Chief of Operations Headquarters, Downtown Brooklyn (served as Chief of Department 2001–2002)

Firefighters searching the pile
Firefighter Kevin Lynch Engine 257 looking out over vast piles of debris and rising smoke during rescue and recovery operations.
Public domain (U.S. federal government). Suggested credit: Andrea Booher/FEMA News Photo, September 17, 2001. U.S. Federal Emergency Management Agency

“I guess four or five days later I was driving in. I was thinking about how the last few days I was really overwhelmed about the number of guys I knew who were killed and what was going on at the site. Then I started thinking about all the things that needed doing in the firehouse. Then I realized that I really wasn't doing my job as far as the firehouse was concerned.

—Captain Kerry Hollywood, then in Engine 53, Spanish Harlem, Manhattan; Commanding Officer Family Assistance Unit

“After a few days he [captain Hollywood] says, ‘I want to talk to everybody.’ He brought us all into the kitchen and he talked. He apologized for not being the captain. He meant he wasn't acting like a captain. Everybody was looking to him for leadership and he apologized for not being able to do it. He said, ‘I got it and I'm back and from now on I'm going to take care of things.’ Which I thought was very noble and honest and the right thing to do.

—Firefighter Louis Giaconelli, then in Engine 53, Spanish Harlem, Manhattan; FDNY IMT

“The fire department immediately went to what we call an A, B chart. A, B chart is work 24 [hours], go home and rest, work 24, go home and rest. That impacts your life dramatically, because everything that you had planned, or whatever you were doing, family stuff, everything was just – the test [promotional exam] was canceled, the Fire Tech school shut down, there was no test, there was nothing to study for at that point. And then when you reported to work in the A, B chart, sometimes you're just working in your division, sometimes you were working at the site. It just varied, but all you know is after you work 24 hours, you came home and you were exhausted, and the next day you were going in again for 24 more hours.

—Deputy Chief Jim DiDomenico, then in Division 13, South Jamaica, Queens

“We stayed in a full-blown rescue mode, looking for survivors, for [two] weeks, and we weren't finding them. That was traumatic. We had issues with the search dogs. FEMA brought in search dogs who were trained to be rescue dogs, looking for live victims, and they weren't finding them. All they were finding were bodies. The dogs got depressed because they weren't doing their determined mission. It was happening to firefighters. We were uncovering bodies, but we were hoping for survivors.

—Deputy Assistant Chief John Norman, Chief of Special Operations, then a Battalion Chief in Battalion 16, Harlem, Manhattan; FDNY USAR

Stairway B: A miraculous exception

Even the seemingly straightforward was not. What was simple before wasn't anymore. Bearings and landmarks had vanished, turned to dust. Literally and metaphorically, getting oriented took time and collaboration, as these tales of rescue and recovery from Stairway B convey.

A structural peculiarity and happenstance created a sanctuary in Stairway B of the North Tower, the second tower to collapse. The tale of how the FDNY recognized and seized the rare opportunity presented by that pocket illustrates many of the forces at play and the efforts to counteract them.

“ The biggest concern at the time, well, one, was rescuing people that ended up trapped in a stairway [Stairway B]. When they told me that they were in a stairwell in the North Tower, I thought they were

Working on the pile
Firefighters search "the pile" with the help of a dog.
Shared with permission from the Daniel Quinn private collection

confused and were in a different building because it didn't appear that there was a North Tower, and that was a miracle. Took a while to get those people out safely, and we did.

—Chief of Department (2004–2006) Pete Hayden, then a Deputy Chief in Division 1, SoHo, Manhattan

“ He [Captain Jay Jonas, Ladder 6] was getting through to me again, intermittently, trying to explain to me that in his mind, ‘Well this is pretty simple, I'm in Stairway B.’ We're at a moonscape trying to make heads or tails of where possibly Stairway B could even possibly be.

—Chief of Operations Pat McNally then a Deputy Chief in Division 3, Midtown, Manhattan

“ I knew where he was. I'm thinking if we find these people in a stairway, how many stairways are in this building? 80? There's got to be other people alive and it just wasn't happening. They're going to study that for centuries. Why that one stairway, why? I'm sure those guys asked themselves that all the time. ‘How did that happen?’

—Captain Glenn Rohan, then a Lieutenant in Ladder 43, Spanish Harlem, Manhattan

Treacherous operating environment
Firefighter stretching a hoseline across an I-beam to extinguish underground fires.
Andrea Booher, Public domain, via Wikimedia Commons

" He had this electronic bullhorn. It's the first time they were carrying it. It had this electronic wail on it, I'm going, 'I hear it, but it's so far'. Oh my God. It's not like you're walking on dirt or ground. This is steel, fires and voids. Chief Ferran [Battalion Chief Mark Ferran, Battalion 12] says, 'I'm going to go this way to the left, split half of our crew, and you take the other half.' We're going to keep telling him, 'Hit it again,' and we'll hone in on where you guys are because they were stuck in the stairway. They could see an opening and point this thing towards it.

I said, 'Show me where.' He brings me to the stairway and there's tons of debris on the landing. 'They're down there.' There's a little opening at the corner where the standpipe riser is in the stairway and you could yell to them. I go, 'Okay.' Jimmy's [FF Jim Lanza L-43] like, 'Glenn, we need rescue here. We need the Hurst tool' [Jaws of Life, commonly used at auto accidents for victim extrication]. 'Jimmy, Jimmy look. That stuff's a long way away. We got hooks and halligans and axes with us.' I said, 'We'll get them. We'll get them.'

I'm leading men into a bad – asking them and they never hesitated. They never questioned me. I said, 'We got to go down there.' Jimmy was the first guy behind me to not hesitate. We went down the rope that they came up and then Mark Carpiniello came down. Another guy that was with 53 Engine and I could see the doorway, and they said, 'He's somewhere back there.' I said, 'Mark, you're smaller than me, you're thinner than me. Get up in there and see what we got. What's back there?' It's really tight in there. It's like a rabbit hole.

He says to me, 'Lou [Lieutenant], I got him. I'm standing over him.' He was a battalion chief and he had fallen and he got stuck in the vertical position. I said, 'Mark [firefighter Mark Carpiniello, Engine 53], is he alive? He's not talking. His radio is dead but check his pulse.' I get on him and I said, 'He's gone. He's dead.' I said, 'But we'll get him out.'

For over two hours, we're trying to extricate this guy who's a big man from this incredibly tight spot above him, the size of him, he's stuck. I don't think we moved him more than a couple of inches in two hours and they're screaming at me. They're saying they want you out. Building 7's going to come down. You got to get out. I'm like, 'Give me 10 more minutes. Give me 10 more minutes. Cut that pipe, cut this.' We got saws coming down. We got electric battery-operated tools coming down.

Dave Rayner from Rescue 4 came down, very knowledgeable fireman, and we're all in this tight little spot and we're trying to move this guy and we couldn't. Then the guy says to me, 'Lou, I'm getting dizzy. I think I smell fuel.' I said, 'Okay, I said, I'm calling it. We're out.' We said a prayer. Left. You want to talk to me about September 12th and 13th, I was a little crazy because I wanted to go get that man and they wouldn't let me. They wouldn't let me and I was out of my mind.

—Captain Glenn Rohan, then a Lieutenant in Ladder 43, Spanish Harlem, Manhattan

7 World Trade Center

" The water mains were broken from the collapse [of 1 WTC and 2 WTC]. What ended up happening, 7 World Trade Center, which is a 50-story high-rise...caught fire. One deputy chief went in and took a look at it for us and said it was already beyond what we could probably handle, and certainly beyond what we can handle because we didn't have the resources and the water right there. The Office of Emergency Management [NYC OEM] had their offices there. What had happened was when the North Tower collapsed, it sheared off about six or eight floors of the corner of the building. Structurally, it didn't even look real good, but it also had a pretty good fire going on many floors. Basically, this deputy chief came back and said, 'It's too far gone. We won't be able to do anything with that.' Ultimately, we had to pull back again because that collapsed later in the afternoon.

—Chief of Operations Pat McNally then a Deputy Chief in Division 3, Midtown, Manhattan

" At some point early in the day I get a call from Frank Fellini. He wants me to know...several battalion chiefs had concerns about the stability of 7 WTC. There is fire in it. This is a 50-story building. Frank lays this out. He says, 'What I want is, create a collapse zone big enough for a 50-story building to fall in whatever direction it may fall.' Sounds perfectly logical and easy. However, we need to put this in the context of not only are our firefighters looking to fight the fire and save civilians, they're looking for their own. In order to establish that broad a collapse zone, basically you are giving up area where both civilians and firefighters and police officers might be.

—1st Deputy Commissioner (2004–2010) Frank Cruthers, then an Assistant Chief at Headquarters, Downtown Brooklyn (served as Chief of Department 1996–1997, 2002–2004)

" I made the decision to stop rescue attempts [in 7 WTC]. Some people were not happy. Most people I think would've made the same decision, but it's hard to give up while you still think there's people trapped, people alive. Around 5:00, 7 World Trade collapsed, much in the same manner as the two towers in a really straight down pile. Thankfully, we didn't have a single injury with that collapse, which I think had the Trade Center not collapsed, that would've been the tallest building ever to collapse in a fire by itself. It was 50 stories perhaps.

—Fire Commissioner (2014–2022) Dan Nigro, then Chief of Operations Headquarters, Downtown Brooklyn (served as Chief of Department 2001–2002)

" So 12:00, that's when the decision is made to pull back. We pulled back almost two blocks [from 7 WTC], I guess we were in the last block before the river. It collapsed, luckily just as both towers had collapsed in a pancake fashion, one on top of the other. We didn't have to deal with any other buildings that it hit or anything like that. We were lucky enough. We had everybody out of the way; the building had been completely evacuated, so the life risk was much reduced. During that time, we tried to get a handle – there's a lot going on here – on what all the risks could have been.

—Chief of Operations Pat McNally then a Deputy Chief in Division 3, Midtown, Manhattan

" From my vantage point, there's a lot of urgency in that situation. There's a lot of high-level decisions being made. Should we commit to this building? I saw some very senior chiefs gathering around, there was another building that had, 7 World Trade Center. There was a lot of fire in that building. Should we keep them in the building? Should we pull out of this building? I saw some very high-level, incredible courage, to make decisions based on construction, based on their experience. They pulled everybody out of 7 because they thought the building was coming down and it did. Came down shortly after that. They saved some lives there. I saw numerous members trying to save life, searching, desperately looking for people and firefighters that were trapped. Again, chiefs controlling those actions so that unnecessary risks would not be taken.

—Deputy Chief Jim DiDomenico, then in Division 13, South Jamaica, Queens

“ 7 World Trade was, I believe, a 47-story building. The interesting thing about it is it's the third-largest structural collapse in history and nobody ever talks about it. It's also the building that the Mayor's Command and Control Center was in.

—Captain Paul Brown, then a Lieutenant covering in Division 15, Brownsville, Brooklyn; FDNY IMT

“ That's how hard it was to walk, but as you walk by, we found people then we found this one, and that, so you are kind of trying to get everybody to safety, but you don't want to leave anybody behind, so it was kind of touch and go, but at that point, I think we had made the right call because 20 minutes off the pile, the building [7 WTC] fell down. It came down pretty hard. That was the right call.

—Battalion Chief Fred LaFemina, Chief of Rescue Services, then Captain of Squad 270, South Jamaica, Queens; member FDNY USAR

“ It was quite something to see that come down and at least that was the immediate collapse danger. Other buildings were being looked at and were for a couple of days. Buildings around there had people skittish. It was the next day or day after, I was at the scene and people thought one of the buildings on the east side was moving and it caused a bit of a stampede. I know one member broke their leg running north, but it was a long time before people were comfortable either at the World Trade Center site or in Manhattan.

—Fire Commissioner (2014–2022) Dan Nigro, then Chief of Operations Headquarters, Downtown Brooklyn (served as Chief of Department 2001–2002)

FEMA photographer Andrea Booher
FEMA Photographer Andrea Booher overlooking the remains of the Marriott Hotel. The only section to survive the collapse had been structurally reinforced following the 1993 bombing.
Doug Welty, Public domain, via Wikimedia Commons

> After 7 World Trade came down, we did have – we had folks looking at the surrounding buildings at all times to see if any of the other buildings were sufficiently damaged that we might have another building come down. That went on for a few days. The priority, of course, first priority was putting out the fires, a couple of them were quite large, supplying water, which was not easy, and searching for people who were still alive.
>
> *—Fire Commissioner (2014–2022) Dan Nigro,*
> *then Chief of Operations Headquarters, Downtown Brooklyn*
> *(served as Chief of Department 2001–2002)*

Communications with the families

> They said, 'We're setting up a hotline in Fort Totten [FDNY training facility in Queens]. Go over there and run the hotline. The hotline will be for family members.' I went over to Fort Totten. Now it's like six in the morning. Again, there were greater minds than me doing this. When I got there, the idea was already set up. They were going to have these calls that were going to roll. Now, the technology at the time was different. For whatever this building was being used for, there were computers that were at each desk. We had no access to the computers.

What we had was stick-em notes that we're actually sticking onto the computer screen. The only thing that we had operational were the phones and the fax.

I started calling people that retired and that I knew were not at the trade center. I asked them if they can come to Fort Totten and answer the phones. I knew that they would be the best people because they knew half the people that were under the pile. I knew that they knew the way the department worked. I don't think I got a no. Our job was, when a family member called, to tell them if they were officially on the missing list. We had the phones ready to be staffed. We had the list of missing and deceased incomplete. Then I called headquarters and said, we are ready. They started scrolling on the bottom of the local networks and CNN, the number for FDNY family members.

One of the heartbreaking things that happened, I went back to the call center a few days after and there was a woman whose husband had been killed. She was saying that her husband was seen on television after the collapse, and I knew he was dead. I knew he was dead.

Where we operate best is in chaos. Somebody had the foresight that this needed to be done [family hotline], and then they followed through with plan.

—Captain Frank Leto, then Deputy Director, Counseling Services Unit, Bayside, Queens

Federal plaza meeting; FDNY WTC Task Force

Organizing key resources prepared the way to launching a counterattack on the rubble...and what it might yield.

“Within just a couple of days, I want to say, Thursday morning, we had a meeting at 26 Federal Plaza [Federal office building] and the Commissioner was coordinating the meeting, and basically said, 'Okay, Frank Cruthers is now the Incident Commander. Pete Hayden is going to be the XO. You're going to be the Search and Rescue Manager. We want Bobby Ingram for HAZMAT input.' I think that was it. Initially, we didn't have Charlie Blaich immediately, but within a day or two, we recognized we needed somebody for logistics, so Charlie Blaich was pulled in as the chief of logistics, and we built the command task force from there. That was done, I believe, Either Thursday or Friday morning.

—Deputy Assistant Chief John Norman, Chief of Special Operations, then a Battalion Chief in Battalion 16, Harlem, Manhattan; FDNY USAR

The Southwest All-Hazards Incident Management Team

Dan Oltrogge had spent about five weeks on a large wildfire on the North Rim of the Grand Canyon fighting a succession of wildfires. With limited communications, he had little information regarding events in NYC and DC. Following the collapse of the second tower, Dan Oltrogge as a member of the South West Incident Management Team (SW-IMT) received a call to mobilize. By 8:30 a.m. Mountain Time [11:30 EDT], the team received orders to deploy to New York. It reported to Albuquerque, New Mexico, for a government flight to New York.

“ Well, [the Southwest Incident Management Team] got on the airplane [in Albuquerque], there was already an incident management team on the airplane. They were a team from California. So, the charter jet had flown to California, picked up one of the California incident management teams. They were going to the Pentagon, and we were headed for New York. And so, we got on the airplane, as I recall, it was dark, and I think it was maybe around midnight or so by the time we left Albuquerque, on the 11th.

So at some point in the night when we looked out of the airplane window and, saw the fighter jets, o-o-okay, thi-this-this is very real, and then what really sunk into us is that we landed in Baltimore, to let off...the Pentagon team, but as we did, you could look and see the fires at the Pentagon. You know, now television has become real. So we dropped them off and then we hopped up to New York, and we got to Newark (airport). We arrived I think right around sunup because you could look over across the river and you could see the smoke.

We get over towards the Javits Center (used as a staging area, 3.8 miles north of the WTC) and there’s people standing around everywhere. That was an interesting thing over the next week, the number of people from around the country who just showed up looking to help, you know. And that was somewhat gratifying, but it was also a logistical nightmare – trying to deal with that.

Getting into the Javits Center and the chaos that was occurring – it was just a lot. What – those first probably 48, 72 hours of that it was really just trying to figure out who's who in the zoo and what – who we needed to pay attention to and who we didn't. We had a number of people come up to us initially, and we knew, we had been through this before, so we knew these weren't the real people we needed to deal with. But people came up and tried to give us directions and tell us what to do, and asked things, requested us to do things.

As we begin to kind of get things at the – at the Javits Center, which is where we were initially. Our logistics section and our medical section and, finance, those things set up like we would typically do it. We began to interact with the different USAR [Urban Search and Rescue] teams that were there.

As that began to occur, we began to realize there's – there were really two things going on. One is, you had the Urban Search and Rescue teams who were at the Javits Center, who were deploying every day going down to the – to the Trade Center site and were doing stuff and were coming back to the Javits Center at night. On the other side, you had all of NYPD, FDNY, and all those folks who owned the site who were there doing their own thing. And-and they were not gonna give up. Uh, and so you had these-these two operations going on. Uh, and they weren't necessarily, in that first week or two, communicating too well with each other.

We get there and it's, of course, and this is very normal. Nobody knows you're coming; nobody knows who ordered you. They don't know what you do. They don't know who you are. That first day on the 12th, we had no work. We didn't have it. We didn't have a tasking. We spun our wheels during that and then went back. It was by Rutgers University somewhere. We got a hotel.

I remember myself and one of our ops guys [Operations Section], we said, 'We're gonna walk down to the Trade Center from the Javits

Center.' And so we just started walking down Manhattan, and we just walked and we got down there. Ran into a barrier that NYPD had put up and talked our way through that. We were wearing uniform. We had a couple of credential IDs with us. They let us through. We got to another one, we got through. We got down to the marina there, and then it really became real. You saw the rubble, you saw the exhausted people, you saw the debris. The – just the – the frantic activity that was occurring, and we were able to take that back to the team and give them kind of, okay, this is what we're up against. This is what we're seeing.
—Paul Summerfelt, Commander National Area Command Team (2013–2020), then Planning Section Chief Southwest-IMT, Deputy Chief Flagstaff, AZ Fire Department (served as Type-1 IMT Incident Commander 2008–2012)

“ I was not the incident commander of the team. I was the incident commander trainee. In fact, that was my first trainee assignment. The incident commander was a guy named Van Bateman. Van and I and these two representatives, Forest Service and GSA [General Services Administration], were having a little huddle and Van made an on-the-spot decision that I thought was brilliant, and it's pretty simple. He said, 'No, we're not going to look to get out of here. What we're going to do is we're going to go back and I'll get logistics to find us a hotel somewhere. We're going to sleep tonight, and then we are going to get on the bus tomorrow morning, we're going to go across the Hudson and we're going to go to that big Convention Center.'

Once we got to the Javits Convention Center we started visiting with a few folks, the local jurisdiction needed help [with] the urban search and rescue teams.... They don't need any help tactically or operationally but support. For whatever reason, they were having a hard time getting them fed, they were having a hard time getting a decon [decontamination], they were having a hard time getting a decent sleep, things like that, having a hard time with the ordering system and getting your pipeline or supply chain to keep them response-ready. They [USAR Teams] knew that we are those guys, that we could access stuff. They knew we had an ordering system that likely may be better than theirs. That was it. We just found some blank space in the Convention Center, we set up our command post and we started supporting the urban search-and-rescue teams.

At the convention center, getting traction, what we call catching a rhythm. Shortly after arrival next day or two at the most, it was myself and the plans Chief [Paul Summerfelt], we just got off the escalator coming into our incident command post. We got approached, the representatives from FEMA and the US Fire Administration, Bill Lokey and Hugh Wood.

They asked us, because at this point we did not have any operational or consistent presence down at the pile, they asked us to do that, go down there to the pile and take a look and see what they could do to provide some assistance to the FDNY.

Of course, it was glaring. There was a lot of opportunity for us to lend a hand, to help with this. We just got back and reported that to the US Fire Administration. In fact, we met with the US Fire Administration and informed them why we were down there at the pile on that first day. Then they lined out what they wanted us to do. What they were scope locked on was, they being the US Fire Administration, to get the FDNY to use the Incident Command System. We were reluctant, executing ICS in an operational environment without training would be problematic.

—Dan Oltrogge, Commander National Area Command Team (2009–2011), then Incident Commander Trainee SW-IMT, Chief of Fire and Aviation Grand Canyon National Park (served as SW-IMT Incident Commander 2003–2007)

“ In our world....[w]hat that was at the time we didn't know.... I think that we recognized the value of the work that we did as a collective team [SW-IMT is a multi-agency federal resource]. And we were from all different agencies.

—Paul Summerfelt, Commander National Area Command Team (2013–2020), then Planning Section Chief Southwest-IMT, Deputy Chief Flagstaff, AZ Fire Department (served as Type-1 IMT Incident Commander 2008–2012)

Doing their part

“ Each person there, you might have been in a position of leadership, but everyone did their part and then some to get these things done. People said, 'Well, I'll do this. I'll take care of the schedule for folks.' I think we had them going to, at the time, Shea Stadium, [now Citi Field] taken by bus to the site. It was somewhat overwhelming the amount of things. The president came two days later and made his famous speech there on the little pile of debris. It's a bit of a blur.

—Fire Commissioner (2014–2022) Dan Nigro,
then Chief of Operations Headquarters, Downtown Brooklyn
(served as Chief of Department 2001–2002)

“ I think the initial first several days were very much caught up with the rescue efforts at the site and trying to ascertain who was missing and field phone calls from people calling about loved ones as well as take care of the most immediately seriously injured people.

—Dr. Kerry Kelly MD, then FDNY Chief Medical Officer,
Bureau of Health Services, Headquarters Downtown Brooklyn

“ On the second day, they assigned me to notification phones. You would answer calls coming in, wives looking for their husbands, crying and upset. You would know some of the wives who called. They would say, 'John, tell us where he...' I said, I don't know where they are. You kind of knew in your mind that they were already gone, and you can't tell them that. It was calls like that back to back to back. The kids – I just need to take a second.... The kids would call up crying hysterically, looking for their father. I guess that was one of the traumatic days for that. Those calls, those types of calls kept coming in. I would say like every 20 minutes, I'd be on the phone talking to the wives and talking to the kids the best you can. You can't go overboard in telling them what you already know the truth is. That was pretty hard trying to keep that together. The kids, the voices calling on the phone looking for their parents, looking for their father, I still hear the voices at times.

—Fire Alarm Dispatcher John Lightsey, then in Manhattan
Communications Office, Central Park, Manhattan

“ A few days after September 11th, the fire department started running two parallel operations, in essence. One was the site itself, and the other was the missing firefighters and their families. They ran parallel for virtually months.... You had two jobs. You had your day job, in a sense, that was the site. Because I worked at the site at least every other day, if not every day. Then I got a job being the night commander at the site for about five or six weeks. On your off time, it became very apparent that the firehouses, the families, the local units needed attention also. I'm a deputy chief in Midtown Manhattan, and many of my units lost all their members. I can't go to the site and then go home. I have to go tend to the units, in a sense. That's what myself, Chief Tom Galvin and many others did. Then the offshoot, the third function, was going to the funerals. That started a week or two later, too. Go down, work the site, go to a funeral. Go down, work the site, go to a funeral. That's how it worked. Fall asleep in the car on the way home, and then come home for a couple hours, go to the site, go to another funeral.

—Chief of Department (2010–2014) Ed Kilduff, then a Deputy Chief in Division 3, Midtown, Manhattan and past IMT Incident Commander; was IC for FDNY deployment to Hurricane Katrina

“ I think the other thing too [was] recognizing that this incident was going to change our world.... I think that was a kind of a shadow that was over the entire thing...that what we were doing was a small part of some things that were going to change in a big way.

—Dan Oltrogge, Commander National Area Command Team (2009–2011), then Incident Commander Trainee SW-IMT, Chief of Fire and Aviation Grand Canyon National Park (served as SW-IMT Incident Commander 2003–2007)

“ What was difficult with this is trying to get a handle on what the problem really was. In other words, the scope was so gigantic. In the military, they would be like what's the intelligence on this? What are we dealing with? We don't know what we're dealing with. Are these gigantic pockets of fire that are going to collapse on us still? How are we going to work around this? What resources can we bring to bear?

On 9/11, we lose the top part of the fire department command structure. Who's standing in the street next?

—Chief of Operations Pat McNally, then a Deputy Chief in Division 14, Flushing, Queens

“ It was hard to fathom that we lost the people that led our job.... These are the people that are supposed to lead us through this, these are the people that are supposed to get us through this crisis, working with them, helping them but working together naturally, and they're not here to do it.... [It was] daunting in knowing what we had to do, and the people that were supposed to be leading us doing it weren't there.

—Fire Commissioner (2010–2014) Sal Cassano, then Assistant Chief at Headquarters, Downtown Brooklyn (served as Chief of Department 2006–2010)

Rebuilding order

FDNY leadership in the two weeks post 9/11 acted to restore order, clarify purpose, and enable coordinated action. The FDNY's actions offer lessons for leaders working out of chaos and trauma. Tragically, Ground Zero offered purpose and, ironically, a balm for the injury and trauma resident in the members of the FDNY. The balm came in the form of nearly endless physical labor to the point of numbing exhaustion, clear immediate objectives, and the blunt agency of doing something - and doing it together. In those first days, so many firefighters wanted to be there. The work continued, day and night.

Firefighters battling smoldering fires
Firefighters continue to battle smouldering fires amidst World Trade Center wreckage.
Public domain (U.S. federal government). Credit: Andrea Booher/FEMA News Photo, September 13, 2001. U.S. Federal Emergency Management Agency

At first, all efforts centered on rescue: listening for signs of life, people and dogs digging for survivors. But gradually, resignation took hold. The mission shifted – grudgingly, painfully – from rescue to recovery, and then to removal. All the while, the rest of the city still needed its firehouses staffed, emergencies answered, and calls responded to. There was the work itself, and then the work of enabling the work–setting orders, assigning responsibilities, creating domains, and restaffing depleted units.

Rebuilding order from the bottom-up through basics, improvisation, and increasing coordination

Amidst disaster and devastation, firefighters returned to the foundations of their training and their shared experience – firefighting, building collapse, chain of command – and applied it at a scale and intensity far beyond anything they had faced before. Over time, ad hoc and improvisational efforts interconnected, organically or by direction. Leaders across ranks identified gaps, pulled in expertise, and began to coordinate dispersed efforts into something more systematic.

> “ [Y]ou can never plan for every eventuality. The best you can do is prepare in your basic skill sets.... As far as what you do? Why do you do what you do? You go back to your experience and your training...and be good at them and then just be prepared to adapt and overcome.... We were good at the basics.... We reverted back to what we do well. We started with those basics. That got us to the point where we could bring in the experts to get us further along to where we needed to be.
>
> *—Deputy Assistant Chief John Norman, Chief of Special Operations, then a Battalion Chief in Battalion 16, Harlem, Manhattan; FDNY USAR*

> “ What you do?.... You have to go back to what you've been taught.... You don't make it up as you go along? That's our structure. That's what you study. You study how to work at a fire scene, how to work in a collapse scene. There's a couple of steps to take, but you go back to that. What we did was basically taking this scene and magnifying it because of the size of it.
>
> *—Chief of Operations Pat McNally, then a Deputy Chief in Division 14, Flushing, Queens*

“ Basically, we did it ourselves and worked through things. Slowly but surely, the leadership rose to the top. Either the senior guys or the officers started taking charge.

—Firefighter Louis Giaconelli, then in Engine 53, Spanish Harlem, Manhattan; FDNY IMT

“ [T]his old fireboat [Former FDNY Marine 2, the John J. Harvey] ended up supplying a tremendous amount of water to us.... You use the resources you have at hand, but sometimes they are limited.... You have to go back to what you've been taught. No one was taught that, there's no book on how to fight a hundred-ten-story office pile that's been hit with jet fuel. You make it up as you go along.

—Chief of Operations Pat McNally, then a Deputy Chief in Division 14, Flushing, Queens

“ You don't even know if they're accomplishing what you set out to accomplish for that period of time.... This is going to take months and it's going to take a lot of equipment. So you're going to have to bring in people who are not firemen...

—Assistant Chief Bob Maynes, Queens Boro Commander, then a Battalion Chief in Battalion 41, East Flatbush, Brooklyn, and past IMT Incident Commander

“ Another thing that struck me, I think this was that morning of the 12th...I remember being up at the firehouse...my battalion was virtually destroyed. We had no real equipment, even the breathing apparatus that the members were wearing was all missing along with them.... [B] ut seeing all this breathing apparatus laying all around [later that day at WTC] probably because people didn't need it, this was responders that had come later. I remember walking up to one of the staff chiefs that was running things and said, 'Hey, there's no equipment back in the firehouse, it's all laying on the ground here.' He was so focused on a rescue effort, he just said, 'Okay, pick it up, and bring it back.'

—Battalion Chief George Maier, then in Battalion, 9 Hell's Kitchen, Manhattan; FDNY IMT

“ We were taking people in by bus from the Shea Stadium [now Citi Field] parking lot and developed a working schedule that was a living schedule.

It could be adjusted from week-to-week. Members were advised of the changes. That schedule stayed until the end of May. People were there continuously until the very end. That's how that site got cleared.

—Fire Commissioner (2014–2022) Dan Nigro,
then Chief of Operations Headquarters, Downtown Brooklyn
(served as Chief of Department 2001–2002)

Rebuilding order by rebuilding the command structure

In the immediate aftermath of 9/11, the FDNY had to reconstitute itself. Firehouses were reeling, the upper command decimated. To counter losses, the department promoted 130 to ranks from Lieutenant to Chief of Department on Sunday, 9/16. A class of just over 300 probies took their oaths on October 22nd and began their training. A class of 246 completed their training and graduated the Fire Academy on November 1st. Rebuilding proceeded at all levels and across diverse tasks, some brand new – such as finding fencing or ever more massive and powerful construction cranes. The rank-and-file stepped up to be sure and FDNY leadership worked to reestablish the operational command structure. The surviving leaders attempted to repopulate the department. Top-down efforts met bottom-up efforts.

Assignments often happened quickly, even spontaneously, to meet a need or to fill a void. Responsibilities as assigned together with responsibilities as assumed. As the situation stabilized, order evolved. Basic sectoring and incident command appeared, scaled to meet an unprecedented challenge and unprecedented initiative.

One interviewee characterized the FDNY as a complex-adaptive system. It healed initially like the body trying to close multiple, searing wounds.

“ They undertook that mission on their own. Now we just started coordinating all of those teams.

—Deputy Assistant Chief John Norman, Chief of Special Operations,
then a Battalion Chief in Battalion 16, Harlem, Manhattan;
FDNY USAR

“ Our command structure in the fire department kind of collapsed. The chief of the department was killed.... A lot of good men died that day.... The responsibility of caring for the guys, of actually getting things done, it fell to the company level. Yes, our battalion chief would come by and he would try to tell us what to do, but you know in the army when everyone else is killed and it goes down to the corporal, he has to take charge. That's what actually happened in the New York City Fire Department the days after that catastrophe.

—Captain Jeff Simms, then a Lieutenant in Engine 58, Harlem, Manhattan; FDNY IMT

“ If you have a big fire, you sector it off into different spots. Ultimately in the weeks that follow we'd sector, often into four quarters.

—Chief of Operations Pat McNally, then a Deputy Chief in Division 14, Flushing, Queens

“ We began writing an action plan, an incident action plan, with the help of an incident management team that came in from the Southwest. Things became more coordinated from that perspective that there was actually a daily plan that was taking place.

—Chief of Department (2010–2014) Ed Kilduff, then a Deputy Chief in Division 3, Midtown, Manhattan, and past IMT Incident Commander

“ In the firehouse, we just became like, ‘Let's try and get organized here. You guys do this, you guys do this.’ There was plenty to do. Everybody had to be fed. We had to get equipment.... One of our own officers didn't even tell us to do it. We did it on our own. That's what we did.

—Firefighter Louis Giaconelli, then in Engine 53, Spanish Harlem, Manhattan; FDNY IMT

“ I always said that the proudest moment for me was that rebuilding part. Rebuilding as a group, as a department, was important, but that secondary part of getting the firehouses back to being functioning and trying to collect them and get them to be functioning firefighters.

—Chief of Department (2010–2014) Ed Kilduff, then a Deputy Chief in Division 3, Midtown, Manhattan, and past IMT Incident Commander

“ As command structure started getting rebuilt, we started capturing the information that those people were telling us.... They undertook that mission on their own. Now we just started coordinating all of those teams that were doing things on their own and said, 'Okay, do we have all the basics covered?'

—Deputy Assistant Chief John Norman, Chief of Special Operations, then a Battalion Chief in Battalion 16, Harlem, Manhattan; FDNY USAR

“ Again, every day, we have to respond, right? We have to respond. It wasn't easy getting them up and running again with all of the distractions and the families and everything that were constantly looking for attention from them. That was an important part of our job. I really wasn't thinking about myself. I was very fortunate. My daughter was in college. My son was working. My wife was extremely understanding. I got home when I got home. We'd have dinner for a night and then I go back out the next day. She was very understanding, and it was just carte blanche, whatever I needed to do. I wasn't home a lot, so whatever I needed to do, we did. She understood that.

—Chief of Department (2010–2014) Ed Kilduff, then a Deputy Chief in Division 3, Midtown, Manhattan, and past IMT Incident Commander

“ The command [Special Operations command] is getting built up, we keep getting new guys in every day and we're training them.

—Battalion Chief Fred LaFemina, Chief of Rescue Services, then Captain of Squad 270, South Jamaica, Queens; member FDNY USAR

“ Within just a couple of days, I want to say Thursday morning, we had a meeting at 26 Federal Plaza. The fire commissioner was coordinating the meeting, and basically said, 'Okay, Frank Cruthers is now the Incident Commander. Pete Hayden is going to be the XO [Executive Officer]. You're going to be the Search and Rescue Manager. We want Bobby Ingram for HAZMAT input'.... Within a day or two, we recognized we needed somebody for logistics, so Charlie Blaich was pulled in as the chief of logistics, and we built the command [of the] task force from there.

—Deputy Assistant Chief John Norman, Chief of Special Operations, then a Battalion Chief in Battalion 16, Harlem, Manhattan; FDNY USAR

❝ We needed construction equipment and we knew it right away.... Then very quickly...they realized this isn't a bucket situation (debris removal by hand).

—Assistant Chief Bob Maynes, Queens Boro Commander, then a Battalion Chief in Battalion 41, East Flatbush, Brooklyn, and past IMT Incident Commander

❝ [We're] trying to make searches without disturbing the debris for fear of further injuring someone who might be alive. If you're going to get anywhere with this, even as far as finding people is concerned, you really have to start fully engaging the heavy equipment.

—1st Deputy Commissioner (2004–2010) Frank Cruthers, then an Assistant Chief at Headquarters, Downtown Brooklyn (served as Chief of Department 1996–1997, 2002–2004)

The following two extended interview quotes describe the top reaching down and lower down reaching up, feeding off one another, complementing one another in full view of the work to be done. The FDNY remained in "response mode," hence with a much higher accepted level of risk than in routine operations.

❝ One week after the incident, I'm at a funeral and John Norman, in command of Special Ops says to me, 'You're going to Rescue One as the captain.' I said, 'John, that's not a good idea. I'm on the Chief's (promotion) list.' I said, 'I'm going to be promoted. I'm not going to be there long.' He said, 'No, you're going there and you're going to rebuild that company for as long as you're going to be there.' He said, 'What do you think about that?' I said, 'I'm going to do whatever you want me to do.'

—Battalion Chief Fred LaFemina, Chief of Rescue Services, then Captain of Squad 270, South Jamaica, Queens; member FDNY USAR

❝ Three-star chief, Frank Fellini, came up and said, 'You're in charge of opening up the bridge that's collapsed on West Street.'... I came to him with one question. I came to him again, and the third time I came to him he said, 'Chief, that's your job. Use whoever you need because it's not going to be firemen, you're going to be working the trade [Iron Workers], but that's your job. Make a decision and just realize, if you fuck up, you'll be responsible.'... I ended up having a couple hundred guys working for me and only four were firefighters. Everybody else was an ironworker and operating engineer types. I still remember there was a man there, very polished from the trade industry and he started telling me what we needed, meaning cranes and things like that. He said, 'Just give me the authority to order them.' I was like, 'Order it.' I thought it was ironic that two days before you would have been fired for making a decision like that.

—Assistant Chief Bob Maynes, Queens Boro Commander, then a Battalion Chief in Battalion 41, East Flatbush, Brooklyn, and past IMT Incident Commander

Rebuilding order as the job expands and the mission changes

In the weeks after 9/11, the FDNY's responsibilities stretched far beyond firefighting and rescue. The scope of its work expanded rapidly, requiring occasionally fraught coordination with other agencies, control of a massive site, and attention to widespread trauma magnified by a dearth of rescues and then even of recoveries. The recovery of firefighter remains and the growing sense that many would never be recovered blistered individual and collective wounds. Leaders continued to improvise within an evolving mission. As anticipated, the shift from rescue to recovery took place – grudgingly, regretfully, and painfully.

“ After September 11th...we stayed in a full-blown rescue mode, looking for survivors for three weeks, and we weren't finding them.... The dogs got depressed.... It [depression] was happening to firefighters.

—Deputy Assistant Chief John Norman, Chief of Special Operations then a Battalion Chief in Battalion 16, Harlem, Manhattan; FDNY USAR

“ They brought in the four biggest construction firms in New York City, gave them to a sector, and then we worked with them. We took a tremendous hit in individuals. Guys like me had to step up and do a job. Maybe they wouldn't have been given that much responsibility, but they did. They overexerted themselves if anything, but you do keep your command structure. You try to keep communications in place.

—Chief of Operations Pat McNally, then a Deputy Chief in Division 14, Flushing, Queens

Urban search and rescue
Then Battalion Chief John Norman FDNY-USAR (on left) coordinating search operations with Jay Coon Sacramento Fire, USAR CA TF-7.
Andrea Booher, Public domain, via Wikimedia Commons

> When it becomes recovery, it was using more large equipment.... Really, to this day, I think that 40 percent of the people were never found. Not even a piece of them.
>
> —*Fire Commissioner (2014–2022) Dan Nigro, then Chief of Operations Headquarters, Downtown Brooklyn (served as Chief of Department 2001–2002)*

> My company, we knew where our guy had been.... We made a diligent search.
>
> —*Captain Jeff Simms, then a Lieutenant in Engine 58, Harlem, Manhattan; FDNY IMT*

> We just couldn't have chaos of people coming in wanting to go to work. You just can't have people all over the place with no organization. That's how people get hurt.
>
> —*Chief of Operations Pat McNally, then a Deputy Chief in Division 14, Flushing, Queens*

“ I said, ‘We fence it in.’ He [Nigro] looks at me and he says, ‘It’s 16 acres.’ I said, ‘We’re in New York City, Chief. We must have 1500 fence companies. We’ll get a fence up.’

—Battalion Chief Fred LaFemina, Chief of Rescue Services, then Captain of Squad 270, South Jamaica, Queens; member FDNY USAR

“ In our world...[w]hat that was at the time we didn’t know.... I think that we recognized the value of the work that we did as a collective team [SW-IMT is a multi-agency federal resource]. And we were from all different agencies.

—Paul Summerfelt, Commander National Area Command Team (2013-2020), then Planning Section Chief Southwest-IMT, Deputy Chief Flagstaff, AZ Fire Department (served as Type-1 IMT Incident Commander 2008-2012)

“ We had a meeting, almost a daily meeting, with geological experts and collapse recovery experts at three o’clock in the morning. It was my first experience with maybe 10 or 15 people from around the world at the same time discussing the recovery and the rescue effort. Things just slowly developed from there.

—2nd Deputy Commissioner Tom Fitzpatrick, then Headquarters, Downtown Brooklyn

“ The lowest medical leave in the history of the fire department was the days after 9/11. Everybody came to work, but there was a lot of tension.

—Fire Commissioner (2014–2022) Dan Nigro, then Chief of Operations Headquarters, Downtown Brooklyn (served as Chief of Department 2001–2002)

“ One of my regrets is that I never got to work down at the site [due to injuries and hospitalization].... I never called it Ground Zero and I still don’t refer to it as Ground Zero.... [I]t was The Site.... It’s a graveyard.

—Lieutenant Ray Brown, then in Ladder 113, Crown Heights, Brooklyn

“ I remember thinking that we’re going to lose people driving home.... I had a whole process where I wouldn’t go to the bathroom when I left so that I had that urgency going on to keep me awake.

—Assistant Chief Bob Maynes, Queens Boro Commander, then a Battalion Chief in Battalion 41, East Flatbush, Brooklyn, and past IMT Incident Commander

> “They broke [companies] into four groups.... If your day was in the firehouse...you couldn’t go down to Ground Zero. That lasted quite a few months.
>
> *—Firefighter Lois Mungay, then in Engine 235, Bedford Stuyvesant Brooklyn*

> “I think people would have stayed there. If you weren’t ordered to go back, I think guys would stay there until they dropped, which is a pretty awesome bunch of people that would do that.
>
> *—Captain Kerry Hollywood, then in Engine 53 Spanish Harlem, Manhattan; Commanding Officer, Family Assistance Unit*

> “There was a gradual time...between seven and 10 days, where the FDNY went from tactical to strategic...cooperation with the IMT.... [T]he men and women of the FDNY went from hope to resignation.
>
> *—Denis Onieal, then Senior FEMA Rep., Superintendent, National Fire Academy*

> “My biggest job was to try to make sure the guys were safe. That to me will always stay with me. We have it easy. That was our job.
>
> *—Chief of Operations Pat McNally, then a Deputy Chief in Division 14, Flushing, Queens*

Dignified Removal
Emergency personnel in a crane basket transport a flag-draped stretcher past the skeletal remains of the World Trade Center.
Shared with permission from the Daniel Quinn private collection

Leadership and grieving

The grieving began immediately – privately, as the horror unfolded, and collectively, as the scale of the loss became clear – a jumper killed a firefighter before either tower came down. From firehouse kitchens to home kitchens, sorrow and shock coursed through the city's tight-knit firefighting families. Pain's river ran deep and wide. More than one-third of the department lost family – fathers, sons, cousins. A legendary FDNY father lost both of his sons – one a firefighter, the other a police officer.

The work of recovery demanded both urgency and reverence. At Ground Zero, each recovery of remains brought all work to a halt. Every instance was treated as a "dignified removal," a U.S. flag draped over the remains and a solemn salute marking the moment. Heavy machinery silenced. Uniformed personnel stood at attention. All others stood in silence.

Firefighters juggled shifts at the pile with seemingly round-the-clock wakes and burials. Exhaustion and grief intermingled. The work of grieving– like the work of rescue and recovery – was massive. It required time, presence, and leadership that could honor both the dead and the living. For FDNY leaders, that meant confronting not a single, shared loss, but thousands of overlapping personal ones – distributed unevenly across companies and units.

Leadership and grieving – the pain: organizational, familial, and individual

Decades of shared service – reinforced by the FDNY's rotation system – meant that most firefighters lost people they knew. Some companies were hit especially hard. Special Operations, for example, home to some of the department's most highly trained units, was nearly wiped out. Loss upon loss produced staggering grief. And families needed help navigating the legal, financial, and emotional chaos. Firefighters were often the ones to step in.

> A poster came out with all the guys' faces and names. I'm like 'I know him, I know him.' It was unbelievable. I'll say, we were constantly going to funerals.
>
> —*Battalion Chief Bill Moore, then in Battalion 10*
> *Yorkville, Manhattan*

Dignified Transfer
Rescue workers stand at attention as firefighters carry the flag draped remains of a fallen firefighter.
Shared with permission from the Daniel Quinn private collection

> At that time a little less than 40 percent of the people on the job had [FDNY] relatives. They could have been an uncle, could be a father, brother whatever, cousin but a relative.
>
> *—Malachy Corrigan NP, then Clinical Director Counseling Services Unit, SoHo, Manhattan*

> [I]t was unbelievable...working 24 on, 24 off, but we started recovering remains. In fact, we had recovered two of the remains from my firehouse within the first couple days. We had funerals for those two and it seemed like every time we were off not working the 24-hour shift I was going to funerals.
>
> *—Battalion Chief Bill Moore, then in Battalion 10, Yorkville, Manhattan*

> One of my children was very, very scared...it kind of got into their head...I never really went to counseling. I counseled with my brother and sister firefighters.... But there were a lot of my friends who didn't. I was trying to coax them to go to counseling. And several of them, their marriages fell apart.
>
> When we found a firefighter, it was a big deal for firefighters. And police and fire worked together. And if we found a cop, we would tell the cops. They would come over, and we'd let them do what they needed to do. Same, vice versa. Took a little while to get that established, but we did.
>
> *—Chief of Department (2020–2022) Tom Richardson, then a Battalion Chief in Battalion 53, Bayside, Queens*

"We found a Scott [breathing apparatus] bottle...and it wasn't FDNY we thought it's either a Port Authority cop's bottle or an ESU [NYPD Emergency Service Unit] cop's bottle. I said 'Why don't we get a cop or two here and I'll meet them coming in so I can tell them what's going on.' After a while a cop car pulled up and out pops John Vigiano [Retired FDNY Captain] he is one of our legends, and a Marine veteran.... He saw the bottle and he goes, 'What do you got, Bob?' I said 'We found a bottle.' He goes, 'Ahh, Scott 3...that's Joe's [NYPD Detective Joseph Vigiano]. We recovered his partner's [Scott] yesterday. You're right on top of my son.' That was surreal. A little while later they found remains. They ended up recovering Joe Vigiano...John never interfered.... He just gave us a little nod of thank you. I always thought that was 100 percent dignity and class. [FDNY Captain John Vigiano lost both of his sons: NYPD Detective Joseph Vigiano and FDNY Firefighter John Vigiano II. John was never found.]

—Assistant Chief Bob Maynes, Queens Boro Commander, then a Battalion Chief in Battalion 41, East Flatbush, Brooklyn, and past IMT Incident Commander

Captain Tom Behan FDNY Pipes & Drums
Captain Tom Behan of the FDNY Pipes & Drums playing the Bag Pipes.
With permission from the private collection of Paul Brown

> The 11 surviving widows, girlfriends...they were the concern of the unit that I was in.... There were money issues, child issues, spousal issues.... They were just nonstop.
>
> *—Battalion Chief Fred LaFemina, Chief of Rescue Services, then Captain of Squad 270, South Jamaica, Queens; member FDNY USAR*

> It was a difficult time.... [N]o one thought this was a once-and-done attack.... There was a lot of angst...especially amongst the units that had lost.... Everyone feels...the next attack...will take place in Manhattan.
>
> *—Fire Commissioner (2014–2022 Dan Nigro, then Chief of Operations Headquarters, Downtown Brooklyn (served as Chief of Department 2001–2022)*

Leadership and grieving – emotional presence as leadership

Following 9/11, the FDNY's challenge extended well beyond the rubble of Ground Zero. The department faced emotional wreckage within its own ranks and among the families of the fallen. Leaders held open the space

Firefighter Jack Clark FDNY Pipes & Drums
From left to right, firefighters Al Schwartz, Jack Clark with the FDNY Pipes & Drums Playing the bass drum.
With permission from the private collection of Paul Brown

for grieving and for supporting those in grief. In the face of such loss, structure and work also became lifelines. With the chain of command shattered, leaders didn't wait for perfect information, but rather plugged holes and moved ahead. As noted, they started with what they had: people, purpose, and the ability to create order. Even small acts – reassigning roles, organizing units, setting staging areas – led the healing.

> “ Out of the 343 firefighters that died, I think over 90 of them were in Special Operations. [That was] 25 percent of the members [killed]. Just about every SOC company [Special Operations Command, comprised of specialized Rescue and Squad Companies] got killed, except for my old company, Squad 270 in Queens. All the rescue companies got wiped out.... Some people sometimes don't understand it completely, the amount of training that they have, hundreds of hours of training in all different disciplines [collapse, technical and high-angle rescue, water and confined space rescue]. So Special Ops that day, we learned a lesson, a bad lesson, all our Special Operations units went. So they all got killed, the ones that were there. And the others came after the fact. So I wind up spending 15 months in Special Operations as they're trying to rebuild.
>
> *—Chief of Department (2020–2022) Tom Richardson, then a Battalion Chief in Battalion 53, Bayside, Queens*

> “ Our job was to reach out to our firefighters and our fire officers and try to make them whole, try to make them functional. By doing that, you had to visit the firehouses every day that you were working on duty there and ask, 'What's going on? Where are the problems?'
>
> *—Chief of Department (2010–2014) Ed Kilduff, then a Deputy Chief in Division 3, Midtown, Manhattan, and past IMT Incident Commander*

> “ The families were spending an awful lot of time in the firehouses because they didn't have any place to go. Some of them were still hopeful. They were not easy to deal with, though you wanted to help them along.
>
> *—Chief of Department (2010–2014) Ed Kilduff, then a Deputy Chief in Division 3, Midtown, Manhattan, and past IMT Incident Commander*

> “ You’d sit in there with other first responders – cops, fire, all different agencies– just talking to people. They made a point of coming and talking to you.
>
> *—Chief of Department (2020–2022) Tom Richardson, then a Battalion Chief in Battalion 53, Bayside, Queens*

Leadership and grieving – clarity and structure as lifelines

Structure provided firefighters focus, something to hold on to. It helped focus energy that might otherwise have dissolved into paralysis. When people knew the next step – however small – they could begin to move. That movement restored a sense of control, allowing firefighters to act in the face of the unthinkable, and to believe that their actions still mattered.

Without direction, even the most dedicated teams can drift. But with clarity – even temporary, imperfect clarity – leaders gave their people a way forward. They didn’t suppress the grief. They created a structure strong enough to work through the grief, to get the job done. Structuring the work at the site helped. So too did structuring the work of supporting the grieving...and the grievers.

The pipe band’s commitment became symbolic of the department’s broader effort to treat every family’s loss with dignity. The FDNY Counseling Services Unit began scaling its work to match the unprecedented need. The city, with help from the department, created family information centers on Manhattan’s West Side. Help came from many quarters: colleagues and counselors, city agencies and volunteer organizations, clergy, community centers, and a network of professionals.

Yet, all the goodwill in the world couldn’t erase the magnitude of the loss. Emotional complexity swirled beneath the surface.

> “ [I]n the weeks that followed, we over-supervised. We had battalion chiefs doing jobs that maybe captains and lieutenants would normally be doing. We got them right down in there.
>
> *—Chief of Operations Pat McNally, then a Deputy Chief in Division 14, Flushing, Queens*

> “ We ended up having many more than 343 funerals and memorials. There were duplicates of some, and the department attended as many

Mangled steel beams
Close-up view of mangled steel beams at Ground Zero that naturally formed a cross shape amidst the wreckage of the World Trade Center. This "World Trade Center Cross" a symbol of hope and a makeshift memorial for workers during the recovery efforts.
With permission from the private collection of Daniel Quinn

as we could. I had said to somebody, 'There's no way the [Pipe]band will be at every funeral.' But somehow, they split up. There was some representation from the [FDNY Emerald Society Pipes & Drums Band] at every single funeral and memorial.... [The band] takes care of their own business.... They were given the schedule of funerals and memorials and figured out how to ensure that we would have a presence there.

—Fire Commissioner (2014–2022) Dan Nigro,
then Chief of Operations Headquarters, Downtown Brooklyn
(served as Chief of Department 2001–2002)

“ On the Thursday after the event, we opened our first [counselling] satellite.... [O]n Friday we opened the next one. Two weeks later, we opened the third one. It wasn't like we were wasting time. A lot of community centers helped us. And in Long Island, volunteer firehouses opened their doors to our members.

—Malachy Corrigan NP, then Clinical Director, Counseling Services Unit, SoHo, Manhattan

“ I think relative to coping and handling, it kind of developed on its own. A self-sustaining system where brothers and sisters in the fire department quietly counseled themselves, counseled each other, especially at the unit level.

Our counseling service unit now is so robust.... Probably the best in the business. And that's in part – maybe mostly – because of what we learned out of 9/11.

—Chief of Department (2020–2022) Tom Richardson, then a Battalion Chief in Battalion 53, Bayside, Queens

Leadership and grieving – crosscurrents and unexpected gifts

The pain didn't end with towers collapsing or extinguishing fires. For months – and in many cases, years and decades – members of the FDNY carried emotional burdens that were often invisible but deeply scarring. Grief showed up in many forms: anger, silence, guilt, fatigue. Some reached out for counseling and took advantage of respite centers set up near the site, offering a place to pause, to eat, and to re-group. Others found support in small, surprising acts of kindness. And while not everything done in the name of help actually helped, many gestures – especially the quiet, unheralded ones – became treasured moments of connection in an otherwise overwhelming, potentially isolating time.

“ Thankfully, many of our members reached out for help, which was good. Some didn't. They probably should have. People shouldn't go through these situations by themselves. For the most part, professional help helps.

—Fire Commissioner (2014–2022) Dan Nigro, then Chief of Operations Headquarters, Downtown Brooklyn (served as Chief of Department 2001–2002)

“ This may be one of the few positive results of September 11th.... Eventually it brought an openness to getting some help aside from a medical doctor.... I think how it started is the infrastructure was not in place to give counseling to thousands of firefighters.... Immediate federal funding was put in place.... I went to counseling though I thought I was coping very well.

—Captain Paul Brown, then a Lieutenant covering in Division 15, Brownsville, Brooklyn; FDNY IMT

“ I didn’t like the celebrities coming down there.... My answer was, ‘Did you give them a shovel? Is he down here to work?’...Then, there was the other end of it...these bikers from North Carolina.... ‘You guys eating? We’re going to make ribs tonight’.... Just do-gooders who do a good one, no recognition.... On September 12th...I’m walking down West Street and I’m thinking to myself.... ‘I’d kill somebody for a pair of socks right now.’ This woman walks out of nowhere.... She says, ‘Well, what can I do for you?’ I said, ‘I can use a pair of socks.’ She said, ‘You’re in luck.’ She had a pair of socks in her bag.... I talk to her, every 9/11, she calls me.... I put those socks on, [and] it felt like a million dollars.

—Battalion Chief Fred LaFemina, Chief of Rescue Services, then Captain of Squad 270, South Jamaica, Queens; member FDNY USAR

“ The community did what they could for us...even in my Battalion. Most of the other companies...were in very affluent areas. They were inundated with supplies, food.... It became like one big—actually, that part of the story is actually a good part of the story, how all the communities came together.

—Firefighter Louis Giaconelli, then in Engine 53, Spanish Harlem, Manhattan; FDNY IMT

“ I remember the poor guys at 10 and 10 [Engine 10, Ladder 10]. People were putting flowers outside their door saying thank you, and they’re like, ‘Get away from me. I want my friends back. I want my health back. I want those buildings back. I want my job back.’

—Stephanie Gaskell, then a journalist, Associated Press, New York (covered WTC site for duration of FDNY operations)

> It was not just the families, but their firehouse families that were terribly affected. You had people—like the chauffeur of the engine who didn't go into the building [as per protocol]—carrying this guilt. 'Why is he still alive?' It took its toll.
>
> *—Fire Commissioner (2014–2022) Dan Nigro,*
> *then Chief of Operations Headquarters, Downtown Brooklyn*
> *(served as Chief of Department 2001–2002)*

Leadership and grieving – tending to self

Even the most seasoned commanders felt the weight of 9/11 in many, often idiosyncratic ways, ways they weren't always prepared to share. Being present for others took a toll. They had jobs to do, people to protect, and standards to meet. But underneath the command presence, they were human – carrying pain, guilt, and exhaustion of their own.

A week after 9/11, Captain Kerry Hollywood gathered his unit in the firehouse kitchen. He apologized for not acting like a captain since the attacks, for not being able to provide the leadership people needed. Then he said, "I got it and I'm back, and from now on I'm going to take care of business." One of the firefighters, his voice cracking years later, recalled his reaction: "That was very noble. And honest. And the right thing to do."

> You tried to keep that part of it as private as you could or between yourself and your immediate family, and perhaps somebody, a counselor that you might have been speaking to, to talk you through some of these issues so you could keep going.
>
> *—Fire Commissioner (2014–2022) Dan Nigro,*
> *then Chief of Operations Headquarters, Downtown Brooklyn*
> *(served as Chief of Department 2001–2002)*

> I was kind of beat up just being there every day and seeing all the death.... I said to John Norman, I said, 'Listen, man, you've got to get somebody to take my place down there. I can't work there every day'.... It got to me after a while.
>
> *—Chief of Department (2020–2022) Tom Richardson,*
> *then a Battalion Chief in Battalion 53,*
> *Bayside, Queens*

Part B: Summary, Lessons, and Commentary

Summary

Firefighters were in an all-out battle to save lives. They remained in response mode for a painfully extended period of frenzied, nonstop work, risking much to save lives. Each was confident in the knowledge that their brother and sister firefighters would give their all searching for them were their roles reversed.

Radio communications at the unit level did not exist. Staff chiefs and deputy chiefs were posted around the perimeter of the site. Battalion chiefs supervised the work. Firefighters received verbal orders to operate in a certain area reporting to the chief there.

Chief of Operations Dan Nigro had made his way back to the, now relocated, command post at West and Chambers Streets. As the ranking uniformed survivor he took command. After being briefed by chiefs Cruthers and Fellini, Nigro gathered his staff chiefs. As he related "I took all of the surviving bosses that were there north on West Street. We had a little meeting as to how we would operate. We sectored the job, and put different people in charge of whoever was in those quadrants. Under them, deputy chiefs and battalion chiefs would work with each of those chiefs."

Their next issue was concern that 7 WTC would collapse. Earlier commanders had come to the realization that fighting the fires would be futile as they did not have adequate resources or available water supply. Hoses supplied by water tanks in nearby buildings could protect search operations but not much beyond that. Fires inside had burned unchecked for hours. The collapse was coming. All operations in and near the building were halted and a collapse zone surrounding the building was cleared of civilians and firefighters.

Keeping firefighters out of the potential collapse zone around 7 WTC continued to be an active ongoing concern until the building collapsed at 5:20 p.m. The air movement from 47 stories of building falling lifted the dust and debris from the towers into the air. The dust cloud pushed in every direction pulsing against windows, people – everything in its path. Miraculously, there was only one serious injury in the collapse or running from the debris cloud.

When the dust settled, 7 WTC no longer loomed as a threat. Firefighters could re-enter the area for searches. Chief Nigro convened all staff chiefs once again. They needed to develop a plan for the overnight and the following day. The chiefs who survived the towers collapse would go home, clean up, rest, and return in the morning. Assistant Chiefs Frank Cruthers and Harry Meyers would share command for the next few hours. Meyers would then have command of all FDNY operations for the overnight. Assistant Chiefs Fellini and Callan returned in the morning.

The day after the attacks, in firehouses throughout the department phone calls came in and went out. Lists of the deceased and the missing were written and verified. Paul Brown recounted receiving a faxed list of the missing mid-morning on 9/12: "The page came out: we did a quick count, about 50 names. The pages kept coming out; there were seven.... They asked us to check the list and cross off anyone we saw [alive]. We crossed a few names off. I found out later that my name was on an early list sent to my old firehouse."

At headquarters, staffers began contacting apparatus and equipment suppliers. No accounting of material loses had been made, however headquarters staff knew replacement equipment was needed and a lot of it, now. Dispatchers in each of the cities five boroughs struggled to provide coverage for the remainder of the city. Fire departments from as far away as Virginia and Massachusetts had responded to FDNY's mutual aid requests. Beginning early morning of 9/12, mutual aid units were located inside FDNY firehouses to provide fire protection to the people of New York City.

Within a day, the FDNY was divided into two working platoons: 24 hours on, 24 hours off schedule. In the working platoon, fire companies were covered at minimum staffing levels. All excess firefighters, officers, and chiefs were either at the site or minding the families of the missing.

A workforce traumatized and suffering still had work to do. But how to begin? "You have to go back to what you've been taught. That's our structure. That's what you study. You study how to work at a fire scene, how to work in a collapse scene. What we did was basically taking this scene and magnifying it because of the size of it," Chief Pat McNally reasoned.

The first funerals were held on Saturday, September 15. Chief Ed Kilduff saw FDNY's mission expand once again. "A few days after September 11, the fire department started running parallel operations. One was the site itself, and the other was the missing firefighters and their families. The third function was going to the funerals."

In the immediate aftermath the FDNY simply did not have the capacity to honor our fallen as tradition dictated. The ceremonial unit and the pipe band were spread thin yet facilitated every firefighters funeral. Many of the same departments that responded on mutual aid requests assisted with funerals outside NYC.

That same day, the FDNY World Trade Center Task Force began operating as a separate command within the department. This was the fifth time FDNY would reorganize its command and control at the World Trade Center.[41]

Chief Frank Cruthers was Incident Commander and Chief Pete Hayden was Deputy Incident Commander. Relieved of their respective "day job" duties. Firefighters were detailed from field units for each respective tour. The work continued as it had from the 11th: searching, fighting fires, and recovery and removal of victims. For the most part, it was familiar work.

The FDNY WTC Task Force was created to address the scale of the operation, and to facilitate on-scene continuity and efficiency of effort. The task force developed and improved over time. As Chief Pat McNally saw it, "The first few weeks, you're making this up as you go along. It's never been done before." The FDNY flew solo in its first attempt at large-scale incident management. Denis Onieal, FEMA, saw the shift: "There was a gradual time, I'm going to say it's between 7 and 10 days, where the FDNY went from tactical to strategic."

On Sunday 9/16 the FDNY held a promotion ceremony. 166 were promoted to fill leadership positions and meet the challenges facing the department. Dan Nigro officially became the chief of department. 29 to Battalion chief, 61 to captain, and 70 to lieutenant. All ordered immediately into field assignments. The urgency of the need precluded normally required training for the new Lieutenants.

By the 18th, Chief Cruthers began leading morning agency briefings at the Duane Street firehouse. Chief Hayden recalled, "There were agencies I never heard of. There were federal agencies, state agencies." Chief John Norman, part of the WTC TF management team, concluded: "We started with those basics. That got us to the point where we could bring in the experts to get us further along."

The funerals began and continued unabated. Searching continued. Digging continued. Grief continued. Dignified, respectful removal of the dead continued.

Leadership and grieving – a closing illustrative tale

The following story from the interviews captures an overarching lesson for leaders trying to support healing: diagnoses, commitment to department member health, innovation, and, as with much of managing, following up to learn and to get it right.

The FDNY mobilized psychological services, even stationing psychologists and psychiatrists in firehouses. Leadership did this despite a culture of independence and emotional toughness. This time, they recognized that the magnitude of the loss, of the hurt, required something more and something different. As Malachy Corrigan, Clinical Director of the Counseling Services Unit, put it, "The determining event was the actual placement of professionals in the firehouse."

Yet, few firefighters availed themselves of these resources. Leadership persisted, and sought to understand why. Rather than check the box of "resource provided" and move on, leaders went to the firehouses, to what one later described as the emotional *gemba*. Corrigan recalled a telling encounter: a psychiatrist sat behind a fully opened copy of the *New York Times*, waiting for someone to approach him. "You've got your back to the wall," Corrigan said. "You're watching the only entrance and hiding behind the paper." That wasn't outreach.

The department shifted course. The FDNY found retirees with experience in psychological services and crash-trained volunteers. These care providers had street (or firehouse) cred. They could provide initial assistance and referrals. The issue of utilization went away – just the wrong receptors. That shift proved fundamental and lasting.

Lessons for Leaders

1. **Rebuild structure as you use it.** Repopulate command, establish boundaries and roles, organize the work – even as everything remains in flux, perhaps convulsing. Clarity, even temporary clarity, affords an object to grip.

2. **Move toward the loss and the grief.** Don't wait for people to approach you. Visit every firehouse. Assure taps at every funeral. Presence matters more than perfect, formal words. Be visible and real. Like Chief Pete Hayden on 9/11, climb up where people can see you. Name the reality, tend to the pain, organize the work – day after day.

3 **Care for the caregivers.** Those doing the tending need tending too, at least by themselves of themselves. Scale the resources, particularly the support resources, to match the need – counseling services, peer support, places and occasions to sit and talk.

4 **Precipitate the coexistence of work and grief.** Don't ask people to compartmentalize the incomprehensible or the unbearable. Create structures and feed relationships strong enough to work through grief, not around it.

5 **Honor each loss individually.** The death of one person equals a tragedy. Hold tight to that truth. Pause whenever a body is found.

6 **Stay alert for miracles.** Remember Stairway B.

7 **Don't rush what can't be rushed.** Big challenges require time and stamina. Patience is not avoidance – it's commitment. Recovery comes from all directions – operational, emotional, relational. Encircle the wound.

8 **Change norms that need changing.** Old attitudes can facilitate or inhibit. Old attitudes toward counseling, toward just asking for help or showing vulnerability – crisis can provide the crucible for transformation.

Dealing with crisis requires accepting its inherent qualities: ongoing uncertainty, looming disorder, and at times debilitating chaos. What needs doing changes over time. Scope can change. Even the mission can change. Toiling amidst chaos is inherently messy and disorderly.

In such conditions, leaders benefit from a workforce selected not only for skill, but for adaptability, shared purpose and values as well as for what some call "sand." Next, shared training and shared experience matter. They, in turn, can facilitate development of a collective backbone of skill and trust. If conditions degrade into chaos, then leaders can rely on that backbone – what everyone knows how to do and trust that others do as well…and with one another. Return to the basics. Rely on muscle memory. Regroup and recover from there.

Leaders should consistently and reliably ensure that people have the resources they need. Crises deliver a pounding. Leaders should understand what their people need and help them get it. That may mean identifying, procuring, and deploying expertise quickly – whether in firefighting, logistics, construction equipment, perimeter control, fencing...or emotional support.

Progress often comes step by step. Moving the spotlight, deliberately shifting focus helps channel energy toward purpose. Orderly, productive action, even on a limited scale, generates momentum. When people understand the next step they can take, they begin to believe that their efforts matter. That belief fosters collective recovery. Leaders should recognize effort expended and impact made. They should acclaim effort expended and impact made. They should support people across the entire range and process of personal and organizational healing. The battered and beleaguered can easily exhaust all energy in the face of the daunting. Progress and praise restore and recharge.

Reestablishing order, competency, and a strong sense of agency happens incrementally. Clarity facilitates order and bolsters a sense of agency. Simple, concrete questions need answers: What needs doing now? Who's doing what? In a shattered landscape, small acts of organization – assigning roles, setting priorities, defining immediate next steps however tactical – begin to generate and guide motion. Helping people regain footing helps them regain a sense of agency, a critical requirement for moving on, for moving forward.

Prominent and powerful steps also matter. Rebuilding formal structure – quickly – helps to combat uncertainty and disorder. Rebuild with clarity at the top and initiative from below. Fill the most important gaps, at least for now, right now. Rebuild while remaining operational. Keep moving. Fold work back into the official chain of command, however temporary. Above all, give and take leadership moment by moment: accept the assignment, or, if none is given, then assume the task that needs doing, assigned or not.

Leaders can further restore agency by sectoring the chaos, breaking the work into more manageable parts. Progress, even when small, renews confidence and agency. Create roles, assign tasks, and organize people using the language and logic of the work itself. Adapt to the situation. Leaders should model problem identification and resolution – innovatively when required – and as quickly as possible.

Throughout, leaders should keep purpose in full view. Small steps matter, but so does the "why." For the FDNY, that purpose remained clear and unchanged: rescue. Find the living. Save who could be saved. That shared, practiced, and simple 'why' animated action and helped keep paralysis at bay. People, especially those suffering and exhausted, benefit from connecting action to meaning. Purposeful, shared action restores agency.

Crises can also dictate changes in mission and purpose. Leaders should guide such transitions carefully. Restated, alter mission with care. When reality demands a shift in purpose – as it did when the work transitioned from rescue to recovery – leaders should guide and pace that change with compassion. The deeper people's commitment to mission, the more important that leaders recognize and accept the difficulty inherent in such transitions. In this case, transitioning from a rescue mission to a search mission, of transitioning from looking for survivors to recovering the dead qualified as not just unusual, but as profound, painful, and potentially deeply dispiriting. That collective and individual reality required serious weighting by leaders wrestling with a decision about moving from one mission to another, by leaders considering not just whether to move, to change, but also when and how.

FDNY leaders shepherded a gradual transition, allowing the unsettling truth to settle in before officially reorienting the work. Effective leadership respects deep, shared emotional burdens. In this instance, that meant the burden of declaring a fundamental change in mission. Where possible, leaders influence the pace of metabolization of such change.

As for grieving, lead it. Acknowledge it. Accept the reality of loss and the process of healing, in yourself and in others. Do not outsource leading grieving. FDNY leaders understood this. They showed up at every funeral and visited families. Hard work. Sometimes very hard work. Leadership work. As Nigro noted, "I visited every firehouse that lost somebody at some point. Some of them were very difficult meetings. Members were angry. Some asked, 'What are you going to do if this happens again?'"

Leaders can use formal or positional authority to hide or to engage. It affords those of higher rank the opportunity to amplify personal presence in the grieving and in the healing process. Far better for leaders to use their position to gain access to events, to authorize visits, and to signal that anguish matters and requires addressing. Presence also matters. Leading through grieving requires persistence, compassion, thoughtfulness, and learning – without making compassion feel institutional. It demands structure and coordination, but also heart – the band members appear at every memorial, training psychologists appear in the firehouses, and Chief Nigro visits every firehouse that lost a firefighter – personal presence combined with organizational support, institutionalization without depersonalization.

Small gestures matter. Help doesn't always arrive in grand packages. Clean, dry socks can matter more than eloquently scripted speeches delivered by luminaries. Use moments of shared pain to foster community. Don't seek closure. Aim instead for healing – integrating what happened into individual lives and into the leader's connection with his or her people and thereby into the organization. This work, this complex, deeply personal and yet shared, and ongoing work benefits from informed and committed leadership.

In short, intent, resources, heart, and organization all matter. For the FDNY, this meant expanding commitments to the injured and fallen as required, moving beyond precedent as necessary. Longstanding commitment to families of the fallen evolved and became more formalized, not by consulting manuals, but by blending need and core values. Compassion, not just empathy or sympathy, guided the actions of listening, assisting, and acting in the service of healing.

Leaders must also care for themselves, for their own well-being and as human resources key to the well-being of others. Model this openly. Seek support before reaching a personal breaking point. A depleted leader cannot sustain others. Limit tours of duty. Allow no-fault exits. Prolonged crises require paced leaders.

Leaders, like others, can fall short. If they do, then they should stop and reset. Stop to start over. An apology, honestly offered, can repair trust and restore the leader:follower relationship. Name the failure. Own it. Fix it. People often remember such moments with respect and gratitude. Hence, initiate the repair, the healing. Lead it.

In the end, leadership in acute – and prolonged – crisis rests on two commitments: protecting each person's sense of agency and honoring the heart of each person, including one's own. In matters of the heart, move at its pace.

Commentary

Long ago, in the 1940s, the Ohio State Leadership Studies identified two key factors of leadership and labelled them "initiating structure" and "consideration."[42] Much of leadership literature up to today crisscrosses the same terrain, often refining these ideas, sometimes without explicit reference. At its core, the insight endures: effective leadership both creates clarity and order, defining what needs doing and how, while also attending to relationships and the well-being of those being led.

The FDNY's navigation of the tower collapses and their aftermath illustrates the continuing relevance of the Ohio State study, particularly the value of both factors during the transition from rescue to recovery portrayed. That transition demanded both structure and care, often simultaneously.

Interviewees repeatedly described the rebuilding of a command structure, the reestablishment of direction, and the organization of daily work (including basic but essential tasks such as securing the perimeter with a fence). These key tasks exemplify *initiating structure*. They occurred from the top down, as leaders reconstituted formal command, and from the bottom up, as firefighters created pockets of self-organized work. Both generated order amid disruption.

Consideration emerged just as clearly. Interviewees spoke of attending to trauma and exhaustion in others, and, as necessary, in themselves. Leaders moved toward the grieving and the grievers. Leaders introduced new forms of support, changed norms and practices, and adjusted policies to reflect changed realities. They advocated for and modeled flexibility and self-care. By doing so, FDNY leaders connected, in some cases reconnected, with those they led. They maintained and restored leader:-follower relationships, perhaps even strengthening them through shared grieving. Thus, grieving that could easily have distanced people from one another instead became something borne together.

Consideration, in this context, went well beyond the normal attention to human needs, well beyond resilience in the narrow sense of "bouncing back." Well beyond. It included recognition of the need for healing – individual and organizational, emotional and psychological. Healing, of course, begins with acknowledging the injury: naming the wound, recognizing its depth, and accepting the consequences–including the very need to heal.

After 9/11, overtaxed and often just-promoted FDNY officers were called to lead their people through grief – raw, personal, and pervasive. Some companies had been decimated. Special Operations, one of the department's most elite units, had lost nearly everyone. Because of the FDNY's tight-knit culture and rotation system, nearly every member had lost someone they knew. Crews weren't just missing colleagues. They were missing brothers, mentors, and lifelong friends.

In any organization, the loss of team members – especially in sudden, traumatic ways – creates a vacuum of energy, identity, and trust. But the FDNY's response offers a powerful example of what emotional leadership can look like in the face of that kind of rupture. Officers didn't try to suppress, or override, grief, or rush past grief. They recognized that leadership in crisis means connection, not just coordination. That connection required presence. Officers showed up in the firehouses – not to deliver speeches, but to listen. To witness. To acknowledge the full spectrum of pain, both shared and personal.

In any organization staggered by loss – whether from tragedy, mass layoffs, scandal, or sudden change – leaders should engage with the emotional aftermath. That means going to the emotional gemba—meeting people where they are, not just physically but also emotionally and psychologically, namely active trauma and associated deeply individual grief.

Officers still had to rebuild teams and make decisions. But they understood that progress in the work and in the healing required permission to grieve.

That emotional honesty did not distract from the mission. Rather, it provided groundwork for renewed commitment to it. Leadership looks like this when so much lies about broken: clarity and presence. Not just moving on or bouncing back – but moving through and moving forward, together.

Leading out of crisis, as with leading through crisis, means doing the fundamentals of leadership well – even amid crushing loss and a prolonged and evolving aftermath. Reestablishing order meant organizing the work that needed doing and caring for those who did it: firefighters, families, and the broader community. Leadership after 9/11 involved tending to the loss and to the lost. It required giving people something to hold on to as they, and the FDNY, climbed back on their feet. In short, leaders working out of crisis should delineate the work, support the work, and attend to the people performing it, including themselves.

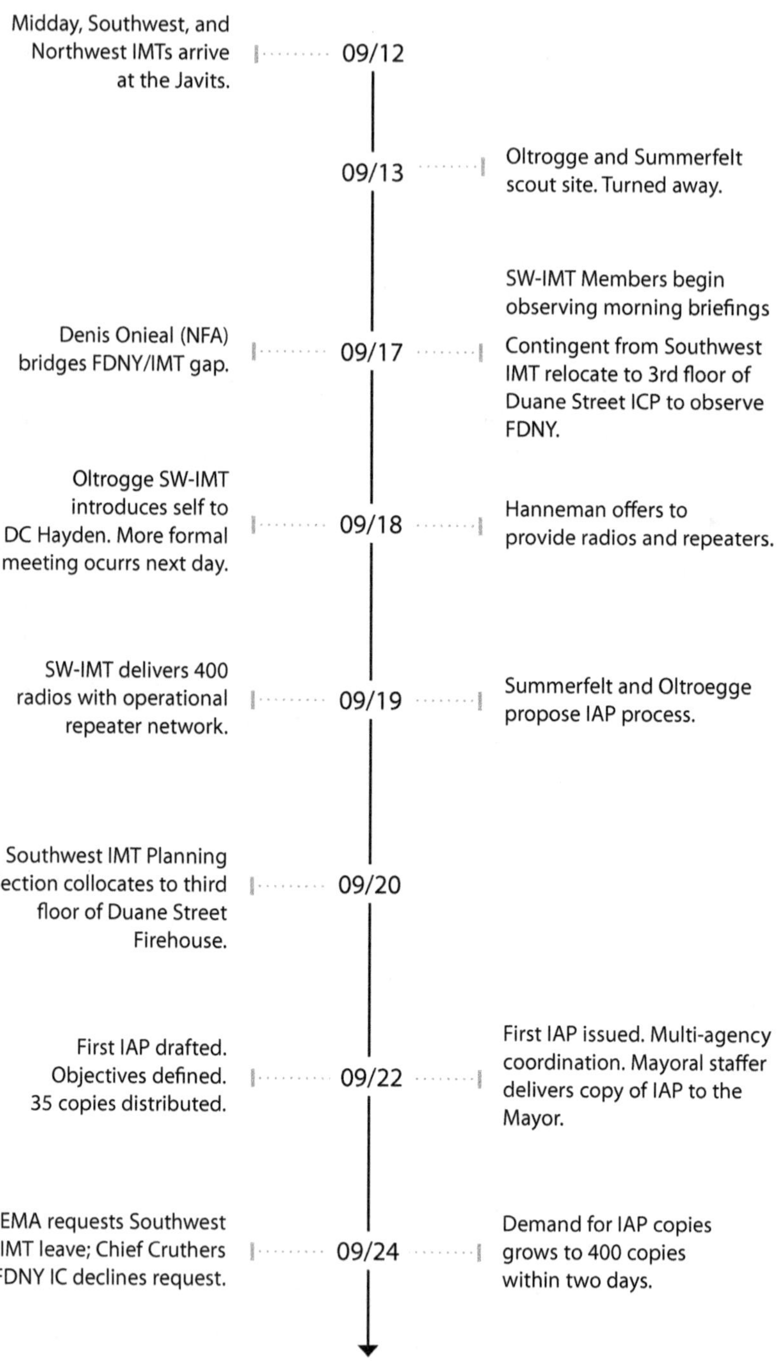

Midday, Southwest, and Northwest IMTs arrive at the Javits.
09/12
09/13
Oltrogge and Summerfelt scout site. Turned away.
SW-IMT Members begin observing morning briefings
Denis Onieal (NFA) bridges FDNY/IMT gap.
09/17
Contingent from Southwest IMT relocate to 3rd floor of Duane Street ICP to observe FDNY.
Oltrogge SW-IMT introduces self to DC Hayden. More formal meeting ocurrs next day.
09/18
Hanneman offers to provide radios and repeaters.
SW-IMT delivers 400 radios with operational repeater network.
09/19
Summerfelt and Oltroegge propose IAP process.
Southwest IMT Planning Section collocates to third floor of Duane Street Firehouse.
09/20
First IAP drafted. Objectives defined. 35 copies distributed.
09/22
First IAP issued. Multi-agency coordination. Mayoral staffer delivers copy of IAP to the Mayor.
FEMA requests Southwest IMT leave; Chief Cruthers FDNY IC declines request.
09/24
Demand for IAP copies grows to 400 copies within two days.

Chapter Seven

A Study in Effective and Enduring Helping

> "Early on, I'm going to say probably, the 13th thereabouts, I began to realize that the leadership of New York City Fire Department, as talented as they are, couldn't comprehend what they needed.... This was beyond anything that they had ever conceived of, in my opinion. I know it was far more than I ever could conceive of.
>
> *—Denis Onieal, then Senior FEMA Rep., Superintendent, National Fire Academy*

> "So the three of us went down to the pile (Dan Oltrogge, Paul Summerfelt, Pruitt Small SW-IMT). We just did that and came back. Of course, it was glaring. With all due respect...there was a lot of opportunities for us to lend a hand, to help with this.
>
> *—Dan Oltrogge, Commander National Area Command Team (2009–2011), then Incident Commander Trainee SW-IMT,*

Chief of Fire and Aviation Grand Canyon National Park
(served as SW-IMT Incident Commander 2003–2007)

“ They [FDNY] had no idea what federal resources were available. The only person that had a really, really good handle on it was dead. That was Ray Downey [Chief of Rescue Services and FDNY USAR Commander].

—Denis Onieal, then Senior FEMA Rep., Superintendent, National Fire Academy

“ When I tell this story, I always say...the one thing we can take credit for is once it was explained, we weren't dumb enough to say no.

—1st Deputy Commissioner (2004–2010) Frank Cruthers, then an Assistant Chief at Headquarters, Downtown Brooklyn (served as Chief of Department 1996–1997, 2002–2004)

By mid-September, the FDNY arrived at a sobering realization: the distinctness of the work at the World Trade Center site. The FDNY response would last for far more than the customary hours or even a few days. This work was unlike anything it had ever faced. This was no longer an emergency response that would resolve in hours or at most in a few days, nor even a prolonged firefighting operation. This one was not governed by familiar tactics. Vastness of scale, technical complexity, and open ended duration all set this challenge apart from anything that the FDNY had ever faced.

Normally, firefighters arrive at incidents well trained, well equipped, as well as well connected with one another and organized around well-honed methods. Bigger fires mean more personnel but using the same tactics modularized and scaled as befit the incident. When the fire is out, the assignment ends. Responsibility for the site transfers. The department moves on. Perhaps a battalion commander staffs a shift to watch smoldering ruins, perhaps two or three such shifts run in succession, each with their own method of operation. Still, soon, as soon as possible, the FDNY mitigates the emergency and the NYPD or Buildings department assumes responsibility for the scene.

Not this time. Ground Zero was different – the oft referenced big one. Fires smoldered for days and burned deep within the debris for months. The rubble field covered more than 10 city blocks. Firefighters were missing. The dead, including many of the FDNY's own, lay unrecovered under stories of rubble. This work stretched out over an indeterminate period. This work did not allow handing off and demanded continuous presence.

Additionally, 9/11 had stripped the FDNY almost down to its organizational studs. Unprecedented numbers of dead especially among the ranks of senior leaders. Thousands of years of experience gone. Thousands of pieces of equipment destroyed.

Ground Zero was different.

This time the FDNY stayed on site. This time the FDNY owned the site...for months.

The volume and complexity of the work proved knee buckling and mind numbing. Tactics applied improvisationally from deep know-how proved insufficient. The FDNY tried to plan the work and work the plan, but this was new work and the plan needed to encompass new magnitudes of breadth and depth. New work at a new scale. Complicated, overarching work needed doing and identifying and the countless initiatives at the site needed coordinating.

On Saturday morning, September 15, the FDNY took its first major step toward a more formalized approach to reorganize its response to the incident – the FDNY's first attempt at large-scale incident management. It established a World Trade Center Task force and sent approximately 1,200 firefighters to the site each day across eight-hour shifts, 400 firefighters per eight-hour shift. Assistant Chief Frank Cruthers served as Incident Commander (IC), Deputiy Chief Pete Hayden as Deputy IC, being relieved of their normal duties. They divided the incident site into four sectors each commanded by a Deputy Chief. On Saturday morning, 9/15, the FDNY-WTC-TF began operation. Assistant Chief Frank Cruthers convened the first interagency briefing and assumed the role of Incident Commander. Deputy Chief Pete Hayden assumed the role of Deputy Incident Commander.

The reorganization marked progress. Still, FDNY leaders increasingly recognized that they now confronted new forms of work. As for just how to do that work, the FDNY did not yet know how much they did not know. They did know that this recovery and cleanup effort required capabilities beyond those the department possessed on its own. Fortunately, others had experience with precisely this kind of work. The challenge? To connect with them – and to learn how to work together.

Part A: Responder Voices

Prelude to collaboration

> “ The purveyors of knowledgeable assistance needed to connect, meaningfully connect, with those who needed it, namely the FDNY. Denis Onieal from the National Fire Academy urged Bill Lake from FEMA and Hugh Wood from the National Fire Administration to meet with members of the SW-IMT at the Javits Center. Lake and Wood tasked the SW-IMT to connect with assist and support the FDNY.
>
> We had people come in from the outside and said to us, ‘This is not your field of expertise. You're trying your best, but it's not your field of expertise.’ There was a group that dealt with airline crashes and things like that. They knew how to manage specific things. They had expertise in it. We were just helping each other as best we could. It went from there....
>
> *—2nd Deputy Commissioner Tom Fitzpatrick, then in Headquarters, Downtown Brooklyn*

> “ I knew about the federal response, but a federal response comes on many levels. The reason he [Mike Byrne from FEMA] came to see me is because we anticipated that we would need command posts. We knew that FEMA was coming...and how FEMA would respond to all these things in California (wildfires).
>
> *—2nd Deputy Commissioner Tom Fitzpatrick, then in Headquarters, Downtown Brooklyn*

> “ We went down prior to that request from FEMA and the National Fire Administration just to try and get a feel for what was occurring, how was it happening, you know, just kind of trying to get our-our legs under us. Well, at that point, there wasn't a command post on Duane [Street]. That didn't happen for a little bit, but for them to even get access to assist on the pile, they were turned away by whatever sector they were going into, likely by a sector chief. So that-that had occurred.
>
> *—Dan Oltrogge, Commander National Area Command Team (2009–2011), then Incident Commander Trainee SW-IMT, Chief of Fire and Aviation Grand Canyon National Park (served as SW-IMT Incident Commander 2003–2007)*

> “As I recall, it was Mike Byrne who took me down to [FDNY's] Brooklyn headquarters and started listening in and the kind of issues that they needed. The problem was they didn't know what they needed. They had no idea what federal resources were available. The only person that had a really, really good handle on it was dead. That was Ray Downey [Deputy Chief, Chief of Rescue Services and FDNY USAR Commander]. He was the guru in New York City on FEMA resources.
>
> —*Denis Onieal, then Senior FEMA Rep., Superintendent, National Fire Academy*

> “Denis Onieal...attached himself to us in those early days as our liaison to the FDNY. Even though Denis was at the academy [National Fire Academy], he had spent a career across the river in Jersey City, so he knew a lot of ‘em. He knew the culture and we did not know the culture.... I don't know who Denis met with, my guess would be it was either Frank Cruthers or Pete Hayden. I'm not quite sure how that all evolved. But we came in and helped them do that. Essentially, we just found a warm corner for ourselves up on the third floor, FDNY on the second floor, and the ground floor was the meeting space. So we didn't just walk in unannounced.
>
> —*Dan Oltrogge, Commander National Area Command Team (2009–2011), then Incident Commander Trainee SW-IMT, Chief of Fire and Aviation Grand Canyon National Park (served as SW-IMT Incident Commander 2003–2007)*

> “He [Denis Onieal] and I were in a conversation on the street. We're going over, ‘Well, I've requested this, this, this, and this.’ He says, ‘Do you want incident management teams?’ I said, ‘Denis, I have to confess my ignorance. What do they do?’ He explained very briefly how they manage large-scale disasters, wildfires, et cetera. When I tell this story, I always say...the one thing we can take credit for is once it was explained, we weren't dumb enough to say no. Oh, I knew we needed more help. It was a matter of I didn't need the same kind of help that I already had. Our communications on scene were verbal over a period of hours, sometimes into the next day, rarely more than that. I have said over and over again, of all of the help that we

got from outside the city, I thought, from my perspective, they were the most helpful.

—1st Deputy Commissioner (2004–2010) Frank Cruthers, then an Assistant Chief at Headquarters, Downtown Brooklyn (served as Chief of Department 1996–1997, 2002–2004)

“ Then we talked about – we knew the USAR teams would be coming from all the other states. That was the search and rescue people, who had a long history in FEMA. Some of our own people were already engaged in that. That was a tactical thing. We knew they would be on the ground, at Ground Zero, doing all those things to search and rescue and whatnot. The second piece of it, which we both agreed on, was the IMT. The IMT was the glue between the federal response and the city at Ground Zero. They have a well-established process and a well-established interface between governments or between tactical units and FEMA.

—2nd Deputy Commissioner Tom Fitzpatrick, then in Headquarters, Downtown Brooklyn

“ That's an interesting story there. So we were – we were kind of anchored at the Javits Convention Center and just found a niche for ourselves to help with the USAR support activity, and then there were other things we could do. And you had to have a name tag by FEMA to access the site, and FEMA was handing those out, but we didn't really understand what that process was.... [W]e're really good at improvising. So some of the folks on our team, we made our own ID tags and we just put them around our neck and we went down there and we got through all the security.

We got back from our recon at the pile, I recommended to Van Bateman that he go down to the pile, because that would be the focal point in short order. He [SW-IMT IC] told me, ‘No, you're going to go down to the pile and I'm going to stay here, so I want you down there.’ [We] then split the team, so I took a component of the team, again we went light. As we began to catch more work and get more traction over the weeks that followed, we grew, but we went in pretty light. I had the component of the team down at the pile, and Van had a component of the team up at the Javits Convention Center.

They asked us to do that, go down there to the pile and take a look and see what they could do to provide some assistance to the FDNY. We went again, we went in real light, it was myself, our plans chief Paul Summerfelt, and we took an operational person whose name was Pruitt Small, so the three of us went down to the pile. We just did that and came back. Of course, it was glaring. With all due respect, Paul, but there was a lot of opportunities for us to lend a hand, to help with this.

> We were aware 'cause we've been down there reconnoitering for probably at least a day or so and you kind of had a feel for what was occurring and we got the request to go down to the pile and see if we could help the FDNY, and that came from FEMA and the National Fire Administration and the FEMA rep was a gentleman named Bill Lokey and the National Fire Administration was a gentleman named Hugh Wood. And so that was the authority. We went down to the pile to begin to see what we may be able to do.
>
> We went back, reported, and then came the official tasking at a FEMA mission assignment to create a presence down at the pile. Get with the FDNY and help. Well, the problem with that was, we didn't quite grasp it as clearly as we should have, but on those initial days there was some agencies asking us to go down and directing us to go down there and lend a hand and help but there was one that was not asking us, and that was the FDNY. We shortly found out that there were reasons for that. Now, we're going down there and know what we have to do.
>
> *—Dan Oltrogge, Commander National Area Command Team (2009–2011), then Incident Commander Trainee SW-IMT, Chief of Fire and Aviation Grand Canyon National Park (served as SW-IMT Incident Commander 2003–2007)*

> “ This meeting kicked off, and that's where we got introduced to the administrator [IMT-speak for Incident Commander]. Just not formally introduced, just watching what was occurring, it was not like any meeting we had ever been in. And I say that because there was there wasn't a lot of – uh, there was no smiling. There was, you know, there was no joking. There was – it was business, but it was answer the question – there's no time for storytelling. And a 'no' answer or 'I don't

> know' answer, was very apparent[ly], was not a good answer. Because people were cut off. They were told that's enough, and it moved right to the next person, you know.... This was the environment to help and- and just develop relationships and then good things will come out of that. We had no idea what was gonna be at the time, because we recognized if we didn't have the relationships the door was gonna get slammed in our face and we were going home.
>
> *—Paul Summerfelt, Commander National Area Command Team (2013–2020), then Planning Section Chief Southwest-IMT, Deputy Chief Flagstaff, AZ Fire Department (served as Type-1 IMT Incident Commander 2008–2012)*

A meeting of consequence

Initially ignored, federal representatives observed the FDNY and worked their way into the FDNY's view. People like Mike Byrne, Thomas Fitzpatrick, and Denis Onieal personally connected FEMA, IMTs, and the FDNY. Southwest Incident Management team (SW-IMT) relocated to the third floor of the Incident Command Post at Duane Street on 9/17. On Tuesday, September 18, immediately following the morning inter-agency briefing

FDNY WTC Task Force Command Post
FDNY WTC Task Force Command Post office on 2nd floor of Duane St firehouse.
Left to right: DC Pete Hayden FDNY, AC Frank Cruthers FDNY, DC Charlie Blaich FDNY, Bob Gear PNW-IMT, Mike Lowry NW-IMT (Deceased due to 9/11 illness).
Shared with permission from the John Norman private collection

at Duane Street Incident Command Post, a brief meeting occurred. It wasn't accidental, but neither was it formal. Representatives from from the U.S. Fire Administration and FEMA had prompted the conversation, and a key FDNY leader was prepared to listen – barely.

Pete Hayden took the lead with Frank Cruthers and Charlie Blaich also in attendance for the FDNY. Dan Oltrogge, Paul Summerfelt, and Mike Hanneman represented the Southwest Incident Management Team (SW-IMT).

> “We had learned that they went to Motorola to help them fix their problem. Motorola was agreeing to do that, but it was going to take a very long time and it was going to cost a whole bunch of money so, they balked at that. That was a major issue they had. Denis set up the meeting and so it's myself and our plans chief (Summerfelt), and then I had the communications leader (Hanneman) there with me.
>
> *—Dan Oltrogge, Commander National Area Command Team (2009–2011), then Incident Commander Trainee SW-IMT, Chief of Fire and Aviation Grand Canyon National Park (served as SW-IMT Incident Commander 2003–2007)*

The meeting

> “There was a moment. Denis Onieal, the superintendent of the National Fire Academy, set up a meeting between myself and Pete Hayden, their [FDNY] deputy Incident Commander. The story goes from Pete is that I initiated that. I didn't. Denis Onieal did. We sit down at the table and I've got my plans chief with me, Paul Summerfelt. I've got our communications unit leader from the team with me because the issue was their communications down there at the pile was a train wreck when World Trade Center went down the afternoon on 11th, that was the majority of their communication capabilities. You'd see piles of handheld radios, portable radios that had just died and they had no way to replenish, to resupply, and communications was killing them.
>
> *—Dan Oltrogge, Commander National Area Command Team (2009–2011), then Incident Commander Trainee SW-IMT, Chief of Fire and Aviation Grand Canyon National Park (served as SW-IMT Incident Commander 2003–2007)*

> After one of the [interagency] meetings, Daniel [Oltrogge] comes up to me... and he goes, 'Chief, can I have five minutes of your time and talk to you?' I'm trying to be polite, 'Sure, okay.' I'm looking at him and he says, 'I'm from out west, Grand Canyon and like that, really.' I remember saying to myself, 'Here's a guy from the Grand Canyon.' I said, I'm in the canyons of New York City, how is this guy going to help me?
>
> He starts, we go up into the office and he tells me about incident management teams. I had never heard of these teams. We didn't have them. He starts telling me about the incident management teams like that.
>
> *—Chief of Department (2004–2006) Pete Hayden, then a Deputy Chief in Division 1, SoHo, Manhattan*

> Then, it was Pete Hayden, and then their logistics chief, identified as their logistics chief because I remember even back then, FDNY couldn't – the mnemonic we use for the incident command system is ICS. Well, back then FDNY couldn't spell ICS and they didn't want to learn how. They could have cared less.
>
> *—Dan Oltrogge, Commander National Area Command Team (2009–2011), then Incident Commander Trainee SW-IMT, Chief of Fire and Aviation Grand Canyon National Park (served as SW-IMT Incident Commander 2003–2007)*

> And we were up in the second floor of the firehouse, and Pete Hayden had a minute, uh, and I think he was – I think he may have – in retrospect, I think he was just doing it to satisfy the National Fire Academy guy [Onieal] and he was gonna have this meeting and walk out the door, and that was it. And he had the meeting and we were dismissed. And he walked in and his first – as I recall, his first thing was, 'What do you guys – what can you do for me?' And – there's about six of us. Dan Oltrogge, myself, and a couple of the planning staff are there. Uh, no real introductions, just what can you do for me?... 'You know, we can help with some – we can help some with some planning efforts.' And-and really generic answer to him. And he paused for a second and he said, 'Okay, we're having a meeting – in an hour or so, why don't you come to that, bring a couple people to the meeting.' And he spun around and walked out. It's like, okay. So we kinda looked at

each other and we said, 'Well, Dan [Oltrogge] will go, I'll go.' And we had recognized that FDNY was having a big communication problem at the time in terms of their ability to talk with each other on the pile. The radios and the batteries and stuff piled up on street corners was just a mountain of stuff. You know, they weren't able to recharge it. So they were just tossing radios. It was just an amazing thing. So we brought our communications guy with us for the team. The three of us went into that meeting, and that's the meeting that got us in, and it was all about our ability to help with the communication.

—Paul Summerfelt, Commander National Area Command Team (2013–2020), then Planning Section Chief Southwest-IMT, Deputy Chief Flagstaff, AZ Fire Department (served as Type-1 IMT Incident Commander 2008–2012)

“ Mike Hanneman [Communications unit leader]...goes, 'You know, I think—.' He's thinking out loud and he goes, 'I think I can have the plane on the tarmac at Newark tomorrow morning 400, I can have 400 portables up and running with a couple of repeater sites by tomorrow afternoon and repeater sites are where the signal will bounce and so you don't have to do line of sight by tomorrow afternoon.' There's a pause and Pete looked at me and he goes, 'You know—.' For him, he's like, 'These guys are really from Mars! Well, they can't do that.' He just looked at me goes, 'Okay, do it.'

—Dan Oltrogge, Commander National Area Command Team (2009–2011), then Incident Commander Trainee SW-IMT, Chief of Fire and Aviation Grand Canyon National Park (served as SW-IMT Incident Commander 2003–2007)

“ Mike said, 'We can have a communication system in X number of hours.' And as I recall...that was the point at which you talk about a razor-thin edge. I mean, okay, now we're on the head of a pin here, we do it and it'll lead to other things, or we fail and we're back at the Javits Center, and we'll never see these people again. You know Mike pulled it off. We had the radios there. And they had communications the next day. And it was at that point Pete Hayden came back and he said, 'What else can you do for me?' And that was the moment that, 'Okay, now we can help.'

—Paul Summerfelt, Commander National Area Command Team (2013–2020), then Planning Section Chief Southwest-IMT, Deputy Chief Flagstaff, AZ Fire Department (served as Type-1 IMT Incident Commander 2008–2012)

> Now the impetus is on us, but – which is exactly what we wanted because we knew we could do it. I knew Mike Hanneman, we just got out of his way and he made that happen. Now it's tomorrow afternoon. He's got a repeater site set up on the Empire State Building. He's got a repeater site set up on the Hudson called the Intrepid. He's got one up on the mast of the Intrepid and he's handing out radios, and he's tracking, and he's got a coms [communications] plan with frequencies, and this and that, and we're rolling. Pete sees me downstairs that afternoon, he looked at me and goes, 'What else can you guys do?' That was the moment and it was because it's that typical thing, don't talk about what you can do, don't hold a bunch of meetings, you got to act, you got to prove, show value-added, you got to display competence on a consistent basis. That was the first real thing that got our foot in the door. Then things after that, more things began to happen and you just feel – we did anyway, just a little decompression.
>
> —*Dan Oltrogge, Commander National Area Command Team (2009–2011), then Incident Commander Trainee SW-IMT, Chief of Fire and Aviation Grand Canyon National Park (served as SW-IMT Incident Commander 2003–2007)*

Duane Street Firehouse
Location of FDNY WTC Task Force Command Post at firehouse of Engine 7 and Ladder 1 on Duane Street.

> After that was accomplished, and then the-the question that Pete asked was, 'What can you do next?' And Dan and the crew, well, let's – we can start helping you put your arms around this – this planning effort, that up to that point did not have a written document that we were aware of. And you know, it-it's gonna take us a few days of working on this to get it into the correct format and acceptance and use, but we got to start, and so that probably happened within 24 hours of the radios. Uh, us beginning to do that. And that's when our interaction with Pete Hayden became, uh, much more consistent and much more on a daily, uh, throughout the day basis.
>
> *—Paul Summerfelt, Commander National Area Command Team (2013-2020), then Planning Section Chief Southwest-IMT, Deputy Chief Flagstaff, AZ Fire Department (served as Type-1 IMT Incident Commander 2008-2012)*

A tenuous beginning...

The FDNY's nascent SW-IMT structure and growing comprehension of the work at hand produced receptors and receptivity to an offer of help made to a proudly stand alone department in a proudly independent city. A head smacking display of ability to resource (radios) built credibility and eventually led to a long lasting collaboration. A unique, customized working relationship emerged, one that simultaneously recognized FDNY ownership of the site and Incident Management Team competency in managing massive and complicated disaster settings such as wild fires and hurricanes.

The first FDNY-IAP (Incident Action Plan) entered use on Friday, September 21.

> From that day forward, we were moving forward with the organization because they would draw up a written what they call an IAP, Incident Action Plan, every day for all the meetings. Every day we had this plan, the daily plan, every day, everybody, every agency was issued the plan.[43]
>
> *—Chief of Department (2004–2006) Pete Hayden, then a Deputy Chief in Division 1, SoHo, Manhattan*

CP Meeting Room
1st floor meeting area at FDNY WTC TF CP on Duane Street where daily interagency briefings were held.
With permission from the private collection of John Norman

" You see most of it in the early stages was on the fly. A perimeter was established. I remember we had to have IDs. People had to have IDs to get on the site. At some point, that was established. There were regular meetings, probably, I think, daily early on, and I don't know what the schedule was later on, so that we could have an idea, 'This is what we expect for today. This is your part. This is our part.'

—Fire Commissioner (2014–2022) Dan Nigro,
then Chief of Operations Headquarters, Downtown Brooklyn
(served as Chief of Department 2001–2002)

" We all wanted to get in here and search, but there were a lot of other competing agencies. 'We need this and that.' All these, you need to address this. You need to address sanitation, ConEd [the local power company] needs to get into things that are underground. If the transit authority wanted to get into one of the subway stations underneath there, we would be alerted that, we'd make sure that proper safety because we're like that. If the construction guy wanted to pull down a piece of steel or something like that, we would make sure that everybody knew about that, that there's going to be stuff pulled down and that we would set up a half-hour before we would – our chiefs would set up a collapse zone, we had an alert, warning established and things like that. If the telephone company needed to get into a manhole on West Street, we arranged to have them access to them and get in over there. We also know that this operation was going to be a long, drawn-out operation. It was going to go on for as long as a year, which it did.

—Chief of Department (2004–2006) Pete Hayden,
then a Deputy Chief in Division 1, SoHo, Manhattan

“ That's how we got them starting to come. I'm pretty sure Pete met with them on their arrival. I don't know if I was there that day or I was doing something else. Basically, they were divided up into smaller groups and a group was assigned to each sector. They got together at the end of the day and they came up with a very, very helpful, useful log of information that we used the next morning.

—1st Deputy Commissioner (2004–2010) Frank Cruthers,
then an Assistant Chief at Headquarters, Downtown Brooklyn
(served as Chief of Department 1996–1997, 2002–2004)

“ Well, using the management teams [IMT], they went and got this stuff. They fulfill both the planning function and also the logistics function of incident command.... I was relieved of that planning and logistics part of it, and eventually even some of the finance administration.

Daily meetings would start, and it had to be about, at the beginning, it was like 60 agencies there, agencies I never heard of. They were there. Federal agencies, state agencies.

We would have two meetings. One, 6, 6:30 in the morning, and this was the plan for the day at the site there. At 5:30 at night, we had another meeting and we would look at the day's work and the plan, and what was achieved, what was accomplished. If the task and the plan was accomplished, all right, we'd check that off. If it wasn't completed, it was only half through, then we would roll it over to the next day in the plan. What it did is it gave a tactical approach to the strategy that we were employing.

Initially, everybody was cooperating and knew the immensity, the tragedy that occurred and they need to set everything right... There's always inter-agency disagreements but that gets resolved now. Everybody wants to do their own thing, and do what they think is best.

At one point in time, at the height of it, we had 19 cranes operating. Before we allowed them to permanently place their the cranes there, we had to make sure that we had completed a search there. All that went into the incident action plan, daily plan, all the agencies were aware of that going on.

—Chief of Department (2004–2006) Pete Hayden, then a Deputy Chief in Division 1, SoHo, Manhattan

" Because throughout the day, we were building the plan to kind of go over at the planning meeting and, you know, filling in the last-minute details that we needed to. So, at those – at those late afternoon planning meetings, uh, which was primarily Pete Hayden and and there were a couple of other folks there. We were just kind of laying out the – what we had put together and what information gaps we needed to fill, and they were filling those for us. What cover photo we were gonna use, who was on the organizational chart, you know, all of those kind of things. Getting thumbs up from Pete, and then we were – we had a – we were – we were putting it together that, you know, the finalizing it within an hour or so of that meeting, and that-that meeting always happened like at 5:00 or 6:00 in the evening as I recall.

Well, I think initially, it was a little difficult. Uh, number one, people didn't know what we were after, and we didn't necessarily know what we were after. But as the acceptance of the document grew, and we measured that by the fact that over the first day we produced it, three-quarters of them were left in the room at the end. The next day, half of them. The next day there were only a few. The next day we didn't have enough. And the fact our operations people who were out on the four different sectors, would go into the sector and the sector commanders from FDNY would say, 'Where's our plans?' and so, that shifted the dynamic of, okay, now we know it's being used. That took – that took a few days, after we started producing the plan. So it probably wasn't until maybe two weeks into the incident that we felt the plan's accepted, the document. And maybe it became somewhat of a comforting thing for people, too, that there is structure to this chaos. Maybe-maybe there was some of that, in addition to whatever it said on the inside, uh, of the plan. But the fact that there is a written plan, you know, I think that that-that-that provides a sense of calm, uh, for-for some people.

—Paul Summerfelt, Commander National Area Command Team (2013-2020), then Planning Section Chief Southwest-IMT, Deputy Chief Flagstaff, AZ Fire Department (served as Type-1 IMT Incident Commander 2008-2012)

" Basically, they were divided up into smaller groups and a group was assigned to each sector. They got together at the end of the day and they came up with a very, very helpful, useful log of information that we used the next morning. It was an overall report...that was produced. Basically, a daily action report, which was: What did we accomplish yesterday? Who's going to do what? What are we going to do today? Greatly to their credit, the quality of it all was what caused the mayor to request the copy of those for daily use in his dealing with other branches of government and with the press.

—1st Deputy Commissioner (2004–2010) Frank Cruthers, then an Assistant Chief at Headquarters, Downtown Brooklyn (served as Chief of Department 1996–1997, 2002–2004)

Reflections and implications: learning about IMT and learning about learning

The SW-IMT and the FDNY learned how to do incident management in the canyons of New York City, at a scene of mass destruction and death. They learned together – Forest Service offering and adapting, FDNY receiving and changing.

" I don't recall who suggested or how they ended up here even, but I found out, we had the Forest Service and they were going to help us with incident management. I was a little befuddled about how could the forest service be of any use to us in this urban environment.

—Fire Commissioner (2014–2022) Dan Nigro,
then Chief of Operations Headquarters, Downtown Brooklyn
(served as Chief of Department 2001–2002)

“ All I was picturing is, oh my God. I know they can do it, but if one of them comes in here with that sort of a cowboy attitude, and maybe a steel helmet from the Forest Service, it's going to be like, 'Stop right there. You're not going to tell us what to do.' That would have been the end. The IMT was a perfect fit. We know the upside of the IMTs. The downside is you don't know, as in life, if the wrong guy shows up in charge of the IMT, it's done. It's cooked. It's finished. If the right guy shows up, it'll sound like a finely tuned symphony in a short time, because they don't come in and dominate, they come in and blend, educate, show the benefits of all of those things. That was Dan [Oltrogge]. Dan was the guy. It was just all I could picture when I said, 'Sure, let's roll the IMTs.'

—2nd Deputy Commissioner Tom Fitzpatrick,
then at Headquarters, Downtown Brooklyn

“ I think I was curious as to – I guess I'm very territorial too. I wanted to make sure we're still running things. We're not turning this operation over to the Forest Service by any – this is still Fire Department operation. Let me make that very clear by showing up and making that point. They had no intention of managing the job. They did all the nuts and bolts and weaned our people out of our old ways and into the new method of managing a long, long, long complex operation.

—Fire Commissioner (2014–2022) Dan Nigro,
then Chief of Operations Headquarters, Downtown Brooklyn
(served as Chief of Department 2001–2002)

“ That period was our introduction, although we didn't know it at the time. We were going to be introduced to the incident management system of the – wildfire service. That was our introduction to that and that's first time to hear about the limitations on how long you can work, what is going to happen, the stages of recovery, almost like the grief thing when someone you know passed away.

—Firefighter Louis Giaconelli, then in Engine 53, Spanish Harlem, Manhattan; FDNY IMT

“ I know the whole IMT issue, when they came in, and I do remember meeting them at Duane Street at the firehouse. I had my doubts. I had no idea what they did but once I learned, I thought they would be helpful. Of course, they were, and helped us develop a system.

—Fire Commissioner (2014–2022) Dan Nigro, then Chief of Operations Headquarters, Downtown Brooklyn (served as Chief of Department 2001–2002)

“ They [the IMT] spoke FEMA, they spoke the language, they did all that stuff together. We didn't have that. We had incident command, but we had never exercised or trained people to the finite levels within the incident command system to be able to fill in and do those functions, which we knew would be necessary. I think if we had had a class on September 10th and said, 'Who's going to be the logistics officer? Who's going to be in charge of getting widgets from some other state? Who's going to be in charge?' That would be like, 'What are you asking us that for? Somebody will do that.' We couldn't conceive of that happening. Some other agency must do that. They probably do, but those other agencies never had the experience of trying to reach out on this scale.

—2nd Deputy Commissioner Tom Fitzpatrick, then at Headquarters, Downtown Brooklyn

“ We never had this sort of a checklist of items and who's going to do what segment of incident command that comes so natural to the incident command team now. Little by little, you appreciated that this was a good thing which is why we copied it. Anything that was going on, whether it was the pandemic, or the incident command team, when we started running out of people, we used the incident command team to help us make sure we could staff all our engines, trucks, and ambulances.

—Fire Commissioner (2014–2022) Dan Nigro, then Chief of Operations Headquarters, Downtown Brooklyn (served as Chief of Department 2001–2002)

“ Part of that is all working under one management system. The [Forest] service has been following an incident command system since 1970. We were the only agency in the city that followed it. We were operating under one management system, for handling emergencies, and the other agencies didn’t understand the jargon, the language, and the structure of this and that. They were operating differently, which in many times, throughout operation of city, led to ineffective operations.

—Chief of Department (2004–2006) Pete Hayden,
then a Deputy Chief in Division 1, SoHo, Manhattan

“ I was still overall commander. I think Frank Cruthers might have been running the operation at that time on-site. We went up to the third floor, and these folks were there, and then we met with them, and I was – it took me a little time to appreciate what it is they were going to do for us. I think it helped that they won over some of the members like Frank and some of the others who worked with them daily. I think they would start their mornings there. The leadership at the Trade Center site would start their mornings on Duane Street [FDNY-ICP] with these folks, and they would go over these lists that we never had before.

—Fire Commissioner (2014–2022) Dan Nigro,
then Chief of Operations Headquarters, Downtown Brooklyn
(served as Chief of Department 2001–2002)

“ It’s pretty nebulous. It was Frank Cruthers and Pete Hayden being comfortable with us going out the door, and it was Frank Cruthers and Pete Hayden understanding that we could bring in another organization that we trusted that would be able to carry on because the work itself that was such a long duration, especially when we went from rescue to recovery. I think recovery probably ended in like the spring of the following year. It’s a long duration. Frank [Cruthers] wanted to keep us till Christmas and we were not interested in that, so we started working on and educating them on how we did business and how we transitioned and transferred command.

—Dan Oltrogge, Commander National Area Command
Team (2009–2011), then Incident Commander Trainee SW-IMT,
Chief of Fire and Aviation Grand Canyon National Park
(served as SW-IMT Incident Commander 2003–2007)

“ They stayed there for 30 days, and then they were relieved by the Alaskan incident management team. They got an extra 30-day extension. They were there for 60 days, so the total of 90 days, we had the incident management teams there. A tremendous asset to any organization.

—Chief of Department (2004–2006) Pete Hayden, then a Deputy Chief in Division 1, SoHo, Manhattan

“ Anne [Venemen, US secretary of Agriculture] had come to the Trade Center, and I escorted her around to her people and so on. At one point, in a light conversation, I said ‘If somebody told me six weeks ago that we were going to have the biggest disaster we’ve ever had, and the Forest Service was going to bail us out, I’d have had that person committed, but thank God you’re here.’

—1st Deputy Commissioner (2004–2010) Frank Cruthers, then an Assistant Chief at Headquarters, Downtown Brooklyn (served as Chief of Department 1996–1997, 2002–2004)

“ I knew if somebody from the [forest] service talked to Chief Hayden, it will work. Maybe for somebody else, they would say, ‘It’s not going to work.’ For the most part, the majority of people recognized, I think, Chief Hayden said it. We needed to accept help when we needed help. That’s the way it worked.

—2nd Deputy Commissioner Tom Fitzpatrick, then at Headquarters, Downtown Brooklyn

“ I have said over and over again, of all of the help that we got from outside the city, I thought, from my perspective, they were the most helpful.

—1st Deputy Commissioner (2004–2010) Frank Cruthers, then an Assistant Chief at Headquarters, Downtown Brooklyn (served as Chief of Department 1996–1997, 2002–2004)

“ In this case, it exposed a new generation of people to what was possible, that they might have not thought possible before 9/11. It gave the department a chance to accept things that needed to change. Before that, it was just, ‘No, we don’t want that,’ or, ‘We don’t do that.’ I think it matured, it was a new development of emergency management that shocked the city [New York government officials]. I’m sure it did, because even the city probably thought, ‘We’re the city, we have the greatest fire department in the world, the greatest police department in the world, biggest sanitation department in the world, the best parks department in the world. We got it all. What do you want to tell us?' I think it all got everybody's attention. It was sad that a tragic event, as throughout history, tragic events are the things that bring out the best.

—2nd Deputy Commissioner Tom Fitzpatrick, then at Headquarters, Downtown Brooklyn

" I said, 'Pete' [Hayden], who looked 'really worn out. I said, 'Hey, just –' Because I had great respect for him and I wanted to – I certainly didn't want to try and big-time him, but I said, 'We've done one or two of these, not like this, but long duration.' I said, 'What we've learned over the years is you have to pace yourself. This is a marathon. You cannot outwork these things. It's not going to happen.' He just looked at me and just said, 'Danny, I got no choice. That's my world,' and he walked away.

—Dan Oltrogge, Commander National Area Command Team (2009–2011), then Incident Commander Trainee SW-IMT, Chief of Fire and Aviation Grand Canyon National Park (served as SW-IMT Incident Commander 2003–2007)

Part B: Summary, Lessons, and Commentary

Summary

Within New York City, Mayoral Directives determine which agency has the lead for different categories of emergencies. Responsibilities may shift with changes in administrations, as agency heads lobby each mayor for increased responsibilities.

As of 2001, the FDNY was lead agency for response to and mitigation of fires, aircraft crashes, building collapses, and consequences of terrorism, among others. The FDNY responsibilities clearly covered all aspects of the WTC incident. However, FDNY's hold as lead agency was tenuous at best. Multiple agencies at all levels of government could potentially make a case for incident lead. The Mayor could simply sign a new directive assigning another agency.

Which agencies? It could have been the Port Authority of NY and NJ. The WTC was not built under NYC jurisdiction or building codes. It was constructed under the jurisdiction of the Port Authority. The complex was patrolled by the Port Authority Police Department, which lost 47 officers. Or it could have been the NYPD, the largest police department in the country, which lost 23 officers. They felt they should manage the site. At the federal level, there was precedent for FEMA taking control. Paul Summerfelt of the SW-IMT explained: "Typically, when we were called to an incident, where local responders were unable to manage the incident, it got too big, they were overwhelmed, regardless of what the reasons, they just needed help. When we arrived, typically local responders stepped back, [the IMT] take command of an incident."

It was up to FDNY leadership to retain control. But top commanders are appointed based on their tactical excellence and strong leadership. Ultimately, they are firefighters not politicians. That distinction, usually a point of pride within the department, could become a liability when navigating among authorities with overlapping jurisdictions and with several aspiring to control the site.

At the same time, the FDNY is an organization steeped in some traditions, firefighters, viewed as non-negotiable. Captain Paul Brown, a third-generation New York City firefighter, explained one of the most sacred: "We carry our own out. When a firefighter falls, they are carried out by their own unit. It is a debt of honor. At the WTC, if the firefighter's family was on the job, they were involved. But, in the end, firefighters carry firefighters out." The idea that another agency might exert control over how the FDNY recovered its own was beyond repugnant.

Layered onto these institutional realities was profound loss—of people, of equipment, of operational capacity. The scale of the trauma created a rare moment of vulnerability for the department. Could an organization that had suffered so deeply still function effectively as the unprecedented work continued?

History had proven that the FDNY held enough resources to rotate units through several days or even a week at any incident. The WTC operations were of a scope, tempo, and duration not seen before. Direct operations on site would continue for months. Recovery from departmental losses compounded with on-scene challenges were daunting. Taken individually, each challenge would be the most complex task in the history of the department.

Outside resources continued to arrive, including Incident Management Teams from the Department of the Interior. Initial forays by IMTs met with mixed reaction and impact. The approach to working directly with the FDNY would change quickly and to significant effect.

The FDNY relieved Frank Cruthers and Pete Hayden of their regular daily duties and assigned full responsibility for the site. They were charged with managing all FDNY resources while simultaneously filtering an overwhelming influx of volunteers and external assistance. The volume of help itself became a problem. As Chief Cruthers recalled: "It was a matter of I didn't need the same kind of help that I already had." He continued: "Over the course of the next few days, the plan would change many, many times as to how we were going to go about this, how we were going to use our manpower – how many people we would have there. We had no experience in operating a scene for weeks and months. We were used to operating at scenes for up to a day or two."

What transpired next would forever change the FDNY. Chief Cruthers had a conversation with Denis Oneial from FEMA who was recommending Incident Management Teams. He had to confess complete ignorance regarding their function, but he was willing to listen.

A group from the Southwest Incident Management Team had been observing FDNY operations on the pile. With Deputy Commissioner Tom Fitzpatrick's cooperation the SW-IMT moved into a small room on the third floor of the Duane Street firehouse. They would spend the next few days quietly observing FDNY command inside the Task Force Headquarters.

Oneial then facilitated a meeting between the FDNY and the SW-IMT. But agreeing to that meeting carried risk. Had Cruthers exposed the FDNY's vulnerability? Would "The Feds" take command of the site? Chief Hayden understood the concern – but also the necessity. "I knew down deep I needed the help," he acknowledged. They agreed to meet. Hayden remembered the first exchange: "He's [Oltrogge] basically, like, 'Can I speak to you? I may be of some help to you.'" Oltrogge explained the capabilities of Incident Management teams. The parties then agreed to meet later. When they sat in the office, Hayden listened, and it became clear that the IMT was there to help, not take over.

In fact, SW-IMT members had already been quietly observing FDNY operations for several days. They learned from their earlier attempts to connect with the FDNY. They studied not only the physical operations, but also took notice of behind-the-scenes issues. Dan Oltrogge, from the SW IMT, observed: "We were impressed with how the FDNY planted their flag and kept it there 'cause we knew there had to be a lot of pressure coming from elsewhere to take that flag." Paul Summerfelt added, "We recognized immediately we were not taking command of this situation. There was way too much ownership, rightly so."

What the Southwest Incident Management Team offered was not control, but capacity. They introduced the New York City Fire Department to the discipline of modern incident management – systems designed to sustain large workforces over extended periods, support leaders under prolonged stress, and bring structure to incidents that no longer fit traditional response models.

Lessons for Leaders

1 **Recognize when your world changes.** The FDNY first needed to understand that the scope and nature of the challenge before it made this time different. Significantly different.

2 **Embrace the fact of your ignorance.** That's cognitive and it's emotional. It's external reality based and it's a felt need born of humility. Embracing ignorance about something of importance leads to openness to assistance and to learning...and to the change that they might precipitate.

3 **Stay proactive.** Use what you know while you figure "it" out. Carry on doing what you know how to do until further notice... and learn from using what you know. Use the known approaches to inform your search for what else you need, to demonstrate what you need.

4 **Remember the importance of relationships in making anything complicated work...today and especially tomorrow.** Notice damage to relational networks that accompanies the loss of people. Reach anew into established relationships, relationships perhaps used differently in the past, including with federal agencies.

5 **Experiment.** "Try stuff," including watching for possibilities to help and to be helped. Recognize a possibility when it occurs.

6 **Offer and look for competent helping.** Rushing in and declaring "I'm from...and I'm here to help" creates an added "to do." Calling "help!" provides insufficient guidance. If you want to help, then study – Who are you looking to help? What, concretely, can you provide that would help? Help the recipient understand what you offer that they would most likely find of value.

Major forest fires leave behind smoky, charred wastelands. And yet, after a seemingly impossibly short stretch of time, sprouts shoot through

FDNY

INCIDENT ACTION PLAN

OPERATIONAL PERIOD

SEPTEMBER 27 - 28, 2001

0700 - 0700

IMT Action Plan
Front cover of September 27 to 28 IMT Action Plan. The full Action Plan appears in Appendix 6.
Public Record

blackened soil and reach toward the sun. The same forest may not return, but something living and verdant usually does.

Crises can yield the same phenomenon. Even amid pressure and loss, new possibilities – small at first – can emerge from the wreckage. Leaders should notice these early "sprouts" and nurture them. New people may arrive, bringing the potential for beneficial relationships. Pay attention. Encourage what works. Invest in it. When something promising appears, consider how to sustain it...and perhaps how to scale or transplant it elsewhere.

New possibilities may also emerge from established relationships. Ask not only what people know, but whom they know and who might help now, under these conditions. Seek and offer assistance deliberately. Random offers rarely land. Search for the right receptors and go to them. Proceed respectfully and concretely, step by step. People under the duress of crisis, especially ongoing crisis and extended hard times, have low tolerance for disrespect. Weariness and strain make people edgy. Hence, potential recipients of help should demand – and potential providers of help should provide – proof of value. They should proceed step by step. Developing proof of value promised and delivered spawns credibility...and trust.

Effective collaboration takes time. Time pressures notwithstanding, patience can make the difference in both the development of key relationships and the production of consequential outcomes. Relationships often need time to form, trust to develop, and roles to clarify. Accordingly, leaders should stay alert, adjust as they learn, and keep listening. In short, leaders should look not only to rebuild, but to recreate – renewal often begins with relationships, old and new.

Commentary

This chapter offers a case study in what makes effective help possible. Federal agencies offered significant aid to the FDNY. Also, the FDNY received significant aid from federal agencies. The Southwest Incident Management Team facilitated connecting the FDNY with highly beneficial assistance. Assistance it did not know existed. Together, these combined efforts made help happen and reveal a fundamental truth: effective help is relational. No relationship, no effective help.

The meeting described in this chapter evidences the creation of such a relationship. Neither inevitable nor scripted, the meeting opened the door to ongoing collaboration and lasting change. Edgar Schein's analysis of helping, articulated in his book by the same name, provides a way to understand how the helping took hold.[44]

Schein writes about individual, group, and organizational helping primarily from the perspective of the helper or consultant. This case, by contrast, underscores the interdependence of helper and recipient. Effective help emerges when both sides play their part.

> **Principle 1:** "Effective help occurs when both giver and receiver are ready." The Forest Service did not give up after its initial, unsuccessful attempt to assist, nor did it simply repeat it. Rather, its personnel studied the situation and the FDNY. They observed and adapted their approach toward helping as the FDNY moved toward a readiness to receive help.
>
> **Principle 2:** "Effective help occurs when the helping relationship is perceived to be equitable." Equitable does not mean equal. Both the Forest Service and the FDNY had contributions to make and needs to meet.
>
> **Principle 3:** "Effective help occurs when the helper is in the proper helping role." In the case at hand, Forest Service personnel figured out what the FDNY needed – such as field communications support and incident action planning – and, equally important, what it did not want: namely, a boss.
>
> **Principle 4:** "Everything you say or do is an intervention that determines the future of the relationship." For example, wearing casual attire rather than agency uniforms reduced signals of differentness and competing authority. Taking time to listen, politely and intently, amid overwhelming demands demonstrated respect and helped to shape the future of the relationship.
>
> **Principle 5:** "Effective helping starts with pure inquiry." Pure inquiry means "accessing your ignorance." Forest Service personnel went to the site to learn. They learned not only the help needed but also how to proceed in offering it.

They learned that the FDNY controlled the site and had no intention of relinquishing that control. Characteristically, FDNY leaders began this meeting with very New York directness: “What can you do for me?” Offputting? Perhaps. Ground clearing? Absolutely.

Principle 6: “It is the client who owns the problem.” The FDNY firmly gripped the problem of work at the WTC site. The Forest Service did not seek to take the problem away. Instead, it helped to loosen and then change the grip enough to enable the FDNY to work the problem differently, more effectively.

Principle 7: “You never have all the answers.” Both helper and client came to that conclusion. Mutual acknowledgment of limitation, both cognitive and emotional, creates the conditions for utilizing complementarity and, ultimately, even synergy.

This helping relationship evolved and deepened over time. It endures to this day. The collaboration between the Forest Service and the FDNY grew into a national resource, an ongoing and valuable local and national legacy of a searing tragedy.

That legacy began with a meeting of a handful of individuals officially representing thousands of others. That encounter yielded deep organizational change in how the FDNY did its work and, eventually, how it defined itself. The story illustrates how individual behavior can produce effective helping between and within organizations – across units, professions, departments, agencies, and even national borders. The story bears remembering. It illustrates a set of principles worth remembering as well, worth remembering especially in times of disruption and uncertainty, in critical times and in times of prolonged crisis and protracted hard times.

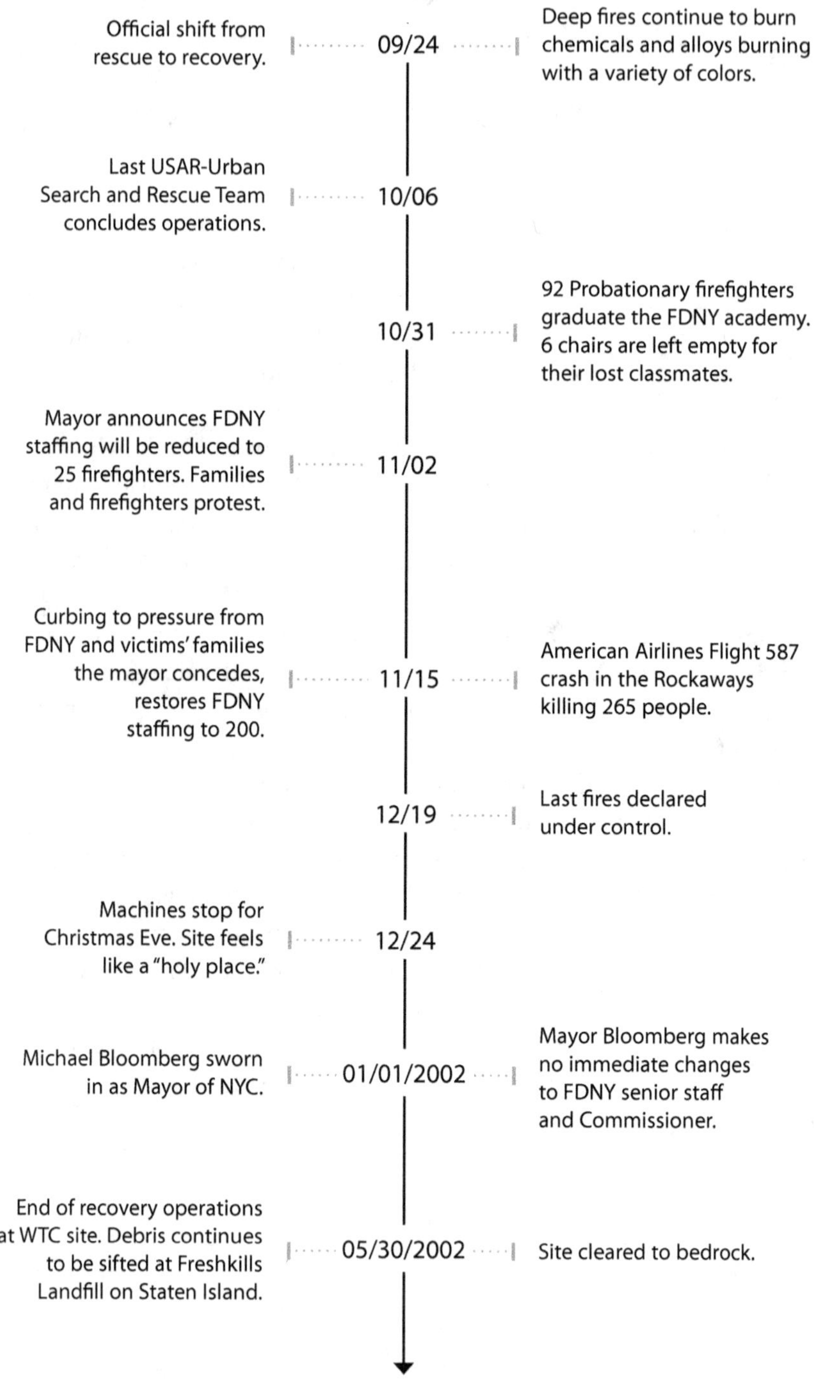
Official shift from rescue to recovery.
09/24
Deep fires continue to burn chemicals and alloys burning with a variety of colors.
Last USAR-Urban Search and Rescue Team concludes operations.
10/06
10/31
92 Probationary firefighters graduate the FDNY academy. 6 chairs are left empty for their lost classmates.
Mayor announces FDNY staffing will be reduced to 25 firefighters. Families and firefighters protest.
11/02
Curbing to pressure from FDNY and victims' families the mayor concedes, restores FDNY staffing to 200.
11/15
American Airlines Flight 587 crash in the Rockaways killing 265 people.
12/19
Last fires declared under control.
Machines stop for Christmas Eve. Site feels like a "holy place."
12/24
Michael Bloomberg sworn in as Mayor of NYC.
01/01/2002
Mayor Bloomberg makes no immediate changes to FDNY senior staff and Commissioner.
End of recovery operations at WTC site. Debris continues to be sifted at Freshkills Landfill on Staten Island.
05/30/2002
Site cleared to bedrock.

Chapter Eight

The Recovery and Cleanup: Two Weeks to Eight Months Post-9/11

> I remember after 9/11, there's a national wildfire organization.... As New Yorkers, we always know that they had these big incident management teams...We thought we were so big that we couldn't learn a thing from these people, but we did.
>
> —*Captain Jeff Simms, then a Lieutenant in Engine 58, Harlem, Manhattan; FDNY IMT*

> When we find one of our brothers and sisters, when you're asking how long is it going to take, it's going to take as long as it takes. And that's it. That's it.
>
> —*Chief of Department (2020–2022) Tom Richardson, then a Battalion Chief in Battalion 53, Bayside, Queens*

> “When I was down on the site supervising firefighters, trying to dig their brothers and sisters out of there, and civilians. It was so disgusting, the stuff that we saw.
>
> *—Chief of Operations Pat McNally, then a Deputy Chief in Division 14, Flushing, Queens*

> “The community, the volunteer people came from all over to help. Whatever they could do.... It was a good time to be in the city. I got to say that.
>
> *—Captain Kerry Hollywood, then in Engine 53, Spanish Harlem, Manhattan; Commanding Officer Family Assistance Unit*

> “I think of all the health issues that are confronting the firefighters today, there were times where the smoke was green coming up out of those piles. It was terrible. It was really terrible.
>
> *—Chief of Department (2004–2006) Pete Hayden, then a Deputy Chief in Division 1, SoHo, Manhattan*

The FDNY imported and adapted a system to manage the monstrous task before it. The Southwest Incident Management Team would support the department through October 15 remaining 2 weeks longer than typical deployments. The Alaska Incident Management followed and remained for an extended 4 week deployment. The last FEMA dispatched Urban Search and Rescue team (USAR) left on 10/06. The FDNY then had a new chief and a rebuilt chain of command. Its firefighting onsite would last until December 19, 2001. Recovery operations on site would run until May 30, 2002.

Healing would take much longer. Its early contours appeared on October 31, 2001, as symbolized by six empty chairs at the first post-9/11 graduation ceremony, six chairs reserved for classmates killed when the towers collapsed. Everything had to scale, everything from incident management and operations to the work of honoring and tending to the dead.

Part A: Responder Voices

Organizing

Early Operations

> “ What was happening was there was no continuity of the operation. One chief officer would come in on one day and he wanted this done and that done. The next guys come in and they wanted something else done. At the time, I was the division commander and there were staff always above me. It was a little delicate because I was giving orders and staying there, I wouldn't go home till 9, 10 o'clock at night and be back at six o'clock in the morning.
>
> *—Chief of Department (2004–2006) Pete Hayden, then a Deputy Chief Division 1, SoHo, Manhattan*

> “ I think what worked is we didn't try to totally reimagine the department. I think we all accepted the fact that we did a good job that day. We did everything we could and then some for the sake of the poor people that were trapped that day. We didn't try to recreate the wheel, but we tried to just streamline it, and people accepted that that way.
>
> *—Fire Commissioner (2014–2022) Dan Nigro, then Chief of Operations Headquarters, Downtown Brooklyn (served as Chief of Department 2001–2002)*

Shift from Rescue to Recovery

> “ We never said we're in recovery, it's always just ‘rescue and recovery’ because you just would never say that to the victims' families and staff that we weren't on recovery, but we were at a time.
>
> *—Chief of Department (2004–2006) Pete Hayden, then a Deputy Chief in Division 1, SoHo, Manhattan*

> “ At the three-week mark, we had to make that transition because there is a difference between rescue and recovery. I will risk injury if I can recover a live victim. I'm not going to risk injury to dig out a body. That was one of the biggest challenges, making people understand,

why we're doing it. That was important.

—Deputy Assistant Chief John Norman, Chief of Special Operations, then a Battalion Chief in Battalion 16, Harlem, Manhattan; FDNY USAR

" Now, as this time goes on, as [NYC Mayor] Giuliani says, 'If you want a death certificate, we'll issue one, but you don't have to take one. If you want one, we'll give it to you.' When they move from that brilliant statement into accelerated debris removal using the cranes, that's when that whole thing changed. That's my observation. Again, the realization after about seven days of finding body parts, the bodies, that this isn't going to have a happy ending.

—Denis Onieal, Senior FEMA Rep., then Superintendent, National Fire Academy

" That was when they decided to cut the manpower, fire department manpower that was down at the [site] digging. There was a big protest, and they showed the guys getting locked up [on TV].

—Battalion Chief Bill Moore, then in Battalion 10, Yorkville, Manhattan

Utter devastation
Last standing Remnants of the North and South Towers.
Shared with permission from the Daniel Quinn private collection

"There was a period [when]...the mayor...wanted to shut the site down.... Guys got arrested. There were fights on the street....[T]hey didn't want to do that.

—Fire Commissioner (2014–2022) Dan Nigro,
then Chief of Operations Headquarters, Downtown Brooklyn
(served as Chief of Department 2001–2002)

"They [the firefighters] wanted to keep it a recovery operation.... [T]he mayor...got beat up for that...but they came to their senses.

—Chief of Department (2020–2022) Tom Richardson,
then a Battalion Chief in Battalion 53,
Bayside, Queens

"After two weeks, after three weeks, I'm like, there's nobody alive here, man. There's no way. So when the rescue part was clearly over, only the recovery. If you remember back, there was a period of time where the Mayor, he wanted to shut the site down and make it strictly a recovery operation. Guys got arrested. There were fights on the street. There was protests, Cops, firemen. It got very ugly.

—Chief of Department (2020–2022) Tom Richardson,
then a Battalion Chief in Battalion 53,
Bayside, Queens

"We're three weeks into this, which then got us into a huge political issue because the mayor now wants to – if there are no survivors, why do I have 1,000 people, 1,000 firefighters on scene every day looking when there are no survivors? The mayor's office made the decision, we're going to shrink the workforce. We're going to cut it from 1,000 firefighters to[25] firefighters per shift. Those same people are still looking for their relatives. They're not going to find live relatives, but they're still looking for their bodies and they didn't want to give up. They did not want to say, 'Okay, you stay over in what we call the bullpen. When the construction worker unearths a body with an excavator, we'll let you go out and retrieve the body parts.' We had almost a mutiny on scene.

—Deputy Assistant Chief John Norman, Chief of Special Operations,
then a Battalion Chief in Battalion 16, Harlem, Manhattan;
FDNY USAR

BC John Norman
Battalion Chief John Norman supervising search operations.
Andrea Booher, Public domain, via Wikimedia Commons

> I know at one point, not too long after we switched [from rescue to recovery], the City made a decision to severely cut the number of people we had at the site, and that did not sit well with the members or their families, and that was shut down right away. That idea, it actually never actually happened. The backlash on that was such – it was a semi-riot that occurred with the members storming the site with some family members. They were going to go to the site, to pray, and it was obvious that this was a poor decision, poor thought-out decision.
>
> —*Fire Commissioner Dan Nigro (2014–2022, then Chief of Operations Headquarters, Downtown Brooklyn (served as Chief of Department 2001–2022)*

Recovery

> I'm foggy on the date, but one important bit of information that came from outside and down, I think somebody contacted the commissioner, and it was a person who's – I don't recall but not from anywhere

around here, who had dealt with major catastrophes and said, 'Basically, I know the thought process that you're trying to make searches without disturbing the debris for fear of further injuring someone who might be alive. If you're going to get anywhere with this, even as far as finding people is concerned, you really have to start fully engaging the heavy equipment.' That was a bit of a relief, because we knew we had to use the heavy equipment, but whoever he was, he was exactly right on the reluctance.

—1st Deputy Commissioner (2004–2010) Frank Cruthers,
then an Assistant Chief at Headquarters, Downtown Brooklyn
(served as Chief of Department 1996–1997, 2002–2004)

“ It's very clear that this hand digging is just a waste of manpower, because they're mining body parts and no survivors. The challenge is that we've got these huge pieces of steel that are impeding a lot of the digging, and so we had to get a crane in to start to lift the steel. We knew that once we brought a crane in, the firefighters are going to have to be taken off the pile, because it's too dangerous.

—Denis Onieal, Senior FEMA Rep., Superintendent,
National Fire Academy

“ It was probably the most stressful time I spent in the fire department... guys are digging with little hand tools...and like, you're not getting them out with hand tools, bro. Like, we've got to get a machine in here. And sometimes when you did that, it didn't go well...it was very, very upsetting for a lot of people.

—Chief of Department (2020–2022) Tom Richardson,
then a Battalion Chief in Battalion 53,
Bayside, Queens

“ As the backhoes and the heavy construction material were pulling out, the debris was so heavily impacted – we were finding nothing but body parts.... It was quite an unsettling period of time for the firefighters, emotional.... They saw a lot of stuff that was just terrible. It really was terrible.

—Chief of Department (2004–2006) Pete Hayden,
then a Deputy Chief in Division 1,
SoHo, Manhattan

Learning

“I was assigned to stay down there. Every day, there were firefighters and companies coming in and chief officers coming in and executing whatever strategy we had implemented to work for the rescue operations. After 17 days, we went from a rescue operation to strictly recovery.

—Chief of Department (2004–2006) Pete Hayden, then a Deputy Chief in Division 1, SoHo, Manhattan

“I remember after 9/11, there's a national wildfire organization. They're the ones that put out those wildfires out West. As New Yorkers, we always knew that they had these big incident management teams. We never really applied it to us because we are structural. We go inside. We thought that our department was so big that we couldn't learn a thing from these people, but we did. How to organize something large. How do we expand it as necessary. They stood to the side and told us, how they could help, and this is what they're capable of doing.

—Captain Jeff Simms, then a Lieutenant in Engine 58, Harlem, Manhattan; FDNY IMT

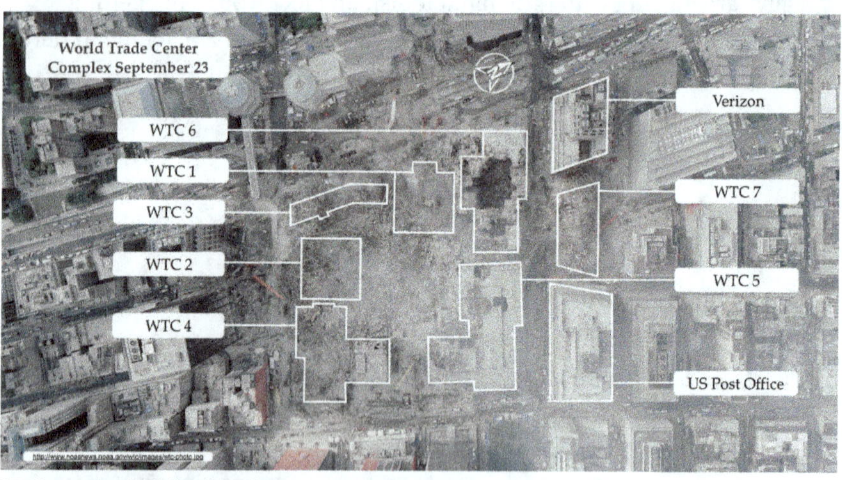

WTC complex building locations

Building outlines superimposed on the NOAA image recorded on September 23, 2001.

National Oceanic and Atmospheric Administration (NOAA), Public domain, via Wikimedia Commons
Edited by the authors

“ They finally said, you know what, let's just take a contingent of firefighters of all the ranks and assign them down to the World Trade Center, not do this piecemeal detailing of people day in and day out, which helped.

—Battalion Chief George Maier, Battalion 9, Hell's Kitchen, Manhattan; FDNY IMT

“ [We were] continuing to gain traction on being helpful. And now our organization down there at the pile with us is beginning to grow. So, we took our operations people, since we didn't have any tactical responsibilities, the FDNY held tight to that, and urban search-and-rescue [USAR] and that was fine because that's not our expertise. We took our operations people and we put one of them on every shift in a sector command post. They were there to simply gather intel. Then intel would come back to us at the Incident Command Post [Duane Street], so we could factor that into the next day's incident action plan. We could validate and verify with FDNY: Is this a significant piece of business? Do we want this included [in the IAP], do we need to share this or that?

—Dan Oltrogge, Commander National Area Command Team (2009–2011), then Incident Commander Trainee SW-IMT, Chief of Fire and Aviation Grand Canyon National Park (served as SW-IMT Incident Commander 2003–2007)

“ Before that, we were really moving by Braille, we didn't really have any intel because FDNY was not used to, in their system, any intel coming back, that would be outside of their chain of command. That wasn't in the cards, but now it was. That was occurring. It was a big deal to us; it was very helpful. Now we also had in each sector a command post. We have a resource tactical asset tracking mechanism that we used in that incident command system and we were allowed to set that up and staff that in each sector command post, and that would allow them to track on a minute-by-minute basis exactly where all of their assets were at any given time.

—Dan Oltrogge, Commander National Area Command Team (2009–2011), then Incident Commander Trainee SW-IMT, Chief of Fire and Aviation Grand Canyon National Park (served as SW-IMT Incident Commander 2003–2007)

Aerial view of 6 World Trade Center
Aerial view of crater in the center of the U.S. Customs House (6 WTC) caused by collapse of the North Tower.
U.S. National Oceanic and Atmospheric Administration (NOAA). Aerial view of the World Trade Center site showing damage to Building 6. September 23, 2001. Public Domain

> “ For the fire department, it was an easy move to adopt incident management. Other agencies fought tooth and nail. There were ridiculous arguments just below municipal level with the police department, who absolutely refused, and the basic reason is because they believe they should be in charge of everything.
>
> *—1st Deputy Commissioner (2004–2010) Frank Cruthers, then an Assistant Chief at Headquarters, Downtown Brooklyn (served as Chief of Department 1996–1997, 2002–2004)*

Becoming more organized

> “ I'd go to these meetings in the morning, it was like 80 people from all different agencies, the contractors, the ironworkers. There were politicians there. And I remember one time, there was a big to-do going on. This is right at that time, when the mayor's thinking about shutting it down. Because the contractors and some people were

saying, 'you know, these firemen and these cops, once they find a body, they're taking forever, it's slowing the operation down'. I got up and I said, listen, when we find one of our brothers and sisters, when you're asking how long is it going to take, it's going to take as long as it takes. And that's it. That's it. I said, so I know that you have work to do. We have work to do. And quite frankly, we can't do our work without you.

—Chief of Department (2020–2022) Tom Richardson, then a Battalion Chief in Battalion 53, Bayside, Queens

“ What we found, at least I found, particularly when I went out the second time, [rotated into WTC-TF] the first few weeks, you're making this up as you go along. It's never been done before. We went back, run it back in April, it's fairly well organized. We really were focusing on giving the families who were missing people, who didn't have a body to bury. The Catholic Church can't have a funeral if you don't have a body. People were dealing with that.

—Chief of Operations Pat McNally, then a Deputy Chief in Division 14, Flushing, Queens

“ I think it was a pretty squared away operation for such a big field and so many missing. It was separate commands in different areas. I think it was well done, the search pattern and the marking of remains and the GPS things. It's such an overwhelming event, it was pretty well coordinated.

Not only the fire. The community, the volunteer people came from all over to help. Whatever they could do. It got to a point that there had to be some control. Volunteers with food, volunteers with this. You need a place to sleep for three hours. Anything you wanted.

—Captain Kerry Hollywood, then in Engine 53, Spanish Harlem, Manhattan; Commanding Officer, Family Assistance Unit

“ I did go down for a month. It's different, but it's more advanced because they got it down, how they're going to do things. There was a roadway built to get out and stuff. When you met it, you found a member or found something of significance. It was a very solemn way that was handled. I specifically remember around two, three o'clock in the morning, we had – I got a call on the radio from, 'Hey, chief, we found somebody. It's a member.' I went, 'Okay,' because this was handled a very specific way. I said, 'Look, don't do anything until I get there.' They go, 'No, we're waiting for you.'

—Deputy Chief Jim DiDomenico, then in Division 13, South Jamaica, Queens

“ They found something, anything with remains, they would put a flag down and check a marking on it. The flag had a code on it where it was, they take a mark – this particular body part or whatever it is, at this spot. I don't know exactly where it all went. They put this number on this piece of a human being and they said, 'Okay, this is where we found Joe.' I'm assuming that's how it worked. GPS, I had no idea what it was at the time.

—Captain Kerry Hollywood, then in Engine 53, Spanish Harlem, Manhattan; Commanding Officer, Family Assistance Unit

“ The eight months until the end of May was a learning curve. Nobody had ever been through this before. We hadn't done it and hadn't even anticipated, but all right, we made a commitment that we're going to stay there and we're going to recover every human remains that we can find. That became the mission now.

—Deputy Assistant Chief John Norman, Chief of Special Operations, then a Battalion Chief in Battalion 16, Harlem, Manhattan; FDNY USAR

“ I think the members needed a little space and they needed…I was going to say less discipline. They needed room. They didn't need to be under the thumb as much as under normal times. I think gradually, as the weeks and months went by, that leash got reeled in a little bit more, but allowing people to maybe say or do things you wouldn't normally allow, but it's just something they needed.

—Fire Commissioner (2014–2022) Dan Nigro, then Chief of Operations Headquarters, Downtown Brooklyn (served as Chief of Department 2001–2002)

South Tower remnant
Last standing remnant of the South Tower.
Shared with permission from the Daniel Quinn private collection

Incident lead

> "Well, I think certainly, immediately after the planes went into the buildings, there was no issue as to who was in charge: it was the fire department. Other agencies were there and operating, but obviously, we were in charge, and after the buildings came down for that short-term period, I don't think there was any issue as to who was in charge.... Later on, over the course of the days, weeks, and months that followed, there were some issues. The Port Authority, they had a phrase, 'This is our house.' I think they felt as if they were being pushed aside somewhat and they should be in charge because it was their property at some point.
>
> The city agency, DDC [Department of Design and Construction], at some point felt and I think – I saw somewhere, somebody there wrote a book or an article and touted how they were running the operation. They were bringing in the heavy equipment and organizing that part of it. All in all, we felt as if we were the primary. We were supplying most of

the manpower before and after, and up until the end of May, we felt as if it was our operation and did our best to work with the other agencies and other people on hand, but it wasn't always easy.

Early on...I do recall National Guard folks being at the perimeter. NYPD started, I think, at maybe Canal Street, and then the perimeter was reduced over time.... The police always want to be in charge... they had their part to play. I think we were able for the most part to work with them okay.

Fires burned there for so long, and actually the fire burning underground went on, I think, until November, but it's just a recollection of mine. Oddly enough, I heard the fire – usually, the fire chief places any fire under control. I had the radio on one day. I think the governor said the fire was under control, which I thought was curious, but not that he was wrong. He was right. It was at that point under control.

—Fire Commissioner (2014–2022) Dan Nigro,
then Chief of Operations Headquarters, Downtown Brooklyn
(served as Chief of Department 2001–2002)

Fires burned until December 7
Grapplers operate on "The Pile" as underground fires continue to burn.
Shared with permission from the Daniel Quinn private collection

“ The emotional processing probably took quite some time. I think having a mission and engaging in work that you feel has a purpose helps tremendously. I talked to some of the other people who went through that and I think that was a common denominator that you have to put aside some of that mourning and that feeling of the loss and focus on, here's where we are. Here's where we need to go and we need to stay on point. I think that helped.

—Chief of Operations Pat McNally, then a Deputy Chief in Division 14, Flushing, Queens

“ I wound up staying and working at the site for several months, and my job, I was a liaison between special operations and the fire department and the building trades. I was doing 12-hour tours for the next several months.

—Chief of Department (2020–2022) Tom Richardson, then a Battalion Chief in Battalion 53, Bayside, Queens

“ I worked the overnight shift.... It was so peaceful down there in the middle of the night. Then the sun would come up and...everyone would just descend again.

—Stephanie Gaskell, then a journalist, Associated Press, New York (covered WTC site for duration of FDNY operations)

“ I remember telling my wife, 'You don't understand. We're still putting the fires out. They're still burning. It's not on the news, but they're still burning.' At that point, I was pretty angry about the complete inaccuracy of the information getting out. I did not appreciate being told that we couldn't do our job the way that we knew we should be doing their job. Particularly based on bad information.

—Captain Paul Brown, then a Lieutenant covering in Engine 234, Crown Heights, Brooklyn; FDNY IMT

“ It was terrible. I was a pretty new battalion chief. I was only in the field two months before 9/11 happened, so I'm pretty new to the rank still, but it was probably the most stressful time I spent in the fire department as a supervisor. Because, picture being down on the site, supervising firefighters, trying to dig their brothers and sisters out of there, and civilians. It was so disgusting, the stuff that we saw.

—Chief of Department (2020–2022) Tom Richardson,
then a Battalion Chief in Battalion 53,
Bayside, Queens

“I think of all the health issues that are confronting the firefighters today, there were times where the smoke was green coming up out of those piles. It was terrible. It was really terrible. People don't realize that we officially declared the fires out on December 7th. As the backhoes and the heavy construction material were pulling out, the debris was so heavily impacted. We would pull out 30, 40, 50-foot long pieces of steel, and they were cherry red, and they would light up once the oxygen hit them.

—Chief of Department (2004–2006) Pete Hayden,
then a Deputy Chief in Division 1,
SoHo, Manhattan

Volunteering at first responder dining canteen
Susan Sarandon (left) and Tim Robbins (center) volunteering at a responder canteen on Liberty Street.
Andrea Booher, Public domain, via Wikimedia Commons

“ In the nighttime, you couldn’t get enough help.... During the day...you couldn’t manage it. We picked up a trick.... ‘Your scent will interfere with the dog’.... We made this up.

—Assistant Chief Bob Maynes, Queens Boro Commander, then a Battalion Chief in Battalion 41, East Flatbush, Brooklyn, and past IMT Incident Commander

Recoveries

“ [W]e’re going to bring everybody home and treat every body part with dignity and respect that you would want your family member to be given. Again, that was not what they originally wanted to do, what they originally thought they were going to be doing. Okay, it’s another mission that needed to be done.

—Deputy Assistant Chief John Norman, Chief of Special Operations, then a Battalion Chief in Battalion 16, Harlem, Manhattan; FDNY USAR

“ When they would identify a [firefighter] who passed away. Signal 5-5-5-5, you transmit it over the radio. You’d see the names of people that you know. Now, you’d have to do that in the morning and evening time, and continuous for days. I don’t know, it just felt weird. As far as everyday operation, you still handled everything that was coming in before 9/11, you handled the basic calls, fires, rescues, all that stuff.

—Fire Alarm Dispatcher John Lightsey, Manhattan Communications Office, Central Park, Manhattan

“ But now when they found a body, it would be like a swarm of people. Is it a firefighter, is it a cop, is it a civilian? So firefighters looking for firefighters. And of course, they treated everybody with the deepest respect, any people or parts of people that we found.

—Chief of Department (2020–2022) Tom Richardson, then a Battalion Chief in Battalion 53, Bayside, Queens

“ There was one particularly bad day, it was right after Thanksgiving, right by the revolving doors, the exits to the North Tower, and we found a 33 Engine there and a number of other companies of firefighters, as many as 12 I think, in one spot.

—Chief of Department (2004–2006) Pete Hayden, then a Deputy Chief in Division 1, SoHo, Manhattan

The Woolworth Building
The Woolworth Building, world's tallest 1913–1930, seen through the wreckage of the WTC.
Shared with permission from the Daniel Quinn private collection

> “I came down and you could clearly see the helmet. You could clearly see the body. The recovery of – when I say clearly see the body, you saw the bunker gear, right? A tremendous amount of dirt had fallen where this member had passed. That's why everything was intact. It wasn't steel and concrete and stuff. It was a tremendous amount of dirt that covered him literally more than anything else. We were able to figure out which unit it was. We called them up three o'clock in the morning. They go, ‘Yes, we're missing one guy.’ We called the family, we called the company and we waited until they all got down there to let them carry their brother out. That was just particularly a very moment of interest in a lot of ways. Sad, but also special.
>
> —*Deputy Chief Jim DiDomenico, then in Division 13, South Jamaica, Queens*

> “There were a lot of remains being recovered. It was pretty well organized. When a body was discovered, it was marked. Then a contingent would come, the remains were removed in a ceremonial way, covered in a flag in the very beginning. After the second or third

day, it was more organized, more formal. That's when you're finding more then.

—Captain Kerry Hollywood, then in Engine 53, Spanish Harlem, Manhattan; Commanding Officer, Family Assistance Unit

" I remember being there one night. It's dark, it's 8, 9 o'clock at night. We find Timmy [Lieutenant Tim Higgins, Squad 252], one of my good buddies. I worked with him in Rescue 2. His father [Captain Ed Higgins, Engine 227, retired] was my first captain. Timmy had three brothers on the job [firefighters Mike Higgins, Ladder 108, Joe Higgins, Ladder 111, Bob Higgins, Ladder 103, Matt NYPD]. His body was intact. His brothers were there earlier but they left. The one brother said, 'If you find Timmy call us, please.' [Joe left to work his first tour in the firehouse since 9/11.] I called Joe on the phone. I said, 'Listen, we got Tim.' Joe said, 'We're coming back. Please, wait till we get back.' The guys at the makeshift command post, the chief, was starting to get antsy. Like, what are you doing up there? I was stalling, stalling, and stalling. 'Take your time, guys. We're going to put him in the stokes. We're going to cover him with a flag.' And I waited for them to come back. Timmy's family carried him out. Every time I saw him after that, his father would say to me, 'My boys will never forget what you did for them.' I waited, because I wanted them to take him out. And it was their brother. But that one hit me pretty hard, that one hit me pretty hard.

—Chief of Department (2020–2022) Tom Richardson, then a Battalion Chief in Battalion 53, Bayside, Queens

" I don't think I got back down to the World Trade Center until I guess it was February when they found the folks from Four truck, [Ladder 4] my firehouse. I was working. We went down and carried them out. It was several of them anyway.

—Battalion Chief George Maier, Battalion 9, Hell's Kitchen, Manhattan; FDNY IMT

" April, there was still stuff going on, I remember, but it really was scaled down then. But they were no longer taking in battalion commanders and sending them down. Then you were starting to run your battalion.

—Assistant Chief Bob Maynes, Queens Boro Commander, then a Battalion Chief in Battalion 41, East Flatbush, Brooklyn, and past IMT Incident Commander

New normal: at work

“ Our apparatus floor, you'd come in, and there would be all this donated stuff, somehow word got out, right or wrong, we needed gloves and there were boxes of gloves with messages from kids written on them. The food we'll give to St. Malachi because they had a pantry or soup kitchen. You'd clear some of the stuff out and come back in, and it was filled up again and you just couldn't move.

—Battalion Chief George Maier, Battalion 9, Hell's Kitchen, Manhattan; FDNY IMT

“ That was another focus of getting the unit up and running as an integral part of the fire department. That was a main focus. That was one of my things. The other one was taking care of the widows.

—Battalion Chief Fred LaFemina, Chief of Rescue Services, then Captain of Squad 270, South Jamaica, Queens; member FDNY USAR

“ They went through a terrible experience, and I knew that eventually, they would get back to being the department that we were with the discipline that we had. For the most part, that's exactly how it worked. I think doing it any other way would've been inviting backlash or more serious issues, individual issues with what was going on in our members' psyches and they were given time to maybe be a little more out of control than they normally are.

—Fire Commissioner (2014–2022) Dan Nigro, then Chief of Operations Headquarters, Downtown Brooklyn (served as Chief of Department 2001–2002)

“ I was working my first tour in a firehouse after two weeks at the site. It was just an emotional time. I was filling in at Engine 214; they had lost their entire crew. It was tough because I knew them all; I had covered [filled in] at that firehouse a lot. Their rig was undamaged and sent back to the firehouse. We went on a run, hit a pothole, the entire cab was filled by a cloud of WTC dust. It came out of every crack and crevice, we had to drive with the windows open. Later on, I'm alone in the office and a fax came in. It was an assignment for an elementary school 'Please write a note thanking our first responders, police, fire, and EMS.' The notes from kids were always nice to see and usually lifted our mood. Then I read the next page.... in little kid handwriting.... I can't even spit it out.... It said.... 'Thank you for looking for my Dad. It was signed Keith Kerwin Grade 4 Abbey Lane Elementary School, Levittown.' I immediately recognized the last name. I knew Lieutenant Ron Kerwin from Levittown was gone. I just paused for a second, I put the paper down. I walked into the restroom, I turned on the sink, I turned on the shower, I turned on the air conditioner and I just sobbed and cried for probably 20 minutes. I still have those papers. [Keith Kerwin is currently a Firefighter in Ladder 55, The South Bronx.]

—Captain Paul Brown, then a Lieutenant covering in Division 15, Brownsville, Brooklyn; FDNY IMT

Thank you for Looking for my Dad.

Keith Kerwin Grade 4
Abbey Lane School
Levittown, N.Y. 11756

Thank You
A child's note thanking responders. (Keith Kerwin is now a firefighter in Ladder 55, The Bronx.)
Used with permission Paul Brown private collection

“ Maybe two or three weeks after the actual incident. John [Hemsley], the captain of 13 truck [Ladder 13] came in for a night tour and he tells the guys, close the door. Get everybody who didn't belong out of the firehouse, walked to the kitchen with a garbage pail to get [donated] food that was on the table with the garbage pail. He says, 'Tonight we are going back to our routine.'

—Battalion Chief Bill Moore, then in Battalion 10, Yorkville, Manhattan

" The divisions where members were heavily lost, which was Brooklyn and Manhattan in particular, there was tremendous pressure for the companies that lost members to be down at the site looking for their guys.

—Deputy Chief Jim DiDomenico, then in Division 13, South Jamaica, Queens

" I was shocked at how many people, as I made my way around and went to fires and firehouses and so on, how many people came up and told me about a conversation that they had with me on that day that I had absolutely no recollection of it at all. I cannot tell you on that day, whether more firefighters came up and asked, 'Have you seen my son?' or…'Have you seen my father?'

—1st Deputy Commissioner (2004–2010) Frank Cruthers, then an Assistant Chief at Headquarters, Downtown Brooklyn (served as Chief of Department 1996–1997, 2002–2004)

" Yes, straight through the winter, and then around January, February we started going back to regular – if you wanted to go down, if you wanted to work at the landfill in Staten Island, they could send you there but they would give you overtime for going, instead of doing it on your own time.

—Firefighter Lois Mungay, Engine 235, Bedford Stuyvesant, Brooklyn

" Right after Thanksgiving, I went into the chief operations and I said, 'You got to get me out of here. I have been down here since September 11th.' He says 'You gotta stay. You know what's going on down there.' I said, 'Well, I'm taking a couple of days off,' and I did. I took a couple of days off and I went back and then after that, my head was great, and we finished that up. Tough times, it was for the firefighters, that's for sure.

—Chief of Department (2004–2006) Pete Hayden, then a Deputy Chief in Division 1, SoHo, Manhattan

“I know by April, it became business as usual more in the firehouses. Before that, a lot of our guys volunteered and went to the firehouses that lost a significant amount of people. One of my jobs there was to make a decision; it's time for this guy to come back. We need him here. I'd make the call.

—Assistant Chief Bob Maynes, Queens Boro Commander, then a Battalion Chief in Battalion 41, East Flatbush, Brooklyn, and past IMT Incident Commander

“I lost the ability to play it [Taps] musically, to put feeling into a horn. I went to a music store and I said, ‘Look, I need to sit down with somebody and play the trumpet, take some lessons.’ It took probably five to 10 times where I could feel again. It was some emotion coming out of me into the horn. I remember him telling me, he's like, ‘You got it, You got it back.’ Then my phone rang, I answered the phone, I hung up, and he goes, ‘Did somebody just die?’

—Lieutenant Joe Minogue, Commanding Officer of Ceremonial Unit; Department Bugler; then a firefighter in Engine 289, Corona, Queens

Heavy machinery and contractors on the pile
FDNY and Construction crews oversee grappler operation.
Shared with permission from the Daniel Quinn private collection

New normal: at home

“ In February of that year, my first social event outside the fire department. This is the first time I'm with people that are not firefighters. They were going on with their life. I walked in the front door and I said hello to everyone, and I walked out the back door. I couldn't handle it. It was still September 12th for me.

—Captain Frank Leto, Deputy Director, Counseling Services Unit, Bayside, Queens

“ I said that to myself – I just want my simple little life back. I didn't want to be a celebrity. I wanted to be Louis, firefighter Louis, bike rider, skier, family, part of my little world again.

—Firefighter Louis Giaconelli, Engine 53, Spanish Harlem, Manhattan; FDNY IMT

“ I was sitting in the kitchen and I was talking to my wife. My emotions were pretty raw, and I said to her, 'You know, I should have died there.' Those three kids [young firefighters] that died from [Artie's firehouse], they were all young. One just had a baby. At least my kids would have remembered me. I had survivor guilt, no doubt about it. My daughter was in the hallway listening to me and I didn't know it. She gave me a card the next day and said, 'We're so happy you didn't die, Dad.'

—Lieutenant Artie Riccio, then a firefighter in Ladder 119 South Williamsburg, Brooklyn working in Ladder 110

“ Every once in a while, you have your little private moment and you let out the tears and you let out some sobs and then you're renewed afterwards. Then you realize that part of the process is not to fight it, let it come.

—Captain Paul Brown, then a Lieutenant covering in Division 15, Brownsville, Brooklyn; FDNY IMT

“ I used to use the term 'I was living a Jimmy Buffett lifestyle' right up to then and then it all became a lot more serious. Life, it changed me, and then looked at the danger in the world through your kid's eyes. It's so much different, you worry more about your kids than you used to, and it definitely took some of the fun out of me, without a doubt. I thought my wife, if she was listening, she'd be happy to tell you that

I am not as much fun as I used to be. She might say that I'm a little too thin, mentally.

—Assistant Chief Bob Maynes, Queens Boro Commander, then a Battalion Chief in Battalion 41, East Flatbush, Brooklyn, and past IMT Incident Commander

" Well, you got to stay in the game. It would not have been a good move to say, 'I can't do this anymore.' Sure it happened to some guys. Their wife said, 'You got to retire, you got the time in, you could get a pension, you can't have this again.' I didn't get any of that from my wife. She knows I love being a fireman. I guess, how I dealt with it, was by just staying busy. I worked all the time. I loved to go to work.

—Captain Glenn Rohan, then a Lieutenant in Ladder 43, Spanish Harlem, Manhattan

New normal: funerals

" A few days after September 11th, the fire department started running two parallel operations.... One was the site itself, and the other was the missing firefighters and their families, and they ran parallel for weeks and virtually months.

—Chief of Department (2010–2014) Ed Kilduff, then a Deputy Chief in Division 3, Midtown, Manhattan and past IMT Incident Commander

" Firefighter funerals are enormous events, 'specially in Manhattan. Eight to ten thousand uniformed firefighters from all over the country, even in parts of the world, line up for block upon block. Early on, I went to a friend's funeral [firefighter Bill Henry, Rescue 1]. There were maybe 150 people in uniform. It wasn't close to my house either. By the time I got home, it was time to go to sleep and then get up and go back to work.

—Captain Paul Brown, then a Lieutenant covering in Division 15, Brownsville, Brooklyn; FDNY IMT

" Then I think it was December 1st, they were going to have a Memorial service for a guy. It turned into a funeral. A day or two before, the medical examiner did more testing and discovered they had misidentified another firefighter from the same company, who had been buried. They had the wrong guy. They exhumed that body and buried him as a different [the correct] person. There were some assumptions made, I guess, from the medical examiner, but that just threw the firehouse sideways for a week.

—Battalion Chief George Maier, Battalion 9, Hell's Kitchen, Manhattan; FDNY IMT

" The fire department didn't do a thing. They told us, 'You can't tell them he's dead.' They left it like that. We had a personal relationship with her, so we would go by her house every day and tell her what had happened that day. He was listed as missing. We took it upon ourselves to go contact his widow. We didn't know she was a widow at the time. We could never say that he's gone. She made that call after two months. We had a big memorial service for him. He had been a Vietnam veteran. Being a combat vet, he was supposed to be buried in National Cemetery. Because there were no remains ever found, he was denied that burial.... We had a bed of flowers to represent a coffin. We did a memorial service for Bobby without Bobby [Lieutenant Bob Nagle, Engine 58].

—Captain Jeff Simms, then a Lieutenant in Engine 58, Harlem, Manhattan; FDNY IMT

" When playing Taps, everybody pretty much knows that song, 35 seconds, 40 seconds, depends on how long you play it. I tried to play it different for everyone. You have the military da, da, da, but everybody's different. Everybody needs something special. I have to give something to the families that they can take away and say, 'That was special.' Then when we had the helicopters, the police department helicopters coming [Missing Man formation flyover], we coordinated with the police department that my last notes were taken away by the helicopter wash.

—Lieutenant Joe Minogue, Commanding Officer of Ceremonial Unit; Department Bugler; then a firefighter in Engine 289, Corona, Queens

New normal: counseling

" I think later on they really expanded their counseling. I think they realized that they had this other bigger problem that they were going to have to deal with. They expanded that exponentially and then it became known that, 'Yes, if you are struggling or dealing with 9/11 related things, definitely, come down, speak to us.'

—Firefighter Louis Giaconelli, Engine 53, Spanish Harlem, Manhattan; FDNY IMT

" From 9/11 to the end of September, we saw 1,000 people, individuals in a workplace where we had seen more or less 900 in the previous 12 months. Couldn't grow the staff that quickly. We had to create a way to identify licensed professionals who could adapt themselves to the Fire Department culture.

—Malachy Corrigan NP, Clinical Director, Counseling Services Unit, SoHo, Manhattan

" I thought, 'I'm doing okay.' I didn't think it's anything pressing. But you know what? I don't want to suffer down the road and I want to minimize the lasting effects. I found someone who was near where I lived who specialized in grief counseling. I went once a week for a month or so. I almost get the impression that she finally worked up the courage to ask me how many people I knew who died. When I said, 'More than 70,' she gasped, stammered, got up and stood with her back to me, wiping tears. She said she expected me to say two or three.

—Captain Paul Brown, then a Lieutenant covering in Division 15, Brownsville, Brooklyn; FDNY IMT

" I would say to guys, 'Listen, you need to talk to a therapist, you're going to get destroyed by this.' Guys would turn, including myself, more heavily into alcohol. Guys have gone out on psychological disabilities. They've gotten help, professionally, and they're okay today. One of the guys with me [on 9/11] died of brain cancer last year, he was my first dead of my guys.

—Captain Glenn Rohan, then a Lieutenant in Ladder 43, Spanish Harlem, Manhattan

" I knew I had to get healthy. I had to get healthy for my daughter, and she needed to see me getting healthy. There was so much help and love and support there, and I'm still going to funerals. There came a point where I was like, 'I got to stop.'

—Lieutenant Ray Brown, Ladder 113, Crown Heights, Brooklyn Conclusion of operations

New normal: incident management

"There was a push by FEMA, their federal coordinating officer, to get us out of there as soon as possible and have the FDNY begin to execute the incident command system. So Cruthers and Hayden said, 'No, they're staying right here, we'll let you know when we're good.'

—Dan Oltrogge, Commander National Area Command Team (2009–2011), then Incident Commander Trainee SW-IMT, Chief of Fire and Aviation Grand Canyon National Park (served as SW-IMT Incident Commander 2003–2007)

"It [the transition to the Alaska IMT] went well. We left; I'm going to say about the 15th of October, I think, we were out of town. They stayed till about through the first week of November, something like that. They didn't bring in another team behind them. It went well. We do that in that team world. Well, that's very normal business for us. We just took more time because of all of the anomalies and the innovations that were in place that we needed to get them to understand. They picked it up right away. It wasn't a big deal.

—Paul Summerfelt, Commander National Area Command Team (2013–2020), then Planning Section Chief Southwest-IMT, Deputy Chief Flagstaff, AZ Fire Department (served as Type-1 IMT Incident Commander 2008–2012)

Volunteer Dan Quinn with Paul Brown

Volunteer Dan Quinn with Lieutenant Paul Brown standing in front of the pile.

Shared with permission from the Daniel Quinn private collection

> They [Alaska IMT] probably stayed for another month. They were home by Thanksgiving, And by that point the-the incident had stabilized and FDNY picked it up and went from there on their own.
>
> *—Dan Oltrogge, Commander National Area Command Team (2009–2011), then Incident Commander Trainee SW-IMT, Chief of Fire and Aviation Grand Canyon National Park (served as SW-IMT Incident Commander 2003–2007)*

> When I was asked in March when I was pulled off, and I was asked to work with the McKinsey consultants in writing the report, one of the things is we need to get one of these incident management teams in the department. And we did, we moved forward with it. We wound up training a lot of guys and it's become an integral part of the department operation.
>
> *—Chief of Department (2004–2006) Pete Hayden, then a Deputy Chief in Division 1, SoHo, Manhattan*

Conclusion of WTC site operations

> May 30th of 2002. They had the ceremony, the last beam. They cut that last beam off and they put it on a truck, and they ceremoniously drove that truck up the ramp, and that was the official end of the recovery effort. It was quite moving.
>
> *—Fire Commissioner (2014–2022) Dan Nigro, then Chief of Operations Headquarters, Downtown Brooklyn (served as Chief of Department 2001–2002)*

Part B: Summary, Lessons, and Commentary

Summary

Most firefighters knew rationally that the shift from rescue to recovery had in fact already occurred. But that didn't mean they could accept that conclusion in their hearts. They clung to hope, if not for themselves, then for the families of the missing. Denis Oneial, Senior FEMA representative, recounted, "They believed that they were going to find others. Then they realized after about seven days of finding body parts, the bodies, that this isn't going to have a happy ending."

Being mindful of the families and firefighters was foremost for Deputy Chief Pete Hayden: "They've been under this for a week, there's been no sound, no nothing. We never said, 'we're in recovery.' It's always just 'rescue and recovery' because you just would never say to the victims' families or staff, that we're on recovery, but we were."

The official announcement of the shift from rescue to recovery came on Monday, September 24th. For many within the FDNY, the announcement shredded all hope that their comrades or civilians had survived. Denis Onieal recalled the Mayor telling the families, "'If you want a death certificate, we'll issue one.' When they move [into] accelerated debris removal using the cranes, that's when that whole thing changed. That's my observation."

New York City had lost nearly 800 firefighters in the line of duty from its founding through September 10, 2001. Historically, they had experienced death within their ranks with a frightening regularity. As with most uniformed organizations, the FDNY had deeply established traditions for honoring its fallen and taking care of their families.

Lieutenant Jeff Sims explained, "Taking care of fallen firefighters' families became priority. It's dignified, it's respectful. That's the most you

Daunting task
Last remnant of the North Tower amid debris.
Shared with permission from the Daniel Quinn private collection

could really do. You can't really make miracles, but you can be there for them, make sure the family's needs are met."

That same ethic extended to the recovery of the fallen themselves. We had lost the battle to rescue more survivors. All we had left was to find and respectfully remove our fallen. We all felt honorbound to return our fallen to their families. Battalion Chief John Norman remembered, "We're going to bring everybody home and treat every body part with dignity." Within the FDNY, that mission was grounded in a generations-long tradition: a fallen firefighter is carried out by their own company. At the World Trade Center, deference was given to family members who were themselves FDNY, or members of another uniformed service, to be part of the dignified removal.

"You found a member or found something of significance. It was a very solemn way that was handled," said Jim DiDomenico. He remembered one such event: "We were able to figure out which unit it was.... [W]e called the company and we waited until they all got down there to let them carry their brother [brother firefighter] out. That was a moment of interest in a lot of ways. Sad, but also special."

As the incident became more organized, so too did the removal process. A supply of American flags of adequate size was on hand to drape over found remains. Lieutenant Paul Brown remembered the oft-repeated ritual: "Once they were ready for the carryout, word would spread, over the radio but mostly person-to-person: 'line up, line up.' Everyone in the area stopped working. All the machinery stopped. It was so quiet. By the time you got into position, you'd know the firefighter's name and unit. We stood to the side along the path out and saluted. Not all at once, more like the wave at a stadium as the firefighter was carried past. Then we just went back to whatever work we were doing."

Whenever remains were positively identified by the Medical Examiner, a Line of Duty death announcement would be made, transmitted over all FDNY radio frequencies and voice alarm systems using signal 5-5-5-5, then announcing the firefighter's name and unit.

The pace continued, taking its toll, physically and emotionally. Firefighters, feeling duty-bound, spent their off hours at funerals and memorials. Paul Brown continued, "Our culture tells us that if there's a line of duty death, you are either working or you're at the funeral, period." The emotional and physical pace was crushing. "Word got out through the union that the counseling unit said we should just go to the funerals near

Aircraft parts
"The Pile"
Shared with permission from the Daniel Quinn private collection

where we lived," said Brown. "That being said, officially, kind of relieved people of the burden. I still feel guilty for the funerals I missed."

Once the shift from rescue to recovery was announced, City Hall ordered staffing reduced and more heavy equipment brought in. This escalated after November 1. The City seemed to be in a rush to "clean up" the site. Over 200 firefighters and hundreds more civilians remained entombed in "The Pile." Media were reporting that firefighters were slowing the cleanup. They were: respectful removal of remains is deeply ingrained in FDNY culture. Once a person was found, digging would be done by hand, eschewing large equipment that could potentially cause more damage to the remains.

The city announced that it would reduce FDNY staffing to 25 firefighters per shift. This amounted to a gut punch to the department's rank-and-file. Firefighters viewed the reduction as a shift to a "scoop and dump" operation, meaning that recovering of remains, would entail sorting through debris at a landfill on Staten Island. Firefighters saw this as disrespectful. Families saw it as outright cruel. After impassioned pleas from victims' families, City Hall compromised.

Perhaps no way exists to convey accurately the immense size and complexity of on-site operations, the sheer number of activities simultaneously going on. The searching and digging continued around the clock for eight months. "The Pile" slowly became "The Pit." The search for the fallen unabated, the dignified removals continued. It was relentless.

The elements with the greatest impact on site operations were the Incident Action Plan [IAP], and the National Incident Management System [NIMS]. These were introduced to the FDNY by the Southwest Incident Management Team. Deputy Incident Commander Pete Hayden explained what came next: "From that day forward, they would draw up a written Incident Action Plan. Every day, everybody, every agency was issued the plan."

Returning to the site sometime later, Captain Kerry Hollywood recognized the change: "I think it was a pretty squared away operation for such a big field and so many missing. It's such an overwhelming event. It was pretty well coordinated."

While work at the site continued, the emotional toll on responders was not overlooked. Malachy Corrigan, Director of the Department's Counseling Services, worked to build up capabilities. "From 9/11 to the end of September, we saw 1,000 people, where we had seen 900 in the previous 12 months. [We] couldn't grow the staff that quickly. We had to create a way to identify licensed professionals who could adapt themselves to the Fire Department culture."

What followed for FDNY firefighters was the attempt to regain normalcy. But in the firehouse, returning to old routines would prove difficult.

Battalion Chief Bill Moore saw one step toward normalcy: "The captain of 13 Truck came in for a night tour and he tells the guys, 'Close the door. Get everybody who didn't belong out of firehouse.' We're going to go back to firehouse routine."

For some who had spent extended time enmeshed in the event, the return to their outside life proved difficult. Lieutenant Frank Leto hadn't been to a non-FDNY gathering in months. "My first social event I couldn't handle it. It was still September 12th for me."

On May 30, 2002, recovery operations in "The Pit" were concluded with the Last Beam Ceremony. But while operations at the WTC site in lower Manhattan had concluded, the job for FDNY was far from completed. Tons of debris continued to be sifted at the Staten Island landfill. This debris would give up fragmented remains for months. Care and support for the families continued. The departments' efforts to restore, rebuild, and replace would carry on for several years. And there were still more funerals each time a firefighter's remains were identified. They would continue steadily through 2003.

The remains of nearly 60 percent of the firefighters killed at the WTC have never been recovered or identified. The idea that FDNY would have firefighters MIA (missing in action) was incomprehensible. Without remains, some families held memorial services. Other families chose to wait in hope, as their religious beliefs preclude a Funeral Mass without remains. A few families clung to hope for years, hoping that one day their loved one would be identified.

Years prior, a simple act, carried out in the spirit of giving by their firefighter loved one would provide comfort and healing for their family. In 1989, Firefighter Mark Kalwasser was in search of a bone marrow donor for his sister. He reached out to his brothers and sisters in the FDNY. Since then, nearly every firefighter in every FDNY Fire Academy class has joined the registry.

A funeral mass was held in September 2003 for Firefighter Michael Ragusa of Engine 279. Vials of blood served as the vital remains buried. The blood samples had been stored at the NY Blood Center Bone Marrow Registry since collection in probie school four years earlier. The family of Battalion Chief Larry Stack would similarly hold a funeral mass in 2016 with blood samples from the bone marrow donor registry. To date, his was the last New York City Fire Department funeral for a firefighter killed at the World Trade Center on 9/11.

Lessons for Leaders

1 **Focus on what comes next.** Good crisis management gets people through the crisis. The required "next" step involves cleaning up the debris and repairing the damage.

2 **Care for the care givers.** In the case of the FDNY, more than in many other cases, rescuers were also victims. Identify and treat their wounds. Survivors of natural disasters, pandemics, and even organizational traumas such as layoffs or closings; those who provide care, also need care.

3 **Post crisis, settle into the methodical.** The methodical, the orderly, the routine will support victims (i.e., firefighters, responders and others). The predictable will foster the unpredictable release of the bottled up and of the unaddressed.

Leaders should expect that the press coverage will fade away, along with the celebrity visits. The work of clearing the ground, both literally and metaphorically, will still need doing. Hence, no victory laps. It's not over. Not by a long shot. Leaders should minimize the distraction of all the visitors in order to maintain focus and routine.

Neither the physical nor the emotional work has ended. Leaders should prepare accordingly. They should embrace the wounded as they discover their wounds. Methodical leadership creates the space necessary for reconfiguration of a place, a community, an organization, and, as necessary, of individuals themselves.

Commentary

On September 10, 2001, the FDNY ranked among, if not at the very top of, the list of the world's premier fire departments. Over 11,000 of its members tended to arguably the most complex city on earth. They responded to over one million calls each year. Now, that same department turned to the work of clearing away the rubble and extinguishing persistent fires. All in the field of tragedy.

As the city chose not simply to rebuild two towers, the FDNY chose not just to rebuild itself. Instead, the FDNY chose to transform itself in multiple ways. Its sustained success in purposefully changing itself as an organization stands in contradistinction to many, indeed the majority, of attempted organizational changes. Simply stated, most change efforts, especially those involving culture, fail. The FDNY's did not and has not. This exception merits examination

First and foremost, the FDNY focused on behavior such as using management tools and support services. It did not speak in fuzzy or abstract terms. Rather, it worked to strengthen its use of tools such as Incident Management and to increase requests for mental health and emotional support. Specificity helps to focus efforts to change.

Second, change requires energy. The energy to change arises from human emotion. The energy can flow from a desire to move away from something, to move toward something, or, most likely, a combination of the two. The energy may stem from a simple but heartfelt desire to minimize the risk of losing senior commanders when hell's gates open or from a broader, more complex felt need to widen and deepen the department's incident management capability. Change begins with, indeed requires, energy. It begins with a felt need to change.

Next comes the consideration of alternatives: different approaches, different ways of acting that might address the felt need. The more specific the alternative, the easier to assess what it requires for conversion into reality. For example, the Wildfires Department provided a proven model for incident management at scale. The FDNY took notes. Finally, successful change requires that people believe that a given change can occur.

The following model provides a way of understanding why the FDNY changes succeeded. In effect, the FDNY used this model to change itself, its competencies, and to develop its external focus. For example, to make Incident Management Teams central to the department and to encourage training, particularly outside the department, it reshaped its internal environment and drove specific behavioral change. A sample of how this played out in practice appears immediately below.[45]

Commentary

The Eight Levers of the Work Systems Model

1. **Workplace:** Layout of physical and virtual space; available work tools and technology
   - Incident Management Teams (IMTs) provided with dedicated space and radio interoperable with NYPD
   - Partnership with climbing equipment company Petzl to develop the Personal Safety System

2. **Task:** Work processes, protocols and practices, including timelines
   - Approval of travel no longer required by the mayor's office: easier to go places and to learn

3. **People:** Selection, training, development of talent in areas such as task competency and process skills, such as stakeholder mapping as well as key stakeholder ties, and training in group processes,

including conflict management and evolving team membership and roles, including leadership:

- Selection of IMT personnel based on skill sets outside of those normally used to select personnel for structural firefighting (e.g., accounting, computer-related, restaurant and catering, supply logistics and transportation)
- Training facilities, integrated IMT training (within and outside FDNY)
- Open training programs to "outsiders" such as the U.S. Coast Guard to facilitate cross-fertilization
- Partnerships with external institutions, including Columbia University, the Naval Postgraduate School, the U.S. Military Academy at West Point, and the Wharton School of the University of Pennsylvania)
- NIMS (National Incident Management System), and Guardians Center training (private and military) as well as ship fire training at the FDNY Randall's Island simulator (including Coast Guard personnel)
- Joint training with NYPD, OEMs, hospitals (e.g., simulations), New York City Transit, the Metropolitan Transportation Authority, and ConEd

4. **Rewards:** Rewards and punishments of any sort (intrinsic and extrinsic), including success, recognition, financial incentives, skill development, promotion and future assignments
   - Full compensation plus overtime pay for outside IMT personnel working within and outside New York City
   - Opportunities in the IMT based on training and competency rather than exclusively on FDNY rank
   - Attachment professional value to NIMS certification
   - Exposure to senior officers and cross-functional collaboration with firefighters, EMS personnel, and dispatchers through IMT assignments

5. **Measurement:** Outcome and process metrics or scorecards
   - Adequacy of staffing: maintaining three-deep coverage for each IMT position
   - Member certification levels

6. **Information Distribution:** Ease and comprehensiveness of access to external information, who gets to know what, when, and how
   - Free flow within IMTs, including post-incident reviews, morning briefings, and daily incident action plans
   - "Day Challenge" programs that brought local businesses into FDNY settings to learn about leadership, problem-solving, decision-making, and team-building

7. **Decision-allocation:** Who participates when, in which decisions and in what way? In responsibility or RACI charting terms, nature and clarity of decision-making steps and both individual and group roles in each of them
   - IMT "founding" principle that the IMT manages the IMT, not the incident itself – focusing on resources, coordination, and support under the authority of the agency administrator

8. **Organization:** Overall vertical and horizontal organizational structure (e.g., organization chart), such as geographic, functional or matrixed as well as task forces, project teams and committees or other regular meeting groups
   - Creation of a separate and independent IMT organization and the Center for Terrorism and Disaster Preparedness
   - Reestablishment of borough commands with authority to act as independently as needed, reinforcing decentralized operational capacity

In short, the FDNY did what only a minority of organizations, let alone broadly acclaimed organizations, manage to do: it changed itself – and sustained that change. Not surprisingly, it did so consciously and systematically. It also did so, not knowingly, but, nonetheless, according to the model described above and presented in the figure on the next page.

Meanwhile, the FDNY moved in a similar manner along an arc of healing similar to that described by Tedeschi and Calhoun in their work on post-traumatic growth:[46] deepening connection with others (emotional openness, sometimes expressed simply by hugging); the creation and installation of the new (IMTs, the Center for Terrorism and Disaster Preparedness, and expanded formal support services); a heightened sense of collective strength; an enhanced appreciation of life (including

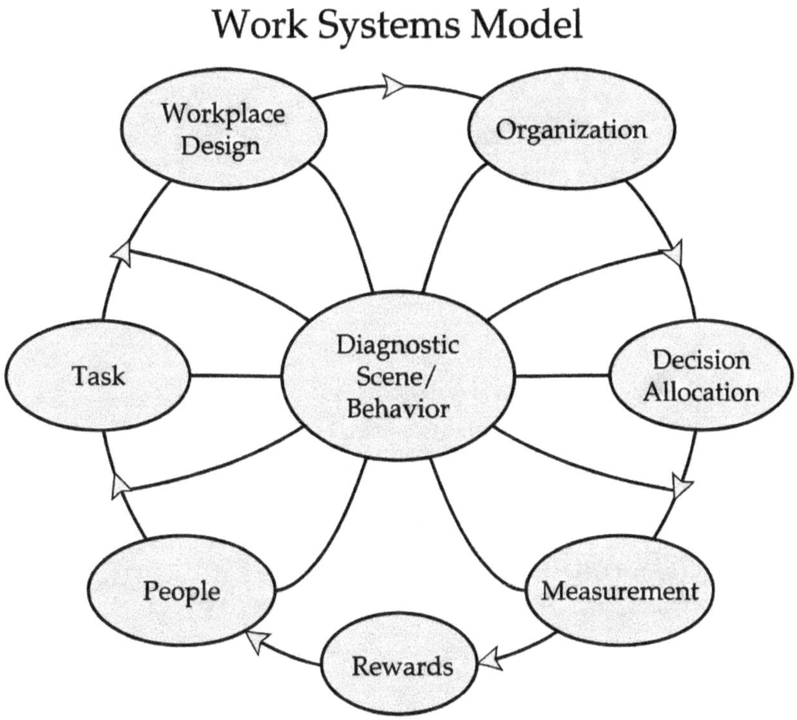

Work Systems Model

The Work Systems Model (Shea and Associates). A diagnostic tool used to analyze the alignment between organizational structure, people, and task environments.
Copyright Shea and Associates, Inc.

tears of all kinds); and a deepened (even spiritual) reverence for the mission and for the memory. Beyond resilience. Beyond closure. After 9/11, the FDNY evinced ongoing commitment to work of stitching back together and, ultimately, of healing – an integration of scarring and learning under the balm of thoughtful and heartfelt attention.

Still, “The Body Keeps the Score.” As Bessel van der Kolk reminds us, trauma lives in the body as well as the heart and mind.[47] In this instance, it lives in every first responder – in the daily medications, the doctor visits, the anniversaries, and in the continuing toll of 9/11-related illness and death. As one interviewee said, simply, “It’s in the eyes.”

Section Four: Today

“

Life can only be understood backwards;
but it must be lived forwards.

—Søren Kierkegaard

“

I am not afraid of storms,
for I am learning how to sail my ship.

—Emily Dickinson

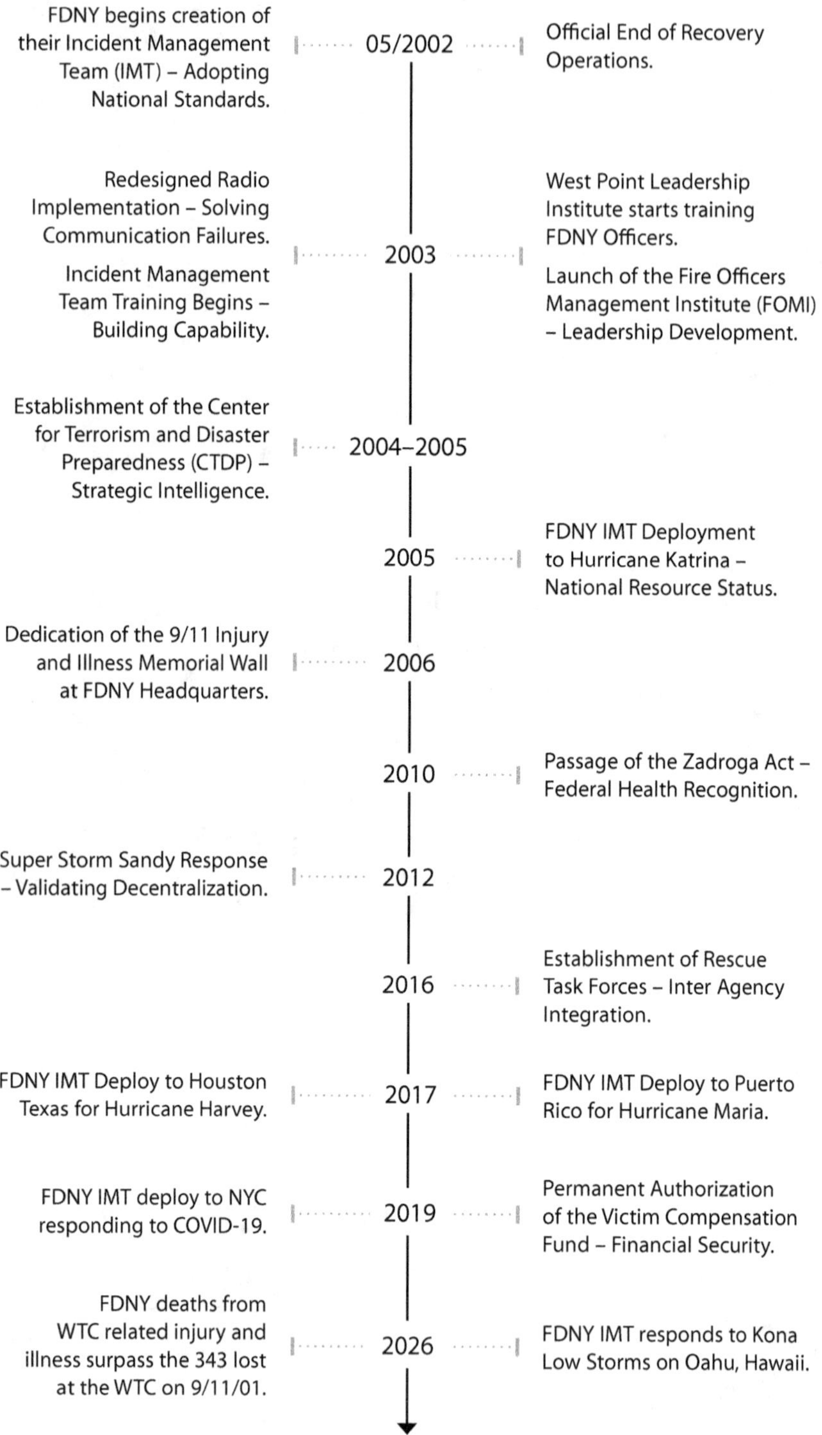
FDNY begins creation of their Incident Management Team (IMT) – Adopting National Standards.
05/2002
Official End of Recovery Operations.
Redesigned Radio Implementation – Solving Communication Failures.
West Point Leadership Institute starts training FDNY Officers.
2003
Incident Management Team Training Begins – Building Capability.
Launch of the Fire Officers Management Institute (FOMI) – Leadership Development.
Establishment of the Center for Terrorism and Disaster Preparedness (CTDP) – Strategic Intelligence.
2004–2005
2005
FDNY IMT Deployment to Hurricane Katrina – National Resource Status.
Dedication of the 9/11 Injury and Illness Memorial Wall at FDNY Headquarters.
2006
2010
Passage of the Zadroga Act – Federal Health Recognition.
Super Storm Sandy Response – Validating Decentralization.
2012
2016
Establishment of Rescue Task Forces – Inter Agency Integration.
FDNY IMT Deploy to Houston Texas for Hurricane Harvey.
2017
FDNY IMT Deploy to Puerto Rico for Hurricane Maria.
FDNY IMT deploy to NYC responding to COVID-19.
2019
Permanent Authorization of the Victim Compensation Fund – Financial Security.
FDNY deaths from WTC related injury and illness surpass the 343 lost at the WTC on 9/11/01.
2026
FDNY IMT responds to Kona Low Storms on Oahu, Hawaii.

Chapter Nine

Legacy

On Riverside Drive at 100th Street in Manhattan stands the Firemen's Memorial. Each October, the FDNY gathers there for its Memorial Day ceremony, honoring all of the members of the department who passed away, whether in the line of duty or not. Dedicated in 1900, the Memorial bears an inscription that reads:

TO THE MEN OF THE FIRE DEPARTMENT
OF THE CITY OF NEW YORK
WHO DIED AT THE CALL OF DUTY.
SOLDIERS IN A WAR THAT NEVER ENDS

> “Yes. It was forever; we were forever scarred.
>
> *—Captain Glenn Rohan, then a Lieutenant in Ladder 43, Spanish Harlem, Manhattan*

> “I'm trying to make sense of it. There's no sense to it. Then my sister [NYPD Officer Laura Brown-Amodeo] like, boom, 9/11 cancer, a rare cancer, gone. I remember being angry and resentful. Who am I angry and resentful at? God? No sense in that.
>
> *—Lieutenant Ray Brown, then in Ladder 113, Crown Heights, Brooklyn*

> “I think the emotional processing probably took quite some time. I think having a mission and engaging in work that you feel has a purpose helps tremendously.
>
> *—Chief of Operations Pat McNally, then a Deputy Chief in Division 14, Flushing, Queens*

The Timeline at the beginning of this chapter makes clear that the legacy of 9/11 and its aftermath extends well beyond a single day. It stretches out through a set of sustained changes – organizational and individual. The changes have compounded over time – to today and likely to tomorrow.

Measures abound. More firefighters have now died from illnesses caused as a result of 9/11 and working at the site after 9/11 than died on the day itself. That number exceeds 400 and increases year by year with more than 11,000 firefighters now diagnosed with at least one WTC-related chronic medical or psychological condition, including over 3500 with 9/11 related cancer. These numbers continue to grow. The legacy also includes nearly 100 new firefighters known as “9/11 Legacies.” These firefighters lost a firefighter parent on or as a result of 9/11. This number also continues to grow.

Other elements of the legacy prove less easily quantifiable if no less identifiable or consequential. For instance, the FDNY changed how it saw itself and its place in the city, America, and the world. Succinctly stated, the FDNY changed the work it does and how it does it. For example, it adopted use of internally developed Incident Management Teams because it now sees itself as managing incidents, including fires. The FDNY also significantly altered its support of firefighter mental health and the support of families of firefighters injured or killed in service. It expanded, formalized, and institutionalized that support.

The following quotations capture how the FDNY came to define itself and its mission differently in the wake of 9/11. That redefinition reshaped what the department did and how it did it. Probably most significantly, that redefinition reflected and fostered greater openness to change, education, breadth of mission, and cooperation. In short, an expanded openness to world.

The FDNY changed its ways of working notably. The voices that follow highlight several of the most consequential shifts, from expanded training – ranging from simulation-based exercises and leadership training to new approaches to ongoing education to deeper partnerships beyond the department. At the same time, the FDNY broadened and strengthened its commitment to caring for firefighters and their families, institutionalizing once informal or ad hoc forms of support.

In the years after 9/11, the FDNY's Counseling Services Unit developed deep experience and competency in supporting its members, leading to requests for its expertise from departments across the country.[48] One of those requests came from New Orleans post-hurricane Katrina and this year from Hawaii...along with IMT support.

Part A: Responder Voices

The people

Mental health

“ A little thing that changed too, is everybody used to say, ‘Hey, I'll see you at the big one,’ and we stopped saying that.

—Lieutenant Ray Brown, then in Ladder 113, Crown Heights, Brooklyn

“ When you have brothers lose brothers and fathers lose sons and sons lose fathers, and we lost a father and son – the Angelinis – that takes an awful lot out of you, an awful lot out of you. We knew that we were going to have to rebuild psychologically as well as physically with tools and equipment, and training and procedures, and we did that.

—Fire Commissioner (2010–2014) Sal Cassano,
then Assistant Chief at Headquarters, Downtown Brooklyn
(served as Chief of Department 2006–2010)

“At the 15-year anniversary, I was asked to speak at a dedication of a memorial in Massachusetts. You saw a team over there build this beautiful memorial and I was asked to speak. I like being prepared. I wrote a 10 minute nice, short and sweet, and I couldn't get through the first line. I said to somebody, 'I can't believe this.' My body was saying, it got you, it has finally got you.

—Battalion Chief Fred LaFemina, Chief of Rescue Services, then Captain of Squad 270, South Jamaica, Queens; member FDNY USAR

“We got through it because it was all of us and not just me, and I'm not alone. We're all in it together, and we all suffered together.

—Captain Paul Brown, then a Lieutenant covering in Division 15 Brownsville, Brooklyn; FDNY IMT

Counseling Services Unit (CSU)

“That was something that was very new. Prior to that [9/11], any counseling basically revolved around alcohol rehab, and that if you went for any type of psychological counseling or anything it was viewed with stigma.

—Captain Paul Brown, then a Lieutenant covering in Division 15, Brownsville, Brooklyn; FDNY IMT

“I think it was 18 months when we started to peak after the Trade Center [CSU intakes], but really the influx was May of 2002 when we closed the site. That's when people came in; it was therapy being at the Trade Center. That's where we needed to be because we needed to be able to have those conversations. We needed to be with people that had the similar experience.

—Captain Frank Leto, then Deputy Director, Counseling Services Unit, Bayside, Queens

“It absolutely changed it in that it was okay to seek help. It was okay to be afraid, to have nightmares, to feel like 'I'm not okay, I'm just not being myself,' drastically after that. It also changed in training. They're definitely training a lot more than we used to and they do a lot more building inspection which is good, but more that mentality, and it is okay to hug a guy. We became a department of we all hug now.

—Lieutenant Ray Brown, then in Ladder 113, Crown Heights, Brooklyn

FDNY Squad Company 1

Quarters of FDNY Squad Company 1 in Brooklyn, New York. Banner lists the names of the 12 fallen firefighters of Squad 1.

Oleg Yunakov, CC BY-SA 4.0, via Wikimedia Commons

> From my perspective, clearly, many, many more members are open to mental health interventions, and actually support them. The lieutenants and captains...[t]heir whole perception of what's good for them and their co-workers is a lot different.
>
> *—Malachy Corrigan NP, then Clinical Director, Counseling Services Unit, SoHo, Manhattan*

Legacy mental health: helping outside NYC

> They sent me down to New Orleans post hurricane as part of the mental health team, there was no mental health service in New Orleans in the fire department. They sent a bunch of us from FDNY down there...I went there for what I was good at. I was good at it. In terms of outcome.
>
> *—Malachy Corrigan NP, then Clinical Director Counseling Services Unit SoHo, Manhattan*

> The health and safety division of the IAFF would call me. and say, Frank, we have this. Can you pull people together from FDNY? Why? Because, they're gonna be trusted and they were seasoned. and that was it. Thank goodness, that's not the case anymore...a wildfire in California, we have people that can do that, and be effective behavioral health coordinators of a disaster. I would say from 2001 to 2015, that was it. I would call the chief of department. Can I go and can I bring these people? And he would say, yes. And off we would go and it was basically us.
>
> I was behavioral health coordinator for Surfside [Surfside, FL condo collapse (2001)]. So I ran the program for both the urban search and rescue teams and the IAFF [International Association of Firefighters].
>
> *—Captain Frank Leto, then Deputy Director, Counseling Services Unit, Bayside, Queens*

Shift from reactive to proactive mental health response

> After the Trade Center, the big one was the Black Sunday fires [January 23, 2005; two firefighters killed in the Bronx, one in Brooklyn]. The counselling was there for the troops that were around the scene and

for the firehouses. It is different. Before: 'Deal with it,' that was it. Now, they'll send counselors into the firehouse, so if anybody needs anything, and it's all private anyway.... I think that's a lesson learned. Hey, listen do you want people beating themselves up or killing themselves over some incident that they had to experience that nobody has any business experiencing? I think they handle things better than in the past.

—Captain Kerry Hollywood, then in Engine 53, Spanish Harlem, Manhattan; Commanding Officer Family Assistance Unit

“ We had our own peer counselors here. They were excellent at going to firehouses. Again, not to, per se, give counseling, but to help people acknowledge and tell their story. At the same time, let them see there was a value to going to counseling. That program is very successful. The people realize that the expression was 'this was a new normal.'

—Dr. Kerry Kelly, MD, FDNY then Chief Medical Officer, Bureau of Health Services, Headquarters Downtown Brooklyn

10th Anniversary Commemoration Lieutenant Joe Minogue playing Taps at the base of the World Trade Center site ("Ground Zero"). Lieutenant Minogue played Taps at nearly 500 funerals for those who died at or as a result of the WTC collapse.
CC BY-SA 3.0, via Wikimedia Commons

“Now, anytime you respond to a traumatic incident, you can call and get a team to come to the firehouse. I had an incident a few years later where we did CPR on an infant, and the infant passed. I noticed that the guys were very quiet on the way back. Every one of us was a father, so I called up the counselors, had them come to the firehouse. Nobody said a word about it. There was no negativity, completely accepting of it. Two peer counselors came, older guys, war-years firemen. They told us about what we might experience and that there was always someone available to talk to. On the way out he put a stack of cards on the table. We still had not gotten away from the stigma by this point; it was still early. I didn’t want somebody being afraid to be seen taking the card. So I handed the cards out. One guy protested. I leaned in and said ‘Take it for the guy who needs it and doesn’t want to be seen.’ Through the years, there were repeat appearances by the counselors, and I did the same thing every single time. Years later, a firefighter told me, ‘You made us take those cards,’ he said. ‘I used that card, but if I had to get up in front of the guys and take it, I never would have grabbed it.’

—Captain Paul Brown, then a Lieutenant covering in Division 15, Brownsville, Brooklyn; FDNY IMT

“If there was one complaint I would hear it’s that the person [counselor] was too young, had never been at the site and didn’t know what it was like to be a firefighter. Then that was seen as a barrier, because it’s impossible to have every single counselor be a firefighter or had been at the site, which is where the peer counselors I think were very useful.

—Dr. Kerry Kelly MD, then FDNY Chief Medical Officer, Bureau of Health Services, Headquarters Downtown Brooklyn

Physical health: FDNY-WTC medical monitoring

“Acknowledging health concerns both short-term and long-term. We didn’t have all the answers, but we will continue to take care of people moving forward. We were advocates for health in terms of getting funding, making sure that we could get the federal government on board.

—Dr. Kerry Kelly MD, then FDNY Chief Medical Officer, Bureau of Health Services, Headquarters Downtown Brooklyn

“ In October of ‘01, we started to do a baseline on all of us knowing – thanks to Dr. Prezant and Dr. Kelly, they knew that we were in a cauldron of chemicals there and that somewhere along the line, this was going to affect us all. I get my results back and my blood work looked like I had been in a chemical factory for three weeks, just sleeping there. It was all over the place. My numbers were crazy.

—Fire Commissioner (2010–2014) Sal Cassano,
then Assistant Chief at Headquarters, Downtown Brooklyn
(served as Chief of Department 2006–2010)

“ The monitoring and the health program that we developed after 9/11 is still continuing [FDNY-WTC Medical Monitoring] and I think it's stronger than ever because we brought back all our retirees who were exposed. We have probably about 16,000 people we would count as exposed and we still every year we get people back for an annual monitoring. That program has really been able to pick up some early cancers. We're also able to, I think, serve the scientific community by letting people know how our members are doing because we had the preexisting data from our medicals, we were able to show real changes in the health patterns of our members.

We've been able to, through that monitoring again, pick up problems for the individual but also help people understand health trends that have impacted on how the federal government has now recognized these conditions, certified these conditions and provided long-term health care for our members. I think that is very important.

It may be almost 20 years, but the reality is this department is still seeing the effects of that day or those days. It's stark when you see the numbers of people who have developed cancers, people have other ongoing pulmonary problems, and it impacts on, again, the mental health of members who worry, are they going to get something? How do I protect myself? I think that's an important message that we give to stay healthy.

—Dr. Kerry Kelly MD, then FDNY Chief Medical Officer,
Bureau of Health Services, Headquarters Downtown Brooklyn

“ I think every fireman who lived through 9/11 is a hypochondriac because we have to be. Because we never know what is going to get diagnosed into cancer. If something hurts or doesn't feel right – straight to the doctor. It's an underlying thing we're always going to carry. My sister was NYPD, she died from 9/11 cancer. Guys I was down there with and guys I grew up with died from 9/11 cancer. So it's still our reality. It's still every day, you get the posts of this firefighter died, this police officer died. We don't talk about it, but it's that always, ever-present in the back of your head, what if. I look at the kids, our little one, am I going to be healthy? Is something going to take me out because I was there. For me, I always think,' I was there a lot longer than my sister was,' so there's some survivor's guilt.

—Captain Paul Brown, then a Lieutenant covering in Division 15, Brownsville, Brooklyn; FDNY IMT

Family Assistance Unit, firefighter family transport

" I don't recall if we had a family assistance unit, or even a family assistance person, prior to 9/11. That also developed out of this, I guess, starting right afterwards. The fire department set up a unit, which now working with the ceremonial unit, is incredibly helpful in dealing with the needs of the families. You have a line of duty death, both of them are there right from the beginning at the hospital, both of them are there to assist the family, to assist them in setting up the funeral, and seeing to their needs, every need, and then following up forever, really, the needs of these families. Some of them have needs ongoing for the rest of their time. We're lucky enough to find good people to staff that. Those two, Ceremonial Unit, Family Assistance Unit, all this coming out of 9/11 has made the department just so much better.

—Fire Commissioner (2014–2022) Dan Nigro, then Chief of Operations Headquarters, Downtown Brooklyn (served as Chief of Department 2001–2002)

" The firehouse used to take care of the family if a guy was in the hospital. Guys would stay with the family while other guys covered their shifts in the firehouse. The family would be taken care of, we'd drive them back and forth to the hospital or the kids to school, we'd mow their lawn, shovel snow. The firehouse would chip in to cover any expenses. Since the Trade Center, the department officially took that over. Everything is coordinated by the Family Assistance Unit. A firefighter is taken off the chart [removed from firehouse responsibilities] and assigned to the family for as long as it takes.

—Captain Paul Brown, then a Lieutenant covering in Division 15, Brownsville, Brooklyn; FDNY IMT

“ Now Family Assistance Unit is dealing with all of our World Trade Center deaths. We have 253 [now over 400] people that have died since September 11, due to illnesses contracted at the World Trade Center.

—Fire Commissioner (2010–2014) Sal Cassano, then Assistant Chief at Headquarters, Downtown Brooklyn (served as Chief of Department 2006–2010)

“ My time in the Family Assistance Unit was the most rewarding of my time on the job, out of 35 years.

—Captain Kerry Hollywood, then in Engine 53, Spanish Harlem, Manhattan; Commanding Officer Family Assistance Unit

Ceremonial Unit

“ If somebody died, then we would put a bunch of people together and do it. It’s been around for a long, long, long time. Unfortunately, we always lose people. It’s the line of work we’re in. Then, because we were so busy doing it, we had to come up with a unit just to take care of ceremonies and funerals. I was the commanding officer of the ceremonial unit. I got my staff together, I said, ‘Okay. What do you know?’ ‘Joe, we know funerals.’ ‘No. No. No. What about doing graduations? What about doing promotions? What about this? What about that?’ ‘Joe, we do funerals.’... Well, we’re going to build a ceremonial unit. Besides doing just funerals, we’re going to build a unit that can function. If we lose a whole company, if we have another September 11 again, if we have to do promotions, graduations, we will become self-contained.

—Lieutenant Joe Minogue,Commanding Officer of Ceremonial Unit; Department Bugler; then a firefighter in Engine 289, Corona, Queens

“ It was quite moving how it was done. The department had a history in this, certainly not on the level that we were faced after 9/11. Now, it's a ceremonial unit. Before it was a person, perhaps, and some volunteers and whatnot. Now, there's a full-fledged ceremonial unit that has plans and procedures that make it, because we have a funeral almost, I'm going to guess, every few weeks for a post-9/11 [9/11-related illness death] member. These funerals are every bit as moving as line-of-duty funerals.

—Fire Commissioner Dan Nigro (2014–2022), then Chief of Operations Headquarters, Downtown Brooklyn (served as Chief of Department 2001–2022)

“ A body is brought in on an apparatus, and every step is choreographed the way the last one was. It is quite a tribute to the member, to the family, in how that's done. The plaque dedications. Ceremonial unit now, to see how they operate, and how they run things. It's incredible. Swiss precision, I would say, how every one of our events is handled, thanks to the members of the ceremonial unit.

I had said, 'After 9/11, there's no way the band [Pipe Band] will be at every funeral.' The band proved me wrong. I've told them that many times they made a liar out of me. Maybe it wasn't the whole band. It might have only been a few because there were more than one funeral on some days. Somebody from the pipes and drums was at every funeral after 9/11. That's an amazing thing.

—Fire Commissioner (2014–2022) Dan Nigro, then Chief of Operations Headquarters, Downtown Brooklyn (served as Chief of Department 2001–2002)

“ I had to change the wall [Memorial for WTC health related deaths] that they had the names on. [It] was already too small midway through my tenure, we had to put up a larger memorial wall in headquarters knowing that it's going to far exceed the 343. [FDNY WTC health-related deaths surpassed 343 in September, 2023.]

—Fire Commissioner (2014–2022) Dan Nigro, then Chief of Operations Headquarters, Downtown Brooklyn (served as Chief of Department 2001–2002)

“Every five years, interviews and all this other stuff. It's just non-stop. Sometimes I just wish it would just disappear.

—Fire Alarm Dispatcher John Lightsey, then in Manhattan Communications Office, Central Park, Manhattan

“I never went up to the site. Never been there since everything's been rebuilt. What I do down here in Florida now, I'm with the FDNY retirees in Spring Hill. I work on a 9/11 memorial with them. Every year we have a memorial honoring everybody, not just the firefighters but everybody who perished that day. Plus I do stuff with Tunnels to Tower a lot now. It seems to help more. A lot of people know my story and everything. Just by being around people who understand, it makes it easier. Doing what I'm doing to honor everybody and never forgetting, it drastically helps. Funny part is when it was time to leave the job, I used to drink. June 1st, 2013, when I retired, I haven't had one drink since then, and I still haven't.

—Fire Alarm Dispatcher John Lightsey, then in Manhattan Communications Office, Central Park, Manhattan

“I don't know what I'm going to do for this anniversary (of 9/11). Some years I've gone to memorials. Some years not. Some years I'm with other people. Some years I'm alone. Some years I drink. Some years I don't. I don't know what I'll do this year.

—Stephanie Gaskell, then a Journalist for Associated Press, New York (covered WTC site for duration of FDNY operations)

“At the 10th anniversary [as FDNY Bugler for the ceremony] I wanted to be out of sight on the lower-level parking garage. I chose that spot for myself because I didn't want to be up in the limelight. I wanted to be in the back. A photographer took the picture. I'm going to work on the 12th. I get the newspaper, and there's a picture of me in Newsday.

—Lieutenant Joe Minogue, Commanding Officer of Ceremonial Unit; Department Bugler; then a firefighter in Engine 289, Corona, Queens

FIRE DEPARTMENT • CITY OF NEW YORK

Supplement No. 90 to Department Order No. 101

September 8, 2025

Edited Online Edition

2.1.1

FDNY MEMORIAL SERVICES AND CEREMONIES COMMEMORATING THE 24th ANNIVERSARY OF WTC ATTACKS

The FDNY will host or participate in a number of commemorative ceremonies to honor the 343 members lost by the Department on September 11, 2001.

At the National September 11th Memorial Plaza at the WTC Site:

On Thursday, September 11, 2025, the City will commemorate the 24th anniversary of the attacks on the World Trade Center. The observance will take place at the National September 11th Memorial Plaza at the WTC Site at Liberty Street and Trinity Place on the morning of September 11th.

The ceremony will observe six moments of silence:

0846 hours: In observance of the time the first plane struck the North Tower. Houses of worship throughout the City will be encouraged to toll their bells at this time.

0903 hours: In observance of the time the second plane struck the South Tower.

0937 hours: In observance of the time Flight 77 struck the Pentagon.

0959 hours: In observance of the time of the fall of the South Tower.

1003 hours: In observance of the time Flight 93 crashed near Shanksville, PA.

1028 hours: In observance of the time of the fall of the North Tower.

On September 11th, the Officer on Duty shall cause the National Flag to be displayed at half-staff on company quarters. This mark of respect shall continue until sunset.

At sundown, the "Tribute of Light" will return as a tribute to the memory of those lost. This poignant symbol will carry us through the night and into the next day.

At Field Locations:

On September 11th, as a mark of respect to those members of the Department who made the Supreme Sacrifice on September 11, 2001, all Firehouses and EMS Stations shall affect the following:

1. A few minutes before 0846 hours, Department Apparatus (where applicable) shall be pulled onto the apron of quarters.
2. At 0845 hours, the Company officer may read the Remembrance a few moments before the 0846 hours moment of silence, before placing apparatus back in quarters.
3. Companies shall observe additional moments of silence at 0903, 0937, 0959, 1003 and 1028 hours.

At Fire Headquarters:

1. At 0845 hours, the Remembrance shall be read over the public address system a few moments before the 0846 hours moment of silence.
2. Building personnel shall observe additional moments of silence at 0903, 0937, 0959, 1003 and 1028

At Tribute Wall:

On September 11th, from 0800 hours to dusk, an Honor Guard will be stationed at the Tribute Wall located on the outer wall of Engine 10 / Ladder 10.

At Firemen's Monument:

On September 11th, at 0930 hours, members of Battalion 18 will host the annual Memorial Services at the Firemen's Monument on Riverside Drive and 100th Street (Upper West Side of Manhattan). A Mass at St. John the Divine will follow at 1215 hours.

At EMS Bureau of Training:

On September 11th, at 0800 hours, the EMS Academy will host its annual September 11th Memorial Service in front of the EMS Academy at Fort Totten, Building 325.

Other September 11th Related Ceremonies:

On September 11th, at 1800 hours, the Office of the Staten Island Borough President will host a Memorial Service at the Staten Island September 11th Memorial located adjacent to the Staten Island Ferry Terminal.

Remembrance

To be read by the Company Officer a few moments before the 0846 hours Moment of Silence on September 11th.

Today, we remember the bravery of the 343 members of this great Department, who made the Supreme Sacrifice Twenty-four years ago today, so that others could be saved.

Twenty-four years ago today, members gathered in their firehouses and EMS Stations to begin another day of service to the people of this city not knowing what the day would bring. This can be said about every day in the life of career First Responders.

On September 11, 2001, the Department lost not simply 343 Members, but we lost One Member 343 times. Today, we come together to remember each of these individuals. We also come as a Fire Department Family to give strength and support to each other.

We continue to honor the memory of our 343 fallen members and their contribution to the Department, the City, and the country. We Will Never Forget.

Let us bow our heads for a moment of silence.

By Order of: **Robert S. Tucker**, *Fire Commissioner*
John M. Esposito, *Chief of Department*

FDNY 9/11 Anniversary Commemoration
Supplement No. 90 to Department Order No. 101, issued on September 11, 2025, for the FDNY Memorial Services and Ceremonies commemorating the 24th anniversary of the 9/11 attacks.
Public document

“ I go back to the firehouse a lot, every year we have a memorial mass, I usually try and make that. We have a great retirees association, and a neighboring town put a good memorial up for the five guys from the area that got killed, and we have a big service there.

—Battalion Chief Bill Moore, then in Battalion 10, Yorkville, Manhattan

“ Now, as I've been a member of the pipe band for some time, we continue to play [at] funerals. It's every two weeks we're doing a funeral for somebody from 9/11 or 9/11 cancer. The 9/11 thing with the New York City fire department is just, at least for now, it's still visceral. It's still right there because we're losing people from these cancer deaths now, and many of whom I work with now at this point, these are people I know.

The pipe band has a really nice tradition. It was one of the best things that we do. We play the pipes at sunset at the Trade Center. Some guys in the pipe band 15 years ago decided, 'Let's go down and play a couple of sets at sunset at the Trade Center.' It started just like that – very, very unofficial, very organically. We still do it. It's unsanctioned. It's unofficial. There's a huge crowd that comes there now, where we are no longer mindful of real sacrifice, we have people in the pipe band whose parents were killed. It's an incredibly emotional, personal event for them, and it's a spectacle for others.

—Battalion Chief Tom Winship, then a District of Columbia FD firefighter; responded to the Pentagon on 9/11; appointed to FDNY 2003; FDNY Pipes and Drums; IMT

Giving back, staying in

“ It was a lot of rebuilding a lot of different areas. It was a sheer picture of dedication and commitment that they helped us to do this, and I can't be more proud of the staff that stayed on and helped us through this.

—Fire Commissioner (2010–2014) Sal Cassano, then Assistant Chief at Headquarters, Downtown Brooklyn (served as Chief of Department 2006–2010) [Stayed an additional 13 years.]

> I did feel a tremendous responsibility for surviving. Maybe that's the survivor's guilt that they talk about. I had and still have a responsibility to - people call you fireman for the rest of your life. If I was busy, I was no busier than the guy who had training and no busier than the guy who was in operations; they were all working. It just had to be done. In choice, you can say no, but in our culture, you wouldn't do that. The only guys that left [Staff Chiefs] were guys who had heart attacks or cancer, literally. They were the only guys who of the 15 guys [Staff Chiefs] that nobody retired.
>
> *—Chief of Operations Pat McNally, then a Deputy Chief in Division 14, Flushing, Queens [Stayed an additional eight years.]*

> I had just hit my 20th anniversary, 20, you can retire and at that time, I was looking to leave, and then after 9/11, it became clear there was a reason to stay.
>
> *—Dr. Kerry Kelly MD,FDNY then Chief Medical Officer, Bureau of Health Services, Headquarters Downtown Brooklyn [Stayed an additional 19 years.]*

LODD Memorial Wall FDNY HQ
The memorial Wall inside the lobby of FDNY headquarters. The names of all firefighters killed in the line of duty since the department's founding in 1865. Additional panels were added following 9/11 to accommodate the additional names.
Shared with permission from the private collection of Paul Brown

20th Anniversary of 9/11
Uniformed member of New York City Fire Department standing solemnly at the 9/11 Memorial during the 20th anniversary commemoration.
Photo by Todd Maisel

“ The guys with time on, like myself, we band together to make it better. The chiefs, they all knew they had to step the game up. They had to do better training. All the deputies and the current chiefs, I would say 90 percent of them all knew that we have to band together and work together with these young kids who were coming on the job to make them do the right thing.... I was very lucky that my wife never asked me to retire after that. I felt in my heart I wanted to make the Fire Department better. I wanted to bring it back to where it was. That if I could touch these young kids' hearts and teach them something. I've felt that in my heart that I wanted to make these guys better firefighters, the New York City Fire Department better.

—Lieutenant Artie Riccio, then a firefighter in Ladder 119
South Williamsburg, Brooklyn working in Ladder 110
[Stayed an additional 19 years.]

“ As far as the job and everything else, FDNY, I really love the job and really didn't want to leave but had no choice. But I'm still part of it, and

I still love it. I can't say anything bad about it. The guys are great. It was a great job, and I loved it a lot.

—Fire Alarm Dispatcher John Lightsey, then in Manhattan Communications Office, Central Park, Manhattan [Stayed an additional nine years.]

The organization

Tactical change

❝ They came with McKinsey and they knew nothing about the fire department. When I was asked to help do the report, and work with them - we told them what needed to be done, and they just wrote it all out.

—Chief of Department (2004–2006) Pete Hayden, then a Deputy Chief in Division 1, SoHo, Manhattan

❝ The department itself, I think the McKinsey report had said that we needed to be more prepared for an event like that, if it should happen, and to be able to break up into mini departments, if you will. If there was a catastrophic event in South Queens, I would come in and I would run South Queens as if it was its own small fire department.

—Deputy Chief Jim DiDomenico, then in Division 13, South Jamaica, Queens

❝ McKinsey gave us a blueprint. Here's your operations on September 11th. Here's from working with our subject matter experts what we think needs improvement and certainly you got to move on it if you want to get better as a department.

—Fire Commissioner (2010–2014) Sal Cassano, then Assistant Chief at Headquarters, Downtown Brooklyn (served as Chief of Department 2006–2010)

❝ After the Trade Center, I think everybody understood that fire rescue was extremely critical. We can rescue all the people we want, but if we don't have the EMS people to treat our people and get them to the hospital, we didn't do our job. Commissioner Scoppetta made EMS an integral part of the department.

—Chief of Department (2010–2014) Ed Kilduff, then a Deputy Chief in Division 3, Midtown, Manhattan and past IMT Incident Commander

Incident Management Team (IMT)

" [In] '02, I go to the commissioner and say, 'This is something we need to do.' There's the Federal People who came here and they were very impressive. They did something that we were clearly lacking the ability, or at least lacking the resources, to do.... 'What if the Feds don't give you the money?' 'I'll tell you right now, I will find the money.' We did the training, and then they agreed to take individuals out and shadow their people in various functions. Then later on, that built up into us sending groups of people, and eventually, even being employed not as a student or a shadower, but actual participant. Then it was used in the city for a disease outbreak and made a great impression on the Mayor.

—1st Deputy Commissioner (2004–2010) Frank Cruthers, then an Assistant Chief at Headquarters, Downtown Brooklyn (served as Chief of Department 1996–1997, 2002–2004)

FDNY IMT Deployment: New Orleans post Hurricane Katrina
FDNY IMT first deployment outside of NYC: Hurricane Katrina, September 2005, New Orleans, LA. At FDNY IMT command post L to R President George W.Bush, Battalion Chief George Maier, Battalion Chief Bob Maynes.
Photo credit: Firefighter Ben Cotton FDNY IMT. With permission, FDNY IMT commanding officer Battalion Chief Rich DePrima

“What I was really impressed with when we started that training program with the FDNY at their request, that they didn't try and shortcut. They really drank the Kool-Aid that our system is performance-based. It's not based on day job or rank structure. That's huge for us. That means in whatever position you choose, you have to be able to be technically proficient in that. You have to go through this training, whatever that is. It took them a while, but they checked all the boxes and did that. Then chose to deploy to the field their own IMT.

—Dan Oltrogge, Commander National Area Command Team (2009–2011), then Incident Commander Trainee SW-IMT, Chief of Fire and Aviation Grand Canyon National Park (served as SW-IMT Incident Commander 2003–2007)

“I think the lesson of 9/11, of having this incident management team, if we had that developed IMT at the time, they would have been right there in place.... They would have been the number one tool that we would have used to manage this overwhelming scene. That's a big change in the department. There's a lot of changes, but that change is monumental.

—Fire Commissioner (2014–2022) Dan Nigro, then Chief of Operations Headquarters, Downtown Brooklyn (served as Chief of Department 2001–2002)

“I think one of the biggest things, on a larger scale, on a more global scale, was to understand the need for support. The command and operations are running the incident, but there's also so many things at the higher levels you can't be thinking of. You can't just have somebody down there who's not trained trying to wing it. Now, we have people who got this incredible training on large-scale events and how to operate the logistics, the finance, and all that. We were good at command and we were good at operations, and now we got better at that, thinking more globally and needing those teams behind the scene.

—Deputy Chief Jim DiDomenico, then in Division 13, South Jamaica, Queens

“I was working with them at Katrina. That was a huge operation. I think that was their first deployment as an incident management team. It was really striking for me. I was in a meeting with their [FDNY] incident commander, a guy named [Deputy Assistant Chief] Mike Weinlin, and then he was talking to senior chief officers of the New Orleans Fire Department. Mike Weinlin is trying to get them to understand, and extolling the positive attributes of the Incident Command System to the New Orleans Fire Department. Four years back, Mike probably couldn't spell Incident Command System, and now he's on the other end of that conversation, in an operational capacity.

—Dan Oltrogge, Commander National Area Command Team (2009–2011), then Incident Commander Trainee SW-IMT, Chief of Fire and Aviation Grand Canyon National Park (served as SW-IMT Incident Commander 2003–2007)

“ They [FDNY Firefighters] go to Katrina and basically, they take over fire protection. While they're off duty, they're out rehabbing the homes of the New Orleans Firefighters who also had been affected by the storm, and nobody told them to do that, nobody asked them to do that. Firefighters, over the years, have continued to greatly impress me but rarely surprise me because I know how much they can do.

—1st Deputy Commissioner (2004–2010) Frank Cruthers, then an Assistant Chief at Headquarters, Downtown Brooklyn (served as Chief of Department 1996–1997, 2002–2004)

“ The Fire department can do this stuff. We have a team that can plan all the things you want to plan, have an incident action plan, ready to go.... Then during [Hurricane] Sandy, our Incident Management Team was heavily involved.... [It] is used now for all major emergencies. During the pandemic, our [IMT] was heavily involved in planning and how we were going to handle it.

—Fire Commissioner (2010–2014) Sal Cassano, then Assistant Chief at Headquarters, Downtown Brooklyn (served as Chief of Department 2006–2010)

“ As far as going forward, it's like when you discover there's a tool that you could use, and say, this just makes life so much easier. After Katrina, we had a couple of crane collapses in the city, we were able to put a small IMT in there to help organize with other agencies, and it released the day-to-day burden of bringing in a new chief every day. I looked at it as it made our life easier by being more organized.

—Assistant Chief Jim Manahan, then a Battalion Chief in Battalion 50, Jamaica, Queens and past IMT Incident Commander

“ Eddie Kilduff [Chief of Department] would always tell us, ‘We’re not just firefighters anymore, we’re emergency managers. We manage emergencies.’ I really believe this, there’s nobody better than us to do it [in] the city of New York and probably the country, because the training that we give people. We send them all over the country now, to help out wildlife fires. We sent them to help out floods in Houston and Florida, and they are not getting involved in the operations, but they get involved in the planning of it.

—Fire Commissioner (2010–2014) Sal Cassano, then Assistant Chief at Headquarters, Downtown Brooklyn (served as Chief of Department 2006–2010)

“ We [FDNY IMT][49] work with DOHMH, [NYC] Department of Health and Mental Hygiene. They are tasked with the canvassing operations, like what we did during Sandy. We are their IMT. They cannot stand up their own IMT. We have that ongoing relationship with them. I would say if you wanted to take COVID, it lasts almost two years. We handled the largest temporary morgue mission for the medical examiner. We worked with fire prevention, helping get them back up and running. Then we helped vaccinate the homebound people. First, it was vaccinate FDNY members, then FDNY family members. Then all city workers, we helped vaccinate. Then the people stuck in their homes.... That would probably be the biggest.

—Battalion Chief Rich Deprima, then a Firefighter in Ladder 154, Jackson Heights, Queens and IMT Incident Commander

“ The FDNY, I think, was very well known because of the fires in the late ‘60s and ‘70s. Now we’re known as just an incredible brand all over the world. We’ve become the forefront agency for all-hazards incident management around the country. For any incident, large-scale event that might happen in New York City, we have a team of folks that are ready to go. We're the only Type 1 Incident Management Team in an urban environment in the country.

—Chief of Training Mike Meyers, then a Lieutenant covering in Division 15, Brownsville, Brooklyn; FDNY IMT

Leadership and training

" The turnover, we hired 7,000 people in a relatively short period of time after that [9/11]. We almost turned over the entire firefighting force. Officers not as much, but firefighters had just a huge turnover. A lot of it was based on what this did to them, both physically and mentally and emotionally. The toll it took on people and on families. To this day, there are people that are not the same.

—Fire Commissioner (2014–2022) Dan Nigro, then Chief of Operations Headquarters, Downtown Brooklyn (served as Chief of Department 2001–2002)

" Now when I became Commissioner, it was a matter of making sure that we weren't complacent in thinking we were done, because you're never done. You're never done rebuilding, you're never done looking at what's out there to make your department better.

—Fire Commissioner (2010–2014) Sal Cassano, then Assistant Chief at Headquarters, Downtown Brooklyn (served as Chief of Department 2006–2010)

FDNY-IMT Sandy morning briefing
Sean Johnson FDNY IMT Public Information Officer at Hurricane Sandy morning briefing. November, 2012
Photo credit: Battalion Chief Walter Kowalski FDNY IMT. With permission, FDNY IMT commanding officer Battalion Chief Rich DePrima

“ I think part of it is, as people move up in the fire department, I think they shouldn't forget where they came from. Unfortunately, now people are moving up faster and faster. It's easy to forget because you never spend as much time. In the past, you spent more time in the different ranks to season a little bit. I'm hoping, for the most part, that the higher echelons don't forget where they came from. I think that's very important.

—Captain Kerry Hollywood, then in Engine 53, Spanish Harlem, Manhattan; Commanding Officer Family Assistance Unit

“ When we would have deployments, our members would go down to Puerto Rico or an area that there was a hurricane, I would be on the tarmac, giving out shots with the nurses because, the message I wanted to give was, ‘We're here for you and we care about you.’

—Dr. Kerry Kelly MD, then FDNY Chief Medical Officer, Bureau of Health Services, Headquarters Downtown Brooklyn

“ Well, one of the biggest pluses that came out of it was Tom Galvin became the Chief of Training, very highly respected in the field, and his commitment to make training the best that it could possibly be. [He said,] ‘We're going to think outside the box.’ He developed the Mobile Training Teams with vehicles that were capable of delivering [Division of Training]-level training out at remote sites. Tom Galvin stepping into that role was hugely, I thought, transformational.

—Deputy Assistant Chief John Norman, Chief of Special Operations, then a Battalion Chief in Battalion 16, Harlem, Manhattan; FDNY USAR

“ We increased our training in every rank, we put people in the right spots that we knew we would use their skill sets.... We increased our probie school training because we had to teach them new things, and lieutenants' training went up. We never had a captain's course, we had started a captain's course. A battalion chief's course was a couple of weeks, it's now eight weeks. We have a course with deputy chiefs and we even have a course for command chiefs as well.

—Fire Commissioner (2010–2014) Sal Cassano, then Assistant Chief at Headquarters, Downtown Brooklyn (served as Chief of Department 2006–2010)

> FOMI is Fire Officers Management Institute, Columbia University, [it was developed] after 9/11 to teach leaders specialized training with [in] a different type of mindset. Thinking three to five years out as a department, to understand how government worked, to understand terrorism on another level. [P]ut together in 2003, that program is still in effect today. They gave an overview of things that we [fire officers] didn't normally think about, it ranged from talking to the media to government history in New York City. That was part of our changing as a department. We had never done that high-level training before.
>
> *—Deputy Chief Jim DiDomenico, then in Division 13, South Jamaica, Queens*

> I was asked with four or five other members to put together a Deputy Chief Command Course. I ended up, with five, six guys, put it together, we taught it. Then I ended up taking over the whole program five, six years later. I still teach it today, even though I'm retired.
>
> *—Deputy Chief Jim DiDomenico, then in Division 13, South Jamaica, Queens*

FDNY-IMT Covid vaccine-Homebound Mission Briefing
FDNY IMT Covid response briefing. L to R: FDNY Chief of Department Tom Richardson, Unknown, FDNY 1st Deputy Comm. Laura Cavanaugh, NYC Mayor Bill DeBlasio, Tom Carrera FDNY IMT.
Photo credit: Lieutenant Kyra King FDNY IMT. With permission, FDNY IMT commanding officer Battalion Chief Rich DePrima

“We provided a couple of other levels of education for people as far as West Point training some of our folks, as far as the Naval War College training some of our folks. We demonstrated to folks that education is good.

—Chief of Department (2010–2014) Ed Kilduff, then a Deputy Chief in Division 3, Midtown, Manhattan and past IMT Incident Commander

“In many ways, September 11th was a liberating event for the FDNY. It coerced us into accepting the mission that is so much broader than just fire and rescue. The awareness of the other threats in the environment, we have to deal with it. There's no way that you could say, ‘Okay, well, yes, that's a law enforcement issue.’ Everybody has to play their part of the mission, and it's changing. The world is constantly changing around us, and we have to adapt to those changes, like it or not.

—Deputy Assistant Chief John Norman, Chief of Special Operations, then a Battalion Chief in Battalion 16, Harlem, Manhattan; FDNY USAR

“So we didn't have a problem getting people at the end of the day. We had plenty of people that wanted to come [to Special Operations]. And then it was a matter of selecting the right people. So, the folks that became the captains and the officers, were able to select good people, solid. And they rebuilt the staffing. They got people in the companies pretty quickly after.... But then it was the process of training them. That was a whole multi-year process, right? But I would argue, you know, within five years after, at least from my perspective, they were back up and running.

—Chief of Department (2020–2022) Tom Richardson, then a Battalion Chief in Battalion 53, Bayside, Queens

Center for Terrorism and Disaster Preparedness (CTDP)

“[I]t could never happen,’ or, ‘There's no way that could happen.’ That was a lesson that we learned on September 11th: that it could. When we look at threats, and today we're looking at cyber, we're looking at drones, we're looking at complex coordinated attacks. I think, from September 11th on, we look at it through a different lens. How is this going to impact the fire department? How do we prepare for this? How do we train for this? That's the biggest change, I think, is the focus on keeping us safe, keeping us prepared, because prior to September 11th, we were never a target, and on September 11th we were. That put us on the path of making sure that we knew that there were people who had no problem harming firemen, and preparing for that. That, I think, is one of the most important lessons.

We established partnerships with West Point. We established partnerships with the FBI. We established partnerships with the NYPD. That probably never would have occurred if not for 9/11.... Living in those silos doesn't exist anymore. The relationship we have with NYPD today is far different than it was in 2001.... It's not only just preparing, but hearing what these other outside agencies have to say and, identifying emerging threats. Two, three years ago, we met with the Secret Service about increasing our presence with respect to our Rescue Task Force that stands by while the United Nations are in session.... Same thing with the FBI reaching out to us, and now we sit on the Joint Terrorism Task Force, where they say...they're looking at information, they're looking at something, and they go, 'Well, it'd be really nice to have a fireman to tell us what would happen in this situation.'

West Point was our first partner, the Combating Terrorism Center. We run their cadets through an exercise. We give them a class in incident management. In return, they come down, and they lecture our officers, fire officers, and EMS officers at our Counterterrorism Leadership Program in the current threat environment in the world of terrorism. It's just having an open dialogue.

If you're responding to a car fire, or it says there's a fire at a church, we're not saying it's terrorism, but put that in the back of your mind that maybe, because it's a house of worship, it's a synagogue, it's a mosque, it's an Episcopalian church, it's a Catholic church. Consider, just think about it on your way as you approach this. Could it be terrorism?... I think that just changes the mindset. It's a more cautious approach. I think guys are a lot more trained these days.

—Deputy Assistant Chief Paul Miller, Chief in Charge Center for Terrorism and Disaster Preparedness, then a Firefighter in Ladder 48, Hunts Point, Bronx

Covid Vaccine Administration Mission
FDNY IMT Covid response briefing. L to R: Dean Koester FDNY IMT, FDNY 1st Deputy Commissioner Laura Cavanaugh, Rich DePrima FDNY IMT, Fire Commissioner Dan Nigro, Jim Long FDNY PIO
With permission, FDNY IMT commanding officer Battalion Chief Rich DePrima

Shifting culture, attitude

“ There's an old expression in the fire service: 'Don't let progress get in the way of a tradition.' Well, we changed that. We made progress get in the way of a tradition. I don't care if we did it that way for 30 years, but in the same respect, I knew I had to have people a lot smarter than me working for me. A lot of them said, 'We can't go into a high-rise building anymore and fight the fire.' We're going to have to change the way we operate.

—Fire Commissioner Sal Cassano, then an Assistant Chief at Headquarters, Downtown Brooklyn

“ One of the guys who I was closest with died, Joe [Angelini Sr.] and, Joey, his son, died also. I worked with Joe. He was the senior-most man to die in the job. I remember giving him a hug just a couple of weeks before that. He didn't really like being hugged, but after September 11, that's the simple way to fit in. We became a department of huggers and we all hugged, we all hug now. [Joe Angelini III graduated from the FDNY Fire Academy in May 2025.]

—Lieutenant Ray Brown, then in Ladder 113, Crown Heights, Brooklyn

“ One of the things that was unique about September 11th was, I don't believe we had thought about high-rise buildings collapsing. Because that had never really happened. Now we were all thinking, in the field, because we were worried about another attack, 'What if this happens again? Do I leave the guys in the building? Will this building come down?' There was a lot of discussion about construction, and a lot more deeper look into how to handle collapse, how to anticipate collapse.

—Assistant Chief Jim Manahan, Assistant Chief of Operations, then a Battalion Chief in Battalion 50, Jamaica, Queens and past IMT Incident Commander

“ If there was anything to learn from that was know what kind of building you're dealing with. Don't commit all your resources at once. I think the fire department for a while afterwards kind of got into that frame of mind of like, 'We're not going to send everybody so quickly right away.' I would say definitely, do not commit all your resources at once. No matter what the situation is, definitely hold back.

—Firefighter Louis Giaconelli, then in Engine 53, Spanish Harlem, Manhattan; FDNY IMT

“ We got a great boost from Homeland Security as far as all the grants they gave us. I believe with 17.5 million dollars later, we got the state-of-the-art operation center. That operation center is put to full use. There is a management team that we bring in, that we developed after September 11. There were feeds coming from helicopters. We have plans for subways and high rise buildings and that plays a big part in us running the city.

—Fire Commissioner (2010–2014) Sal Cassano, then Assistant Chief at Headquarters, Downtown Brooklyn (served as Chief of Department 2006–2010)

“ That center CTDP was a big part of the cooperation we got working with other city agencies, state agencies, federal agencies, the military, so that if and when this happened again, [the] first time we see each other, wouldn't be at the operation. It would be at the center, having a big drill, or someplace else out in the field, having a big drill, and knowing that, this is the way we did it. When we were training, just the way we're going to do it while we're actually here. It was more about not rebuilding only but redesigning, what didn't work or what do we need to change to make it work?

If we pull up to the scene of a bridge or tunnel where there was an explosion, how to report to the people in headquarters so that they could be talking to building engineers, bridge engineers, people like that. 'What's damaged?' so we can assess whether we should commit to the bridge or not commit to the bridge? A lot of that stuff has evolved out of September 11th.

—Deputy Chief Jim DiDomenico, then in Division 13, South Jamaica, Queens

“ What else did we do and how do we change after this event? You know that we lost Chief Ganci, Chief Barbara, Chief Burns, Commissioner Feehan, Ray Downey. How many of our stock chiefs and from that we learned that if and when something happens? We're not all going there anymore. We're just not all going to go to the scene and not have anybody left to run the job.

When Miracle [on the] Hudson happened [the successful emergency landing of a disabled airliner on the Hudson River] I was chief of department. You're thinking, 'Oh my God. Here we go, another terrorist event playing out on the water, what do we have?' I see a chief fire marshal. I said, 'Get on with the FAA, talk to the police department, get as much information as you can. Was this a terrorist event? So that we know what we're responding to and for.' I go to FDOC and I have everything at my disposal there, this great center. I can see more on TV than they can see at the scene. I have a nice huge big planning room we can make use of.

—Fire Commissioner (2010–2014) Sal Cassano, then Assistant Chief at Headquarters, Downtown Brooklyn (served as Chief of Department 2006–2010)

Command Post
Command staff coordinate personnel accountability and tactical assignments at a mobile command post. The integration of field communication and visual tracking boards ensures operational safety during large-scale incidents.
Photo by Todd Maisel

"We did a tremendous amount of training, not with just ourselves, but with the airports. The airports were concerned about active shooters at an airport. A lot has been developed, updated, drilled on. We even went as far as giving guys ballistic equipment because they might have to go into the area with the cops.

We had to partner with our emergency management people, our NYPD people, because this is going to be a unified thing. It's not just a fire. A lot of this terrorism stuff is going to be, 'We need the cops, we need the emergency service people, we might need utility people if utilities are involved – gas or electric or something like that, we need fire personnel, we need EMS personnel.' It had to be a collaborative effort.

—Deputy Chief Jim DiDomenico, then in Division 13, South Jamaica, Queens

“When that Trade Center bombing happened [in 1993], it radically changed the way the FDNY viewed training and the world. We used to just deal with fires and emergency. When I first came on that's all we talked about. That's all we drilled on. That first Trade Center attack really changed how the FDNY viewed things because now we had to add in terrorism and hazmat training for all the members of the department. There was a slow process and a slow coming-to-Jesus moment about how they were going to add that in to our repertoire and begin to train up all the troops on that.

—Chief of Training Mike Meyers, then a Lieutenant covering in Division 15, Brownsville, Brooklyn; FDNY IMT

“As a firefighter, we want to put on the gear, put out the fire, dig in the rubble, and help people; where on the Incident Management Team, you're managing resources. That's a different skillset of management, planning, attention to detail.

—Battalion Chief Rich Deprima, then a Firefighter in Ladder 154, Jackson Heights, Queens and IMT Incident Commander

“Prior to 9/11, you used to hear the phrase a lot, the job is fire. I don't think I've heard that in 23 years. Fire is the home run, but we are aware of singles, doubles, and triples now. Whether it's terrorism or HAZMAT or electrical emergencies or gas leaks, because we've had some big gas explosions. I think as an agency, we've come to realize that we're the fire department, but we really are much more than that. You really need to know a lot about a lot of different things.

—Deputy Chief Jim DiDomenico, then in Division 13, South Jamaica, Queens

“The whole department changed. As far as equipment, training, personnel. There was a dramatic change over in the whole department. What did change, is like I said, personnel, training, leadership. We actually advanced ourselves. Firefighters are self-sufficient. We actually took a step forward and started using technology instead of doing everything on our own. Looking at opportunities available to us as far as grants and money and national training. We pride ourselves on we're the best in the world and everybody follows us. That's just the way it is.

I do a lot of national and international work and they always come back to us to see what we're doing and how we're doing it. Dramatic change the day after.

—Battalion Chief Fred LaFemina, Chief of Rescue Services,
then Captain of Squad 270, South Jamaica, Queens;
member FDNY USAR

“ For me personally, I suppose I was a more carefree individual on September 10th than I am in the days that followed. People have said to me, they always can see a little sadness in my demeanor. It's probably true because I do – it comes and goes. That's the biggest change in me. The biggest change in the department, I believe, is its ability to accept change.

—Fire Commissioner (2014–2022) Dan Nigro,
then Chief of Operations Headquarters, Downtown Brooklyn
(served as Chief of Department 2001–2002)

“ You were there on 9/11 or you weren't there on 9/11, and how more and more they weren't on the job. Nobody talks about it in the firehouse, but it's there. You see it with the new kids or new lieutenant that wasn't around in 2001, they're back to that happy place again, you know what I mean?

—Captain Glenn Rohan, then a Lieutenant in Ladder 43,
Spanish Harlem, Manhattan

Part B: Summary, Lessons, and Commentary

Summary

In the aftermath of the attacks on the World Trade Center, the FDNY changed itself. Its people were changed – individually and collectively – but the department also made a conscious institutional choice to evolve. What had long been a highly effective, yet fundamentally traditional, fire department began to reinvent itself as a modern emergency management agency.

The transformation was visible in improved response capabilities for large-scale incidents and for the consequences of terrorism. More consequential, however, was a seismic shift in how the department managed incidents and prepared its people for them. The changes extended beyond tactics and equipment into the culture of the organization itself. Chief Mike Meyers explained: "We used to just deal with fires, that's all we talked about, that's all we drilled on." Regarding terrorism awareness, he continued: "There was a slow process and a slow coming-to-Jesus moment about how they were going to add that into our repertoire and begin to train all the troops."

Firefighters had to confront a difficult truth: going forward, it could no longer be business as usual. At every level of command, the department had to accept that all-out, aggressive, bias-for-action firefighting was no longer a one-size-fits-all proposition. Some conditions would demand a slower, more measured response.

Chief Sal Cassano told firefighters, "We're going to do everything that we did before. We're going to be as brave as we have to be, we're going to be as courageous as we have to be, we're going to be as rogue as we have to be, but we're going to do it most safely." That adjustment applied just as forcefully to senior leadership. Chief Hayden remarked that in the past [Staff Chiefs] "responded to the sound of the guns. Generals can't do that." Someone, he understood, would always need to stay back to maintain overall command.

This shift ran counter to the instinctive culture of fire departments, particularly large urban ones. By design, they are reactive organizations: an event occurs, the department responds, mitigates the emergency, and then waits for whatever comes next. After September 11, FDNY's firefighters came to a stark realization. As Chief Paul Miller explained: "Prior to September 11th, we were never a target, and on September 11th, we were. That put us on the path of making sure we knew there were people who had no problem harming firefighters and preparing for that."

The FDNY's shift from reaction to proactivity became formalized in October 2004 when the department created the Center for Terrorism and Disaster Preparedness [CTDP]. Born directly out of the lessons of September 11, the center operates as a conduit for information sharing. As Chief Paul Miller described, "We established partnerships with the West Point [U.S. Military Academy], FBI, and NYPD – relationships which would not have occurred without the WTC attacks." Those partnerships, he noted, were about awareness: "It's not only preparing but hearing what these other agencies have to say regarding emerging threats."

For the largest fire department in the western hemisphere, past practices dictated calling more people and equipment in as needed then rotating personnel over a period of days. Senior FEMA Rep. Denis Oneial observed: “If you’re the New York City Fire Department, they have 11,000 firefighters. They could stamp out a fire in the World Trade Center if they had to. This was beyond anything that they had ever conceived of in my opinion. I know it was far more than I ever could conceive of.”

FDNY leadership was in unfamiliar territory. Resources were stretched further than in any past experience. The significant resources dedicated to the WTC impacted the department’s ability to provide fire protection for the remainder of the city. Supporting firefighters on scene well into the foreseeable future was a new challenge for leadership as well.

Federal resources were on hand to help, but the FDNY didn’t know how those resources functioned. As Dan Oltrogge of the SW-IMT saw it: “They [FDNY] didn’t need any help tactically or operationally but support. For whatever reason, they were having a hard time getting them fed, they were having a hard time getting decon. [decontamination], things like that. Having a hard time with the ordering system or supply chain to keep them response ready.”

FDNY leadership quickly understood that the Incident Command System (ICS) would be an extraordinarily useful tool for future incidents. In January 2002, the FDNY took steps toward that goal. Ann Veneman, the U.S. Secretary of Agriculture, signed a Memorandum of Understanding at FDNY Headquarters, agreeing to send Incident Management experts to New York City to train FDNY in ICS. Classroom-trained FDNY personnel would then shadow IMTs on wildfire deployments. By the summer of 2005, FDNY had enough qualified ICS personnel to deploy their own team to Hurricane Katrina in New Orleans.

At the same time, the department faced another profound challenge: a surge of retirements. These retirees, all senior firefighters, officers, and chiefs, represented tens of thousands of years of cumulative firefighting experience. To counter the loss, the department raised training capabilities for all ranks. Chief Mike Meyers explained: “They used to train you to be a lieutenant, and that was the last training you got as a fire officer or chief. Now we train captains for five weeks. We train chiefs for five weeks, which I think makes for a much more competent fire officer out there. It also helps build your networking because you’re in training with these folks. If you have an issue or have a problem, you’re better able to reach out to this network of folks from in and around the city who can help you get through that problem."

Training also extended beyond the department. As Chief Ed Kilduff noted, "We provided a couple of levels of education for people; West Point training some of our folks, the Naval Post Graduate School training some of our folks."

Attitudes toward self-care and caring for each other evolved as well. Prior to the World Trade Center attacks, counseling within the FDNY generally revolved around alcohol rehabilitation, and psychological counseling carried significant stigma. Captain Paul Brown noted the changes: "There's no more stigma regarding getting help. None at all. People are involved in it. They talk about it. They don't hide it. As a matter of fact, anytime there's a traumatic event, now you can call up and get a team to come to the firehouse."

The department also formalized long-standing traditions of caring for firefighters and their families. Historically, this support was handled internally and unofficially within each unit. Following the attacks on the World Trade Center, the department established the Family Assistance Unit. Anytime a firefighter is seriously injured or facing a significant health crisis, a firefighter and a privately funded vehicle are assigned to their family. The department also began honoring firefighters who die from 9/11-related illness as line-of-duty deaths. Captain Glenn Rohan put this into perspective: "I think it [the FDNY] recovered when Chief Nigro started this family assistance unit. If you were retired and had cancer; we're giving them an administrative line of duty death. The pipe band, the fire trucks, the flags. When they said, 'We're going to take care of these guys that are dying.' That's when I said, 'We're stronger than we were.' We're stronger, and until that last guy who responded, all who worked down there is gone, and continue to take care of their families. New York's a great city."

The department, with congressional support, has taken great strides to assist firefighters suffering from 9/11-related illness. Dr. Kerry Kelly, retired FDNY Chief Medical Officer, currently works with the FDNY WTC Medical Monitoring Program. She described its reach: "The monitoring and the health program that we developed after 9/11 continues and I think it's stronger than ever because we brought back all our retirees who were exposed. In the past, when you retired from service, you no longer came for your medical [exams]. Now we continue to bring you back. We have probably about 16,000 people we would count as exposed and every year we get people back for annual monitoring. That program has been able to pick up some early cancers. We're also able to serve the scientific community by letting people know how our members are doing. Because we had preexisting data from our medicals, we were able to show real changes in the health patterns of our members."

Despite these changes, the core traditions of the department endured. Firefighters continue to take care of one another and hold deep pride in a job well done. The sense of family inside the firehouse and the generational learning remain central to FDNY culture. Chief Mike Meyers spoke fondly: "I love sitting around a firehouse and listening to the folks that have been there before me talk about it, or some of the older firefighters telling their stories."

Lessons for Leaders

1 **Find and ascribe meaning to what you do.**

2 **Enact that meaning daily**, i.e., breathe meaningfulness into your work.

Nigro on scene
Commissioner Daniel Nigro observing department operations in Queens.
Photo by Todd Maisel

3. **Choose well.** Work with others who share the work and its meaning, – subordinates, colleagues, leaders, and organizations.

4. **Support others in enacting their meaning.**

5. **Continue to spot the meaning enacted**, i.e., when others live it. Call it out.

6. **Doing 1–5 will create your legacy**, individually and collectively, today and tomorrow.

7. **Find and ascribe meaning to what you do.**

Commentary

Sorting through what we mean by "legacy" helps clarify what has emerged in this chapter, both in its complexity and in its power. That sorting holds implications for us and our lives.

A friend of one of the authors lost his firefighter father on 9/11, his remains never found. Several years later he reflected, "I know that my father died an anonymous death in the rubble. I know that we will never be able to place him in the ground. I also know that he died doing what he loved to do." And for us, how might we integrate the legacy laid out by the responder voices quoted above? What does that question even mean?

"Legacy" carries multiple meanings. Merriam-Webster defines it as "something transmitted by or received from an ancestor or predecessor or from the past." In that sense, legacy morphs across time. It arises from what people do, but those who come later determine its meaning. Indeed, more broadly, as Swiss historian Jacob Burckhardt stated, history itself "is the record of what one age finds worthy of note in another."

Importantly, how individuals define the meaning of what they do in any given moment cannot only determine what they do by driving them to act in one way or another but their definition in and of itself can provide a legacy. Their very act of definition can itself constitute a legacy. Meaning drives action; action, in turn, reinforces meaning. Together, they generate legacy. This dynamic helps explain the origin and power of the FDNY legacy described in this chapter. It also points to the importance of cultivating individual and shared meaning – not only in crisis, but in everyday work.

An old Irish adage can provide focus here: "Nothing happened until you respond." These five words affirm the human agency that everyone carries, the power to define the past and thereby the future through present action. The choice of how to respond matters, whether the day is 9/10, 9/11, or any day thereafter. That meaning of the past carried in the present matters because, as Faulkner wrote, "The past is never dead. It's not even past."

Approximately 300 BCE, the Stoics of ancient Greece developed the philosophy and life practice on Zeno of Citium's painted porch (the Greek phrase for which yielded the word Stoicism). Stoicism emphasizes the impact of how people frame events on their responses to those events. Hence, Stoicism foreshadowed many of our currently most advocated approaches to mental health, including Gestalt, cognitive, narrative and logotherapy. More specifically, "how we mentally characterize a situation has a profound impact on how we respond to it emotionally." Stoicism offers a way to approach setbacks, namely "thinking of setbacks as tests of our character...can dramatically alter our emotional response to them. We can...develop our ability to stay calm, even in the face of very significant setbacks."

Calling the collapse of the Twin Towers a "setback" borders on the profane. Still, the collapses did not set the FDNY back for long. The members persevered. A Stoic might say they derived "no small measure of satisfaction from successfully dealing with the challenges presented them by that setback."

Modern psychologist might state it this way: the FDNY members regarded certain actions as meaningful; experiencing performance of them as intrinsically rewarding. Those rewards, in turn, made the actions more likely to recur. A type of self-reinforcing feedback loop. The department supported those behaviors in various ways including through selection, promotion, training, firehouses as gathering spaces, and both formal as well as informal recognition. Co-workers supported those behaviors as well. So did individuals themselves. Key valued actions included both well practiced and intelligently improvised rescue and acts of comradeship – especially when difficult. Irvine might term it "...the Stoic test strategy: when faced with a setback, we should treat it as a test of our resilience and resourcefulness, devised and administered...by imaginary Stoic gods."[50]

Arguably, the firefighters defined the situation faced on 9/11 as, in effect, a challenge from the gods. To paraphrase one interviewee responder, 'whether or not this all happened because we did something to someone who was now doing something to us didn't change what we faced.' The firefighters were the chosen. They had chosen firefighting. The FDNY had chosen them from among thousands of applicants to fight fires. They inherited and shared a legacy arcing over a century and a half. They shared training, values, and experience. Many carried an even deeper meaning, one born of coming from a family of firefighters, of carrying on a family legacy. Individually and collectively they infused what they faced that day and after with a cherished meaning born of a chosen legacy.

The FDNY faced tests and challenges every day. Day after day, firefighters practiced working in a way that they found meaningful. They trained daily – however unknowingly – for 9/11 and its aftermath. They developed deep and shared habits, shared skills, and shared reasons for acting. They embedded meaning not only in what they did and how they did it, but also in why they did it.

The collective mattered, but so did the individual. Before the Stoics, Celtic traditions emphasized a similar ethic of agency, one summarized by Shea and Gunther,[51] "Do not do what you do because you expect some rewards from the gods, for such is not their nature. Do not rage at the gods for not providing a reward for such is the action of a child. Do what you do, choose as you choose because it defines your life – indeed it defines life itself." This bit of Celtic philosophy turned on a sense of agency – your meaning, your choice. Kierkegaard would likely nod agreement.

In this sense, the FDNY provided a modern enactment of ancient wisdom. First responders defined the moment as they climbed the towers, forced open doors, and shepherded civilians out of the impending death trap. They defined it again as summoned and unsummoned firefighters poured into the Plaza and onto its rubble. They defined it again as they doggedly searched for survivors and subsequently for remains, all amid fire and toxic smoke. They defined what the horror meant and would mean. They learned. They changed. They defined the day for themselves and offered a definition for those who came next.

The firefighters proceeded as Stoics. First, understand the moment. Embrace it. Live in it. Second, respond. In this case, fight back. Do what you can do. Control what you can, beginning with one's own internal state and external behavior. Confront the beast. Use what you know, what you know you know, what you know those around you know. Third, learn and adapt. Let building #7 burn and collapse. Accept, provide, and effectively advocate for trauma support. Acknowledge your ignorance and accept outside aid from a WTF source – "tree people" – to manage the scope of an incident humbly understood to exceed FDNY resident knowledge and experience. Skill yourself to manage such incidents in the future, in NYC or anywhere. Alter your practices for next time. Enhance training, the courses, the providers, and the facility. Learn still more.

The FDNY as a whole thereby responded much as a Stoic would: understand the moment, accept it, act upon it. Control what you can control – beginning with one's own mindset and conduct. Use what is known. Learn what is not. Accept outside help when necessary. Change practices. Build new capabilities. Prepare for what may come next.

Victor Frankl posits that the search for meaning supersedes all other human motivation.[52] He further posits that we choose our meaning, our own subjective meaning, and that we can find it in work (perform a deed), love (truly experience another person), and through courage in the face of unavoidable suffering (all humans experience pain and suffering – what sets us apart is what we do with it). Meaning found leads to a by-product, a by-product too often and inappropriately sought in its own right, namely happiness. Frankl sees happiness as resulting from meaning. Meaning discovered yields both happiness and enables coping with suffering.

That sense of agency – of thought, definition and action – anchors the legacy presented in this chapter. A foundational meaning undergirds it, resides at its center. Victor Frankl argues that the search for meaning constitutes the primary human motivation, discoverable through work, love, and courage even in the face of unavoidable suffering. Meaning, for Frankl, entails "becoming aware of what can be done about a given situation," even in concentration camps, a reality that Frankl lived. "In the filth of Auschwitz…individual differences did not 'blur' but, on the contrary, people became different; people unmasked themselves, both the swine and the saints."[53]

Perhaps the firefighters of the FDNY offer a synthesis of Stoic wisdom, Celtic agency, and Frankl's insight, a synthesis echoing Louis Pasteur's famous observation that "chance favors the prepared mind." The mind tooled with skills including an abiding and deeply, personally rewarding meaning. The FDNY firefighters faced 9/11 and the days and years that followed prepared by their form of Stoicism. They pushed through their circle of hell employing tactics driven by discovered and lived meaning. The survivors emerged battered, injured, wiser, more skilled, and recommitted. They reapplied longstanding meaning and purpose to their re-creation and transformation of their department – and their lives. They reasserted a shared sense of what their work meant.

That, ultimately, is their legacy...and their guidance for us.

Chapter Ten

A Whisper in the Ear

Below are interviewee answers to the question, "If you could time-travel and, knowing what you know now, whisper into your ear on September 10, 2001, what would you whisper?" Their answers will conclude this book. The authors offer a few observations to begin.

First, some responses came quickly, but more often than not, interviewees began their response with a pause. Second, most responses eschewed tactics or mentioning (let alone dwelling on) "should haves." Instead, they focused on identity, duty, and what it means to be an FDNY firefighter. Third, the day divides more than a few lives into Before and the long arc After. Few expressed any regrets. Those who did spoke not of the day, but more about how long they tried to carry the load of the day into their future, about what perhaps they neglected at home. Fourth, an unexpected form of shock comes through: of scale, swarming media trucks, political and jurisdictional tensions, and global implications. Fifth, the responses include the need to improvise, constantly, and the need to carry that understanding forward. Even if they had known what was coming, the firefighters still would have had to feel their way through, adjusting in real time.

Most of us will never face anything like September 11, 2001. Yet all of us have lived, or will live, with our own echo of that day, however faint, and therefore our own version of September 10: a day before a phone call, a diagnosis, an auto accident, a market collapse, a global pandemic, a scandal, a storm, a loss. A day when the coffee percolates, the routine holds, and we have no idea of the wave building offshore, or of what will soon wash over our lives.

What follows are recollections from those looking back on their own September 10. These closing words offer guidance not only to themselves, but to us as well.

When asked, Bill Moore laughed.

> “ I'm glad these questions weren't on a test. Is there a multiple choice?
>
> *—Battalion Chief Bill Moore, then in Battalion 10, Yorkville, Manhattan*

Bob Maynes initially joked and then became reflective.

> “ I think I'd probably tell myself to put some money in an IRA instead of just giving it to the tax department. But honestly, I'm not sure what I would say.
>
> *—Assistant Chief Bob Maynes, Queens Boro Commander, then a Battalion Chief in Battalion 41, East Flatbush, Brooklyn, and past IMT Incident Commander*

> “ I don't know. I don't think I have an answer on that one.
>
> *—Captain Kerry Hollywood, then in Engine 53, Spanish Harlem, Manhattan; Commanding Officer Family Assistance Unit*

Dan Oltrogge paused:

> “You know, that's the first time I've ever had that question.
> That's a really good question.
>
> *—Dan Oltrogge, Commander National Area Command Team (2009–2011), then Incident Commander Trainee SW-IMT, Chief of Fire and Aviation Grand Canyon National Park (served as SW-IMT Incident Commander 2003–2007)*

Ed Kilduff had been asked a question like this before by a journalist.

> “Step up and show up, be a student of the job. Understand how you can contribute to the firehouse and the firehouse will contribute to your well-being. Be the guy that says, I can help with that. Show up when there's something going on in the adjoining battalion or for Memorial and Medal Day. Show up in strength, be a part of a great, great group of people, show your pride in the FDNY.
>
> *—Chief of Department (2010–2014) Ed Kilduff, then a Deputy Chief in Division 3, Midtown, Manhattan and past IMT Incident Commander*

> “Myself? I'm not good at giving myself advice. I wouldn't do anything different. That's just another incident that I'm going to be responding to because, it is.
>
> *—Battalion Chief Fred LaFemina, Chief of Rescue Services, then Captain of Squad 270, South Jamaica, Queens; member FDNY USAR*

> “'You know the answer to that already,' Louis Giaconelli said.
> This is the job.
> Yes, I would have gone anyway, of course.
> I was as prepared as I was. I was prepared as I would ever have been.
> There's nothing I could have done differently to prepare me for that day.
> Nothing.
>
> *—Firefighter Louis Giaconelli, then in Engine 53, Spanish Harlem, Manhattan; FDNY IMT*

Arthur Riccio put it even more directly:

> “Listen, my job as a New York City firefighter is to go in and help people. There's nothing I would've changed. Are you not going to go in to help

people? I mean I don't know. To me, there's nothing you can do. This is part of our job.

—Lieutenant Artie Riccio, then a firefighter in Ladder 119 South Williamsburg, Brooklyn working in Ladder 110

Ray Brown reduced it to a single sentence:

“ When the moment arises, do your job.

—Lieutenant Ray Brown, then in Ladder 113, Crown Heights, Brooklyn

“ There would be a few things that I would whisper. First thing I would probably whisper, 'This is going to be a long haul. You need to take care of yourself and your family.' Something I think, in many ways, I neglected for many years. I was running a sprint for years when I should have been preparing and running a marathon.

The other thing I would whisper is that not everyone is you. I worked people to death, because there was too much to do. I regret that. It took me many years to learn that, that people needed to take care of themselves and have boundaries. I had casualties along the way.

—Captain Frank Leto, then Deputy Director, Counseling Services Unit, Bayside, Queens

Pat McNally, thinking about the future, framed it this way:

“ 'Life's going to change, be ready for it.' It did really change. Like I said, just work long hours, responsibilities. I was cruising along pretty good. I had a nice career going.... Be ready for a lot more responsibility and also be willing to change.... I know that I am not the smartest guy in the room. I know what I don't know. I'm willing to listen to people.... Things are going to be different but you don't have to fix all of it.

—Chief of Operations Pat McNally, then a Deputy Chief in Division 14, Flushing, Queens

Paul Miller didn't hesitate long before landing on his answer:

> I would whisper in my ear, 'Be ready for anything.' The next morning, I would understand what that meant.... Never dismiss an idea just because it's too crazy.
>
> *—Deputy Assistant Chief Paul Miller, Chief in Charge Center for Terrorism and Disaster Preparedness, then Firefighter Ladder 48, Hunts Point, Bronx*

Dan Oltrogge listed what no one could have been fully prepared for:

> Expect to improvise on almost a daily basis. Expect resistance from the jurisdictions you're there to help. Try to understand the level of stress and tension. You're not gonna know until you get immersed in it, that is present. Have, best as you can, an understanding of a global implication. You know, satellite trucks for as far as you can see. We're used to satellite trucks, but not 150 of them, you know, that kinda thing.
>
> *—Dan Oltrogge, Commander National Area Command Team (2009–2011), then Incident Commander Trainee SW-IMT, Chief of Fire and Aviation Grand Canyon National Park (served as SW-IMT Incident Commander 2003–2007)*

> My attitude is, never forget the fear.... There is [a] fear factor but you have to override it, but never forget it. Put yourself in that spot. If you know it's dangerous or something, you're going to have to do it but do it as safe as possible.
>
> *—Battalion Chief Bill Moore, then in Battalion 10, Yorkville, Manhattan*

After a pause:

> If I could give myself advice, it would be, 'Holy shit, you're going to see some things that you never thought you'd get through. Take it step by step, day by day. No matter how bad it is, you're going to get through it. You're going to survive it. Process it, feel it, and move forward. If you take it step by step, piece by piece, you will get through it, and you'll get through it successfully.'
>
> *—Chief of Training Mike Meyers, then a Lieutenant covering in Division 15, Brownsville, Brooklyn; FDNY IMT*

Dr. Kerry Kelly said something similar, quieter:

> “I think knowing that things will get better and that you can find happiness and some joy as time goes on, that when that event first happened, I didn't know that I would ever be able to feel that again.
>
> *—Dr. Kerry Kelly MD, then FDNY Chief Medical Officer, Bureau of Health Services, Headquarters Downtown Brooklyn*

Pete Hayden responded with characteristic economy:

> “One of the kids said, ‘Geez, Dad, this is the worst birthday you ever had.’ ‘To the contrary,’ I said, ‘It's the best birthday I've ever had, I'm around to celebrate.’
>
> *—Chief of Department (2004–2006) Pete Hayden, then a Deputy Chief in Division 1, SoHo, Manhattan*

> “We lost the first deputy commissioner. I know Bill. I loved Bill. He promoted me to staff. He's an institution. A world of knowledge. He shouldn't have been there. At least not that close.

Then, asked what he'd whisper to himself, he said:

> “I'd still go and have no regrets.
>
> *—1st Deputy Commissioner (2004–2010) Frank Cruthers, then an Assistant Chief at Headquarters, Downtown Brooklyn (served as Chief of Department 1996–1997, 2002–2004)*

Jim DiDomenico made the point even more directly:

> “The chiefs we had there that day were just unbelievable, and they made some great decisions. No one could have done any better than they did. If I could whisper in my ear, I think, how could you have expected that event and had to think about all we need to know about, I don't think anybody still, on that day, would have done anything different. I just want to be clear. I'm not criticizing or critiquing those guys.
>
> *—Deputy Chief Jim DiDomenico, then in Division 13, South Jamaica, Queens*

Kerry Hollywood, unable to answer what he'd whisper to himself, found his footing when asked what he'd tell a young captain facing a difficult day:

> You do what you think is best and trust yourself. You got to trust many decisions you make. Once you make a decision and whatever comes to be, you got to live with it. Trust yourself and more than likely, you're going to do the right thing.... You're the boss.
>
> *—Captain Kerry Hollywood, then in Engine 53, Spanish Harlem, Manhattan; Commanding Officer, Family Assistance Unit*

Dan Nigro, thinking about the question, reached for a military analogy:

> It would be impossible even, I suppose, before the Marine Corps landed on any of these islands that they island-hopped during World War II, [for] the person in charge [not to have] known that a certain number of people that they're going to put into action will be lost. I guess I'd whisper in my ear to do what we have to do.
>
> *—Fire Commissioner (2014–2022) Dan Nigro, then Chief of Operations Headquarters, Downtown Brooklyn (served as Chief of Department 2001–2002)*

Pat McNally remembered advice from a college teacher:

> It's not important to know everything in the Encyclopedia Britannica, but it is important to know that there is an Encyclopedia Britannica and how to use it, and then maybe you can handle what comes your way.
>
> *—Chief of Operations Pat McNally, then a Deputy Chief in Division 14, Flushing, Queens*

A sanguine Summerfelt, after his interview, wrote:

> Nothing. Anything I could say now would seem insignificant or unbelievable to myself then. Trust in our training and experience, belief in our Team and our process, a shared goal to do good and be flexible, and a desire to partner with others got us to the other side.
>
> *—Paul Summerfelt, Commander National Area Command Team (2013–2020), then Planning Section Chief Southwest-IMT, Deputy Chief Flagstaff, AZ Fire Department (served as Type-1 IMT Incident Commander 2008–2012)*

A highly experienced John Norman looked to first principles:

> We can't fix everything at once. Some things are out of your control. Pick a place to make a positive difference and do that. Then find the next thing you can fix, and do that. We didn't cause the problem, we're only here to do our best to make things better. We are only human.
>
> *—Deputy Assistant Chief John Norman, Chief of Special Operations, then a Battalion Chief in Battalion 16, Harlem, Manhattan; FDNY USAR*

Simms, on point, remarked:

> Get some rest. It's gonna be a long day tomorrow.
>
> *—Captain Jeff Simms, then a Lieutenant in Engine 58, Harlem, Manhattan; FDNY IMT*

Rich Deprima took a long view, reaching for the best possible perspective on a most desperate time in his life:

> I'd say: 'You're going to grow in ways you can't yet imagine – so make sure you enjoy the ride.' I never could have foreseen rising through the ranks of the FDNY to become a Battalion Chief and the Incident Commander of the FDNY IMT. The path was built on sacrifice, dedication, and relentless work. But along the way, I learned something essential: you have to pause and appreciate the journey as it unfolds.... Life is far too short to postpone joy until the next step, the next goal, or the next milestone. Savor the moments in between – they're what shape you just as much as the achievements themselves.
>
> *—Battalion Chief Rich Deprima, then a Firefighter in Ladder 154, Jackson Heights, Queens and IMT Incident Commander*

“

From those who gave in the past
to those who will continue to give in the future:
Be proud, be brave, be strong, but most of all be prepared.
FDNY Never Forget 9-11-01.

Inscription on the plaque at the base of pullup bar built from WTC debris at the Fire Academy of FDNY

Afterword

Closing notes to the reader

We, the authors, wrote to you, the reader, at the very beginning of the book. We wrote about what we tried to do and how we tried to do it. We hoped that you would, eventually, join us here. With our respective work finished, we invite you to share your reactions to the book. We look forward to them. Send them to contact@risingfromgroundzero.com

We offer two reactions of our own to the work that we did: the interviews and our study of them. First, we offer a condensed list of lessons for leaders, our attempt at a master list or, as we termed it, "our distillation." Second, we share how this trek (or as our New Zealand friends would say, "track") most affected us each personally.

Lessons for leaders – our distillation

1 **Ascribe meaning.** Develop and share an overriding and personal sense of why you and others do what you do.

2 **Act.** Reconnoiter as possible, of course. Adapt, of course. But first, get off the mat. Beat the count. Support the sense of agency, yours and others, by moving to impact the surrounding vortex.

3 **Sector the chaos.** Break the madness into pieces. Temporal, psychological, physical, and organizational pieces.
Then take it piece by piece.

4 **Attrit the event.** Persist. Wear it down. Turn it. Stay with it.

5 **Heal, integrate, remember.** Massive life events stay with you. They're foundational. They can reshape the DNA of a person or even an organization. Acknowledge the wounds. Keep in touch with them. Visit them as often as personal or collective need suggests. Place them within the chapters of your life.

6 **Learn and develop.** Reach out and not just in. Take notes. Discuss. Ponder. Above all, listen – to yourself and to others.

7 **Ascribe meaning.** Give it life. Let it breathe. Make it yours. Embrace the suck as required. Share as possible.

How this work most affected each author

Greg

I signed on to this project because André asked me to conduct a few interviews in the service of helping Paul ease into retirement. From such a mustard seed.... Our work affected me in numerous ways, consciously and, I suspect, unconsciously, to date and forthcoming. Here are three highly notable effects of which I am very sure:

Understanding the difference between courage and heroism.
I spent most of 2017 in treatment for multiple myeloma, a blood cancer

commonly attributed to exposure to some carcinogenic agent. The disease killed my father. Surgery reduced the cancerous spinal tumor centered in L4 and enhanced the odds for successful courses of radiation and chemotherapy that filled my spring and summer. A skilled surgeon used cadaver bone and titanium to rebuild my spine so that I could walk and go about daily living. Fall brought my conversion into a petri dish, with the elimination of my immune system to better the odds for success of stem cell transplantation.

A collapsing spine generates exquisite pain as it crushes nerve roots, and the assault of treatments take the body close to the edge of simply too much. I left the hospital after the transplantation with an advisory that the modal response to my year of treatment and the stem cell transplant particularly would be 1–2 months in bed, 1–2 months in bed half time, and then, at around 3 months, resumption of more or less normal activity.

I was in the gym 48 hours after discharge from the hospital. How? Because, unwittingly, I'd spent my life preparing for this year – heavy, heavy

Be proud, be brave, be strong, but most of all be prepared.
FF Morgan Nunez, Ladder 36, detailed to the fitness unit, FDNY Fire Academy working on the pullupbar constructed from WTC steel.
With permission from the private collection of Paul Brown

exercise since junior high school – not unlike how the FDNY had unknowingly spent its 150 years before 9/11 unknowingly preparing for 9/11.

Was I courageous? Perhaps. Courage means facing down extreme personal adversity, in this case, extended acute, life-threatening adversity. Was I heroic? No, because unlike the FDNY, I had fought for my own survival. The firefighters on 9/11 were courageous and fought to survive, of course. They too faced down acute individual adversity, but unlike me, they employed their courage in the service of others, in the service of trying to procure an alternate future for others, indeed to procure for them a future at all. That's the living definition of heroism. That purpose distinguishes it from the merely courageous. Understood. Duly noted. Deeply respected.

The pursuit of healing.

My cancer experience personalizes another aspect of the FDNY's response to 9/11, this one stretching well past the day: enduring great suffering and incorporating it into one's definition of self without allowing it to define

F.D.N.Y. Never Forget 9-11-01
Memorial plaque at the base of an FDNY 9/11 monument focusing on values and remembrance.
With permission from the private collection of Paul Brown

oneself. The FDNY constructed a simple and yet magnificent and living monument to that symbol, one that consumes me whenever I consider it. Probies do their pull-ups outside the Fire Academy on a bar atop the remains from I-beams of the Twin Towers.

A plaque at the base reads "From those who gave in the past to those who will continue to give in the future: Be proud, be brave, be strong, but most of all be prepared. FDNY Never Forget 9-11-01."

In a literal sense, probies (and others) take strength from the remains of 9/11. A "Hirise" simulator opposite the Academy building pictured earlier opened in 2009, funded by the Leary Firefighters Foundation. The teaching inside the Academy reflects expanded and altered training to fulfill a mission altered and expanded in light of 9/11. More fundamentally, probies build physical toughness by training with steel recovered from the Twin Towers themselves – repurposing the remains of 9/11 into preparation for whatever lies ahead.

And the message? Keep it going. Keep the 150 years going. You keep it going. Apply the lessons of 9/11, not only now, but into the future. The future belongs to those who smack their chests against the pull-up bar. Those who do the work.

Remember 9/11, yes – but in the service of what comes next. The training structure stands as a remarkable, symbolic, even poetic, incorporation of a searing event into the definition of the FDNY. Encircle the wound. Heal. Make the event and its impact part of you, body and spirit. Closure? A misguided goal. Integration.

Reasons to cry.

I still cry. I cry when I think of different interviews (especially whenever the interviewees, toughened men and women, cry or just pause to collect themselves, 25 years on): Joe's bent image following one of hundreds of burial deliveries of taps on his trumpet; a firefighter recalling his little daughter's wake up card, "I'm glad you didn't die, Daddy"; the call from Ladder 1 almost immediately to "send every ambulance you got;" Chief Hayden scrambling up on a damaged vehicle to focus the rescuers amidst the wreckage; Senator Mitch McConnell seemingly grudgingly allowing one more year of medical coverage for WTC responders; an FDNY interviewee musing about how to handle the next anniversary; the fire academy plaque; Paul's musing on visiting the 9/11 museum for the first time ("it's just so sanitized"); the 9/11 orphans…my 10-year-old daughter distressed at the rumored prospect that she wouldn't see her out of town father for six months and maybe not forever.

I still cry. I cry for us and, as a reverberation, I cry with those most harmed by 9/11. I cry as a human being for and with other human beings, for the depth and the magnitude of the anguish. I cry for how our failure to heed Mother Teresa's words set the events of the day in motion, "If we have no peace, it is because we have forgotten that we belong to each another." I cry out of respect for the extraordinary effort by the FDNY responders whom we interviewed to follow the therapeutic adage, "Our pain does not differentiate us. We all carry pain. What differentiates us is what we do with our pain." I cry out of gratitude for what so many so deeply hurt by 9/11 did with their hurt– what they planted and what we harvested – firefighters, human beings, acting on and in behalf of nameless others, perhaps on behalf of us all. For the beauty of that gift, I cry.

Paul

I can't describe what writing this book means to me without expressing what "The Job" means to me. It's difficult to convey to non-firefighters the love and respect we feel for the job and for each other. The New York City Fire Department has firehouses, not fire stations. We see our "brother" and "sister" firefighters as family. We are involved in each other's lives, and we know each other's families. We know the people in other firehouses, we know our friends' and relatives' coworkers. Relationships among firefighters exist in a blurred line between the personal and professional. The tragic loss of 343 firefighters was extremely personal. We are all deeply connected, so much so that I have cried at funerals for firefighters I've never met.

On and following 9/11 we did not all suffer equally. The degree of trauma suffered depended on the individual: their experiences, whether they were a survivor or rescuer, who they knew among those killed, and the closeness of those relationships. It also depended on their personal experiences during the rescue and recovery efforts. Just as we did not all suffer equally, we have not progressed toward personal healing equally. Consequently, many firefighters have been guarded about sharing their experiences. With the passage of time, though, it has become less difficult for many to speak about it.

I wasn't there when the towers fell. I arrived later, not knowing whether my brother Ray or so many others that I knew had survived. My story is insignificant compared to the experience of many others. So, what has this project made me feel?

Absolutely honored and humbled; honored to be entrusted with the words and experiences of those who survived, those who dusted themselves off and went back in. Humbled by their openness and willingness to be vulnerable, to speak of still-painful subjects. And ultimately, proud– proud to be part of the incredible family that is FDNY. I have always considered it an honor to have served...I miss it every day.

Reflecting on what this project has meant to me leads me to think about how and why it began. It started at the intersection of my interest in FDNY history and my exposure to executive leadership education. That connection grew through my friendship with André Kotzé. André is an executive coach, educator, military veteran, and good friend. He hired me in various roles to support his work with executive groups.

Through the years, we regularly found ourselves in the classrooms of our now-partner and friend Dr. Gregory Shea at Wharton. Several of his programs examined leadership in the worlds of business, athletics, and the military. I visited Gettysburg with one of Greg's leadership courses, and participated in case studies of Shackleton's 1916 Antarctic expedition in another. Those programs taught leadership through historic moments of crisis and endurance. They helped me to see that the FDNY's experience on 9/11 belonged in that same conversation. I remember regularly remarking "You should study the fire service."

The attacks on the World Trade Center were a historic event of global significance. Everyone knows the basic story of what happened. But few are aware that it wasn't a single-day event for the FDNY. No one knows the boots-on-the-ground stories of those who were there that day and after. Fires burned underground for 99 days. Digging and searching for the remains of the fallen lasted eight months on site, then months more at the landfill. First-person accounts would eventually fade with the passage of time. And the losses are not only in the past – deaths from WTC-related illnesses continue, now almost monthly.

My lifelong interest in department history led me to read extensively about its history and traditions, and many accounts of "the big ones." But much of what I learned also comes from my family history. My grandfather, father, two uncles, two brothers, and four cousins were all New York

City Firefighters. Around our kitchen table, we heard plenty of stories – but they were usually about the job itself, the action, the people, and the humor. They rarely went into specifics about what those experiences cost the men and women who lived through them.

I knew that my father was on the job for quite a few notable events. He worked through the War Years, a period of intense fire activity. He also worked in Rescue 1 in Manhattan, a unit that responded to all large fires in the borough as well as technical rescue calls. I knew he had responded to some important moments in department history, but I didn't know many of the details. I had always assumed that because he was the child of a World War II vet, he had learned not to talk about it. So it wasn't surprising to me that he was not overly talkative regarding the difficult parts.

Dad developed short-term memory issues in his 80s. The doctors told us that speaking with him about older memories would help keep his mind active. So talk about the old stuff we did. We spoke about life and family, but we also spoke a lot about "The Job." I learned so much about his experiences – some I knew small portions of, and others I knew nothing about. All of his experiences were worthy of preserving for future generations of our family.

My Dad spoke about his father, my grandfather. He was a firefighter in the Bronx and a U.S. Navy reservist when World War II began. He transferred to active naval duty, was promoted to lieutenant, and later commanded a firefighting vessel off Omaha Beach on D-day. He came home, went back to work in the firehouse, and never spoke about it.

When asking Dad about "the Big Ones," I was most surprised to learn that he was at the 23rd Street Collapse when it happened. I always thought he arrived there later. The 23rd Street Collapse was the largest loss of life for the FDNY prior to 9/11. Twelve firefighters were killed in a fire and collapse in the Wonder Drug Store on October 17, 1966. He knew all of them.

I asked, and he spoke – in detail.

He told me about going into the basement and miraculously finding an engine company partially buried, and about digging them out. They all survived. He paused a bit before speaking about the search for 18 Engine. He choked up as he described his part in the searching and digging, then finding each of them, one by one. None survived.

I knew more about another fire and collapse that occurred nine weeks later. On December 22, 1966, there was a multiple-alarm fire and subsequent collapse at 43rd Street and 6th Avenue. The newspapers called it the "Miracle on 6th Avenue." Seven firefighters became trapped under the debris when the building on fire collapsed. I had read the news clippings. I knew Dad was there when it happened. I knew the story, but very few of the details. So, I asked.

He remembered hearing the firefighters tapping and calling out from inside the remnants of the building. He spoke of the firefighters by name – he knew all of them. He worked for hours with firefighters from Rescues 1 and 3, tunnelling, cutting, and shoring up the debris until they dug out the first firefighter, freeing him from the wreckage. More tunnelling, more cutting, more shoring. Hour after hour, finding and freeing each of them, one by one, alive. All seven firefighters were from Engine 54 and Ladder 4, a firehouse that would lose 15 firefighters during the collapse of the World Trade Center.

As I listened to Dad's story, I couldn't help but think of the similarity to my brother Ray tunnelling in the lobby of the Marriott WTC Hotel following the collapse of the South Tower. Lieutenant Bob Nagle from Engine 58 was trapped under the wreckage, along with Battalion 12 Chiefs

Greg Shea Interviewing Paul Brown
Paul sits for an interview with Greg while André records, documenting one of the personal histories that shaped our understanding of FDNY.
With permission from the private collection of André Kotzé

Joe Marchbanks and Fred Sheffold. I knew all three. I had fought fires with them. Joe was one of my first Lieutenants.

58 Engine's crew – including firefighters Mike Fitzgerald and John Wilson – Ray, and his firefighters from Ladder 113, were tunnelling, cutting, shoring. Working their way closer and closer. They got so close to Bobby that they were able to pass him a water bottle and a cigarette. More tunnelling, more cutting, more shoring. Then – whoosh.... Three feet away—three feet – on either side of an unseen boundary, determined who survived and who did not. They only had 28 minutes to close the gap between them. If only they had more time before the North Tower collapsed.

As the years passed, I feared that firefighters' stories would be lost, just as my father's stories were becoming lost in the fog of fading memory. Experiences so rich demand capturing, preserving, and mining for lessons learned. In the past firefighters were guarded around any discussion of the WTC. The wounds were still raw, even decades later.

Brown family – 12/1966
Firefighter Ray Brown Sr. receives Hero of the Month Award for December 1966. L to R: Fire Commissioner Robert Lowry, Alice Brown, Future FDNY capt. Paul Brown, Future FDNY Lt. Ray Brown Jr., Future Chief of Rescue Services Ray Brown Sr., Future NYPD officer Laura Brown-Amodeo [EOW 8/29/19, 9/11 illness], Future FDNY firefighter Thomas Brown.
FDNY photo, public domain

The 9/11 Commission Report was critical of the very things which make the FDNY extraordinary. Chiefs were said to have been too close to the scene, and too many off-duty firefighters responded. But FDNY Chiefs lead from the front. Off-duty firefighters responded to enhance the capabilities of their units, assist their on-duty brethren, and help civilians. Those criticisms only served to further shut down open discussion and learning.

Little has been written regarding the tremendous leaps forward the FDNY has made and continues to make, particularly in the areas of training, incident management, mental health, and institutionalizing caring for its own.

With the passage of time, firefighters' hesitancy about speaking of the WTC began to wane. A slow acceptance toward conversation without criticism, and learning from the WTC experience, was growing. Most came to realize the value of sharing. The urgency is very real, as we continue to suffer 9/11 health-related deaths at a frightening pace. When speaking about younger firefighters with senior and retired firefighters, a common sentiment is "They don't know," or "They need to learn about it." Of the more than 11,000 FDNY firefighters on the job on 9/11, fewer than 600 remain on duty. We vow never to forget. The way we help others to never forget is to tell the stories so that their legacy lives on.

I knew many of their stories. I knew there was incredible leadership from all ranks – lessons to be preserved before memory fades or those who lived the moment are gone. I also knew that I had no idea how to organize them. I knew nothing about writing or educational methodology, or interviewing. But I knew people who knew these things.

As more years passed, I continued working with André and Greg. I continued to believe we needed to study the fire service. Gettysburg and Shackleton were generations ago – leadership stories told without a single firsthand account. Time kept passing. People were passing. People were moving away. People were getting older. Memories were fading.

My persistence paid off in 2018. I finally convinced André and Greg of the value of the FDNY lived experience. The FDNY's story was not just what it experienced at the WTC; it was also a story of incredible resilience and perseverance. The story is not simply about how the FDNY rebuilt. It is the story of how the FDNY reconstructed itself stronger and better. I experienced those changes. I knew the big picture. I needed André and Greg, experienced lifelong educators, to help find the themes and deeper learning within the stories.

We began interviewing firefighters of every rank, as well as folks involved with the department. They spoke openly of their experiences and told their stories of the largest event in their lives. Some cried, some choked up, some needed a minute. Their stories are powerful and humbling. It was an absolute honor to be entrusted with them. It was a deeply moving experience.

Initially, we were unsure how to properly honor the material. We worked through that as we captured the memories, insights, and lessons of the people who were there. Many had never shared their experiences before. We quickly found that all of them shared in our desire to preserve and learn from their lived experience. They wanted to tell their stories. They wanted future generations to hear those stories as they remember them – not as they might be written by a historian a hundred years from now.

In being entrusted with their stories, we were reminded of something simple and enduring:

All gave some, some gave all.

That is worth studying, preserving, and sharing with future generations of leaders.

André

I first visited the United States in 1997, arriving as a young educator from South Africa eager to learn more about experiential education. On that work trip, through a circle of friends I had tapped into, I met Paul. Like many firefighters, Paul moonlighted on his days off to afford the privilege of doing the job he loved.

By 2001, Paul and I were close friends, even with an ocean between us. I was still living in Cape Town when the news broke. Like the rest of the world, I turned on the television and watched the horror unfold through CNN's around-the-clock coverage.

Two weeks later, I was back in the U.S., stepping into what has since become the new reality of air travel.

By then, in my 30s, I had completed my military service in South Africa, responded to the St. James Church Massacre, and spent 15 years on a mountain rescue team – 10 of them in the helicopter unit. Even so, I still couldn't imagine what Paul was living through. I understood enough, however, to do what matters most in moments like that: give him space, stay close, and make sure he knew he was loved and supported.

Between 2004 and 2015, I became part of a group of men – mostly firefighters, some from Annapolis, Maryland, others from New York – who found one another in the long wake of September 11, often at the many funerals that followed. When we gathered, it usually involved winter mountaineering, whiskey, and cards. Every trip cost me money. The therapy, though, wasn't in the whiskey. It was in the talk, the fresh air, the adventure, and the laughter.

As I watched the FDNY rebuild and transform from the outside, I sat inside a trusted circle of friends. I watched them advance in their careers. I watched them healing.

Eight years working on this book impressed many things upon me. Details may fade with time. These themes, I suspect, won't.

On Disruption

"You can't outwork this."

Dan Oltrogge passed on that insight to Pete Hayden. Together, Dan and Pete taught me something essential: how to accept help, how to lean on others without losing myself.

The odds of encountering something on the scale of 9/11 may be slim. Even in professions built around crisis, such a time-splitting event is rare. But is it? Perhaps it's part of the deal. I was in Cape Town the day Nelson Mandela was released from 27 years of incarceration on Robben Island. In a New York minute, South Africa transformed from an apartheid state into the youngest and most progressive democracy in the world at the time. History does not always announce itself in advance.

At some point, something will fundamentally disrupt my life: a loss that reshapes my family, an illness that narrows my world, a military service that scrambles my identity, a mistake I can't undo. The details will vary. The pattern won't. Eventually, I will be required to start again – sometimes quietly, sometimes publicly – often before I feel ready. It's not a choice.

That still frightens me. I find courage in the faces of those who ran into those buildings because it was their job and they were ordered to. I also find courage in the quieter confrontations: with grief, alcohol, addiction, shame.

Recovery from disruption is rarely a solo performance. It's a network – support, love, and resources, both practical and emotional – offered at the right moments and, just as crucially, allowed in. A friend who stays on the phone. A mentor who makes room for honesty. A therapist who helps me name the part of my story I keep circling. My dear wife Joyce, with infinite kindness and patience.

I don't get to choose whether life disrupts me. I do get to choose what I build beforehand: relationships that can hold weight, habits that keep me steady, and stories that give meaning to my experience.

And I find hope in my capacity to ask for help, accept it, and let it change me.

On Healing

In my personal experience of trauma, memory rarely arrives as a clean narrative. It comes in shards – images, sounds, smells, a single moment that won't settle – because my mind can't take in every detail while the event is still unfolding and overwhelming. For me, the smell of diesel and dust is one such shard.

Talk therapy gives my fragments a container. It turns raw sensory experience into language, and language into something my mind can place in time. Malachy Corrigan frames healing as an act of repeated telling, not a single breakthrough:

> “ I'm a big believer in verbal therapy.... [T]he person told me the story until they've exhausted their story because maybe I'm hearing a dozen times before the person gets light and connects into something in their life.
>
> —*Malachy Corrigan NP, then Clinical Director, Counseling Services Unit SoHo, Manhattan*

The repetition isn't redundant. It's integration. Each retelling lets me test the edges of what I can bear, say what couldn't be said, and stitch the traumatic loop back into the rest of my life.

Some fragments resist that stitching. They stay lodged as "unfinished work," especially when the memory feels graphic, isolating, or incomplete. Corrigan describes a firefighter caught on a single brutal detail, returning to it whenever life tightens:

> “ Unfinished work psychologically.... That story was told to me more than 1,000 times with the gentleman that's trying to make a connection with that memory and himself.
>
> —*Malachy Corrigan NP, then Clinical Director, Counseling Services Unit SoHo, Manhattan*

Listening to Malachy, Glenn, John, Ray and so many others taught me to see how my stories can stop owning me and start belonging to me.

> They tell me I need to talk about it more. I haven't opened up in years.
>
> *—Fire Alarm Dispatcher John Lightsey, then in Manhattan Communications Office, Central Park, Manhattan*

> I need to talk about it. Because I can't keep things inside. I got to let it out. That would be advice that I would give to anybody, let it out, share it.
>
> *—Lieutenant Ray Brown, then in Ladder 113, Crown Heights, Brooklyn*

On service

I recall our second interview with Commissioner Nigro. This was the interview where he said to us, "You are doing God's work." The commissioner was full of knowledge, memories, and experience, willing to share all of it - even his pain. I watched him visibly tire as the interview progressed. It clearly cost him to give us the answers we were seeking.

Exhausted Dan Nigro
Former Commissioner Daniel Nigro during a poignant moment in an interview, reflecting the heavy burden of leadership and loss.
With permission from the private collection of André Kotzé

To me, in that moment, he was doing more than recalling events. He served a moral center: honoring the fallen. Their lives matter. The institution matters. While he had breath, he would talk to anyone making an honest attempt to learn from his experiences.

And he was not alone. Over and over, we heard their stories, told not to be objectified, but to be useful; not to seal the memory away, but to share it so others can carry what's learned.

> “Listen, if I could help somebody I'm all for it...I'm talking from my heart.
>
> —*Lieutenant Artie Riccio, then a firefighter in Ladder 119 South Williamsburg, Brooklyn, working in Ladder 110*

> “I want the story to be shared, so it's a good thing.
>
> —*Captain Frank Leto, then Deputy Director, Counseling Services Unit, Bayside, Queens*

I am deeply grateful to those who spoke to us. They gave us their stories not because it was easy, but because they believed the telling might help someone they would never meet.

That is the purest form of service I know, and I will seek to pay it forward.

The Fallen

343 FDNY Members Killed on September 11, 2001

Name	Rank	Unit	Date
Joseph Agnello	Lieutenant	Ladder 118	September 11, 2001
Brian Ahearn	Lieutenant	Engine 230	September 11, 2001
Eric Allen	Firefighter	Squad 18	September 11, 2001
Richard Allen	Firefighter	Ladder 15	September 11, 2001
James Amato	Battalion Chief	Squad 1	September 11, 2001
Calixto Anaya, Jr.	Firefighter	Engine 4	September 11, 2001
Joseph Angelini	Firefighter	Rescue 1	September 11, 2001
Joseph Angelini, Jr.	Firefighter	Ladder 4	September 11, 2001
Faustino Apostol, Jr.	Firefighter	Battalion 2	September 11, 2001
David Arce	Firefighter	Engine 33	September 11, 2001
Louis Arena	Firefighter	Ladder 5	September 11, 2001
Carl Asaro	Firefighter	Battalion 9	September 11, 2001
Gregg Atlas	Lieutenant	Engine 10	September 11, 2001
Gerald Atwood	Firefighter	Ladder 21	September 11, 2001
Gerard Baptiste	Firefighter	Ladder 9	September 11, 2001
Gerard Barbara	Assistant Chief	Citywide Tour	September 11, 2001
Matthew Barnes	Firefighter	Ladder 25	September 11, 2001
Arthur Barry	Firefighter	Ladder 15	September 11, 2001
Steven Bates	Lieutenant	Engine 235	September 11, 2001
Carl Bedigian	Lieutenant	Engine 214	September 11, 2001
Stephen Belson	Firefighter	Ladder 24	September 11, 2001
John Bergin	Firefighter	Rescue 5	September 11, 2001
Paul Beyer	Firefighter	Engine 6	September 11, 2001

Name	Rank	Unit	Date
Peter Bielfeld	Firefighter	Ladder 42	September 11, 2001
Brian Bilcher	Firefighter	Engine 33	September 11, 2001
Carl Bini	Firefighter	Rescue 5	September 11, 2001
Christopher Blackwell	Firefighter	Rescue 3	September 11, 2001
Michael Bocchino	Firefighter	Battalion 48	September 11, 2001
Frank Bonomo	Firefighter	Engine 230	September 11, 2001
Gary Box	Firefighter	Squad 1	September 11, 2001
Michael Boyle	Firefighter	Engine 33	September 11, 2001
Kevin Bracken	Firefighter	Engine 40	September 11, 2001
Michael Brennan	Firefighter	Ladder 4	September 11, 2001
Peter Brennan	Firefighter	Squad 288	September 11, 2001
Daniel Brethel	Captain	Ladder 24	September 11, 2001
Patrick Brown	Captain	Ladder 3	September 11, 2001
Andrew Brunn	Firefighter	Ladder 5	September 11, 2001
Vincent Brunton	Captain	Ladder 105	September 11, 2001
Ronald Bucca	Fire Marshal	Manhattan Base	September 11, 2001
Greg Buck	Firefighter	Engine 201	September 11, 2001
William Burke, Jr.	Captain	Engine 21	September 11, 2001
Donald Burns	Assistant Chief	Citywide Tour	September 11, 2001
John Burnside	Firefighter	Ladder 20	September 11, 2001
Thomas Butler	Firefighter	Squad 1	September 11, 2001
Patrick Byrne	Firefighter	Ladder 101	September 11, 2001
George Cain	Firefighter	Ladder 7	September 11, 2001
Salvatore Calabro	Firefighter	Ladder 101	September 11, 2001
Frank Callahan	Captain	Ladder 35	September 11, 2001
Michael Cammarata	Firefighter	Ladder 11	September 11, 2001
Brian Cannizzaro	Firefighter	Ladder 101	September 11, 2001
Dennis Carey	Firefighter	Haz Mat 1	September 11, 2001
Michael Carlo	Firefighter	Engine 230	September 11, 2001
Michael Carroll	Firefighter	Ladder 3	September 11, 2001
Peter Carroll	Firefighter	Squad 1	September 11, 2001
Thomas Casoria	Firefighter	Engine 22	September 11, 2001
Michael Cawley	Firefighter	Ladder 136	September 11, 2001
Vernon Cherry	Firefighter	Ladder 118	September 11, 2001
Nicholas Chiofalo	Firefighter	Engine 235	September 11, 2001
John Chipura	Firefighter	Engine 219	September 11, 2001
Michael Clarke	Firefighter	Ladder 2	September 11, 2001
Steven Coakley	Firefighter	Engine 217	September 11, 2001
Tarel Coleman	Firefighter	Squad 252	September 11, 2001
John Collins	Firefighter	Ladder 25	September 11, 2001

Name	Rank	Unit	Date
Robert Cordice	Firefighter	Engine 152	September 11, 2001
Ruben Correa	Firefighter	Engine 74	September 11, 2001
James Coyle	Firefighter	Ladder 3	September 11, 2001
Robert Crawford	Firefighter	Safety Battalion 1	September 11, 2001
John Crisci	Lieutenant	Haz Mat 1	September 11, 2001
Dennis Cross	Deputy Chief	Battalion 57	September 11, 2001
Thomas Cullen III	Firefighter	Squad 41	September 11, 2001
Robert Curatolo	Firefighter	Ladder 16	September 11, 2001
Edward D'Atri	Lieutenant	Squad 1	September 11, 2001
Michael D'Auria	Firefighter	Engine 40	September 11, 2001
Scott Davidson	Firefighter	Ladder 118	September 11, 2001
Edward Day	Firefighter	Ladder 11	September 11, 2001
Thomas DeAngelis	Battalion Chief	Battalion 8	September 11, 2001
Manuel Del Valle	Lieutenant	Engine 5	September 11, 2001
Martin DeMeo	Firefighter	Haz Mat 1	September 11, 2001
David DeRubbio	Firefighter	Engine 226	September 11, 2001
Andrew Desperito	Lieutenant	Engine 1	September 11, 2001
Dennis Devlin	Battalion Chief	Battalion 9	September 11, 2001
Gerard Dewan	Firefighter	Ladder 3	September 11, 2001
George DiPasquale	Firefighter	Ladder 2	September 11, 2001
Kevin Donnelly	Lieutenant	Ladder 3	September 11, 2001
Kevin Dowdell	Lieutenant	Rescue 4	September 11, 2001
Raymond Downey	Deputy Chief	Special Operations	September 11, 2001
Gerard Duffy	Firefighter	Ladder 21	September 11, 2001
Martin Egan, Jr.	Captain	Ladder 118	September 11, 2001
Michael Elferis	Firefighter	Engine 22	September 11, 2001
Francis Esposito	Firefighter	Engine 235	September 11, 2001
Michael Esposito	Captain	Squad 1	September 11, 2001
Robert Evans	Firefighter	Engine 33	September 11, 2001
John Fanning	Battalion Chief	Haz Mat Operations	September 11, 2001
Thomas Farino	Battalion Chief	Engine 26	September 11, 2001
Terrence Farrell	Firefighter	Rescue 4	September 11, 2001
Joseph Farrelly	Battalion Chief	Engine 4	September 11, 2001
William Feehan	1st Deputy Comm.	Headquarters	September 11, 2001
Lee Fehling	Firefighter	Engine 235	September 11, 2001
Alan Feinberg	Firefighter	Battalion 9	September 11, 2001
Michael Fiore	Firefighter	Rescue 5	September 11, 2001
John Fischer	Captain	Ladder 20	September 11, 2001
Andre Fletcher	Fire Marshal	Rescue 5	September 11, 2001
John Florio	Firefighter	Engine 214	September 11, 2001

Name	Rank	Unit	Date
Michael Fodor	Lieutenant	Ladder 21	September 11, 2001
Thomas Foley	Firefighter	Rescue 3	September 11, 2001
David Fontana	Lieutenant	Squad 1	September 11, 2001
Robert Foti	Firefighter	Ladder 7	September 11, 2001
Andrew Fredericks	Lieutenant	Squad 18	September 11, 2001
Peter Freund	Lieutenant	Engine 55	September 11, 2001
Thomas Gambino, Jr.	Firefighter	Rescue 3	September 11, 2001
Peter Ganci, Jr.	Chief of Department	Headquarters	September 11, 2001
Charles Garbarini	Lieutenant	Ladder 61	September 11, 2001
Thomas Gardner	Firefighter	Haz Mat 1	September 11, 2001
Matthew Garvey	Firefighter	Squad 1	September 11, 2001
Bruce Gary	Firefighter	Engine 40	September 11, 2001
Gary Geidel	Firefighter	Rescue 1	September 11, 2001
Edward Geraghty	Deputy Chief	Battalion 9	September 11, 2001
Denis Germain	Firefighter	Ladder 2	September 11, 2001
Vincent Giammona	Captain	Ladder 5	September 11, 2001
James Giberson	Firefighter	Ladder 35	September 11, 2001
Ronnie Gies	Lieutenant	Squad 288	September 11, 2001
Paul Gill	Firefighter	Engine 54	September 11, 2001
John Ginley	Lieutenant	Engine 40	September 11, 2001
Jeffrey Giordano	Firefighter	Ladder 3	September 11, 2001
John Giordano	Firefighter	Engine 37	September 11, 2001
Keith Glascoe	Firefighter	Ladder 21	September 11, 2001
James Gray	Firefighter	Ladder 20	September 11, 2001
Joseph Grzelak	Battalion Chief	Battalion 48	September 11, 2001
Jose Guadalupe	Firefighter	Engine 54	September 11, 2001
Geoffrey Guja	Lieutenant	Engine 82	September 11, 2001
Joseph Gullickson	Lieutenant	Ladder 101	September 11, 2001
David Halderman	Lieutenant	Squad 18	September 11, 2001
Vincent Halloran	Lieutenant	Ladder 8	September 11, 2001
Robert Hamilton	Firefighter	Squad 41	September 11, 2001
Sean Hanley	Firefighter	Ladder 20	September 11, 2001
Thomas Hannafin	Firefighter	Ladder 5	September 11, 2001
Dana Hannon	Firefighter	Engine 26	September 11, 2001
Daniel Harlin	Firefighter	Ladder 2	September 11, 2001
Harvey Harrell	Lieutenant	Rescue 5	September 11, 2001
Stephen Harrell	Lieutenant	Ladder 157	September 11, 2001
Timothy Haskell	Firefighter	Squad 18	September 11, 2001
Thomas Haskell, Jr.	Battalion Chief	Ladder 132	September 11, 2001
Terence Hatton	Captain	Rescue 1	September 11, 2001

Name	Rank	Unit	Date
Michael Haub	Firefighter	Ladder 4	September 11, 2001
Michael Healey	Lieutenant	Squad 41	September 11, 2001
John Heffernan	Firefighter	Ladder 11	September 11, 2001
Ronnie Henderson	Firefighter	Engine 279	September 11, 2001
Joseph Henry	Firefighter	Ladder 21	September 11, 2001
William Henry	Firefighter	Rescue 1	September 11, 2001
Thomas Hetzel	Firefighter	Ladder 13	September 11, 2001
Brian Hickey	Battalion Chief	Rescue 4	September 11, 2001
Timothy Higgins	Lieutenant	Squad 252	September 11, 2001
Jonathan Hohmann	Firefighter	Haz Mat 1	September 11, 2001
Thomas Holohan	Firefighter	Engine 6	September 11, 2001
Joseph Hunter	Firefighter	Squad 288	September 11, 2001
Walter Hynes	Captain	Ladder 13	September 11, 2001
Jonathan Ielpi	Firefighter	Squad 288	September 11, 2001
Frederick Ill, Jr.	Captain	Ladder 2	September 11, 2001
William Johnston	Firefighter	Engine 6	September 11, 2001
Andrew Jordan	Firefighter	Ladder 132	September 11, 2001
Karl Joseph	Firefighter	Engine 207	September 11, 2001
Anthony Jovic	Lieutenant	Ladder 34	September 11, 2001
Angel Juarbe, Jr.	Firefighter	Ladder 12	September 11, 2001
Mychal Judge	Father	Chaplain	September 11, 2001
Vincent Kane	Fire Marshal	Engine 22	September 11, 2001
Charles Kasper	Deputy Chief	Special Operations	September 11, 2001
Paul Keating	Firefighter	Ladder 5	September 11, 2001
Thomas R. Kelly	Lieutenant	Ladder 105	September 11, 2001
Thomas W. Kelly	Firefighter	Ladder 15	September 11, 2001
Richard Kelly, Jr.	Firefighter	Ladder 11	September 11, 2001
Thomas Kennedy	Firefighter	Ladder 101	September 11, 2001
Ronald Kerwin	Lieutenant	Squad 288	September 11, 2001
Michael Kiefer	Firefighter	Ladder 132	September 11, 2001
Robert King, Jr.	Firefighter	Engine 33	September 11, 2001
Scott Kopytko	Firefighter	Ladder 15	September 11, 2001
William Krukowski	Firefighter	Ladder 21	September 11, 2001
Kenneth Kumpel	Fire Marshal	Ladder 25	September 11, 2001
Thomas Kuveikis	Firefighter	Squad 252	September 11, 2001
David LaForge	Firefighter	Ladder 20	September 11, 2001
William Lake	Firefighter	Rescue 2	September 11, 2001
Robert Lane	Firefighter	Engine 55	September 11, 2001
Peter Langone	Firefighter	Squad 252	September 11, 2001
Scott Larsen	Firefighter	Ladder 15	September 11, 2001

Name	Rank	Unit	Date
Joseph Leavey	Lieutenant	Ladder 15	September 11, 2001
Neil Leavy	Firefighter	Engine 217	September 11, 2001
Daniel Libretti	Firefighter	Rescue 2	September 11, 2001
Carlos Lillo	Paramedic	EMS Battalion 49	September 11, 2001
Robert Linnane	Firefighter	Ladder 20	September 11, 2001
Michael Lynch	Firefighter	Engine 40	September 11, 2001
Michael Lynch	Lieutenant	Ladder 4	September 11, 2001
Michael Lyons	Firefighter	Squad 41	September 11, 2001
Patrick Lyons	Lieutenant	Squad 252	September 11, 2001
Joseph Maffeo	Firefighter	Ladder 101	September 11, 2001
William Mahoney	Firefighter	Rescue 4	September 11, 2001
Joseph Maloney	Firefighter	Ladder 3	September 11, 2001
Joseph Marchbanks, Jr.	Deputy Chief	Battalion 12	September 11, 2001
Charles Margiotta	Lieutenant	Ladder 85	September 11, 2001
Kenneth Marino	Firefighter	Rescue 1	September 11, 2001
John Marshall	Firefighter	Engine 23	September 11, 2001
Peter Martin	Lieutenant	Rescue 2	September 11, 2001
Paul Martini	Lieutenant	Engine 201	September 11, 2001
Joseph Mascali	Firefighter	Rescue 5	September 11, 2001
Keithroy Maynard	Firefighter	Engine 33	September 11, 2001
Brian McAleese	Firefighter	Engine 226	September 11, 2001
John McAvoy	Firefighter	Ladder 3	September 11, 2001
Thomas McCann	Firefighter	Engine 65	September 11, 2001
William McGinn	Captain	Squad 18	September 11, 2001
William McGovern	Battalion Chief	Battalion 2	September 11, 2001
Dennis McHugh	Firefighter	Ladder 13	September 11, 2001
Robert McMahon	Firefighter	Ladder 20	September 11, 2001
Robert McPadden	Firefighter	Engine 23	September 11, 2001
Terence McShane	Firefighter	Ladder 101	September 11, 2001
Timothy McSweeney	Firefighter	Ladder 3	September 11, 2001
Martin McWilliams	Firefighter	Engine 22	September 11, 2001
Raymond Meisenheimer	Firefighter	Rescue 3	September 11, 2001
Charles Mendez	Firefighter	Ladder 7	September 11, 2001
Steve Mercado	Firefighter	Engine 40	September 11, 2001
Douglas Miller	Firefighter	Rescue 5	September 11, 2001
Henry Miller, Jr.	Firefighter	Ladder 105	September 11, 2001
Robert Minara	Firefighter	Ladder 25	September 11, 2001
Thomas Mingione	Firefighter	Ladder 132	September 11, 2001
Paul Mitchell	Lieutenant	Ladder 110	September 11, 2001

Name	Rank	Unit	Date
Louis Modafferi	Battalion Chief	Rescue 5	September 11, 2001
Dennis Mojica	Lieutenant	Rescue 1	September 11, 2001
Manuel Mojica	Firefighter	Squad 18	September 11, 2001
Carl Molinaro	Firefighter	Ladder 2	September 11, 2001
Michael Montesi	Firefighter	Rescue 1	September 11, 2001
Thomas Moody	Captain	Engine 310	September 11, 2001
John Moran	Battalion Chief	Special Operations	September 11, 2001
Vincent Morello	Firefighter	Ladder 35	September 11, 2001
Christopher Mozzillo	Firefighter	Engine 55	September 11, 2001
Richard Muldowney, Jr.	Firefighter	Ladder 7	September 11, 2001
Michael Mullan	Firefighter	Ladder 12	September 11, 2001
Dennis Mulligan	Firefighter	Ladder 2	September 11, 2001
Raymond Murphy	Lieutenant	Ladder 16	September 11, 2001
Robert Nagel	Lieutenant	Engine 58	September 11, 2001
John Napolitano	Lieutenant	Rescue 2	September 11, 2001
Peter Nelson	Firefighter	Rescue 4	September 11, 2001
Gerard Nevins	Firefighter	Rescue 1	September 11, 2001
Dennis O'Berg	Firefighter	Ladder 105	September 11, 2001
Daniel O'Callaghan	Captain	Ladder 4	September 11, 2001
Thomas O'Hagan	Lieutenant	Engine 52	September 11, 2001
Patrick O'Keefe	Firefighter	Rescue 1	September 11, 2001
William O'Keefe	Captain	Engine 154	September 11, 2001
Kevin O'Rourke	Firefighter	Rescue 2	September 11, 2001
Douglas Oelschlager	Firefighter	Ladder 15	September 11, 2001
Joseph Ogren	Firefighter	Ladder 3	September 11, 2001
Samuel Oitice	Firefighter	Ladder 4	September 11, 2001
Eric Olsen	Firefighter	Ladder 15	September 11, 2001
Jeffrey Olsen	Firefighter	Engine 10	September 11, 2001
Steven Olson	Firefighter	Ladder 3	September 11, 2001
Michael Otten	Firefighter	Ladder 35	September 11, 2001
Jeffrey Palazzo	Firefighter	Rescue 5	September 11, 2001
Orio Palmer	Deputy Chief	Battalion 7	September 11, 2001
Frank Palombo	Firefighter	Ladder 105	September 11, 2001
Paul Pansini	Fire Marshal	Engine 10	September 11, 2001
John Paolillo	Deputy Chief	Special Operations	September 11, 2001
James Pappageorge	Firefighter	Engine 23	September 11, 2001
Robert Parro	Firefighter	Engine 8	September 11, 2001
Durrell Pearsall	Firefighter	Rescue 4	September 11, 2001
Glenn Perry	Lieutenant	Ladder 34	September 11, 2001
Philip Petti	Lieutenant	Ladder 148	September 11, 2001

Name	Rank	Unit	Date
Kevin Pfeifer	Lieutenant	Engine 33	September 11, 2001
Christopher Pickford	Firefighter	Engine 201	September 11, 2001
Shawn Powell	Firefighter	Engine 207	September 11, 2001
Vincent Princiotta	Firefighter	Ladder 7	September 11, 2001
Kevin Prior	Firefighter	Squad 252	September 11, 2001
Richard Prunty	Battalion Chief	Battalion 2	September 11, 2001
Lincoln Quappe	Firefighter	Rescue 2	September 11, 2001
Michael Quilty	Lieutenant	Ladder 11	September 11, 2001
Ricardo Quinn	EMS Lieutenant	EMS Battalion 57	September 11, 2001
Leonard Ragaglia	Firefighter	Engine 54	September 11, 2001
Michael Ragusa	Firefighter	Engine 279	September 11, 2001
Edward Rall	Firefighter	Rescue 2	September 11, 2001
Adam Rand	Firefighter	Squad 288	September 11, 2001
Donald Regan	Firefighter	Rescue 3	September 11, 2001
Robert Regan	Lieutenant	Ladder 118	September 11, 2001
Christian Regenhard	Firefighter	Ladder 131	September 11, 2001
Kevin Reilly	Firefighter	Engine 207	September 11, 2001
Vernon Richard	Captain	Ladder 7	September 11, 2001
James Riches	Firefighter	Engine 4	September 11, 2001
Joseph Rivelli, Jr.	Firefighter	Ladder 25	September 11, 2001
Michael Roberts	Firefighter	Engine 214	September 11, 2001
Michael Roberts	Firefighter	Ladder 35	September 11, 2001
Anthony Rodriguez	Firefighter	Engine 279	September 11, 2001
Matthew Rogan	Firefighter	Ladder 11	September 11, 2001
Nicholas Rossomando	Firefighter	Rescue 5	September 11, 2001
Paul Ruback	Firefighter	Ladder 25	September 11, 2001
Stephen Russell	Firefighter	Engine 55	September 11, 2001
Michael Russo	Lieutenant	Squad 1	September 11, 2001
Matthew Ryan	Battalion Chief	Battalion 4	September 11, 2001
Thomas Sabella	Firefighter	Ladder 13	September 11, 2001
Christopher Santora	Firefighter	Engine 54	September 11, 2001
John Santore	Firefighter	Ladder 5	September 11, 2001
Gregory Saucedo	Firefighter	Ladder 5	September 11, 2001
Dennis Scauso	Firefighter	Haz Mat 1	September 11, 2001
John Schardt	Firefighter	Engine 201	September 11, 2001
Fred Scheffold	Battalion Chief	Battalion 12	September 11, 2001
Thomas Schoales	Firefighter	Engine 4	September 11, 2001
Gerard Schrang	Firefighter	Rescue 3	September 11, 2001
Gregory Sikorsky	Firefighter	Squad 41	September 11, 2001
Stephen Siller	Firefighter	Squad 1	September 11, 2001

Name	Rank	Unit	Date
Stanley Smagala, Jr.	Firefighter	Engine 226	September 11, 2001
Kevin Smith	Firefighter	Haz Mat 1	September 11, 2001
Leon Smith, Jr.	Firefighter	Ladder 118	September 11, 2001
Robert Spear, Jr.	Firefighter	Engine 26	September 11, 2001
Joseph Spor	Firefighter	Rescue 3	September 11, 2001
Lawrence Stack	Battalion Chief	Safety Battalion 1	September 11, 2001
Timothy Stackpole	Captain	Ladder 103	September 11, 2001
Gregory Stajk	Firefighter	Ladder 13	September 11, 2001
Jeffrey Stark	Firefighter	Engine 230	September 11, 2001
Benjamin Suarez	Firefighter	Ladder 21	September 11, 2001
Daniel Suhr	Firefighter	Engine 216	September 11, 2001
Christopher Sullivan	Lieutenant	Ladder 111	September 11, 2001
Brian Sweeney	Firefighter	Rescue 1	September 11, 2001
Sean Tallon	Firefighter	Ladder 10	September 11, 2001
Allan Tarasiewicz	Firefighter	Rescue 5	September 11, 2001
Paul Tegtmeier	Firefighter	Engine 4	September 11, 2001
John Tierney	Firefighter	Ladder 9	September 11, 2001
John Tipping II	Firefighter	Ladder 4	September 11, 2001
Hector Tirado, Jr.	Firefighter	Engine 23	September 11, 2001
Richard Van Hine	Firefighter	Squad 41	September 11, 2001
Peter Vega	Firefighter	Ladder 118	September 11, 2001
Lawrence Veling	Firefighter	Engine 235	September 11, 2001
John Vigiano II	Firefighter	Ladder 132	September 11, 2001
Sergio Villanueva	Firefighter	Ladder 132	September 11, 2001
Lawrence Virgilio	Firefighter	Squad 18	September 11, 2001
Robert Wallace	Lieutenant	Engine 205	September 11, 2001
Jeffrey Walz	Lieutenant	Ladder 9	September 11, 2001
Michael Warchola	Lieutenant	Ladder 5	September 11, 2001
Patrick Waters	Captain	Haz Mat 1	September 11, 2001
Kenneth Watson	Firefighter	Engine 214	September 11, 2001
Michael Weinberg	Firefighter	Engine 1	September 11, 2001
David Weiss	Firefighter	Rescue 1	September 11, 2001
Timothy Welty	Firefighter	Squad 288	September 11, 2001
Eugene Whelan	Firefighter	Engine 230	September 11, 2001
Edward White	Firefighter	Engine 230	September 11, 2001
Mark Whitford	Firefighter	Engine 23	September 11, 2001
Glenn Wilkinson	Lieutenant	Engine 238	September 11, 2001
John Williamson	Battalion Chief	Battalion 6	September 11, 2001
David Wooley	Captain	Ladder 4	September 11, 2001
Raymond York	Firefighter	Engine 285	September 11, 2001

Post-9/11 Illness Deaths

Name	Rank	Unit	Date
Robert Dillon	Firefighter	Engine Co. 153	April 30, 2003
Vanclive Johnson	Firefighter	Ladder Co. 135	August 22, 2003
Russell Brinkworth	Firefighter	Ladder Co. 135	August 26, 2003
Edward Tietjen	Firefighter	Ladder Co. 48	November 25, 2003
Walter Voight	Firefighter	Ladder Co. 144	February 2, 2004
Kevin Byrnes	Battalion Chief	Battalion 7	February 4, 2004
Stephen Johnson	Firefighter	Ladder Co. 25	August 6, 2004
Richard Burke	Lieutenant	Engine Co. 97	August 13, 2005
Michael Sofia	Firefighter	Engine Co. 165	September 1, 2005
Joseph Costello	Firefighter	Battalion 58	January 3, 2006
William O'Connor	Firefighter	Ladder Co. 84	January 16, 2006
Reinaldo Natal	Lieutenant	Field Comm. Unit	February 5, 2006
Deborah Reeve	Paramedic	EMS Station 20	March 15, 2006
William Wilson, Jr.	Fire Marshal	Manhattan Base	July 15, 2006
Thomas Hodges	Lieutenant	Engine Co. 313	August 30, 2006
Robert Wieber	Firefighter	Engine Co. 262	October 31, 2006
Joseph Colleluori, Jr.	Lieutenant	Engine Co. 324	January 4, 2007
Michael Shagi	Firefighter	Engine Co. 74	June 22, 2007
William St. George	Firefighter	Special Operations	July 1, 2007
Raymond Hauber	Firefighter	Engine Co. 284	August 4, 2007
Brian Ellicott	EMS Lieutenant	EMS Dispatch	November 26, 2007
William Moreau	Firefighter	Engine Co. 166	March 12, 2008
John Murray	Lieutenant	Engine Co. 165	April 30, 2008
Sean McCarthy	Firefighter	Engine Co. 280	May 27, 2008
Bruce Foss	Firefighter	Ladder Co. 108	June 14, 2008
Jacques Paultre	Firefighter	Engine Co. 50	June 24, 2008
Kevin Delano, Sr.	Firefighter	Ladder Co. 142	July 30, 2008
Vincent Tancredi II	Lieutenant	Ladder Co. 47	August 8, 2008
Clyde Sealey	Paramedic	Bureau of Health Services	April 12, 2009
Timothy Lockwood	Firefighter	Engine Co. 275	May 27, 2009
Edward Reilly, Jr.	Firefighter	Ladder Co. 160	July 23, 2009
John McNamara	Firefighter	Engine Co. 234	August 9, 2009
Thomas Roberts	Lieutenant	Ladder Co. 40	August 12, 2009
Kevin Cassidy	Captain	Engine Co. 320	August 30, 2009
Joan Daley	Firefighter	Engine Co. 63	September 27, 2009
Richard Manetta	Firefighter	Ladder Co. 156	October 11, 2009
Peter Farrenkopf	Lieutenant	Marine Co. 6	October 18, 2009

Name	Rank	Unit	Date
John Vaughan	Battalion Chief	Battalion 3	October 26, 2009
Robert Ford	Firefighter	Engine Co. 284	October 29, 2009
Carene Brown	Paramedic	EMS Bureau of Training	December 22, 2009
James Ryan	Firefighter	Ladder Co. 167	December 25, 2009
Robert Hess	Lieutenant	Ladder Co. 76	May 2, 2010
Freddie Rosario	EMT	EMS Station 4	June 15, 2010
Harry Wanamaker, Jr.	Lieutenant	Marine Co. 1	July 20, 2010
Philip Berger	Supervisor Communication	Outside Plant Operations	July 22, 2010
Vincent Albanese	Firefighter	Ladder Co. 38	July 31, 2010
John Sullivan, Jr.	Firefighter	Ladder Co. 34	December 24, 2010
Roy Chelsen	Firefighter	Engine Co. 28	January 9, 2011
John O'Neill	Firefighter	Ladder Co. 52	February 14, 2011
Randy Wiebicke	Lieutenant	Ladder Co. 1	March 2, 2011
Brian Malloy	Firefighter	Ladder Co. 80	March 28, 2011
John Garcia	Lieutenant	Ladder Co. 5	May 13, 2011
Anthony Nuccio	Firefighter	Ladder Co. 175	June 7, 2011
Steven Mosiello	Fire Marshal	Chief of Dept.'s Office	July 15, 2011
Carl Capobianco	Firefighter	Ladder Co. 87	July 29, 2011
Martin Simmons	Firefighter	Ladder Co. 111	July 21, 2008
Andrew Borgese	Lieutenant	Engine Co. 326	January 25, 2011
Emilio Longo	Captain	Ladder Co. 110	August 29, 2011
Raymond Ragucci	Firefighter	Engine Co. 5	September 4, 2011
Virginia Spinelli	Firefighter	Engine Co. 329	December 19, 2011
Sheldon Barocas	Captain	Engine Co. 251	December 19, 2011
William Guido	Deputy Chief	Marine Division	November 10, 2011
Robert Stegmeier	Lieutenant	Ladder Co.127	February 16, 2012
Mark McKay	Lieutenant	Ladder Co. 45	April 4, 2012
John McFarland	Deputy Assistant Chief	EMS Operations	February 6, 2012
Anthony Ficara	EMT	Station 43	June 15, 2012
Patrick Sullivan	Lieutenant	Ladder Co. 58	June 16, 2012
Michael Mongelli	Firefighter	Battalion 39	August 3, 2012
Lawrence Sullivan	Firefighter	Rescue 5	August 20, 2012
Michael Behette	Firefighter	Ladder Co. 172	September 17, 2012
Joseph Schiumo	EMT	Station 20	December 9, 2012
Ruben Berrios	Paramedic	Station 20	December 10, 2012
John Corcoran	Battalion Chief	Battalion 52	January 11, 2013
Andrew Dal Cortivo	Firefighter	Engine Co. 227	January 13, 2013

Name	Rank	Unit	Date
Martin Fullam	Lieutenant	Ladder Co. 87	January 28, 2013
Charles Jones III	Firefighter	Ladder Co.165	January 29, 2013
William Quick	Firefighter	Ladder Co. 134	January 18, 2011
Willie Franklin, Jr.	Firefighter	Engine Co. 65	February 14, 2011
Thomas Van Doran	Battalion Chief	Battalion 3	November 13, 2012
Walter Torres	Firefighter	Engine Co. 328	December 18, 2012
Richard Arazosa	Battalion Chief	Battalion 19	April 13, 2013
Emil Harnischfeger	Supervising Fire Marshal	Bureau of Fire Investigation	May 6, 2013
Peter Casey	Captain	Engine Co. 212	July 3, 2013
Rudolph Havelka	Paramedic	EMS Bureau of Training	July 9, 2013
Francis Charles	EMT	EMS Station 58	August 27, 2013
John Wyatt, Jr.	Paramedic	EMS Station 22	September 24, 2013
Thomas Greaney	Lieutenant	Ladder Co. 175	January 5, 2014
Keith Atlas	Firefighter	Engine Co. 35	April 4, 2014
Steven Reisman	Lieutenant	Engine Co. 307	June 1, 2014
Joseph Callahan	Firefighter	Engine Co. 245	October 1, 2005
Richard McGuire	Battalion Chief	Battalion 51	December 9, 2012
Douglas Mulholland	EMS Lieutenant	Station 35	May 28, 2013
Luis de Peña	EMT	EMS Station 13	November 7, 2013
Michael Cavanagh	EMS Lieutenant	EMS Station 16	December 2, 2013
James Mandelkow	Deputy Chief Inspector	Bureau of Fire Prevention	December 10, 2013
John Halpin	Lieutenant	Ladder Co. 33	May 29, 2014
William Olsen	EMS Captain	EMS Station 23	June 1, 2014
Keith Loughlin	Lieutenant	Ladder Co. 109	July 31, 2015
John Gremse	Lieutenant	Engine Co. 302	September 16, 2014
Howard Bischoff	Lieutenant	Ladder Co. 149	September 22, 2014
Daniel Heglund	Firefighter	Rescue 4	September 22, 2014
Robert Leaver	Firefighter	Division 3	September 22, 2014
Cornell Horne	Firefighter	Ladder Co.176	October 5, 2014
Thomas Giammarino	EMS Lieutenant	EMS Station 31	October 7, 2014
Eugene McCarey	Firefighter	Ladder Co. 36	November 13, 2014
James Marshall	Firefighter	Ladder 78	November 30, 2014
Charles Szoke	Firefighter	Ladder Co. 21	December 1, 2014
John Cassidy	Battalion Chief	Battalion 40	January 21, 2015
John Graziano	Captain	Ladder 78	March 13, 2015
Gregory Chevalley	Firefighter	Ladder Co. 176	April 24, 2015
Adolfo Otaño	Firefighter	Engine Co. 202	November 8, 2013
Ronald Brenneisen	Firefighter	Ladder Co. 43	September 12, 2014

Name	Rank	Unit	Date
Richard Nogan	Firefighter	Ladder Co. 113	December 20, 2014
Raffaele Scarpitti	Auto Mechanic	Shops	April 24, 2014
George Eysser	Battalion Chief	Battalion 35	June 13, 2015
John Gallagher	Captain	Engine Co. 251	July 26, 2015
Thomas Thompson	Captain	Engine Co. 306	August 17, 2015
Dennis Heedles, Sr.	Firefighter	Engine Co. 151	October 10, 2015
Nicholas DeMasi	Firefighter	Engine Co. 259	October 21, 2015
James Costello	Battalion Chief	Battalion 4	November 25, 2015
Frank Fontaino	Firefighter	Engine 155	December 11, 2015
Harold McNeil, Sr.	EMS Lieutenant	Station 31	September 8, 2015
Gary Gates	Lieutenant	Field Comm. Unit	September 29, 2015
Michael Smith	Firefighter	Ladder Co. 58	December 25, 2015
Thomas Kelly	Firefighter	Ladder Co. 19	January 3, 2016
Joseph Morstatt	Firefighter	Ladder Co. 45	March 5, 2016
Robert Alford	Lieutenant	Engine 231	March 22, 2016
Cruz Antonio Fernandez	Lieutenant	Ladder 111	July 14, 2006
Robert Ventriglia	Firefighter	Engine 207	November 2, 2010
James Hicks	Firefighter	Engine 7	July 25, 2015
Thomas Lynn	Firefighter	Engine 5	October 23, 2015
Norman Valle	EMT	Station 20	January 6, 2016
Thomas Farrell	Firefighter	Ladder 41	March 25, 2016
Robert Johnson	Firefighter	Engine 81	April 10, 2016
Gregorio Morales	Fire Marshal	Bronx Base	July 30, 2016
William Woodlon	Firefighter	Engine 21	August 20, 2016
Ronald Biller	Lieutenant	Engine 151	September 18, 2016
Vincent Ungaro	Captain	Engine 235	October 1, 2016
Paul Santoro	Firefighter	Engine259	October 15, 2016
John Dunn	Firefighter	Engine 230	November 7, 2016
Harry Davis	Firefighter	Squad 18	November 11, 2016
Raymond Alexander	Lieutenant	Engine 70	November 21, 2016
Joseph O'Toole	Firefighter	Ladder 41	December 12, 2016
Kevin Rooney	Firefighter	Engine 42	January 22, 2017
Brian Masterson	Firefighter	Marine 9	January 22, 2017
Robert DiGiovanni	Firefighter	Ladder 144	January 27, 2017
Edith Torres	EMS Lieutenant	Communications	February 8, 2017
Robert Newman	Firefighter	Ladder 18	February 9, 2017
Rose Scott	EMT	Communications	February 15, 2017
Steven Sorger	Lieutenant	Engine 6	March 11, 2017
Mario Bastidas	EMS Lieutenant	Station 58	April 1, 2017

Name	Rank	Unit	Date
Roy Smith	Firefighter	Engine 156	April 2, 2017
James Lanza	Firefighter	Ladder 43	April 6, 2017
Mark Harris	Paramedic	Station 23	May 13, 2017
Raymond Pfeifer	Firefighter	Engine 40	May 28, 2017
William Kelly	Lieutenant	Ladder 116	June 10, 2017
William Gormley	Firefighter	Ladder 174	June 14, 2017
Robert Alexander	Marine Engineer	Marine 1	August 14, 2017
Walter Nelson, Jr.	EMS Lieutenant	Station 31	May 2, 2014
Michael Duffy	Firefighter	Ladder 174	August 8, 2017
Joseph McKeon	Battalion Chief	Battalion 46	August 19, 2017
Michael O'Hanlon	Firefighter	Engine 68	August 28, 2017
Robert Tilearcio	Firefighter	Engine 266	October 25, 2017
Joseph Stach, Jr.	Lieutenant	Ladder 6	January 7, 2018
Raymond Phillips, Jr.	Firefighter	Rescue 3	January 27, 2018
Ronald Svec	Firefighter	Ladder 82	February 2, 2018
Edward Meehan	Lieutenant	Ladder 22	February 2, 2018
Joeddy Friszell	EMS Deputy Chief	EMS Division 3	March 5, 2018
Paul Tokarski	Firefighter	Ladder 164	March 10, 2018
Thomas Phelan	Pilot	Marine 9	March 16, 2018
Keith Young	Firefighter	Ladder 158	March 17, 2018
John Buhler	Marine Engineer	Marine 6	March 24, 2018
George Froehlich	Firefighter	Ladder 87	March 29, 2018
Robert Lembo	Firefighter	Ladder 144	May 29, 2018
Ronald Spadafora	Assistant Chief	Bureau of Fire Prevention	June 23, 2018
Anthony Alese	Firefighter	Engine 9	June 7, 2009
Michael Guttenberg	Doctor	OMA	October 17, 2017
Victor Valva	Captain	Engine 167	February 19, 2018
Brent Crobak	Firefighter	Engine 251	May 8, 2018
Charles Williams	Firefighter	Ladder 111	July 10, 2018
Robert Miuccio	Battalion Chief	Battalion 22	July 12, 2018
Michael McDonald	Firefighter	Ladder 128	August 11, 2018
Jimmy Martinez	Firefighter	Engine 157	August 24, 2018
Dennis Heaney	Firefighter	Ladder 157	September 10, 2018
John Elges	Firefighter	Ladder 134	September 15, 2018
Felipe Torre	EMT	Bureau of Training	October 10, 2018
Martha Stewart	Paramedic	Station 8	November 18, 2018
Joseph Rodriguez	EMT	Station 58	November 23, 2018
Daniel Bove	Firefighter	Engine 251	November 26, 2018
John Moschella	Captain	Engine 26	December 8, 2018

Name	Rank	Unit	Date
Richard Meehan	Firefighter	Battalion 06	January 1, 2019
Timothy O'Neill	Lieutenant	Ladder 5	April 2, 2019
Kevin Lennon	Firefighter	Ladder 175	April 3, 2019
John Moran	Lieutenant	Ladder 41	June 21, 2019
Lloyd Stuart	Firefighter	Engine 3	July 7, 2019
Kevin Nolan	Firefighter	Engine 79	July 16, 2019
Richard Driscoll	Firefighter	Engine 91	July 17, 2019
Owen Carlock	Firefighter	Ladder 122	May 23, 2012
Robert Gless	Firefighter	Engine 329	October 25, 2016
John O'Brien	Firefighter	Engine 329	July 30, 2017
James Hurson	Firefighter	Engine 318	May 22, 2018
Robert Collis	Captain	Engine 304	May 11, 2019
Joseph Walsh	Firefighter	Ladder 32	June 28, 2019
James J. Sottile	Auto Mechanic	Shops	July 24, 2019
Robert Fitzgibbon	Firefighter	Engine 47	August 14, 2019
Walter McKee	Firefighter	Battalion 39	August 18, 2019
John Boyle	Firefighter	Rescue 1	August 24, 2019
Joseph Losinno	Firefighter	Engine 302	September 13, 2019
Roger Espinal	Firefighter	Engine 320	September 14, 2019
Richard Tanagretta	Firefighter	Rescue 5	September 24, 2019
Andrew Gargiulo	Firefighter	Engine 160	November 6, 2019
Richard Estreicher	Lieutenant	Engine 248	November 11, 2019
Clifford DiMuro	Firefighter	Ladder 137	November 22, 2019
Dennis Gilhooly	Captain	Engine 67	November 30, 2019
Brian Casse	Firefighter	Engine 294	December 4, 2019
Michael Feldman	Firefighter	Ladder 161	February 1, 2020
Richard Jones	Firefighter	Ladder 25	February 7, 2020
Paul Deo, Jr.	Lieutenant	Engine 317	February 7, 2020
Joseph Hatzelman	Firefighter	Engine 218	February 18, 2020
Daniel Foley	Firefighter	Rescue 3	February 22, 2020
Dennis Moynihan	Battalion Chief	Battalion 18	March 21, 2020
John Marr	Firefighter	Engine 34	April 7, 2020
Kevin Dunn	Lieutenant	Engine 251	May 6, 2020
Paul Greco	Firefighter	Squad 270	May 6, 2020
Donald Franz	Lieutenant	Engine 329	March 23, 2020
Anthony Iraci	Firefighter	Engine 155	March 26, 2020
Anthony Catapano	Firefighter	Engine 202	May 30, 2020
Paul McManaman	Firefighter	Squad 252	June 5, 2020
Michael Kavolius	Electrical Inspector	Bureau of Fire Prevention	June 29, 2020

Name	Rank	Unit	Date
Rene Sanchez	EMT	Bureau of Investigations & Trials	September 16, 2020
John P. Poulos	Lieutenant	Engine 266	November 1, 2020
William Hodgens	Firefighter	Engine 160	November 17, 2020
Robert J. Kelly	Fire Marshal	ADMBFI	December 20, 2020
Thomas G. Manley	Firefighter	Ladder 113	December 22, 2020
Ronald P. Storz	Firefighter	Ladder 107	January 16, 2012
Gerard C. McGibbon	Firefighter	Engine 217	January 24, 2021
Paige A. Humphries	EMS Lieutenant	Station 16	February 7, 2021
Dennis Farrell	Firefighter	Ladder 59	February 23, 2021
George H. Wilton, Jr.	Firefighter	Ladder 84	March 5, 2021
Joseph M. Boyle	Firefighter	Engine 38	March 10, 2021
Frank A. Portelle	Captain	Division 6	March 13, 2021
Joseph K. Daly	Firefighter	Engine 218	March 24, 2021
James D. Shaughnessy	Firefighter	Battalion 11	April 1, 2021
James J. Winters	Lieutenant	Engine 278	April 11, 2021
John J. Galvin	Captain	Division 8	April 29, 2021
Sean D. Kenny	Firefighter	Engine 155	May 5, 2021
Thomas G. Oelkers	Firefighter	Ladder 44	May 16, 2021
James P. Wind	Firefighter	Ladder 3	October 6, 2020
Dennis J. Reilly	Firefighter	Engine 156	February 14, 2021
Martin K. Farrell	Lieutenant	Engine 253	March 12, 2021
Anthony Malfi	Firefighter	Ladder 168	June 8, 2021
Wayne T. Goehring	Firefighter	Engine 311	July 19, 2021
Stephenson McCoy	Paramedic	Station 22	August 6, 2021
Patrick J. Whalen	Lieutenant	Ladder 83	August 22, 2021
Stephen J. Reilly	Firefighter	Engine 155	August 24, 2021
Dennis B. McClean	Firefighter	Ladder. 137	September 6, 2021
James J. Cody, Jr.	Firefighter	Ladder 24	September 21, 2021
Mark A. Weiner	EMT	Station 43	September 23, 2021
Michael J. Toal	Firefighter	Ladder 20	September 29, 2021
Patrick J. Lauro	Firefighter	Ladder 47	October 19, 2021
Charles Harris	EMS Captain	Station 31	October 23, 2021
Arthur Lakiotes	Battalion Chief	Battalion 32	October 23, 2021
Ronald Kemly	Battalion Chief	Safety Battalion	November 7, 2021
Michael J. Federowski	Fire Marshal	Citywide South	November 8, 2021
Alvin J. Suriel	Assistant Chief	EMS Operations	December 7, 2021
James T. Redmond	Firefighter	Ladder 143	December 11, 2021
Andrew Hornbuckle	Firefighter	Ladder Co. 109	December 12, 2021

Name	Rank	Unit	Date
John P. Raftery	EMS Lieutenant	Station 49	December 27, 2021
Frank Gasparino	Firefighter	Engine 234	January 19, 2022
Christopher P. Viviano	Firefighter	Ladder 157	January 19, 2022
Michael S. Earley	EMS Captain	Division 4	January 26, 2022
Pablo Guzman	EMS Lieutenant	Human Resources	February 1, 2022
Edward Tierney	Battalion Chief	Battalion 11	February 20, 2022
Frederick Gallagher	Firefighter	Ladder 103	March 1, 2022
Richard J. Chatterton	EMS Deputy Chief	Division 7	March 1, 2022
Gregory LaManna	Firefighter	Engine. 313	March 15, 2022
Michael Lyons	Captain	Division 15	March 29, 2022
James Walsh	Firefighter	Engine. 295	March 31, 2022
John Vigliotti	Lieutenant	Engine 159	May 4, 2022
Alfred Artesona	Firefighter	Engine 71	May 11, 2022
John McCauley	Sup. Fire Marshal	QNBAS	May 28, 2022
Robert Reynolds	Firefighter	Engine 96	May 28, 2022
Michael Verzi	Firefighter	Engine 97	May 29, 2022
Vincent Mandala	Deputy Chief	Division 11	May 31, 2022
Dennis Komar	Firefighter	Engine 151	March 31, 2014
Faye Baughman	EMS Captain	Station 58	October 17, 2020
Gloria Gordon	EMS Lieutenant	Station 50	September 10, 2021
Baudon C Malmbeck	Lieutenant	Marine 9	January 5, 2022
Russell Feliciano	Firefighter	Ladder 111	January 10, 2022
Sabina B Ostolski	Doctor	Bureau of Health Services	June 10, 2022
Steven Thorsen	EMT	Station 23	June 19, 2022
Arthur Darby	Lieutenant	Marine 9	June 20, 2022
Richard Toshack	Firefighter	Engine 307	July 6, 2022
James Devery	Sup. Fire Marshal	ADMBFI	August 18, 2022
Edward Hronec	Firefighter	TECHSV/ Engine 229	August 19, 2022
Paul Schmalzried	Captain	Chauffeur School	August 24, 2022
Ronald Kirchner	Firefighter	Ladder 154	August 25, 2022
William Hughes	Firefighter	Ladder 123	September 16, 2022
Gregg Lawrence	Firefighter	Engine 308	September 17, 2022
Joseph McKie	Battalion Chief	Battalion 41	September 18, 2022
James McCauley, Jr.	Lieutenant	Battalion 23	September 20, 2022
Stephen Geraghty	Battalion Chief	Rescue Battalion	September 21, 2022
George Tripptree	Firefighter	Ladder 173	September 23, 2022
Peter Chiodo	Firefighter	Engine 226	November 26, 2022
John McDonnell	Firefighter	Ladder 116	November 27, 2022

Name	Rank	Unit	Date
Brian O'Flaherty	Battalion Chief	Battalion 9	December 3, 2022
Michael Arriaga	Firefighter	Engine 301	December 5, 2022
Thomas Healy	Firefighter	Ladder 25	December 22, 2022
Patricia Scaduto	EMT	EMS Operations	January 2, 2023
Michael Hance	Lieutenant	Engine 302	January 4, 2023
Donald Kelly	Lieutenant	Ladder 161	January 13, 2023
Thomas McDougall	Firefighter	Ladder 117	January 13, 2023
Bruce Peat	Marine Wiper	Marine 1	February 2, 2023
Joseph Brosi	Lieutenant	Engine 88	February 3, 2023
James Hanley	Battalion Chief	Battalion 7	February 4, 2023
Vincent Cantelmo	Firefighter	Engine 236	February 20, 2023
Vincent Lyons	Battalion Chief	Battalion 43	February 23, 2023
Peter Bushey	Paramedic	Station 40	February 23, 2023
Paul Daniels	Paramedic	Station 16	March 14, 2023
Gary Nybro	Captain	Engine 166	April 4, 2023
James Mager	Firefighter	Engine 293	April 8, 2023
Douglas Harkins	Firefighter	Ladder 29	April 21, 2023
Richard Kobbe	Lieutenant	Ladder 133	May 14, 2023
Karl Sederholt	Fire Marshal	BFI Special Operations	May 22, 2023
James Burns	Lieutenant	Engine 46	May 26, 2023
Michael Costa	Firefighter	Engine 328	June 3, 2023
Neil Ferro	Captain	Engine 227	June 4, 2023
James Donohue	Lieutenant	Ladder 8	June 30, 2023
Thomas Anderson, Jr.	Firefighter	Ladder 162	July 7, 2023
Kevin Kelly	Firefighter	Engine 307	July 28, 2023
Robert Hughes	Firefighter	Ladder 134	July 30, 2023
Edward Pecoroni	Firefighter	Engine 70	August 6, 2023
John Fiorentino	Electrician	Bureau of Fire Prevention of Comm.	August 10, 2023
Robert Welsh	Firefighter	Engine 207	August 18, 2023
John Tiska, Jr.	Firefighter	Engine 229	August 24, 2023
Albert Filosa	Firefighter	Ladder 146	August 28, 2023
Andrew Enderes	Paramedic	Station 27	August 31, 2023
Hilda Vannata	EMT	Station 14	September 20, 2023
Robert Fulco	Firefighter	Engine 250	September 23, 2023
Mark Senno	Firefighter	Ladder 50	October 5, 2023
Christopher Scalone	Battalion Chief	Battalion 53	November 13, 2023
John Delendick	Monsignor	N/A	November 23, 2023
Michael Daly	Firefighter	Ladder 87	November 25, 2023

Name	Rank	Unit	Date
Luke Lynch	Captain	Engine 201	December 12, 2023
Michael Higgins	Lieutenant	Ladder 19	July 28, 2022
Harold Johnston	Firefighter	Engine 36	January 28, 2024
Joseph Berardi	Electrician	Buildings	January 29, 2024
Stephen Anthony Asaro	Lieutenant	Battalion 4	February 10, 2024
William R. Bartholomew	Firefighter	Ladder 49	February 28, 2024
Steven Berube	Captain	Ladder 111	February 28, 2024
Michael Cioffi	Firefighter	Engine 165	March 23, 2024
Robert M. Kelly	Firefighter	HAZMOP	March 31, 2024
Frank Caputo	Firefighter	Engine 68	April 2, 2024
Robert DeLeon, Jr.	EMS Captain	Station 3	April 16, 2024
Kevin Blaine	Battalion Chief	Safety Battalion	April 19, 2024
Michael J. Shanley	Lieutenant	Ladder 27	April 21, 2024
Steven Radich	Firefighter	Engine 97	April 24, 2024
Christopher Swierkowski	EMT	EMS Division 3	May 11, 2024
Charles Maniscalco	Lieutenant	Engine 162	May 27, 2024
Peter Quinn	Firefighter	Ladder 106	January 21, 2019
Arill Nyquist	Firefighter	Engine 243	January 6, 2025
Stephen Russack	Firefighter	Ladder 107	February 16, 2024
Jose Hickson	Firefighter	Engine 285	April 9, 2024
Joseph Scaramuzzino	Firefighter	Ladder 113	May 11, 2024
Edward Cosenza	EMT	Medical Supply Unit	June 30, 2024
Joseph Tumulty	Firefighter	Engine 294	July 3, 2024
Michael Wallace	Firefighter	Engine 251	August 3, 2024
Edward Thompson	Firefighter	Ladder 80	August 9, 2024
James Johnsen	Firefighter	Division 14	August 20, 2024
John Tyrrell, Jr.	Firefighter	Engine 75	August 30, 2024
Thomas LaBarbiera	Captain	Division 3	September 1, 2024
Anthony Cozzino	Lieutenant	Station 43	September 7, 2024
Nicholas Visconti	Deputy Chief	Division 14	September 20, 2024
James Cooney	Lieutenant	Engine 254	October 21, 2024
Thomas Ryan	Firefighter	Ladder 33	November 5, 2024
Patrick Ward	Lieutenant	Engine 281	November 5, 2024
Christopher McCormack	Firefighter	Engine 59	November 10, 2024
Mark Steffens	EMS Division Chief	Division 2	November 11, 2024
John Connolly	Firefighter	Ladder 80	November 13, 2024
Anthony Mastrelli	Firefighter	Ladder 56	November 13, 2024

Name	Rank	Unit	Date
Christopher Bach	Firefighter	Engine 329	November 16, 2024
Lawrence Murphy	Firefighter	Ladder 157	November 18, 2024
Richard Sarnes, Jr.	Auto Mechanic	Fleet Services	November 22, 2024
Thomas Gavitt	Firefighter	Ladder 147	November 27, 2024
Neil Gimpel	Firefighter	Ladder 134	December 30, 2024
Michael DeBenedetto	Firefighter	Ladder 167	January 3, 2025
Dennis Collopy	Battalion Chief	Battalion 11	January 30, 2025
Thomas Dunn	Firefighter	Engine 234	February 1, 2025
Frank Leanza	Carpenter	N/A	February 16, 2025
Pamela Hehn	EMS Lieutenant	Station 16	March 3, 2025
James Sweeney	Lieutenant	Ladder 151	March 6, 2025
Brian Fitzgerald	Firefighter	Ladder 137	March 9, 2025
Edwin Steffens	Firefighter	Engine 214	March 15, 2025
Eugene Kelty, Jr.	Battalion Chief	Battalion 10	March 16, 2025
Daniel McCauley	Firefighter	Ladder 45	March 23, 2025
Christopher Revere	Firefighter	Engine 289	March 26, 2025
Ronald Mitchell, Sr.	Fire Marshal	BFI	April 10, 2025
Vincent McMahon	Lieutenant	Ladder 44	April 12, 2025
Robert Okorn	Firefighter	Ladder 158	April 20, 2025
Frederick Simms	Captain	Ladder 58	June 12, 2025
Thomas Tracy	Captain	Marine 1	July 19, 2025
David Burke	EMS Deputy Chief	EMS Division 9	July 31, 2025
Cliff Krug	Fire Marshal	BFI-SOC	August 1, 2025
Michael W. Skody, Jr.	EMT	Station 40	August 5, 2025
John G. McCann	Firefighter	Ladder 26	August 16, 2025
Thomas del Pino	Firefighter	Ladder 85	September 14, 2025
Timothy Westhall	Firefighter	Engine 251	October 12, 2025
Steven Simineri	Firefighter	Battalion 33	October 14, 2025
Robert "Bobby" West	Firefighter	Squad Company 1	October 24, 2025
Kevin Reilly	Firefighter	Rescue 5	November 7, 2025
John J. Brown	Lieutenant	Ladder 165	November 7, 2025
Michael Carter	Firefighter	Marine 9	November 25, 2025
James Riches	Deputy Chief	Bureau of Operations	November 27, 2025
Kevin Roth	Captain	Division 15	December 8, 2025
Pieter Grosbeck	Firefighter	Battalion 7	December 9, 2025
James McGee IV	EMS Lieutenant	Station 54	December 12, 2025
William VanName	Firefighter	Engine 35	December 26, 2025
Gerard Lennon	Firefighter	Ladder 41	December 27, 2025
James Daly	Lieutenant	Engine 251	January 1, 2026

Name	Rank	Unit	Date
Eugene Schramm, Jr.	Firefighter	Ladder 146	January 10, 2026
Andrew DiFusco	Supv Fire Marshal	BFI Specs Ops	January 28, 2026
David Fenton	EMS Captain	Ems Div 2	January 29, 2026
Jeffrey Armstrong	EMS Captain	NYC OEM	February 8, 2026
Jeffrey Halpern	EMS Lieutenant	Station 39	February 13, 2026
Brian O'Hara	Fire Alarm Disp	CADO Unit	February 23, 2026
George Heck	Firefighter	Engine 224	March 4, 2026
Walter Werner	Captain	Ladder 151	March 5, 2026
Thomas Smith	Firefighter	Engine 224	March 26, 2026
David Harney	Chief of Support Services	Planning Unit	April 7, 2026
Steven Lukowski	Marine Pilot	Marine 9	April 7, 2026
Angel Vasquez	Firefighter	Ladder 173	April 12, 2026
Declan Grant	Firefighter	Ladder 48	April 15, 2026
Richard Ruggiero	Fire Marshal	BFI Bronx Base	April 26, 2026
Michael Reutter	Firefighter	Ladder 175	June 20, 2025
James Hartnett	Lieutenant	Ladder 19	August 4, 2025
Arturo Gonzalez	Paramedic	Station 8	May 28, 2026
Daniel Newman	Firefighter	Ladder 5	December 17, 2025
Wiiliam Blaich	Battalion Chief	Battalion 1	June 5, 2026
Andrew Graf	Lieutenant	Engine 167	June 9, 2026
Harold Yodice	Firefighter	Engine 323	June 12, 2026
Israel Hernandez	Firefighter	Engine 74	June 10, 2026
William McLaughlin	Captain	Engine 312	June 2, 2026

Note: Names are listed chronologically by date of death. In instances of delayed certification of 9/11 illness the member is added following certification.

Those Who Continue to Fall

Name	Rank	Unit	Date

Name	Rank	Unit	Date

Appendices

Appendix A: Interviewee Biographies

Captain Paul Brown, was a Lieutenant Covering in Division 15 Brownsville, Brooklyn. Responded to recall. Appointed 1989, retired as Captain of Ladder 158 in Springfield Gardens, Queens in 2016. Served on FDNY IMT. 3rd generation FDNY, grandfather, father, 2 uncles, 2 brothers, 4 cousins all FDNY. Lieutenant Ray Brown's brother.

Lieutenant Ray Brown, was in Ladder 113, Crown Heights, Brooklyn. Dispatched with Ladder 113. Survived both collapses. Appointed 1979, retired 2002 due to injuries sustained at the WTC. 3rd generation FDNY, grandfather, father, 2 uncles, 2 brothers, 4 cousins all FDNY. Captain Paul Brown's brother.

Fire Commissioner (2010–2014) **Sal Cassano**, was an Assistant Chief in Headquarters, Downtown Brooklyn. Responded from Headquarters. Injured in second collapse. Appointed 1968. Served as Chief of Department (2006–2010), retired in 2014. U.S. Army, Vietnam. Brother and son on FDNY.

Malachy Corrigan Nurse Practitioner, was Director Counseling Services Unit. Responded to Headquarters. Appointed 1982, retired 2014. Father FDNY Captain.

1st Deputy Commissioner (2004–2010) **Frank Cruthers**, was an Assistant Chief in Headquarters, Downtown Brooklyn. Responded to recall. Survived both collapses. Served as Incident Commander for FDNY WTC Task Force. Appointed 1968. Served as Chief of Department twice: 1996–1997, 2002–2004. Retired 2010. Father also served as Chief of Department.

Battalion Chief Rich Deprima, Battalion 49, Astoria, Queens, was a Firefighter in Ladder 154 Jackson Heights, Queens. Responded to recall. Appointed 1995. Currently Commanding Officer of FDNY IMT. U.S. Army veteran.

Deputy Chief Jim DiDomenico, was in Division 13 South Jamaica, Queens. Responded to recall. Appointed 1983, retired 2023. Father FDNY.

2nd Deputy Commissioner Tom Fitzpatrick, was in Headquarters, Downtown Brooklyn. Responded from Headquarters. Survived both collapses. Appointed 1968, retired in 2002.

Assistant Chief Tom Galvin, Chief of Training (2004–2015), was a Deputy Chief in Division 3 Midtown, Manhattan. Dispatched with Division 3. Survived both collapses. Tasked with creating FDNY IMT. Appointed 1978, retired in 2015 as Chief of Training. Brother FDNY.

Stephanie Gaskell, Journalist. Associated Press, International Desk, NY, NY. Arrived post collapse. Covered WTC site for the duration of FDNY operations. Later embedded with U.S. military in Iraq, Afghanistan and Guantanamo Bay, Cuba.

Firefighter Louis Giaconelli, was in Engine 53 Spanish Harlem. Dispatched with Engine 53. Survived both collapses. Appointed 1987, retired 2017. Served on FDNY IMT.

Chief of Department (2004–2006) **Pete Hayden** was a Deputy Chief in Division 1 SoHo, Manhattan. Dispatched with Division 1. Survived both collapses. Served as Deputy Incident Commander of FDNY WTC Task Force. Appointed 1968, retired 2006. Brother, 2 sons, 3 nephews, son-in-law all FDNY.

Captain Kerry Hollywood, was in Engine 53 Spanish Harlem. Responded to recall. Appointed 1973, retired 2008. Served as Commanding Officer of Family Assistance Unit. U.S. Army Veteran. Brother FDNY.

Dr. Kerry Kelly MD, was Chief Medical Officer, Headquarters, Downtown Brooklyn. Self-dispatched. Survived both collapses. Appointed 1981, retired 2018. Continues to serve with FDNY WTC Medical Monitoring Program. Father FDNY Lieutenant.

Chief of Department (2010–2014) **Ed Kilduff**, was a Deputy Chief in Division 3 Midtown Manhattan. Responded to recall. Appointed 1977, retired 2014. Served as Operations Chief for FDNY IMT during Hurricane Katrina response.

Battalion Chief Fred LaFemina Chief of Rescue Services, was of Captain Squad 270 South Jamaica, Queens. Dispatched post collapse with collapse rescue apparatus. Appointed 1986, retired 2012. Member of FDNY USAR team. Father, 2 uncles, brother, 7 cousins all FDNY.

Captain Frank Leto, was in the Counseling Services Unit Bayside, Queens. Responded to recall. Appointed 1983, retired in 2022 as Deputy Director of FDNY Counselling Services Unit. Father FDNY.

Fire Alarm Dispatcher John Lightsey, was in the Manhattan Communications Office Central Park, Manhattan. On air dispatcher 9/11. Appointed 1991, retired 2013.

Battalion Chief George Maier, was in Battalion 9 Hell's Kitchen, Manhattan. Responded to recall. Appointed 1978, retired 2013. Served on FDNY IMT.

Assistant Chief Jim Manahan, was Battalion Chief in Battalion 50 Jamaica, Queens. On-duty relocated to cover Battalion 8 Midtown, Manhattan. Appointed 1978. Retired as Assistant Chief of Operations 2014. Served as Commanding Officer of FDNY IMT for Superstorm Sandy in 2012. Father FDNY.

Assistant Chief Bob Maynes, was a Battalion Chief in Battalion 41 East Flatbush, Brooklyn. Responded to recall. Appointed 1983. Served as Commander of FDNY IMT. Retired as Queens Boro Commander in 2014.

Chief of Operations Pat McNally, was a Deputy Chief in Division 14 Flushing, Queens. Responded off duty with Division 14. Survived both collapses. Appointed 1977. Retired in 2008.

Assistant Chief Mike Meyers, was a Lieutenant, covering in Division 15 Brownsville, Brooklyn. Responded to recall. Appointed 1991. Currently Chief of Training, Member of FDNY IMT. Father and brother FDNY.

Deputy Assistant Chief Paul Miller, was a firefighter in Ladder 48 Hunts Point, Bronx. Responded to recall. Currently Chief in charge of Center for Disaster & Terrorism Preparedness. Bayside, Queens. Appointed 1996.

Lieutenant Joe Minogue, was firefighter in Engine 289 Corona, Queens. Responded to recall. Appointed 1997, served as Commanding Officer of Ceremonial Unit; Department Bugler. Retired as Lieutenant Engine 290 East New York, Brooklyn in 2014. U.S. Air Force Veteran.

Battalion Chief Bill Moore, was in Battalion 10 Yorkville, Manhattan. Responded to recall. Appointed 1968, retired 2013. U.S. Army Vietnam. Son FDNY.

Firefighter Lois Mungay, was in Engine 235 Bedford Stuyvesant, Brooklyn. Responded to recall. Appointed 1983, retired as aide-de-camp Battalion 57 Bedford Stuyvesant in 2004. Among the first group of women appointed to FDNY.

Fire Commissioner (2014-2022) **Dan Nigro**, was Chief of Operations, Headquarters, Downtown Brooklyn. Responded from Headquarters. Survived both collapses. Appointed 1969. Served as Chief of Department 2001–2002. Returned to serve as Fire Commissioner 2014–2022. Father and nephew FDNY.

Deputy Assistant Chief John Norman, was a Battalion Chief in Battalion 16 Harlem, Manhattan. Responded to recall, appointed 1977. Retired in 2016 as Deputy Assistant Chief, Chief of Special Operations. Served on FDNY USAR. 2 sons FDNY.

Dan Oltrogge, was an Incident Commander (trainee) with the Southwest Type-1 IMT and Chief of Fire and Aviation, Grand Canyon National Park. Mobilized midday 9/11. Served as National IMT Area Commander (2009–2011), National Type-1 Incident Commander (2003–2007).

Denis Onieal, Senior FEMA representative at WTC, Superintendent, National Fire Academy, Emmitsburg, MD. Retired Deputy Chief Jersey City, NJ Fire Department. U.S. Army veteran.

Lieutenant Artie Riccio, was firefighter in Ladder 119 South Williamsburg, Brooklyn. Responded while working in Ladder 110. Survived both collapses. Appointed 1983, retired in 2018 as a Lieutenant in Engine 311, Springfield Gardens, Queens.

Chief of Department (2020–2022) **Tom Richardson**, was a Battalion Chief in Battalion 53, Bayside, Queens. Responded to recall. Appointed 1981, retired in 2022. Grandfather and son FDNY.

Captain Glenn Rohan, was a Lieutenant in Ladder 43 Spanish Harlem, Manhattan. Dispatched following first collapse. Survived second collapse. Appointed 1987. Retired in 2012 as Captain of Ladder 31, South Bronx. Son FDNY.

Captain Jeff Simms, was a Lieutenant in Engine 58 Harlem. Responded to recall. Appointed 1978, retired as Captain Engine 69 in 2017. Father FDNY. Served on FDNY IMT.

Paul Summerfelt, was Planning Section Chief with the Southwest Type-1 IMT and a Deputy Chief with the Flagstaff, AZ Fire Department. Mobilized midday 9/11. Served as Commander National Area Command Team (2013–2020), Incident Commander Type-1-IMT (2008–2012).

Battalion Chief Tom Winship, Battalion 9, Hell's Kitchen, Manhattan, was a firefighter in the District of Columbia FD, Responded to the Pentagon on 9/11. Appointed to FDNY 2003. Adjunct Instructor National Fire Academy. Member FDNY Pipes & Drums Band, Member FDNY IMT.

Appendix B: Interview Protocol

1. Project Overview and Evolution

The Lessons for Leaders initiative represents a comprehensive effort to capture and distill leadership lessons from the events, aftermath and "long tail" of September 11, 2001 experienced by the FDNY and its members. Initiated in late 2017, the project's methodology has evolved through two distinct phases:

- Phase I (2018): In-person, high-fidelity documentation utilizing documentary-grade audio, video, and still photography to establish a rich baseline of primary material.
- Phase II (2019–Present): Adaptation to the COVID-19 pandemic by shifting to remote recording. While this narrowed the visual scope, the project gained momentum by shifting focus toward the "knowledge capture" from retired leaders – individuals who, like co-founder Paul Brown, possessed the distance and perspective required for deep reflection.

To date, the work has amassed over 90 hours of detailed transcripts from 42 interviews with 37 individuals. These conversations, ranging from one to four hours, constitute a body of primary source material on crisis response and organizational re-creation.

Team roles related to the interviews

- Greg Shea (Primary Interviewer): Project lead and structural architect. Designs the interview arcs and leads the questioning.
- Paul Brown (Subject Matter Expert/Liaison): Scouting, relationship management, and cultural translation. As a peer to many interviewees, Paul establishes the baseline of trust and verifies technical jargon.
- André Kotzé (Archivist/Technical Lead): Librarian of the knowledge base. Focuses on emerging leadership themes and manages the technical integrity of the collection.

2. Governance and Ethical Framework

The authors established Lessons for Leaders as an LLC prior to data collection. This structure was chosen not for commercial gain, but as a protective vessel for the material. Explicitly, we established:

1. Control of Intellectual Property: Ensures the authors maintain absolute control over how sensitive stories are used. No outside entity can dictate the packaging or distribution of these personal accounts.
2. Charitable Commitment: A formalized financial pledge is embedded in the operating agreement. If the project generates profit, 51% of net proceeds are donated to FDNY-related charities (e.g., FDNY Foundation, NY Firefighters Burn Center Foundation).
3. Honoring the Trust of the Interviewees: The LLC acts as a shield against "naked commercialism." It ensures that accounts of trauma are handled with an "appreciative inquiry" lens, preventing exploitation or embarrassment to the department or the survivors.

3. Invitation to Participate

Each respondent was sent an invitation to participate. The following templated letter, sent to Commissioner Sal Cassano, illustrates the project's intent and ethical positioning.

Dear Commissioner Cassano,

We're setting out to build an educational initiative primarily in the service of leadership development. We seek to draw on the wide range of lessons, including in extreme condition/consequences, that events of 9/11 provide. We see 9/11 generally and the role of the FDNY specifically as potentially powerfully instructive. We hope to derive lessons for leaders in a fashion that honors the sacrifices made by the FDNY by learning in detail about 9/11 (and its aftermath) from FDNY survivors of that day and then by constructing educational material based on our learning. We aim to use that material to benefit other current and future leaders. We hope that you will agree to participate. We view the interview with you as a key part of our learning and of the development of educational leadership material.

The interview will last up to two hours. It will begin with background questions about you and the department, then focus mainly on 9/11– the timeline, pivotal events, consequences, and learnings from the day, its immediate aftermath, and over time. The questions are, however, but guides and prompts for our conversation. In the end, we interview you in order to gather your recollections, impressions, and observations about 9/11 and its aftermath for the benefit of others. Should you wish during the interview to alter or to rephrase anything that you say, then you have only to say so and we will reshoot that part of the interview immediately or 'in the moment'. Again, our intention is to capture accurately your experience of 9/11 for the benefit of others.

We are also committed to benefitting the first responders and others who offer their experiences in furtherance of the Work. To this end, we will (a) donate 51% of any net proceeds from any revenue-generating activities to selected non-profit organizations namely the FDNY Foundation, Coalition of 911 Families, Fire Widows and Children's Fund; (b) provide up to two programs/year at cost for FDNY personnel; and (c) provide a channel for the donation of any stipends received by Us or our personnel to a selected non-profit organization.

4. The Interview Protocol

Each interview included questions about before, during, and after 9/11. That said, each interview had its own rhythm and life and each informed subsequent interviews. The time covered touched different interviewees differently. We respected that difference by relying on the interviewee to guide us through their experience. Also, certain topics emerged and precipitated regular follow-up questions. For example, the changes in the FDNY assumed a greater prominence from the start due substantially to their significance to interviewees.

Interview format (FDNY 9/11/01)
Estimated duration: 2 hours
Introduction: Confidentiality defined, interviewee letter of agreement discussed
Thank you for agreeing to be part of this effort.

Paul Brown, André Kotzé–introductions/who we are
We're setting out to build an educational initiative...esp. for leadership development – drawing on the wide range of lessons, including in extreme condition/consequences...we see 9/11 and FDNY as potentially powerfully instructive and we hope to honor the sacrifices made by the FDNY in particular by learning in detail about the 9/11 and constructing educational material and courses based on the FDNY on 9/11 (and after) that will benefit other

leaders...we view this interview as a key part of our learning and the development of educational leadership material.
Additionally, in order to control the use of this material, i.e., so that it is used as just described, we have no plans to relinquish IP.

Finally, just to be clear, as for the commercial side of anything that we might do other than pro bono work (e.g., executive education or writing) – we view the first 51% of any net profit (revenue – sunk costs and expenses) will go to FDNY charities, e.g., Burn Center Foundation, 9/11 Survivors Fund, FDNY Foundation)...we also commit to run up to 2 multi-day programs/year at cost for FDNY...finally, any individual participant in any program can contribute their stipend to these foundations if they wish...

As for this interview itself, it will serve to develop further our understanding of 9/11 and so to develop leadership educational material. The interview will begin with background questions about you and the department, then focus mainly on 9/11, the immediate aftermath, and long-term implications. The questions are but guides. In the end, we seek your recollections, impressions, and observations about 9/11 and its aftermath.

We will assume that we can use the material that you provide us and attribute it to you UNLESS you indicate otherwise.

Do you have any questions about who we are, what we are doing, or what this interview concerns?

Should we begin?

As noted, let's begin with a bit of background, starting with you on September 10, 2001:

- How long had you been a firefighter in FDNY?
- What was your role? How long had you been in it?
- Why did you become a member of FDNY?
- What words would you use to describe the FDNY on 9/10/01?

On 9/11/01,

- Would you walk us through the timeline of events of your day that day?
  [lots of follow-up...ideally, we'd also have some anchor events and time for interviewee to work with/place their day within]
- If you had to indicate the three events, other than the planes crashing into the towers, what three events were most important for you? Why?

On 9/12/01

- Would you walk us through the timeline of events of your day that day?
  [lots of follow-up...ideally, we'd also have some anchor events and time for interviewee to work with/place their day within]
- If you had to indicate the three events, other than the planes crashing into the towers, what three events were most important, most formative for you? Why?

Over the next two weeks,

- What were the three–six most important events?
  Why do you select those?

Beyond,

- In the time since 9/11/01 and the subsequent two weeks, what has happened that you view as most important? Why those events?
- What hasn't happened that you view as particularly important?

For many people, in many different ways, 9/11 and its aftermath were traumatic. Dealing with trauma has at least two aspects, namely the short term which turns on a toughness to push through the trauma as it occurs and a longer term which turns on a resilience, often developed in collaboration with others, to restore and to rebuild one's self in light of the trauma. We'd like to ask a few questions about both aspects of trauma as they affected firefighters professionally, namely as firefighters, and personally, namely as people living lives.

- How did firefighters handle the trauma?
- In the short term
- In the longer term
- How did the department handle the trauma?

Appendix C: The Responders Lexicon

A Comprehensive Guide to FDNY Terminology, Tactics, and World Trade Center Geography

5-5-5-5 – A bell signal transmitted over radio and voice alarm systems to announce a Line of Duty Death (LODD). It is used once remains are positively identified and includes the announcement of the member's name and unit.
10-8 – A radio code indicating a unit is available for assignment.
10-60 – A radio code for a "major emergency." On 9/11, this was famously transmitted by Engine 10 to request all available resources to the World Trade Center.

A
A, B CHART – A specific emergency work schedule implemented after 9/11 involving a "24 hours on, 24 hours off" rotation, splitting the department into two platoons to maintain a constant presence at the site.
ACTING – Temporarily performing the duties of a higher rank.
A.D.V. – Abandoned Derelict Vehicle.
AERIAL – A permanent ladder attached to the top of a fire truck.
AIDE – A Chief's driver and administrative assistant.
APPARATUS – A general term for any fire truck or fire engine.
AQ (At Quarters) – Indicates a unit is back at their home firehouse.
AC (ASSISTANT CHIEF) – A staff-level chief, designated by three stars.

B
BACKUP – The firefighter assigned to be second on the hoseline, assisting the nozzle.
BATTERY TUNNEL – The Brooklyn-Battery Tunnel; an automotive tunnel connecting Brooklyn with West Street, located four blocks south of the World Trade Center.
BC (Battalion Chief) – A field chief officer, designated by an oak leaf.
B.I. – Building Inspection duty.
BORO – The Borough Command; typically overseen by an Assistant Chief.
BUFF – A fire enthusiast or "groupie"; also used as a verb meaning to watch a fire while off-duty.
BUS – An ambulance.

C

CAN – A portable water extinguisher; also the positional assignment of the person carrying it.

CAPTAIN – The commander of a specific fire company.

CHAUFFEUR – The driver of an apparatus. Specifically, LCC refers to the Ladder Company Chauffeur, and ECC refers to the Engine Company Chauffeur.

CHURCH STREET – The eastern boundary of the World Trade Center site.

CSU (Counseling Services Unit) – The unit responsible for the mental health support of FDNY members; scaled up significantly after 9/11 to place professionals in firehouses.

CTDP (Center for Terrorism and Disaster Preparedness) – Created in 2004 to analyze threats and prepare the department for complex attacks based on lessons learned from 9/11.

D

DC (DEPUTY CHIEF) – A Deputy Chief, designated by eagles.

D.A.C. (DEPUTY ASSISTANT CHIEF) – A staff-level chief, designated by two stars.

DEPUTY COMMISSIONER – A civilian title ranking below the Fire Commissioner.

DEUTSCHE BANK – Located at 130 Liberty Street; heavily damaged on 9/11 and later demolished.

DMAT (Disaster Medical Assistance Team) – A federal medical resource dispatched to major emergencies.

DMORT (Disaster Mortuary Operational Response Team) – A federal resource dispatched to handle mass casualty incidents.

E

ECC – Engine Company Chauffeur

ENGINE – A pumper truck; fire apparatus designed to carry water and hose.

F

FAU (FAMILY ASSISTANCE UNIT) – A unit formalized after 9/11 to coordinate support for the families of injured or fallen firefighters.

F.A.S.T. (Firefighter Assist & Safety Team) – A unit whose sole assignment is to stand by for the immediate rescue of trapped or injured firefighters.

F.E. (Forcible Entry) – The act of breaking into a structure; also the positional name of the person assigned this duty.
FIREMAN SERVICE – The use of a special key to manually operate an elevator during emergencies.
FUGAZZI – A term for something jury-rigged, incorrect, or a field expediency.

H

HiRISE – In New York City, any building over 75 feet in height.
HiRISE REPEATER – A device kept inside Chiefs' vehicles used to boost radio transmissions within high-rise buildings.
H.V.A.C. – Heating, Ventilation, and Air Conditioning system.

I

IAP (Incident Action Plan) – A written daily plan organizing objectives and resources. Introduced to the FDNY by the Southwest Incident Management Team during the 9/11 recovery.
ICP (Incident Command Post) – The location from which the overall incident is managed. On 9/11, it was established on West Street.
IMT (Incident Management Team) – A designated team responsible for logistics and administration of large-scale incidents; adopted from the forestry service.

J

JAVITS CENTER – Jacob K. Javits Convention Center; used as a staging area and supply distribution center on 9/11.
JOB – FDNY slang for a structural fire. The Job-The department (FDNY).
JOHNNIE – A junior firefighter.

L

LCC – Ladder Company Chauffeur
LCP (Lobby Command Post) – A command post established inside the lobby of a high-rise to direct operations within that specific structure.
LEAN-TO – A type of structural collapse where the floors are supported on only one side.
LIBERTY STREET – The southern boundary of the World Trade Center site.
LOCAL – Neighborhood residents.
LOO – Slang for a Lieutenant; also abbreviated as L.T.

M

MARRIOTT HOTEL – Also known as #3 World Trade Center; completely destroyed on 9/11.

MASK – An air pack or SCBA (Self-Contained Breathing Apparatus). Also called Scott after the manufacturer.

MAYDAY – An emergency radio transmission signaling a firefighter is in need of immediate assistance.

METROTECH – Located at 9 Metro Tech Center in Downtown Brooklyn; the FDNY Headquarters.

M.U.D. (Multi-Unit Drill) – A training exercise involving multiple fire units.

MULTIPLE – Refers to a greater alarm fire (e.g., a "second alarm").

N

NORTH TOWER – #1 World Trade Center; completely destroyed on 9/11.

NORTH BRIDGE – The pedestrian bridge crossing West Street just north of the North Tower.

NOZZLE – The firefighter assigned to the front of the hoseline.

O

OFFICER – Refers to the Lieutenant or Captain in charge of a unit.

P

PANCAKE – A type of collapse where structural floors fall directly onto one another in a stack.

PILE, THE / THE PIT – Colloquial terms for the WTC debris field. "The Pile" referred to the initial rescue phase; "The Pit" was used as excavation deepened.

PORTABLE – A ladder that can be carried by firefighters.

PROBIE – A probationary firefighter in their first year of service.

R

RECALL – An order for off-duty members to report for duty. On 9/11, a "Total Recall" was issued for the first time in department history.

REPEATER – A device that boosts and retransmits radio signals to increase range.

RESPONSE MODE – An operational mindset of all-out effort and higher risk acceptance to save lives; the FDNY remained in this mode for weeks after 9/11.
ROOF/ROOFMAN – The firefighter assigned to perform ventilation from the roof of a building.
ROOF ROPE – A long rope carried by the roofman to facilitate rescues above the reach of ladders.

S

S.C.B.A. – Self-Contained Breathing Apparatus; also called a Mask, Air Pack, or "Scott."
SCOTT MASK – see S.C.B.A
SEARCH ROPE – A long cord used as a guide to search large areas under zero-visibility conditions.
SHEA STADIUM – Major League Baseball stadium in Queens; used as a muster site for responders on 9/11.
SOC (Special Operations Command) – The command overseeing elite units (Rescue and Squad). SOC suffered catastrophic losses on 9/11.
SOUTH TOWER – #2 World Trade Center; completely destroyed on 9/11.
SOUTH BRIDGE – The pedestrian bridge crossing West Street just south of the South Tower.

T

TENEMENT – A classic walkup-style apartment building common in NYC.
TILLER – The rear section of a tractor-trailer type ladder truck, steered by a second driver.
TRINITY CHURCH – Located at 89 Broadway; served as a site of rest and refuge for responders at Ground Zero.
TRUCK – A fire apparatus equipped with ladders (as opposed to an Engine).
TRUCKIE – A firefighter assigned to a ladder company.
TRUCK CHAUFFEUR (LCC) – Firefighter who drives a Ladder truck.
TRUCK OFFICER – The Lieutenant or Captain in charge of a Ladder company.

U

URGENT – A priority radio transmission used for important but non-Mayday messages.

USAR (Urban Search and Rescue) – Specialized teams of collapse and large-scale disaster rescue experts.

V

V.E.S. (Vent, Enter, Search) – The primary life-saving duties performed by a ladder company.

VERIZON BUILDING – Located at 140 West Street; significantly damaged during the WTC attacks.

W

WAR YEARS – The period from the 1960s to the early 1980s characterized by intense fire activity and arson; forged the leadership of those in charge on 9/11.

WORLD FINANCIAL CENTER – A four-building complex in Battery Park City across from the WTC.

WORLD'S FAIR MARINA – Located in Flushing, Queens; used as a staging area for FDNY-WTC Task Forces.

Appendix D: FDNY Command Structure, September 11, 2001

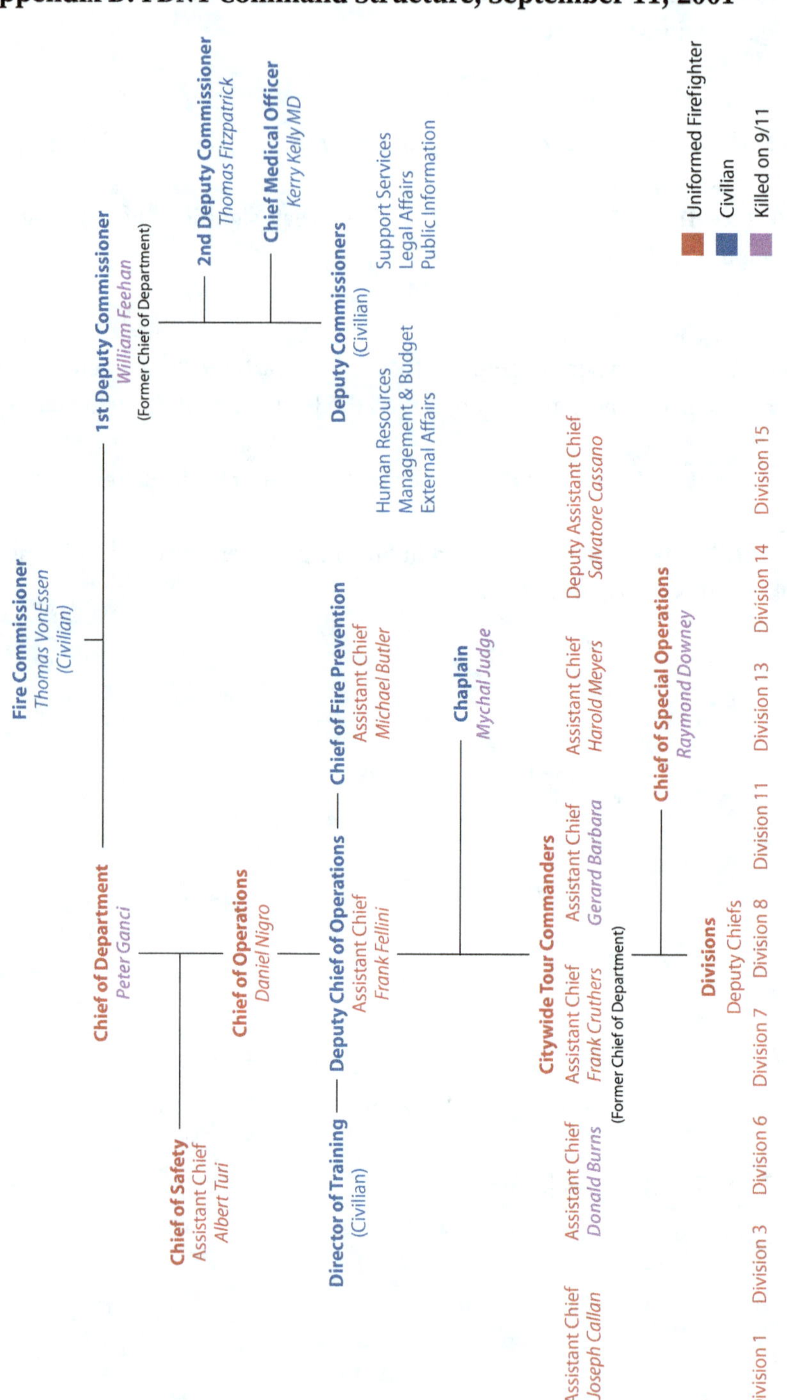

Appendix E: FDNY WTC Task Force 0700 September 15, 2001

FDNY WTC Task Force 0700 September 15, 2001

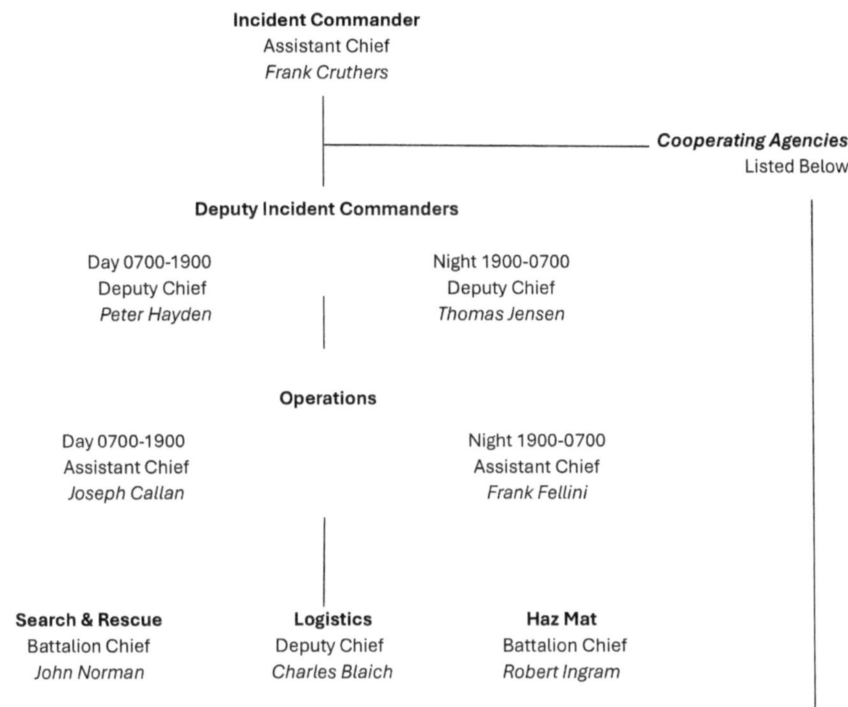

New York City
NYPD
NYCDEP
NYCDOT
NYCDDC
NYCOEM
NYCDOH
NYCDS
New York State
PAPD
NYNG
NYANG
NYSDEC
Federal
FEMA
FBI
Army Corp of Engineers
USPHS

Others
Con Ed
Red Cross

Appendix F: World Trade Center Map

FIRE AND EMS COMMAND POST LOCATIONS

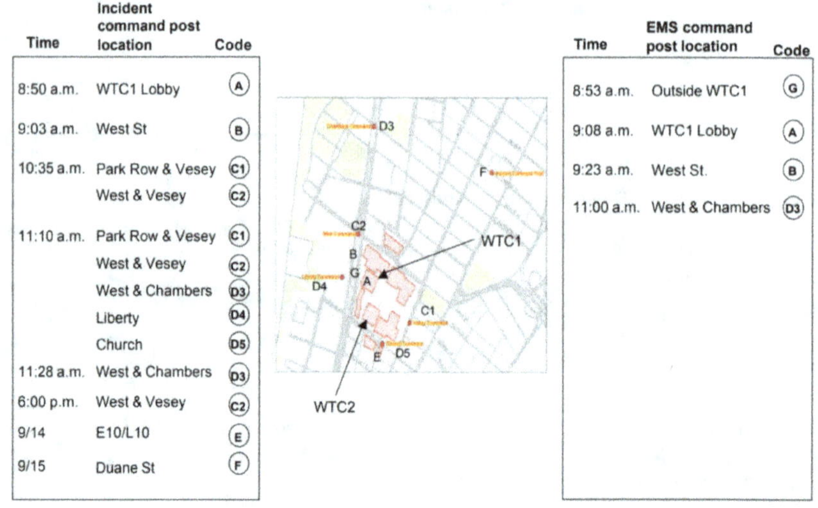

Time	Incident command post location	Code
8:50 a.m.	WTC1 Lobby	A
9:03 a.m.	West St	B
10:35 a.m.	Park Row & Vesey	C1
	West & Vesey	C2
11:10 a.m.	Park Row & Vesey	C1
	West & Vesey	C2
	West & Chambers	D3
	Liberty	D4
	Church	D5
11:28 a.m.	West & Chambers	D3
6:00 p.m.	West & Vesey	C2
9/14	E10/L10	E
9/15	Duane St	F

Time	EMS command post location	Code
8:53 a.m.	Outside WTC1	G
9:08 a.m.	WTC1 Lobby	A
9:23 a.m.	West St.	B
11:00 a.m.	West & Chambers	D3

Souce: Dispatch tapes; Interviews; FDNY Phoenix Unit Geographic Information System

Appendix G: FDNY Incident Action Plan

FDNY
INCIDENT ACTION PLAN
OPERATIONAL PERIOD
SEPTEMBER 27 - 28, 2001
0700 - 0700

Plan 6

Peter E. Hayden

FDNY INCIDENT ACTION PLAN

OPERATIONAL PERIOD

09/27/2001 – 0700 through 09/28/2001 – 0700

OVERALL INCIDENT OBJECTIVES

1. Provide for the health, safety and welfare of all personnel working in and around the incident.
2. Coordinate with all involved agencies to support the operational needs of the incident.
3. Document all critical items and significant events.

Each sector will have Planning and Documentation personnel assigned to support incident objectives. Specifically, they are tasked to update maps, continue to provide resource tracking, record prior and current significant events and provide liaison services at the request of Sector Chief. Interagency cooperation is essential to mission success.

INCIDENT COMMAND

Incident Commander	AC Cruthers
Executive Officer	DC Hayden (day)
Assistant Executive Officer	DC Benson (night)
Operations Section Chief	DC Callan (0700-1900)/DC Fellini (1900-0700)
Logistics Section Chief	DC Blaich
Planning Section Chief	BC Pfeifer
Search and Rescue Chief	BC Norman
Hazardous Materials Chief	BC Ingram
EMS Chief	AC Pascale (0600-1800)/DC Hannafey (1800-0600)

OPERATING FACILITIES AND LOCATIONS

Incident Command Post	100 Duane Street
Operations Center:	1010 Station (Liberty & Greenwich)
Liberty Sector	Liberty & West
West Sector	Vesey & West
Church Sector	Liberty & Greenwich
Vesey Sector	Church & Dey

SECTOR CHIEFS	0530	1330	2130	OFF
Liberty Sector	DC McKnight	ADC Biey	DC McNeela	ADC Ferran
West Sector	DC Rappe	DC Hughes	ADC Jordan	DC Corcoran
Church Sector	DC Jensen	DC Hay	DC Mulrenan	ADC Ievolo
Vesey Sector	DC Didiminica	DC Spadafora	DC Messbauer	DC Esposito

RESOURCES

FDNY WTC TF	300 (Total Firefighters/Officers) per 10-hour shift
PD ESU	100 Officers per 12 hour shift.
FEMA US&R	2 Task Forces – Split shift – 31 persons per task force per 12 hour shift CA-3, CO-1.
FEMA RRTF	NE-1 located off site – operating as a Rapid Response TF to Supplement FDNY capabilities.
SWA IMT	1 to 2 per sector to assist with planning and documentation.

09/26/2001 FDNY IAP – NOT FOR PUBLIC DISTRIBUTION 1

PLANNED ACTIONS AND OPERATING INSTRUCTIONS (Next 24 hours)

1. 300 Ton crane is in place at Washington & Liberty Streets. Debris removal and void search operations will continue. FDNY SOC, PD ESU personnel and (1) FEMA US&R Task Force have been assigned to this location.

2. 800 Ton crane is in place on West St. Debris removal and void search operations will continue in the North tower area. FDNY SOC, PD ESU personnel and (1) FEMA US&R Task Force have been assigned to this location.

3. Based on the anticipated placement of a 1000-ton crane on West St. in the proximity of the Marriott WTC Hotel, contractor is placing required matting to facilitate crane placement and operations.

4. Steel cutting operations with the utilization of oxy-acetylene cutting set-ups (and subsequent removal of debris by rigging and heavy equipment) **is to continue at the most rapid pace possible. FDNY SOC, PD ESU and FEMA US&R personnel are to be utilized as the primary source to accomplish this mission. Ironworkers can be utilized to assist and supplement this function, but keep in mind - this is a rescue operation**. All available cutting set-ups should be utilized on a continual basis as conditions permit. Void search operations will follow these cutting operations as voids are exposed. **These cutting and void search operations will occur in all sectors as required.**

5. All personnel operating on the north and south towers will be in bunker pants as required due to the high heat level being generated on the lower levels of the debris piles. Consideration should be given to stretching protective hand lines as required in all areas of operations. Protective hand lines are in place at the North Tower, continue to operate as required.

6. **NO** void search operations without approval of FDNY Sector Chief in the North and South Towers. Use this time to facilitate the placement and use of large caliber water streams onto areas affected by fire on the north and south towers.

7. NTSB has five camera points and is setting up a sixth one that will assist in locating the flight recorders.

8. Void search operations will continue in the Winter Garden area as heavy steel is removed by crane. A FEMA US&R engineer will be assigned to this area for ongoing evaluation of condition. FD SOC personnel and PD ESU personnel will continue to conduct void searches as required.

9. Review operational / engineering plan to facilitate removal of the South and West façade walls still standing in the South Tower area. FDNY, FEMA US&R, DDC and site construction manager to review plan and evaluate results of recent demolition.

WEATHER FORECAST

Day Party Cloudy, Winds SW 12 mph, 30% chance of showers – up to .1", High of 66 F
Night Party Cloudy with a 30% chance of precipitation – up to .25", Winds W 10 mph, Low of 55 F.
Anemometer Locations: 11th floor of the Verizon Building
1010 Fire Station

SPECIAL INSTRUCTIONS

FDNY Sector Chief's will approve all searches.

Review posted information regarding Minimum Protective Equipment Requirements, Site Safety, Evacuation Warning Signals, Site Hazards, Blood Borne Pathogens and Hazard Markings on Buildings.

Document on the **grid map dated 09/20 or later** and in the sector operations log locations of any victims, public safety personnel, apparatus and equipment found.

When public safety personnel, apparatus and/or equipment are found, please protect the area and notify the appropriate agency for appropriate documentation and removal.

If weapons or ammunition are found, secure the area and immediately notify law enforcement authorities.

Upon approval of FDNY Operations Section Chief, only physicians will perform field amputations.

Individuals within the Green Line must wear minimum recommended safety gear. See attached map.

Damaged SCBA Tanks:

1. If possible, slowly remove air pressure by opening valve.
2. If the valve is damaged or missing – do not remove tank and notify Sector Chief.
3. Sector Chief will notify Operations Command Post for relay to HazMat Operations for further instructions.

As of 1700 hours today (9/27/2001) only white, non-photo credentials will allow access into the site. The new credentials are available at IS 89. Security checkpoints have a list of exempt agencies.

VIPs must be escorted to the OEM command bus at West and Warren before visiting the site.

ANTICIPATED ACTIONS (72 hours)

1. Continue in the above-listed operations.

2. As other crane(s) are set up and / or relocated, continue in the accelerated debris removal and void search operations. Concentration of operations will be in the following prioritized order as conditions permit:
   North Tower
   Marriott WTC Hotel
   South Tower

3. Plan received from DDC is being evaluated on an ongoing basis regarding disposition and process for removing remaining vertical wall sections and limited debris removal process at the Winter Garden building.

4. Perimeter security will continue to be tightened.

5. Four additional wind speed indicators will be operational by Thursday evening at 125 Vesey; West & Warren; one on the SW corner of the site and another on the NE corner of the site.

6. Review and evaluate Draft Freon Removal Plan from Port Authority.

7. 1000 ton crane on schedule for Friday operation.

LOGISTICS

- Access points are as follows:
  - West & Chambers — Vehicle and Pedestrian access
  - Church & Chambers — Vehicle and Pedestrian access
  - Murray & Broadway — Vehicle access only
  - Trinity Place & Rector — Vehicle access only
  - Carlisle Street (West) & Rector — Vehicle and Pedestrian access.
- There are several authorized volunteer EMS agencies in service.
- There will be five (5) authorized meal sites. They are:

  St. John University 101 Murray.
  Spirit of New York cruise ship berthed at the north pier.
  McDonald's on Fulton between Broadway & Church.
  Uncle Ben's between Vesey & Murray
  The Salvation Army on West St and Murray Street

FOOD VENDORS

- The DOH in conjunction with the NYPD will work toward taking down the unauthorized eating / feeding areas

SANITATION

- Personal hygiene stations are in place on Liberty, between Church & Greenwich
- Personal Hand Washing Stations are available at all the above meal sites.
- Boot washes, hand and eye wash stations area available at West and Murray St Johns Univ.
- Additional washes and showers are available on a limited basis at the Liberty Street Marina on a limited basis to augment the entrance/exit facilities

CACHE SITES

- Three sectors now have operational CACHE units.

West Sector-	Port Authority
Liberty Sector-	NYPD
Church Sector-	FDNY

COVERALLS

- Coveralls for FDNY staff will be available at West/Murray/Chambers Street Area.

Tradewinds Laundry Service will pick up & distribute from the World Fair Marina.
The tent will be staffed with their personnel who will collect and size the coveralls.
Pick up and drop off times:

Outbound Crew	In Bound Crew
530	0700-0900
1330	1430-1630
2130	2230-2330

The laundry will be done at their commercial facility in L.I.C.
4000 units shipped to WFM

NOTIFICATION
The E train is now running under Church Street. It will discharge passengers at Chambers Street Station and proceed south at less than 10 mph to WTC station. A switch will be activated and the train will proceed to the north at less than 10 mph to the Chambers Street Station where it will take on passengers. The WTC Station will remain closed.

SAFETY – YOUR PERSONAL RESPONSIBILITY!

Your attitude about safety affects you, your teammates, innocent bystanders and especially your loved ones at home. There are numerous injuries occurring each day. Some we cannot specifically address, but others we can. Injuries to eyes and lungs and lacerations can be prevented or at least reduced by wearing the appropriate personal protective equipment identified below.

Hazards:

- **Due to the instability of Winter Gardens Atrium between 2 and 3 World Financial Center, all personnel shall remain clear of that area. Safety Chiefs for Liberty and West Sectors shall monitor for compliance**
- Potentially pressurized cylinders including: SCBA's; gas cylinders such as propane, ammonia, chlorine, etc.
- Possible live ammunition at WTC 7, Barclay Street Ramp and the Customs House
- Walking, Working Surfaces
- Falling Debris
- Airborne Contamination
- Bio-Hazards, Universal Precautions
- Cutting, Welding-Compressed Gasses
- Cylinder Storage
- Vehicular Traffic
- Backing Vehicles
- Excavation Equipment
- **CRANE Operations- Be aware of swing & stress cables and whipping of broken cables**
- *****On 9/26 at approximately 1430 hours a crane operating in the North Tower area snapped a cable while hoisting a load. This caused the load to drop narrowly missing 4 workers.**
- Sewer Grates, Trenches, Manholes – possible collapse or a vector for the release of toxic gas vapors

Mitigation: LOOKOUTS posted, COMMUNICATIONS reliable, ESCAPE ROUTES planned and known by all, SAFETY ZONES planned and known by all

- **EVACUATION SIGNAL – 3 BLASTS**
- Each Sector Command **MUST** assign a Safety Officer
- Each Sector Command **MUST** assign a **FAST** Truck for Emergency Response
- Treat all cylinders as pressurized & volatile
- Work with a buddy who has visual contact with you
- Control Site Access – allow only authorized, trained & properly equipped personnel inside the "green zone"
- Maintain Site Safety Awareness
- Be aware of changing conditions
- Do not eat or smoke in the work zone (Hand washing prior to eating)
- Scout out, identify, plan, and advise others of escape routes in event of emergency of any type
- Climb with proper protection at all times
- Mandatory head and eye protection at all times
- Look overhead and be aware of all surroundings
- Change respirator filter when resistance is felt from air flow or at least after every shift
- Have a reliable means of communications

Protective Equipment: MUST WEAR MINIMUM RECOMMENDED GEAR WITHIN THE "GREEN ZONE"

- **Hard Hat or helmet**
- **Respirator with replaceable P100 organic vapor/acid gas cartridges**
- **Steel toed boots or equivalent**
- **Coveralls or Long Sleeve Shirts**
- **Safety glasses with side shield / face shield / goggles**
- **Leather Gloves with latex (or nitrile) glove liner**

Site Safety Awareness:

- Your attitude
- As we continue to work the scene, we may often take more chance and risks than necessary.
- Be aware of YOUR surroundings.
- Plan for the HAZARDS of the job.
- USE safety equipment at all times.
- Doing your part to prevent/reduce accidents in the work zone.
- Watch out for your co-workers on the scene

Victim Family Visit to Red Zone

Scheduled Tours

Sept. 26, 2001

15:00

Starting Sept. 27, 2001

Daily 10:30, 12:00, 14:00

Tour Group

Approximately 73 persons per trip

Victim Family

10 Families, 5 members per family

Mental Health Professional

2 PD, 5 DOH, 5 Red Cross

Security

3 NYSP, 3 NYPD

Support

5 Mayor's Community Assistance Unit

Tour Route

1. Depart from Pier 92 to North Cove Marina
2. Disembark at North Cove Marina's New York Waterways dock
3. Walk around Marina to Liberty Street and West Street
4. Lay flowers at the Marina's promenade perimeter
5. Embark at New York Waterways dock
6. Depart from North Cove Marina to Pier 92

Route will be adjusted daily to reflect Red Zone condition

Contacts

Conrad Vazquez	917-682-3469	CAU (Mayor's Community Assistance Unit)
Jose Baptista	917-882-8998	OEM

Victim Family Visit to Red Zone

DR-1391-NY New York City Facility Locations - September 26

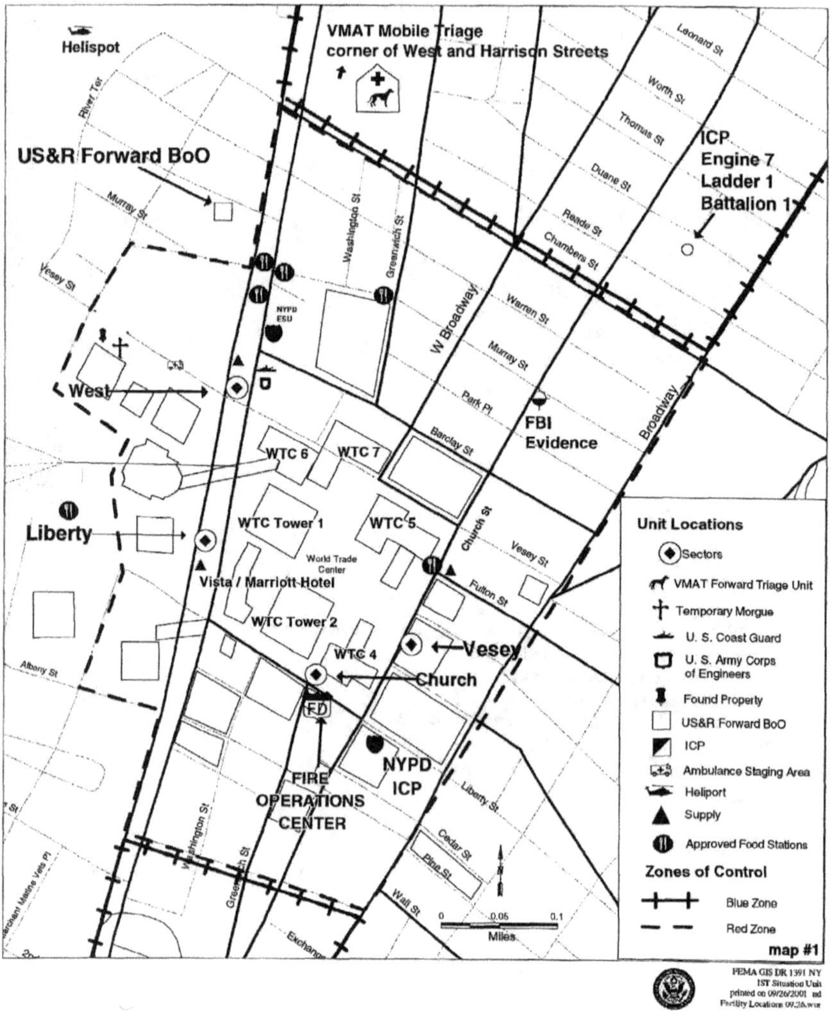

Unit Locations

- Sectors
- VMAT Forward Triage Unit
- Temporary Morgue
- U. S. Coast Guard
- U. S. Army Corps of Engineers
- Found Property
- US&R Forward BoO
- ICP
- Ambulance Staging Area
- Heliport
- Supply
- Approved Food Stations

Zones of Control

- Blue Zone
- Red Zone

map #1

FEMA GIS DR 1391 NY
IST Situation Unit
printed on 09/26/2001
Facility Locations 09.26.wor

9/26/01
0730
VERIZON
WTC 7
VESEY ST
SLURRY WALLS
WTC 6
CUSTOMS HOUSE
#3 W.F.C.
NORTH PROJECTION
NORTH BRIDGE
WINTER GARDEN
#2 W.F.C.
WTC TOWER 1
BASEMENT WALLS
WTC 5
SUBWAY
SOUTH PROJECTION
MARRIOTT WTC 3
WTC TOWER 2
WTC 4
BASEMENT WALLS
CHURCH ST.
SLURRY WALLS
LIBERTY ST
WASHINGTON
GREENWICH ST.
WEST ST.
BANKERS TURST
ON PLAN
APPROXIMATE
LZA / THORNTON - TOMASETTI
J:/WTC-TTDWGS/CRANEPLAN/2001-09-26-AM-CRANEPLAN.D

SAFETY AREA WHERE GEAR IS NEEDED AT ALL TIMES ON, ABOVE, OR WITHIN 25 FEET OF THE RUBBLE PILE

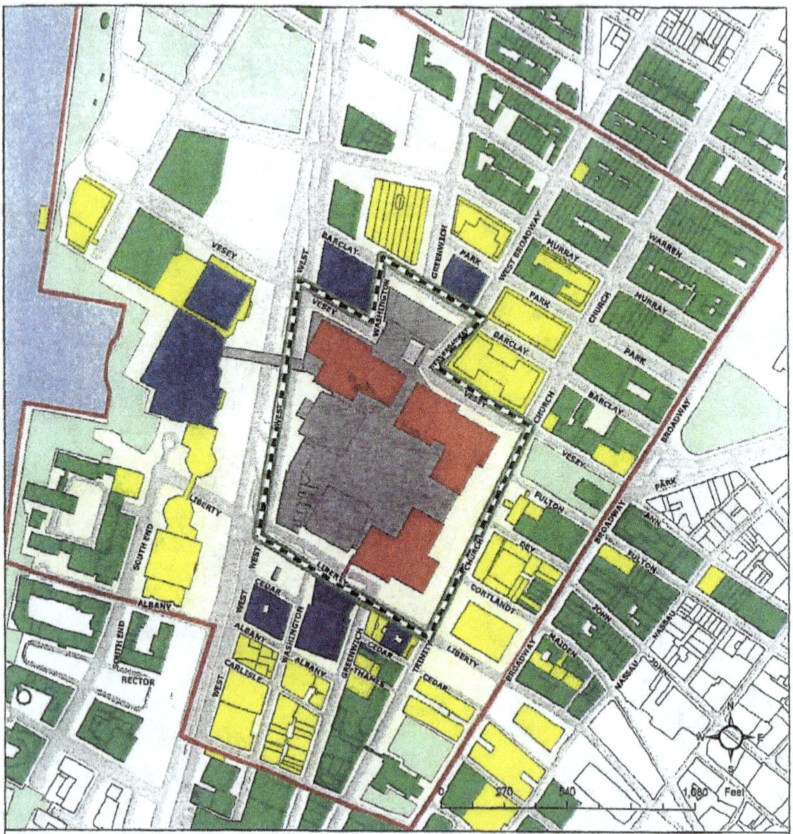

Minimum Safety Gear:

* Hardhat or helmet
* Safety glasses with side shields, Face shields or Goggles
* Half-face re-usable respirator with P100, organic vapor/acid gas (OVAG) cartridges when on, over, or above the rubble pile. P100 or P100 OV can be used when away from the rubble pile. Change Cartridges after every shift.
* Leather gloves with latex (or nitrile) glove liner (or equivalent) when handling human remains.
* Coveralls or long sleeved work shirt
* Steel-toed boots (or equivalent)

Eye and respiratory protection is strongly advised whenever dust or smoke from the rubble occur outside the areas noted above.

Fit-checking is needed to assure proper seal.
Facial hair can prevent an adequate respirator seal.
Entry into confined spaces with unknown or untested atmospheres requires air-supplied respirators.
Welders need appropriate eye protection and leathers.

Do not smoke or eat when on, above, or within 25 feet of the rubble pile.

Legend

- Safety Zone
- Off Limits to Public
- Parks
- Not Affected
- Inspected But Not Affected
- Damaged But Stable Repairs/Cleaning Required
- Major Structural Damage No Occupancy
- Partially Collapsed
- Destroyed

NYC Department of Health

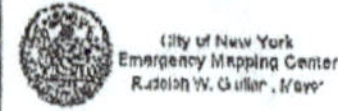

Disclaimer: The City of New York does not certify the correctness of any information provided on this map and is not liable for any actions taken or not taken by any persons.

Revised 9/25/01

Appendix H: Planned Actions and Operating Instructions for the Period September 22 to September 30, 2001

The **World Trade Center Incident Action Plans (IAPs)** are operational documents produced by the FDNY (specifically the Incident Commander and Planning Section) to manage the recovery efforts at Ground Zero. These reports cover specific operational periods, typically running from 0700 to 0700 (24-hour cycles).

The section labeled Planned Actions and Operating Instructions (Next 24 hours) functions as the core of the daily plan. Its purpose is to:

- **Assign Assets:** Detail the specific locations and tasks for heavy machinery (specifically cranes) and specialized personnel (FDNY Special Operations Command, FEMA US&R, and NYPD ESU).
- **Set Priorities:** Establish the immediate goals, such as debris removal, void searches, or structural demolition.
- **Coordinate Safety and Logistics:** Outline specific constraints, such as restricted areas, required protective gear (e.g., bunker pants for heat), and engineering surveys.

Analysis of Operational Evolution

A summary of the included reports reveals how the response evolved from an urgent, rapid-pace rescue operation dependent on incoming heavy machinery to a highly structured, engineering-led recovery effort characterized by command consolidation and long-term site stabilization.

The Mobilization of Heavy Assets (September 22–24)

The initial operational phase was defined by the aggressive acquisition and deployment of heavy lift capacity to facilitate subterranean void searches. On September 22, recovery efforts relied upon a single 300-ton crane positioned at the intersection of Washington and Liberty Streets, with a 700-ton unit anticipated for the North Tower. By the following day, requirements expanded to include an 800-ton crane for the North Tower and the assembly of a 1,000-ton crane near the Marriott Hotel. During this period, the operational tempo was maintained at the highest possible rate. Incident Commanders directed FDNY Special Operations Command and FEMA US&R personnel to conduct steel cutting and void entries immediately as debris was cleared. This phase was further characterized by extreme thermal hazards within the debris piles, necessitating the mandatory use of bunker pants for all personnel operating on the tower footprints.

Implementation of Restrictions and Engineering Controls (September 25–27)

As the recovery progressed, the focus shifted toward site stabilization and the mitigation of secondary collapse hazards. On September 25, a site-wide evacuation was executed to facilitate the controlled removal of unstable steel at the South Tower. By September 26, the risk of falling debris resulted in a total cessation of operations at the Marriott and South Tower sectors. The previous mandate for rapid-pace search operations was superseded by strict command oversight; by September 27, the Incident Action Plan prohibited void searches within the primary tower footprints without the express authorization of an FDNY Sector Chief. During this interval, the role of structural engineering became central to the mission, with comprehensive surveys conducted on the South and West facades to formulate systematic demolition and removal plans for unstable structures.

Infrastructure, Technology, and Long-Term Planning (September 28–October 1)

In the final days of September, the response transitioned into a sustained recovery effort supported by the construction of permanent site infrastructure. Crews began the installation of access roads to allow heavy equipment to reach the Plaza and Pit areas. Technological integration increased with the introduction of GPS for the precise mapping of recovery sectors and structural remnants. Specialized technical teams were tasked with discrete hazard mitigation, including the assessment of Freon tanks and associated plumbing for structural integrity. This period also marked the emergence of formalized site management, as the Department of Design and Construction (DDC) submitted a "Long Range Plan" to the Mayor's office. Simultaneously, the human dimension of the incident was institutionalized through the scheduling of formalized family visits to the "Red Zone."

Consolidation and Stabilization (October 10–11)

By mid-October, the operation reached maturity as a consolidated command structure. The original four geographical sectors were merged into a dual-command system, designated as West Command and East Command. The crane array was fully realized, with 700-ton, 1,000-ton, 550-ton, and 500-ton units operating in synchronicity. Operational priorities shifted toward the stabilization of the "bathtub" and the slurry wall. This required joint DDC and FDNY entries into the Marriott sub-basements to monitor the wall's integrity while backfilling operations commenced to prevent structural failure. Environmental and health controls were likewise formalized; as weather conditions deteriorated, warming tents were established, and the Department of Health implemented rigorous protocols regarding carbon monoxide exposure and mandatory rest cycles for the workforce.

What follows are the Planned Actions and Operating Instructions for the Period September 22 to October 1, 2001. Verbatim and in sequence as they are, they show in detail the kinds of tasks the FDNY, various agencies and organizations were undertaking and make evident the coordinating role the IMT was assuming. They also display how the response unfolded over the period described.

Operational Period: September 22–23, 2001

PLANNED ACTIONS (24 hours) The following areas have been identified to concentrate search & rescue operations in for this operational period based on the recent placement of cranes:

1. Based on the placement of a 300-ton crane at Washington & Liberty Sts. (At 1200 hours on 9/21), debris removal and void search operations are to commence immediately in the South tower area. FDNY SOC personnel and (1) FEMA US&R Task Force have been assigned to this location as of 1130 hours this date.
2. Based on the anticipated placement of a 700-ton crane on West St. (by 1000 hours on 9/22), debris removal and void search operations will commence immediately in the North tower area. FDNY SOC personnel and (1) FEMA US&R Task Force will be assigned to this location when the crane is ready to operate.
3. Steel cutting operations with the utilization of oxy-acetylene cutting set-ups (and subsequent removal of debris by rigging and heavy equipment) **is to continue at the most rapid pace possible.** Special Operations Command personnel and FEMA US&R personnel are to be utilized as the primary source to accomplish this mission. Ironworkers can be utilized to assist and supplement this function, but keep in mind – this is a rescue operation. All available cutting set-ups should be utilized on a continual basis as conditions permit. Void search operations

will follow these cutting operations as voids are exposed. These cutting and void search operations will occur in all sectors as required.

Operational Period: September 23–24, 2001

PLANNED ACTIONS AND OPERATING INSTRUCTIONS (Next 24 hours) The following areas have been identified to concentrate search & rescue operations in for this operational period based on the recent placement of cranes:

1. 300 Ton crane is in place at Washington & Liberty Streets. Debris removal and void search operations are in progress. FDNY SOC personnel and (1) FEMA US&R Task Force have been assigned to this location.
2. Based on the anticipated placement of an 800-ton crane on West St. (0800 hours on 9/23), debris removal and void search operations will commence immediately in the North tower area. FDNY SOC personnel and (1) FEMA US&R Task Force will be assigned to this location when the crane is ready to operate.
3. Based on the anticipated placement of a 1000-ton crane on West St. in the proximity of the Marriott WTC Hotel, contractor will begin placing required matting to facilitate crane placement and operations. Anticipated set up time 72 hours.
4. Steel cutting operations with the utilization of oxy-acetylene cutting set-ups (and subsequent removal of debris by rigging and heavy equipment) **continues at the most rapid pace possible. Special Operations Command personnel and FEMA US&R personnel are to be utilized as the primary source to accomplish this mission. Ironworkers can be utilized to assist and supplement this function, but keep in mind – this is a rescue operation.** All available cutting set-ups should be utilized on a continual basis as conditions permit. Void search operations will follow these cutting operations as voids are exposed. These cutting and void search operations will occur in all sectors as required.
5. All personnel operating on the north and south towers will be in bunkers pants as required due to the high heat level being generated on the lower levels of the debris piles. Consideration should be given to stretching protective hand lines as required.
6. The crane operating in the south tower in conjunction with Oxy-Acetylene cutting equipment shall be used to expedite debris removal.
7. The placement of large caliber water streams onto areas affected by fire on the north and south towers will be facilitated and continued as required.

Operational Period: September 24–25, 2001

PLANNED ACTIONS AND OPERATING INSTRUCTIONS (Next 24 hours)

The following areas have been identified to concentrate search & rescue operations in for this operational period based on the recent placement of cranes:

1. 300 Ton crane is in place at Washington & Liberty Streets. Debris removal and void search operations are in progress. FDNY SOC, PD ESU personnel and (1) FEMA US&R Task Force have been assigned to this location.
2. Based on the anticipated placement of an 800-ton crane on West St. (2000 hours on 9/23), debris removal and void search operations will commence immediately in the North tower area. FDNY SOC, PD ESU personnel and (1) FEMA US&R Task Force will be assigned to this location when the crane is ready to operate.
3. Based on the anticipated placement of a 1000-ton crane on West St. in the proximity of the Marriott WTC Hotel, contractor will begin placing required matting to facilitate crane placement and operations. Anticipated set up time 96 hours.
4. Steel cutting operations with the utilization of oxy-acetylene cutting set-ups (and subsequent removal of debris by rigging and heavy equipment) **is to continue at the most rapid pace possible. FDNY SOC, PD ESU and FEMA US&R personnel are to be utilized as the primary source to accomplish this mission. Ironworkers can be utilized to assist and supplement this function, but keep in mind – this is a rescue operation.** All available cutting set-ups should be utilized on a continual basis as conditions permit. Void search operations will follow these cutting operations as voids are exposed. **These cutting and void search operations will occur in all sectors as required.**
5. All personnel operating on the north and south towers will be in bunker pants as required due to the high heat level being generated on the lower levels of the debris piles. Consideration should be given to stretching protective hand lines as required.
6. The crane operating in the south tower in conjunction with Oxy-Acetylene cutting equipment shall be used to expedite debris removal.
7. Due to the hazards involved, limit void search operations during the night shift in the north and south towers. Use this time to facilitate the placement and use of large caliber water streams onto areas affected by fire on the north and south towers.

Operational Period: September 25–26, 2001

PLANNED ACTIONS AND OPERATING INSTRUCTIONS (Next 24 hours)

1. **At 1400 hours all personnel will be evacuated from the site to facilitate controlled removal of the secondary collapsed hazard at the South Tower. Actual removal is estimated to take 2 hours. Decision about re-entry into the site will occur at 1700. Times may vary based on weather conditions.**
2. 300 Ton crane is in place at Washington & Liberty Streets. Debris removal and void search operations will continue. FDNY SOC, PD ESU personnel and (1) FEMA US&R Task Force have been assigned to this location.
3. 800 Ton crane is in place on West St. Debris removal and void search operations will continue in the North tower area. FDNY SOC, PD ESU personnel and (1) FEMA US&R Task Force have been assigned to this location.
4. Based on the anticipated placement of a 1000-ton crane on West St. in the proximity of the Marriott WTC Hotel, contractor will begin placing required matting to facilitate crane placement and operations. Anticipated set up time 96 hours.
5. Steel cutting operations with the utilization of oxy-acetylene cutting set-ups (and subsequent removal of debris by rigging and heavy equipment) **is to continue at the most rapid pace possible. FDNY SOC, PD ESU and FEMA US&R personnel are to be utilized as the primary source to accomplish this mission. Ironworkers can be utilized to assist and supplement this function, but keep in mind – this is a rescue operation.** All available cutting set-ups should be utilized on a continual basis as conditions permit. Void search operations will follow these cutting operations as voids are exposed. These cutting and void search operations will occur in all sectors as required.
6. All personnel operating on the north and south towers will be in bunker pants as required due to the high heat level being generated on the lower levels of the debris piles. Consideration should be given to stretching protective hand lines as required in all areas of operations. Protective hand lines are in place at the North Tower, continue to operate as required.
7. Due to the hazards involved, limit void search operations during the night shift in the north and south towers. Use this time to facilitate the placement and use of large caliber water streams onto areas affected

by fire on the north and south towers.

8. NTSB will be on site to set up observation points that will assist in locating the flight recorders.
9. Conduct an engineering survey of the South and West facade walls still standing in the South Tower area. Develop an operational / engineering plan to facilitate removal of these unstable structures. FDNY, FEMA US&R, DDC and site construction manager to develop plan.

Operational Period: September 26–27, 2001

PLANNED ACTIONS AND OPERATING INSTRUCTIONS (Next 24 hours)

1. **No operations of any kind to be conducted at the Marriot Hotel or the South Tower area until further notice pending final removal of all overhanging steel hazards.**
2. 300 Ton crane is in place at Washington & Liberty Streets. Debris removal and void search operations will continue. FDNY SOC, PD ESU personnel and (1) FEMA US&R Task Force have been assigned to this location.
3. 800-ton crane is in place on West St. Debris removal and void search operations will continue in the North tower area. FDNY SOC, PD ESU personnel and (1) FEMA US&R Task Force have been assigned to this location.
4. Based on the anticipated placement of a 1000-ton crane on West St. in the proximity of the Marriott WTC Hotel, contractor is placing required matting to facilitate crane placement and operations.
5. Steel cutting operations with the utilization of oxy-acetylene cutting set-ups (and subsequent removal of debris by rigging and heavy equipment) **is to continue at the most rapid pace possible. FDNY SOC, PD ESU and FEMA US&R personnel are to be utilized as the primary source to accomplish this mission. Ironworkers can be utilized to assist and supplement this function, but keep in mind – this is a rescue operation.** All available cutting set-ups should be utilized on a continual basis as conditions permit. Void search operations will follow these cutting operations as voids are exposed. **These cutting and void search operations will occur in all sectors as required.**
6. All personnel operating on the north and south towers will be in bunker pants as required due to the high heat level being generated on the lower levels of the debris piles. Consideration should be given to stretching protective hand lines as required in all areas of operations.

Protective hand lines are in place at the North Tower, continue to operate as required.

7. Due to the hazards involved, limit void search operations during the night shift in the north and south towers. Use this time to facilitate the placement and use of large caliber water streams onto areas affected by fire on the north and south towers.
8. NTSB has five observation points and is setting up a sixth one that will assist in locating the flight recorders.
9. Void search operations will continue in the Winter Garden area as heavy steel is removed by crane. A FEMA US&R engineer will be assigned to this area for ongoing evaluation of condition. FD SOC personnel and PD ESU personnel will continue to continue to conduct void searches as required.
10. Review operational/engineering plan to facilitate removal of the South and West façade walls still standing in the South Tower area. FDNY, FEMA US&R, DDC and site construction manager to review plan.

Operational Period: September 27–28, 2001

PLANNED ACTIONS AND OPERATING INSTRUCTIONS (Next 24 hours)

1. 300 Ton crane is in place at Washington & Liberty Streets. Debris removal and void search operations will continue. FDNY SOC, PD ESU personnel and (1) FEMA US&R Task Force have been assigned to this location.
2. 800 Ton crane is in place on West St. Debris removal and void search operations will continue in the North tower area. FDNY SOC, PD ESU personnel and (1) FEMA US&R Task Force have been assigned to this location.
3. Based on the anticipated placement of a 1000-ton crane on West St. in the proximity of the Marriott WTC Hotel, contractor is placing required matting to facilitate crane placement and operations.
4. Steel cutting operations with the utilization of oxy-acetylene cutting set-ups (and subsequent removal of debris by rigging and heavy equipment) **is to continue at the most rapid pace possible. FDNY SOC, PD ESU and FEMA US&R personnel are to be utilized as the primary source to accomplish this mission. Ironworkers can be utilized to assist and supplement this function, but keep in mind – this is a rescue operation.** All available cutting set-ups should be utilized on a continual basis as conditions permit. Void search operations will

follow these cutting operations as voids are exposed. **These cutting and void search operations will occur in all sectors as required.**

5. All personnel operating on the north and south towers will be in bunker pants as required due to the high heat level being generated on the lower levels of the debris piles. Consideration should be given to stretching protective hand lines as required in all areas of operations. Protective hand lines are in place at the North Tower, continue to operate as required.
6. **NO** void search operations without approval of FDNY Sector Chief in the North and South Towers. Use this time to facilitate the placement and use of large caliber water streams onto areas affected by fire on the north and south towers. Maximize placement of portable monitors for continuous fire extinguishment operations.
7. NTSB has five camera points and is setting up a sixth one that will assist in locating the flight recorders.
8. Void search operations will continue in the Winter Garden area as heavy steel is removed by crane. A FEMA US&R engineer will be assigned to this area for ongoing evaluation of condition. FD SOC personnel and PD ESU personnel will continue to conduct void searches as required.
9. Review operational/engineering plan to facilitate removal of the South and West façade walls still standing in the South Tower area. FDNY, FEMA US&R, DDC and site construction manager to review plan and evaluate results of recent demolition.

Operational Period: September 28–29, 2001

PLANNED ACTIONS AND OPERATING INSTRUCTIONS (Next 24 hours)

1. 300 Ton crane is in place at Washington & Liberty Streets. Debris removal and void search operations will continue. FDNY SOC, PD ESU personnel and (1) FEMA US&R Task Force have been assigned to this location.
2. 700 Ton crane is in place on West St. Debris removal and void search operations will continue in the North Tower area. FDNY SOC, PD ESU personnel and (1) FEMA US&R Task Force have been assigned to this location.
3. Based on the anticipated placement of a 1000-ton crane on West St. in the proximity of the Marriott WTC Hotel, contractor is placing required matting to facilitate crane placement and operations.

4. Steel cutting operations with the utilization of oxy-acetylene cutting set-ups (and subsequent removal of debris by rigging and heavy equipment) **is to continue at the most rapid pace possible. FDNY SOC, PD ESU and FEMA US&R personnel will be utilized to assist and supplement this mission.** Ironworkers can be utilized to assist and supplement this function. All available cutting set-ups should be utilized on a continual basis as conditions permit. Void search operations will follow these cutting operations as voids are exposed. **These cutting and void search operations will occur in all sectors as required.**
5. All personnel operating on the south tower will be in bunker pants as required due to the high heat level being generated on the lower levels of the debris piles. Consideration should be given to stretching protective hand lines as required in all areas of operations. Protective hand lines are in place at the North Tower, continue to operate as required.
6. **NO** void search operations without approval of FDNY Sector Chief in the North and South Towers. Use this time to facilitate the placement and use of large caliber water streams onto areas affected by fire on the north and south towers. Maximize placement of portable monitors for continuous fire extinguishment operations
7. NTSB has six camera points that will assist in locating the flight recorders.
8. Void search operations will continue in the Winter Garden area as heavy steel is removed by crane. A FEMA US&R engineer will be assigned to this area for ongoing evaluation of condition. FD SOC personnel and PD ESU personnel will continue to conduct void searches as required.
9. Continue to review operational/engineering plan to facilitate removal of the South and West façade walls still standing in the South Tower area. FDNY, FEMA US&R, DDC and site construction manager to review plan and evaluate results of recent demolition.
10. Construct an access road to facilitate heavy equipment operations in the Plaza and Pit area between WTC #4 and WTC #5.
11. Access the area of the freon tank to assess structural integrity of the tank and associated plumbing to determine the quantity of product remaining and take appropriate action as required.

Operational Period: September 29–30, 2001

PLANNED ACTIONS AND OPERATING INSTRUCTIONS (Next 24 hours)

1. 300 Ton crane is in place at Washington & Liberty Streets. Accelerated

debris removal and void search operations will continue. FDNY SOC, PD ESU personnel and (1) FEMA US&R Task Force have been assigned to this location.

2. 700 Ton crane is in place on West St. Accelerated debris removal and void search operations will continue in the North Tower area. FDNY SOC, PD ESU personnel and (1) FEMA US&R Task Force have been assigned to this location.
3. Assembly of a 1000-ton crane on West St. in the proximity of the Marriott WTC Hotel is proceeding on schedule. Crane is anticipated to be operational by 9/29 2000 hours.
4. Steel cutting operations with the utilization of oxy-acetylene cutting set-ups (and subsequent removal of debris by rigging and heavy equipment) is to continue. Ironworkers are to be utilized to accomplish this mission. FDNY SOC, PD ESU and FEMA US&R personnel will be utilized to assist and supplement this function. All available cutting set-ups should be utilized on a continual basis as conditions permit. Void search operations will follow these cutting operations as voids are exposed. These cutting and void search operations will occur in all sectors as required.
5. All personnel operating on the South Tower will be in bunker pants as required due to the high heat level being generated on the lower levels of the debris piles. Consideration should be given to stretching protective hand lines as required in all areas of operations. Protective hand lines are in place at the North Tower, continue to operate as required.
6. NO void search operations without approval of FDNY Sector Chief in the North and South Towers. Use this time to facilitate the placement and use of large caliber water streams onto areas affected by fire on the North and South Towers. Maximize placement of portable monitors for continuous fire extinguishment operations.
7. NIJ has six camera points that will assist in locating the flight recorders.
8. Void search operations will continue in the Winter Garden area as heavy steel is removed by crane. A FEMA US&R engineer will be assigned to this area for ongoing evaluation of condition. FD SOC personnel and PD ESU personnel will continue to conduct void searches as required.
9. Continue to review operational/engineering plan to facilitate removal of the South and West façade walls still standing in the South Tower area. FDNY, FEMA US&R, DDC and site construction manager to

review plan and evaluate results of deconstruction process.

10. Construct an access road to facilitate heavy equipment operations in the Plaza and Pit area between WTC #4 and WTC #5.
11. Begin use of GPS for mapping and documentation of recovery operations as well as structural features.
12. DDC is expected to present the long range plan for the site.

Operational Period: September 30–October 1, 2001

PLANNED ACTIONS AND OPERATING INSTRUCTIONS (Next 24 hours)

1. 300 Ton crane is in place at Washington & Liberty Streets. Accelerated debris removal and void search operations will continue. FDNY SOC, PD ESU personnel and (1) FEMA US&R Task Force have been assigned to this location.
2. 700 Ton crane is in place on West St. Accelerated debris removal and void search operations will continue in the North Tower area. FDNY SOC, PD ESU personnel and (1) FEMA US&R Task Force have been assigned to this location.
3. Assembly of a 1000-ton crane on West St. in the proximity of the Marriott WTC Hotel is proceeding on schedule. Crane is anticipated to be operational by 9/29 2000 hours.
4. Steel cutting operations with the utilization of oxy-acetylene cutting set-ups (and subsequent removal of debris by rigging and heavy equipment) is to continue. Ironworkers are to be utilized to accomplish this mission. FDNY SOC, PD ESU and FEMA US&R personnel will be utilized to assist and supplement this function. All available cutting set-ups should be utilized on a continual basis as conditions permit. Void search operations will follow these cutting operations as voids are exposed. These cutting and void search operations will occur in all sectors as required.
5. All personnel operating on the South Tower will be in bunker pants as required due to the high heat level being generated on the lower levels of the debris piles. Consideration should be given to stretching protective hand lines as required in all areas of operations. Protective hand lines are in place at the North Tower, continue to operate as required.
6. NO void search operations without approval of FDNY Sector Chief in the North and South Towers. Use this time to facilitate the placement and use of large caliber water streams onto areas affected by fire on the North and South Towers. Maximize placement of portable

monitors for continuous fire extinguishment operations.

7. NIJ has six camera points that will assist in locating the flight recorders.
8. Void search operations will continue in the Winter Garden area as heavy steel is removed by crane. A FEMA US&R engineer will be available to conduct on-going evaluations of the conditions in this area for the operational period of 0700 hours through 1900 hours. FD SOC personnel and PD ESU personnel will continue to conduct void searches as required.
9. Continue to review operational/engineering plan to facilitate removal of the South and West façade walls still standing in the South Tower area. FDNY, FEMA US&R, DDC and site construction manager to review plan and evaluate results of deconstruction process.
10. Construct an access road to facilitate heavy equipment operations in the Plaza and Pit area between WTC #4 and WTC #5.
11. Continue use of GPS for mapping and documentation of recovery operations as well as structural features.
12. Preliminary Long Range Plan for the site submitted by DDC will be presented to Mayor for approval early next week.
13. Restricted work at WTC 4 due to demolition.
14. Anticipated entry by DDC engineers, FDNY HazMat, PAPD ESU and DEP via path tubes to evaluate slurry walls, perform air monitoring and take selected water samples for analysis. A second entry may take place from the south side of the site Monday 10/01 depending on results of Sunday's recon. Both entries subject to FDNY approval.

Appendix I: FDNY IMT Activation Log

Date	Incident Name	Location	Type	Operations
Sep 2005	Hurricane Katrina	New Orleans	Hurricane	Post storm emergency operations & recovery
Sep 2007	East Zone Complex	McCall	Wildfire Complex	Wildfire operations, support & management
Sep 2008	Hurricane Gustav	Baton Rouge	Hurricane	Storm operations support
Nov 2009	BioPod 2009	New York	Public Health	Support FDNY BHS in medication distribution evaluation
Nov 2010	BioPod 2010	New York	Public Health	Support FDNY BHS in medication distribution evaluation
Nov 2011	BioPod 2011	New York	Public Health	Support FDNY BHS in medication distribution evaluation
Sep 2011	Hurricane Irene NYS	Broome County	Hurricane	Post storm recovery operations
Sep 2011	Hurricane Irene NYC	New York	Hurricane	Pre-landfall operations, post storm recovery (street clearing)
Nov 2012	BioPod 2012	New York	Public Health	Support FDNY BHS in medication distribution evaluation
Oct 2012	Hurricane Sandy Support	New York	Humanitarian	Post storm recovery (street clearing, canvasing, distribution)
Oct 2012	Hurricane Sandy	New York	Hurricane	Pre-landfall operations & during storm operations support
Aug 2012	Governor's Island Vent Exp	New York	Fire Ops	Support FDNY/ NIST in high rise fire/smoke travel experiments

Date	Incident Name	Location	Type	Operations
Nov 2013	BioPod 2013	New York	Public Health	Support FDNY BHS in medication distribution evaluation
Jan 2013	Winter Storm Nemo	New York	Winter Storm	Pre-storm preparation, during storm operations support
Nov 2014	November to Remember	Buffalo	Winter Storm	Post record setting snowfall recovery operations
Nov 2014	BioPod 2014	New York	Public Health	Support FDNY BHS in medication distribution evaluation
May 2014	Nasal Narcan Training	New York	Training	Training all FDNY members in administration of Narcan
Mar 2014	Park Avenue Collapse	New York	USAR	Building explosion operations & recovery
Aug 2015	Legionnaires Incident	New York	Public Health	Reconnaissance & monitoring of NYC legionella outbreak
Mar 2015	2nd Avenue Collapse	New York	USAR	Building explosion operations & recovery
Feb 2015	Kent Avenue Warehouse Fire	New York	Ops Support	Deconstruction, recovery & evidence preservation support
Jan 2015	Winter Storm Juno	New York	Winter Storm	Pre-storm preparation, during storm operations support
Sep 2016	DC Fahy LODD	Yonkers	Funeral	LODD funeral support
Sep 2016	Hurricane Hermine	New York	Hurricane	Pre-storm preparation, during storm operations support
Feb 2016	Worth Street Crane Collapse	New York	USAR/Fire	Operations support post fatal NYC crane collapse

Date	Incident Name	Location	Type	Operations
Sep 2017	Hurricane Irma	Homestead	Hurricane	Post hurricane base camp management
Sep 2017	Hurricane Maria	San Juan	Hurricane	PRFD infrastructure assessment & capabilities evaluation
Aug 2017	Hurricane Harvey	Houston	Hurricane	Post hurricane RSA management & commodity distribution
Apr 2017	Fr Tolley LODD	Bethpage	Funeral	LODD funeral support
Mar 2017	EMT Arroyo LODD	New York	Funeral	LODD funeral support
Nov 2018	Scabies 2018	New York	Public Health	Support and monitoring of scabies outbreak in firehouses
Oct 2018	Hurricane Michael	Panama City	Hurricane	Post hurricane base camp management
Jul 2018	Con Edison Steam Explosion	New York	HazMat	Support operations and hazardous materials decontamination
Mar 2018	Fr Davidson LODD	New York	Funeral	LODD funeral support
Mar 2018	FM Zanetis LODD	New York	Funeral	LODD funeral support
Mar 2018	Lt Raguso LODD	Commack	Funeral	LODD funeral support
Dec 2019	FDNY COVID-19 Response	New York	Pandemic	PPE management to ensure safe field operations
Sep 2019	Measles Risk	New York	Public Health	Monitoring members at risk for measles infection
Aug 2019	Lt Sullivan LODD	New York	Funeral	LODD funeral support
Apr 2019	Fr Slutman LODD	New York	Funeral	LODD funeral support
Jan 2019	Fr Pollard LODD	New York	Funeral	LODD funeral support

Date	Incident Name	Location	Type	Operations
Dec 2020	COVID-19 Vaccine Program	New York	Pandemic	Vaccine administration for FDNY, city employees, and families
Sep 2020	Hurricane Isaias	New York	Hurricane	Assist FDNY & NYC Parks with tree removal operations
Aug 2020	Dolan Fire	Monterey Cnty	Wildfire	Wildfire operations support on Los Padres National Forest
May 2020	BIOPOD Covid Antibody	New York	Pandemic	Assist FDNY CTDP with antibody testing
May 2020	FDNY BFP Reopening TF	New York	Pandemic	Assist Bureau of Fire Prevention with Reopening Taskforce
Apr 2020	NYC OCME Assistance	New York	Pandemic	Assist NY OCME in fatality management of COVID-19
Mar 2020	NYC COVID Testing Sites	New York	Pandemic	Assist NYCEM in set up of testing sites around NYC
Dec 2021	Lt Maiello LODD	New York	Funeral	LODD funerals upport
Sep 2021	Woods Creek/ Balsinger	Helena Forest	Wildfire	Wildfire support on Helena/Lewis and Clark National Forest
Mar 2021	Vaccine Home Bound Mission	New York	Pandemic	Managing mobile nurse teams for home bound residents
Dec 2022	FF William Moon LODD	New York	Funeral	LODD funeral support
Oct 2022	Lt Par Russo-Elling LODD	New York	Funeral	LODD funeral support
Sep 2022	Hurricane Ian	Fort Meyers	Hurricane	Assist Fort Myers Beach Fire District
Apr 2022	Fr Klein LODD	New York	Funeral	LODD funeral support

Date	Incident Name	Location	Type	Operations
Mar 2022	PFF Malveaux	New York	Funeral	LODD funeral support
Feb 2022	MSA TIC Update	New York	Fire Support	Managing software updates for all MSA TICs in service
Feb 2022	Fr Gerhard LODD	New York	Funeral	LODD funeral support
Aug 2023	Louisiana Wildfire	Louisiana	Wildfire	Assist Louisiana State Fire Marshals
Apr 2023	Ann Street Collapse	New York	USAR	Parking garage collapse operations
Oct 2024	Hawthorne Drive Fire	Berlin	Wildfire	Wildfire operations, support and management
Oct 2024	Knoxville SRT	Knoxville	Hurricane	Assisted FEMA with branch operations
Oct 2024	TS Helen	Buncombe Cnty	Hurricane	Assist with post-flood rescue and recovery
Aug 2024	Limepoint Fire	Council	Wildfire	Wildfire support on Payette National Forest
Jul 2024	SQF Lightning	Sequoia	Wildfire	Wildfire support on Sequoia National Forest
Mar 2026	Kona Low	Oahu	Flood	Assist with post-flood rescue and recovery

Appendix J: 9/11 Manhattan Dispatch Transcript

Time	Station	Transmission
	F	Battalion 1 to Manhattan.
8:47	D	Battalion 1.
	F	We just had a plane crash into upper floors of the World Trade Center. Transmit a second alarm and start relocating companies into the area.
	D	Ten-four, Battalion 1.
	F	Battalion 1 is also sending the whole assignment on this box to that area, K.
	F	Engine 6 to ...
	D	Engine 6.
	F	The World Trade Center tower No. 1 is on fire, the whole outside of the building. There was just a huge explosion.
	D	Ten-four. All companies standby at this time.
	F	[inaudible]
	D	Ten-four.
	F	Engine 1-0 to Manhattan.
	D	Engine 1-0.
	F	Engine 1-0, World Trade Center 10-60. Send every available ambulance, everything you've got, to the World Trade Center now.
	D	Ten-four, 10-60 has been transmitted for the World Trade Center, 10-60 for the World Trade Center.
	F	Three Truck to Manhattan.
	D	Three Truck.
8:48	F	Civilian reports from up here a plane just crashed into the World Trade Center for your information.
	D	Ten-four, K.
	F	... available.
	F	Battalion 1 to Manhattan.
	D	Battalion 1, K.
8:48:09	F	We have a number of floors on fire. It looked like the plane was aiming towards the building. Transmit a third alarm throughout the staging area at Vesey and West Street. As the third alarm assignment goes into that area, the second alarm assignment report to the building, K.
	D	Ten-four. Second alarm assignment report to the World Trade Center, second alarm assignment report to 1 World Trade Center.
	F	Engine 1-0 to Manhattan.
	D	Engine 1-0, K.
	F	It appears an airplane crashed into the World Trade Center.

Time	Station	Transmission
	D	Ten-four. Third alarm's been transmitted box 8087, third alarm transmitted box 8087 for 1 World Trade Center.
	F	Squad 1-8 to Manhattan, K.
8:49	D	Squad 1-8, K.
	F	... looked like it was intentional. Inform all unitscoming in from the back it could be a terror attack.
	D	Ten-four. All units be advised –
	F	... to Manhattan.
	F	... to Manhattan, just so you know, this is confirmed, this is confirmed.
	D	This is confirmed. Ten-four, K.
	F	Engine 1-0 to Manhattan.
	D	Engine 1-0, go.
	F	Roll every available ambulance you've got to this position.
	D	Ten-four, K.
	F	Rescue 2 to Manhattan.
	D	Rescue 2, go.
	F	Are we assigned to any of your boxes in lower Manhattan, K?
8:50	D	Rescue 2, standby.
	F	Division 1 to Manhattan, K.
	D	Division 1, K.
	F	... responding, have another rescue squad out.
	D	Ten-four. Rescue 2, start out to box 8087, K.
	F	Rescue 2's responding, K.
	F	Squad 1-8 to Manhattan, K.
	F	Rescue 1 to Manhattan, what do you have in on this?
	F	... 1 to Manhattan.
	D	Division 1, go with your message.
	F	What's the response ... right now?
	D	Division 1, you now have a third alarm assignment to the box, K.
	F	Division 1, 10-4, that's confirmed. We have fire on several floors, the upper floors of the World Trade Center.
	D	Ten-four, Division 1.
	?	K, I've got another siren.
8:51	F	Four-zero Bravo to Manhattan.
	D	Four-zero Bravo ...
	F	Four-zero Bravo's responding to the World Trade Center.
	D	Ten-four, K.

Time	Station	Transmission
	F	Forty Adam[?] to Manhattan.
	D	Forty Adam.
	F	On the way to the Trade Center.
	D	Ten-four.
	D	Third alarm has been transmitted box 8087, No. 1 World Trade Center.
	F	Fire 5 to Manhattan. Engine Fire 5 to Manhattan.
	D	Engine Fire 5.
	F	Please have ambulances respond to West Street, we have several injured people on West Street here.
	D	Ten-four, Engine 5.
8:52	F	Battalion 1 to Manhattan, K.
	F	Two-one-four to Manhattan.
	F	This is Battalion 1 to Manhattan, K.
	F	Three truck to Manhattan.
	D	Three truck, go.
	F	We're at Houston and West Broadway. We can see this from here. We've been directed by numerous civilians. You want us to take this in or you want us to stand fast?
	D	Take that in, K.
	F	[inaudible]
	F	Brooklyn to Manhattan.
	D	Brooklyn, go.
	F	On the ... information Brooklyn is transmitting a box at the Brooklyn end of the Battery Tunnel. We will use this as a staging area for apparatus to respond to Manhattan.
	D	Ten-four.
8:53	F	Division 1 to Manhattan.
	D	...
	F	The staging area at the fire scene here is beyond West Street. All units respond into West Street. Transmit a 10-60 also.
	D	All right, 10-60's been transmitted, box 8087, 10-60, box 8087 for 1 World Trade Center. All units responding into box 8087, the staging area will be at West Street, K.
	F	[inaudible]
	F	... Manhattan.
	F	Four David to Manhattan.
	D	Car 4 David, go with your message.

Time	Station	Transmission
	F	Do we have any report on a fire condition yet from on-scene personnel?
	D	Division 1 reports numerous floors on fire, K.
	F	Is this the second alarm right now?
	D	This is a third alarm, a 10-60 has been transmitted, K.
	F	Four David, 10-4.
	F	Rescue 3 to Manhattan on your frequency.
8:54	F	Three and one to Manhattan, K.
	D	Three and one.
	F	Be advised we're responding. We'll be in the river for water supply. Advise incoming that you have visible flames from the side of the building.
	D	Ten-four. Incoming units, be advised visible flames from the side of the building.
	F	Forty Adam to Manhattan.
	D	Manhattan calling Division 1.
	D	Manhattan calling Division 1, K. Manhattan calling Division 1, K.
8:55	F	Rescue Four to Manhattan, K.
	D	Rescue Four.
	F	... responding, K.
	D	Ten-four.
	F	Battalion 7 to Manhattan, K.
	F	One-one-zero to Manhattan.
	D	Battalion 7 go with your message. Battalion 7 go with your message.
	F	Whatever it was hit the north side of the building. Fire is venting from at least one floor, heavy smoke's all over the front and top of the building, approximately 90-something floor, K.
	D	Ten-four.
	D	Manhattan calling Division 1, K.
	F	Division 1 to Manhattan, go ahead.
	D	Division 1, receiving reports floor No. 106, numerous people trapped, floor No. 106.
	F	Ten-four. We have units on the way up now. Reported fire on the 78th floor. That's unconfirmed at the time. We're going to need the P.D. for security on the entire World Trade Center. We have ... coming from the World Trade Center ... [inaudible]
8:56	D	Ten-four.
	F	Ladder 1-1-0 to Manhattan. We're on your frequency now.
	D	Ten-four.

Time	Station	Transmission
	F	Battalion 7 to Manhattan.
	?	Guys, it was a plane that struck the building.
	D	Battalion 7 go with your message, K.
	F	I'm going to turn on ... battalion car as a back up for the building repeater, K.
	D	Battalion 7, 10-5 that message.
	F	Squad 2-8-8 to Manhattan, K.
	D	Squad 2-8-8.
	F	On your frequency responding. Can you send up a ticket please?
	D	Ten-four.
	F	Car 3 to Manhattan, K.
8:57	D	Car 3, go.
	F	Car 3 and Car 4 are arriving together responding down. Transmit a fifth alarm for this box. Get us a staging area ... somewhere on West Street, K.
	D	Ten-four.
	D	A fifth alarm has been transmitted, box 8087. A fifth alarm has been transmitted, box 8087, for No. 1 World Trade Center.
	F	[inaudible]
	D	Go with your message, K.
	F	[inaudible]
	D	Unit calling, go with your message –
	F	[inaudible]
	F	Battalion 2 to Manhattan.
	D	Battalion 2, go.
8:58	F	Be advised we have jumpers, K, jumpers.
	D	All right, Division 1, be advised, Battalion 2 advised we have jumpers from the World Trade Center, K.
	F	Division 1 to Manhattan.
	F	Three and one to Manhattan, K.
	D	Division 1, go with your message.
	F	Those jumpers, did they already jump?
	D	Battalion 2, have those jumpers jumped, K?
	F	[inaudible]
	D	Battalion 2, do you have jumpers down?
	F	[inaudible] Manhattan.
	D	Division 1, Battalion 2 is advising jumpers down, K.

Time	Station	Transmission
	F	Forty Charlie to Manhattan.
	D	Forty Charlie, go.
8:59	F	Forty Charlie is responding. Be advised you've got all boats available for any transport through the river ... rescue ...
	D	Ten-four, K.
	F	Four David to Manhattan.
	D	Four David.
	F	How many rescues we got here?
	F	Marine 1 to Manhattan with an urgent message, K.
	D	At this time you have three rescues, K.
	F	O.K., 1 want all but one of them here.
	D	Ten-four.
	F	Marine 1 to Manhattan with an urgent message, K.
	D	Unit with an urgent message, K.
	F	This is Marine 1, we're in the river. You've got fire out of the north side and now coming out of the west side of the World Trade Center, the west side.
	D	All right, fire from the north side and the west side of the World Trade Center.
	F	That's affirmative. Fire has penetrated the skin.
	F	Marine 6 to Manhattan.
9:00	D	All right, box 8087, report of smoke 83rd floor, 103 floor, 104 floor. Also received reports of people trapped on floor No. 106, K.
	F	Marine 6 to Manhattan.
	D	Marine 6.
	F	We're getting your frequency underway. You also have fire out of the east side of the building.
	D	Ten-four, Marine 6.
9:01	F	Car 4 David to Manhattan.
	D	Car 4 David.
	F	Ten eighty-four at the World Trade Center.
	D	Car 4 David, repeat that?
	F	Ten eighty-four.
	D	Car 4 David, we're getting reports from the 104th floor, back room, 25 to 30 people trapped. I also have the 103rd floor, northwest room, 103, with people trapped also. I have the 83rd floor with people trapped as well. Car Four David, received?
	F	Car 4 David, 10-4.
	D	All right, 10-4. Time is 09:01.12.61.

Time	Station	Transmission
	F	Car 9 Sally to Manhattan.
	D	Car 9 Sally.
	F	Go to fallback step 3.
	F	Car 4 to Division 1.
	D	Fall back step 3 has been implemented. Fall back step 3 has been implemented, K.
	F	Car 40 Adam to Manhattan.
	D	Car 4-0 Adam, go.
	F	Would you relocate the only rescue that's not going to the Trade Center, put them in Rescue 1 in Manhattan, please.
	D	Ten-four.
9:02	F	Squad 4-1 to ...
	D	Squad 4-1, K. Manhattan calling Squad 4-1.
	F	Squad 4-1 to Manhattan.
	D	Squad 4-1, relocate to Squad 1-8, K.
	F	Squad 4-1, 10-4.
	F	Four-zero Bravo to Manhattan.
	D	Four-zero Bravo, K.
	F	Can you confirm that Hazmat 1 is responding to the 10-60?
	D	They've been assigned, K.
	F	Hazmat 1 to Manhattan.
	D	Hazmat 1.
	F	We are responding. We're just out of the tunnel. Is there a specific route that is set up for emergency vehicles to get through, K?
	F	Marine 6 to Manhattan urgent.
	D	Hazmat 1 standby. Marine 6, go.
9:03	F	You have a second plane into the other tower of the Trade Center, major fire.
	D	Car 4 David, Marine 6 advising a second plane into the World Trade Center, K.
	F	Marine 6, that's the other tower.
	D	That's the second tower at the World Trade Center, K.
	F	Brooklyn to Manhattan.
	D	All units standby unless urgent. Manhattan calling Car 4 David, K. Manhattan calling Car 4 David.
	F	Car 4 David to Manhattan.

Time	Station	Transmission
	D	Be advised, report of a second plane that crashed into the second tower. Be advised on the 83rd floor, room 8311, we have people trapped, room 8311, 83rd floor. Car 4 David acknowledge.
	F	Car 4 David, 10-4.
9:04	F	Marine 6 to Manhattan.
	D	Marine 6, go with your message.
	F	Marine 6, that plane was a large bomber-style green aircraft into the second tower, be advised.
	D	All right, 10-4.
	F	This is mayday, mayday. Engine – another place hit the second tower, K.
	D	All right, 10-4.
	D	Manhattan calling Car 4 David.
	F	Three Adam to Manhattan.
	D	Three Adam, go ahead.
	F	I'm on the F.D.R. Drive. Definitely something hit the second tower, possibly two-thirds of the way up. You've got visible fire showing out there. Suggest to the incident commander, 4 David, to transmit a fifth alarm to Tower 2.
	D	Manhattan calling Car 4 David.
	F	Brooklyn to Manhattan with an urgent.
	D	Standby unless urgent.
9:05	D	Manhattan calling Car 4 David, K. Manhattan calling Car 4 David. Manhattan calling Division 1, K.
	F	Division 1, K.
	D	Division 1, be advised, 3 Adam reports that you have a second plane that crashed into the second tower about two-thirds of the way up. He would recommend you transmit a fifth alarm for that tower as well.
	F	Yeah, 10-4 ... Manhattan. Proceed with your ...
	D	All right, 10-4.
	F	Tactical Support 2 to Manhattan.
	D	Tactical Support 2, go ahead.
	F	Send me a ticket, entering the tunnel.
	D	All right, 10-4.
	F	... Car to Manhattan.
	D	Go ahead ...

Time	Station	Transmission
	F	We're 10-84 this box [or 1 want you to 84 this box?]. Do us a favor, please. Will you call our bosses downtown and have them secure the [M.C.C.?] We're located at Broadway and Maiden Lane, at Broadway and Maiden Lane. Have them ... the [M.C.C.?] to this location. We do need help here.
9:06	D	All right, what is that location?
	F	On Broadway and Maiden Lane. Best to have the [M.C.C.?] and have our personnel be secure here at this location.
	D	The [M.C.C.]?
	F	I'm requesting that at this location, we've got to buildings on fire here.
	F	Unit 4 to Manhattan, K.
	D	Unit 4 to Manhattan, go ahead.
	F	Engine 1-4.
	D	One-four, go ahead.
	F	We're at Houston and Broadway, available for the World Trade Center.
	D	All right. Engine 1-4 remain in service at this time. Standby.
	F	Division 3 to Manhattan.
	D	Go ahead, go with your message.
	F	Division 3 to Manhattan.
	D	Division 3, go with your message.
	F	Are we being assigned to any of these boxes down at the World Trade Center?
	D	Affirmative Division 3. Continue in.
	F	All right, 10-4. Division 3 to Manhattan, call leader Car 4 David on the scene, do they want to institute a recall due to the incident, K?
9:07	D	Manhattan calling Car 4 David. Manhattan calling Car 4 David, K. Manhattan calling Car 4 David.
	F	Division 3 to Manhattan.
	D	Division 3, go ahead.
	F	Did you give me the box that I'm being assigned to, K?
	D	Division 3, you're going to 2 World Trade Center. Box is 9998, K.
	F	Division 3, 10-4.
	F	... to Manhattan.
	D	Units calling Manhattan, one at a time, K.
	F	Division 1 to Manhattan.
	D	One Engine, go.
	F	Division 1 to Manhattan. All incoming units into World 1 and World 2 Trade Center are to bring additional cylinders.

Time	Station	Transmission
9:08	D	Engine 1, repeat that, K. You were totally unreadable.
	F	Division 1 to Manhattan. All responding units responding into No. 1 and No. 2 World Trade Center are to bring additional ... cylinders with them.
	D	All right, all units standby unless urgent in the borough of Manhattan. All units responding into No. 1 World Trade Center and No. 2 World Trade Center, bring all additional S.D.B.A.[?] bottles to the front of the building. All units to box 8087 and 998, No. 1 and No. 2 World Trade Center, bring your extra S.D.B.A. bottles to the front of the building, as per the division.
	D	Other units calling Manhattan.
	D	No problem, go ahead.
	F	Have Field Comm. reports, that they bring vehicles in front of the American Express building on West Street, ... orders with Chief [Ingle?]
	D	Manhattan calling Field Comm.
	F	We got it Manhattan. Thank you.
9:09	D	O.K., 10-4, Field Comm. Thank you.
	F	Four Truck to Manhattan, K.
	D	Four Truck, go ahead.
	F	One-three-one to Manhattan.
	D	One-three-one, standby.
	D	Four Truck, go ahead.
	F	... tower would you like us to be starting into, Tower 1 or Tower 2, K?
	D	Four Truck, go to 2 World Trade Center, K.
	F	Four Truck, 10-4.
	D	One-three-one, go ahead. Ladder 1-3-1. Other units calling Manhattan.
	F	Ladder 11 to Manhattan.
	D	Ladder 11, go ahead.
	F	Which tower are we to respond into?
	D	You're going to 2 World Trade Center, K, two.
9:10	F	All right, we're going to two, 10-4.
	D	And bring all your extra S.D.B.A.'s up with you, K.
	F	Ten-four.
	F	Squad Company 2 –
	F	Engine 2 –
	D	One unit at a time. Two-one-one? The last squad company calling?
	F	Squad 2-5-2 to Manhattan, K, we have our second [piece?] responding to the World Trade Center.

Time	Station	Transmission
	D	All right, 10-4, Squad 2-5-2. When you get there bring up all your extra S.D.B.A. bottles, K.
	F	Ten-four
	F	Division 3.
	D	Division 3, go.
	F	1 can't pick up the five units that you assigned to my system on. Have you got it in the computer yet, K?
	D	They should be on there now. Do you want a rundown?
	F	No, let me try one more time in the computer because all I'm getting is like five units. I'll get back to you in a second.
	D	All right. We're getting them on there as fast as check that.
	F	... 1-0 to Manhattan.
	D	One-zero, go ahead, K.
9:11	F	... 1-0, inform everyone assigned to the scene responding on West Street or Liberty Street not to pull up in front of the building. We have ambulances and everybody else pulling up and we've got debris falling from the building. They have to stop short of the building either north or south.
	D	Ten-four.
	D	Units responding in to the World Trade Center, do not pull in front of the building on West or Liberty, K. Units responding in to the World Trade Center, do not pull in front of the building in West and Liberty.
	F	Division 3 to Manhattan.
	D	Division 3, go ahead.
	F	For some reason it's only giving me a few units. You're going to have to give it to me over the radio. I'm ready to write.
9:12	D	All right: Engine 2-1-1, Ladder 1-1, Engine 4-4, Engine 2-2, Engine 5-3, Engine 4-0, yourself, Battalion 1-0, Battalion 1-2, Ladder 1-6, Ladder 2, Ladder 1-3, Engine 2-2-1, Engine 2-3, Engine 2-0-9, Engine 2-1-2, Engine 2-7-9, Engine 2-3-0, Engine 2-2-9, [interference], Engine 2-1-6, Engine 2-1-7, Engine [interference], Engine 2-1-4, Ladder 12, Ladder 1-1-8, Ladder 7, Ladder 2-4, High Rise 1 and Battalion 1-1. Division 3.
	F	Division 3, 10-4. That's all the units I've got, K?
	D	That's all you've got at this time, K.
	F	All right, 10-4. Thank you.
	D	Ten-four.
9:13	D	Four Bravo, you're calling Manhattan, K? Unit calling Manhattan, K.
	F	Car 9 to Manhattan, K.
	D	Car 9, go ahead.
	F	Would you advise the mobile command vehicle to come in on West and Liberty Street, West and Liberty Street, K.
	D	I already advised them.

Time	Station	Transmission
	F	What's their E.T.A.?
	D	Manhattan calling Field Comm.
	F	Manhattan, that's not the Field Comm. 1 want the mobile –
	F	Division 3 to Manhattan.
	D	Car 9, go ahead.
	F	Manhattan, 1 want the Mobile Command Vehicle, not the Field Comm. The Mobile Command Vehicle is responding also, 1 want them at West and Liberty.
	D	All right, 10-4. I'll advise.
	F	Division 3 to Manhattan.
	D	Division 3, go ahead.
9:14	F	Notify units to get over to the West Side. Eleven Avenue is closed off, they've got a direct route to the World Trade Center. Everything below 24th Street, it's wide open to get down there if they're responding to these locations.
	D	You want them over on the West Side?
	F	If they can get over to the West Side, 11th Avenue, it's wide open from 30th Street all the way south to the World Trade Center, K. The P.D.'s already got it shut down.
	D	All right, 10-4. Units responding, if you can get over to the West Side, 11th Avenue's closed down [interference] 11th Avenue, West Side.
	D	Calling Mobile Command Vehicle, K. Manhattan calling Mobile Command Vehicle, K. Car 9, I'm unable to read them.
	F	10-4, Manhattan. Keep trying.
	F	Car 3 to Manhattan.
	D	Car 3, go ahead.
	F	Get a hold of Field Comm. We need them on West and Vesey Street, K, Field Comm. on West and Vesey.
	D	Ten-four. Field Comm. on West and Vesey, 1 got that.
9:15	F	All right, 10-4.
	D	Manhattan calling Mobile Command Vehicle, K. Manhattan calling Mobile Command Vehicle, K. Manhattan calling Car 3. Manhattan calling Car 3, K.
	F	Car 3, go ahead, Manhattan.
9:16	D	Car 3 are you 84 the box?
	F	We are 10-84 the box. We are at West and Vesey, K.
	D	All right. Listen 1 have some floors for you to check out.
	F	... Go ahead, Manhattan.

Time	Station	Transmission
	D	Mayor's Service, standby. Car 3, in building two, the No. 8-2 floor, the No. 8-8 floor and No. 8-9 floor. On the 82nd floor it's the west. I have other floors. Are you ready to copy?
	F	Ten-four.
	D	O.K., the 83rd floor in building one; the 104th floor; the 103rd floor, northwest corner, room 103; 106th floor; 83rd floor is 8-3-1-1 room; and the 82nd floor, east side, in building one.
9:17	F	O.K. Manhattan, standby for a few minutes. We're going to get Field Comm. set up, we'll be able to copy everything, K?
	D	All right, 10-4. Just advise me when you're ready.
	F	Ladder 1-7 to Manhattan.
	D	Seventeen Truck, go ahead.
	F	... to Ladder 1-5.
	D	All right, 10-4, 17.
	F	Marine 6 to Manhattan.
	D	Marine 6, go ahead, K.
	F	We're the marine division, we will position by the Brooklyn Bridge for a possible transport of men and equipment to Manhattan.
	D	All right, 10-4.
	F	Car 9 to Manhattan.
	D	Car 9, K.
	F	Would you have units responding on the fifth alarm for 2 World Trade Center, that's No. 2 World Trade Center, report to Chief Barbera [sp?] at West and Liberty Street, West and Liberty Street, K?
	D	...
	F	Engine 1-4 to Manhattan, K.
	D	That's correct. That's the command post for No. 2 World Trade Center, West and Liberty Street.
9:18	D	Ten-four, Car 9.
	F	Engine 1-4 to Manhattan, K.
	D	All units standby unless urgent, O.K.?
	F	Four Bravo to Manhattan, K
	D	Four Bravo, go ahead.
	F	Have Field Comm. report in front of the Financial District Building on West Street ... American Express immediately.
	D	Ten-four. They're on their way. All units standby.
	D	Units responding in to 2 World Trade Center, respond to West Street and Liberty and see Chief Barbera. Units responding to 2 World Trade Center, respond to West and Liberty and see Chief Barbera at that location, he's the incident commander at that location.
	F	Engine 1-4 to Manhattan, K.

Time	Station	Transmission
	D	One-four, go ahead.
	F	From the Water Street box we're stuck in massive traffic, we can't get up to 31st and Madison.
	D	All right, 10-4, Engine 1-4.
9:19	F	... to the World Trade Center. We're down there.
	F	Car 9 to Manhattan.
	D	Car 9, go ahead, K.
	F	Give me the company identifications that are coming to 2 World Trade Center. Just read them down.
	D	All right, 10-4: Engine 2-1-1, Ladder [interference], Engine 2-2, Engine 5-3, Engine 4-0, Division 3, Battalion 1-0, Battalion 1-2, Ladder 1-6, Ladder 2, Ladder 1-3, Engine 2-2-1, Engine 2-3, Engine 2-0-9, Engine 2-1-2, Engine 2-7-9, Engine 2-3-0, Engine 2-2-9, Engine 2-3-5, Engine 2-2-0, Engine 2-1-6, Engine 2-1-7, Engine 2-3-8, Engine 2-1-4, Ladder 12, Ladder 1-1-8, Ladder 7, Ladder 2-4, High Rise 1 and Battalion 1-1, Engine 7-4, Engine 7-6, Engine 4-7, Engine 5-8, Engine 9-1, Ladder 2-2, Ladder 2-5, Ladder 3-5, Four Truck and Ladder 2-1.
9:20	F	O.K. Thank you, Manhattan.
	D	Ten-four.
	D	Manhattan calling the Mobile Command Vehicle, K. Manhattan calling Mobile Command Vehicle, K.
	F	Engine 2-3-0 to Manhattan.
	D	Two-three-zero, go ahead.
	F	...
	D	All right, 10-4. You're in front of the 2 World Trade Center. Bring all your extra S.D.B.A.'s to the front of the building with you, K. Respond to West and Liberty and see Chief Barbera, K.
	F	Ten-four, K.
9:21	F	... 2 to Manhattan.
	D	Unit calling Manhattan.
	F	... 2 to Manhattan.
	D	Go ahead.
	F	Manhattan, do you have any special instructions.
	D	What unit was this again, K?
	F	Ladder 1-3-2 to Manhattan. Do you have any special instructions?
	F	... to Manhattan.
	F	Field Comm. to Manhattan, K.
	D	Field Comm., go ahead.
	F	...

Time	Station	Transmission
	D	All units in Manhattan, standby for a ... message. Go ahead, Field Comm.
	F	... [roaring interference]
	D	Ten-four.
9:22	F	Fourth Battalion to Brooklyn.
	F	Staten Island to Manhattan.
	D	All right, all units standby unless urgent. Manhattan to Mobile Command Unit. Manhattan to Field Comm., urgent.
	F	Go ahead, Manhattan. Field Comm.
	D	All right, Field Comm. No. 1 World Trade Center, the 1-0-3 floor, southwest corner and northwest corner, reported to be 100 people overcome at that location. Repeating, No. 1 World Trade Center, 103rd floor, northwest [interference] corner, reported to be 100 people in that location. Also, Ladder 3 is reporting on the 35th floor going up on the stairwell they've got numerous injuries, treating numerous injuries from burns occupied in the stairwell at this time. Field Comm. receive.
	F	[inaudible]
9:23	F	Field Comm. to Manhattan, K.
	D	Field Comm., go ahead. Unit calling Manhattan.
	F	Engine 5-0 is on ... Street.
	D	Engine 5-1, 10-4.
	F	Ladder 4-7 to Manhattan.
	D	Ladder 4-7.
	F	... relocated to Ladder 6.
	D	Ten-four. Unit calling?
	F	...
	D	Unit calling, you're unreadable. What's your message? All right, any other unit calling?
	F	Battalion 8 to Manhattan.
	F	...
	D	All units, standby. Battalion 8, you proceed.
	F	Battalion 8. Which tower are we assigned?
	D	Battalion 8, you're going into No. 1 World Trade Center, K. No. 1 \World Trade.
9:24	F	Battalion 8. 10-4.
	D	Another unit calling Manhattan?
	F	Brooklyn to Manhattan.
	D	Brooklyn unit calling Manhattan.

Time	Station	Transmission
	F	Brooklyn Dispatch. Urgent, people trapped, 5 World Trade on the 8-0 floor; 3 World Trade, that's the 1-0-1 floor and the 1-0-2 floor. Manhattan receive?
	D	That's a 10-4. Receive and acknowledge.
	F	Ten-four.
	D	Manhattan to Field Comm. Manhattan to Field Comm., urgent. Manhattan to Field Comm.
	F	Division 1-1 to Manhattan.
	D	Division 11.
	F	Yeah, do you have a message for Field Comm.?
9:25	D	Ten-four. We've got a report of people trapped No. 5 World Trade Center on the 8-0 floor; No. 3 World Trade Center trapped on the 1-0-2 and 1-0-1 floors at this time, K.
	F	One-one, 10-4, 5 World Trade Center, the 8-0 floor; 2 World Trade Center, the 1-0-2 and 1-0-1 floor.
	D	That's a 10-4, K.
	F	Field Comm. received that Manhattan.
	D	Ten-four, Field Comm.
	F	Ladder 1-0-5 to Manhattan, K.
	D	Ladder 1-0-5.
	F	One-zero-five 10-84 at the box.
	D	Ladder 1-0-5, 10-4.
	F	Car 9.
	F	Engine 2-2-9, 2-2-4.
	D	All right, all units standby unless urgent. Manhattan to Division 1-1. Field Comm.?
	F	One-one to Manhattan.
	D	Division 1-1, No. 1 World Trade Center, the 1-0-6 floor, 100 people trapped at that location, K.
	F	One-one, 10-4.
9:26	D	Another unit calling.
	F	Car 9 to Manhattan.
	D	Car 9, your message.
	F	Present Chief Barbera, have all of the units responding to No. 2 World Trade Center, report in in front of No. 1 World Financial Center, which is on the corner of West and Liberty. All units coming in to No. 2 World Trade Center.

Time	Station	Transmission
	D	That's 10-4. Attention all units responding in to the fifth alarm No. 2 World Trade Center, you're to respond to No. 1 Financial Center, West Street and Liberty Street. Repeating, all units going in to No. 2 World Trade Center for the fifth alarm, you are to respond in to West Street and Liberty Street in front of No. 1 Financial Center. All units going in to the fifth alarm at No. 2 World Trade Center, you are to respond into West Street and Liberty Street. All units going into the fifth alarm for No. 2 World Trade Center, you are to respond to West Street and Liberty Street.
	F	Ladder 1-9 to Manhattan.
	D	Ladder 1-9.
	F	One-four to Manhattan.
9:27	D	Unit standby. Ladder 1-9, your message.
	F	One-four to Manhattan.
	F	Ladder 1-9 to Manhattan.
	D	Ladder 1-9, you go. Ladder 1-9, your message.
	F	Relocating to Ladder 16 on your frequency.
	D	Ten-four. Ladder 1-4?
	F	One-four can't respond into box 6-87 due to traffic. We're stuck by Water Street, the World Trade Center.
	D	Ten-four.
	F	Field Comm. calling Manhattan.
	D	Field Comm.
	F	Have M.S.U. activate all their spares and bring all their spares and all spare bottles to the scene of the fifth alarm, No. 1 World Trade Center, K.
	F	Ladder ... to Manhattan.
	D	All units stand down unless urgent. Field Comm., 10-4. Manhattan to Field Comm., K.
	F	Field Comm., K.
	D	Field Comm., No. 2 World Trade Center on the 8-3 and the 8-4 floors and the 8-2 floor, people trapped at this time.
9:28	F	Ten-four.
	D	Ten-four.
	D	Any other unit calling Manhattan.
	F	Engine 3-3-1 on your frequency.
	D	Engine 3-3-1, 10-4.
	F	Engine 2-1-6 to Manhattan.
	F	Mayor's Service Unit to Manhattan.
	D	Attention all units in the Borough of Manhattan, you are to standby unless urgent. All units in the Borough of Manhattan, standby unless urgent.

Time	Station	Transmission
	D	Attention all units, by the order of citywide tour commander, all off-duty firefighters and all off-duty officers are hereby recalled. Repeating, by the orders of the citywide tour commander, all off-duty firefighters and all off-duty officers, you are hereby ordered to recall immediately.
9:29	F	Four Charlie to Manhattan, K.
	D	Repeating, Manhattan announcing in the Borough of Manhattan, as per citywide tour commander, off- duty firefighters, all off-duty officers are hereby ordered for recall. Repeating, orders of the citywide tour commander, all off-duty firefighters and all off-duty officers, you are hereby ordered for recall.
	D	Car Four Charlie.
	F	Four Charlie responding. Is the Brooklyn-Battery Tunnel available in response to Manhattan, K?
	D	Ten-four.
	F	Ten-four.
	D	...
9:30	D	All right. Any other unit with a message to Manhattan, K?
	F	...
	D	One unit at a time. Are any battalions calling? Any engine companies? Any ladder companies calling Manhattan? Time is 09:30. Manhattan clear.
	F	Marine 6 to Manhattan.
	F	Car 9 to Manhattan.
	D	Car 9.
	F	Contact the units, fifth alarm, coming down for No. 2 World Trade Center, contact them individually and get them to acknowledge the fact that they are to come to Liberty and West, Liberty and West, K.
	D	Car 9, 10-4. Marine 6?
	F	Marine 6 to Manhattan, in the event of a transport problem into Manhattan we can establish a staging area at our quarters.
	D	That's a 10-4.
	F	... to Manhattan, urgent.
	D	Unit calling urgent, go.
	F	... 317 to Manhattan, urgent.
	D	Engine 3-1-7, go.
	F	I've got ... from the Port Authority telling me that the elevators are on the 44th floor. Don't use them, they're about to come down.
	D	Is that going to be for No. 2 or No. 1 World Trade.
	F	Wasn't sure. I'd say go with both.

Time	Station	Transmission
9:31	D	Attention all companies operating at the fifth alarm for both World Trade Centers, the elevators, the Port Authority reports the elevators on the No. 4-4 floor are about to come down. All companies operating at No. 1 and No. 2 World Trade Center at the fifth alarm, do not use the elevators. They are about to come down as per the Port Authority on the No. 4-4 floor. Field Comm, receive that urgent? Manhattan to Ladder 2-1, K.
	F	Field Comm. to Manhattan.
	D	Field Comm.
	F	Repeat that urgent.
	D	As per the Port Authority, the elevators on the No. 4-4 floor, that's 44, are about to come down. Keep all members out, No. 1 and No. 2 World Trade.
	F	Ten-four.
9:32	D	Manhattan to Ladder 2-1. Manhattan to Ladder 4. Manhattan to Ladder 3-5. Manhattan to Ladder 2-5. Manhattan to Ladder 2-2. Manhattan to Engine 9-1. Manhattan to Engine 5-8.
	F	Engine 5-8. We're on - as far as we can get to the scene. We're going to walk down.
	D	Ten-four. You're going to West and Liberty, K.
	F	Ten-four.
	D	Engine 4-7. Engine 7-6. Engine 7-4. Ladder 2-4. Ladder 7. Ladder 1-1-8. Ladder 1-2. Engine 2-1-4. Engine 2-1-8. Engine 2-1-6.
		This concludes Side A. Please turn tape over to Side B for continuation of citywide job No. 1-44.
		END RESPONSE TAPE 1 SIDE A
		RESPONSE TAPE 1 SIDE B, 9:31-10:22 a.m.
9:35	F	Engine 9-4 to Manhattan, K.
	D	All right, all units standby unless urgent. Manhattan calling Field Comm., K. Manhattan calling Field Comm.
	F	Field Comm. Go ahead, Manhattan.
	D	All right, Field Comm., you ready to write? 1 got four for you to check in both building one and building two, everything we have up to now.
	F	Give me building one.
	D	O.K., building one: 9-2 floor; the 106th floor; the 89th floor; 104th floor; the 100th floor, the northeast side; the 8-8 floor; the eighth floor, east side; the 105th floor; the 68th floor; 106th floor, northwest; 103rd floor, room 1-0-3; 83rd floor, room 8-3-11. Let me know when you're ready for building two.
9:36	F	Proceed with building two.

Time	Station	Transmission
	D	O.K. The 82nd floor, west side; the 88th floor; 89th floor; 73rd floor, west side; 105th floor, east side; 104th floor, east side; 47th floor; 73rd floor, west office; 83rd floor, room 8-3-0-0; and 80th floor, northwest. That's what we have at this time.
	F	Field Comm. received.
	F	Squad 4-1 to Manhattan.
	D	Squad 4-1, standby.
9:37	D	Manhattan announcing, as per the citywide tour commander, all off-duty firefighters and all off-duty officers, you are to report to your sector stations and await further instructions. Repeating, all off-duty firefighters and all off-duty officers, you are to report to your respective stations and standby waiting for further orders. Manhattan announcing, all off-duty firefighters and all off-duty officers, you are to sector stations for a total recall and await further instructions. As per the citywide [interference], all off-duty firefighters and all off-duty officers you are hereby total recalled, you will report to your sector stations and standby. Squad 4-1, your message.
	F	Marine Squad 18's response [area?] Do you want us to respond to Tower No. 2?
	D	Standby.
	F	Mass [Mayor's?] Service Unit to Manhattan.
	D	All right, Mass Service Unit.
	F	Mass Service Unit, 10-84 at the box.
	D	Mass Service, 10-4.
	F	Squad 4-1 to Manhattan.
	D	Yeah, Squad 4-1.
	F	1 didn't hear your reply on the last message.
9:38	D	All right, at this time go ahead and respond to No. 2 World Trade.
	F	Ten-four, responding.
	F	Car 9 to Manhattan.
	D	Car 9.
	F	By orders of Chief Barbera [sp?], we want a second alarm assignment from Brooklyn to respond to Albany and West Street. A second alarm assignment from Brooklyn to respond to Albany and West Street through the Brooklyn-Battery Tunnel, no other route, and report to Chief Barbera at that location. When you get the I.D. of the companies, give them to me, K.
	D	Car 9, 10-4.
	F	... to Manhattan.
	D	All units standby.
9:39	F	Rescue 5 to Manhattan.
	F	One-two-four to Manhattan.
	F	Engine 7-1 to ...

Time	Station	Transmission
	D	Engine 7-1.
	F	...
	D	Engine 7-1, your message?
	F	We're on the Manhattan frequency.
	D	Ten-four, make yourself ... Unit calling Manhattan.
	F	Rescue 5 to Manhattan.
	D	Rescue 5.
	F	... on your frequency.
	D	Rescue 5, 10-4, make yourself available, K.
	F	One-two-four to Brooklyn.
	D	All right, Manhattan to Rescue 5, K.
	F	Rescue 5, 10-8 Manhattan.
	D	Rescue 5, you're to respond in to No. 1 World Trade Center. Rescue 5.
	F	Rescue 5, 10-4.
	F	Ladder 1-2-4 and 2-5 to Manhattan.
	D	Ladder 1-2-5.
	F	Ladder 1-2-4 is a couple blocks away.
	D	All right, Ladder 1-2-4 standby.
9:40	F	Ladder 4-3 to Manhattan.
	D	Ladder 4-3.
	F	... is a 10-37. We're below 42 ... south, K.
	D	All right Ladder 4-3, at this time make yourself available, stay in service, we'll notify you.
	F	Ten-four.
	F	... Manhattan.
	D	Ladder 5-9.
	F	We responding to a relocation at 10 Truck, K.
	D	Ten-four. Ladder 5-9, make yourself available, K.
	F	Ten-four.
	D	Any other unit calling Manhattan.
	F	...
	D	All right, everybody standby. Engine company calling.
	F	Engine 83 to Manhattan. What is the location of the station ... on Third Avenue?
	D	Engine 8-3, standby.
	F	Ten-four.

Time	Station	Transmission
	D	Manhattan to Field Comm., K.
	F	Field Comm., K.
	D	Field Comm. Building two, floor 1-0-3 and floor 9-3, floor 1-0-3 and floor 9-3. Acknowledge.
9:41	F	Field Comm., 10-4.
	F	Engine 4-3 to Manhattan.
	D	Engine 4-3.
	F	... available in Engine 4-4's response area, K?
	D	Ten-four.
	D	Manhattan to Engine 8-3.
	F	Engine 8-3.
	D	Engine 8-3, what's your present assignment?
	F	We're reporting to station ... Third Avenue. What's the cross street there?
	D	Standby.
	F	Engine 8-2 to Manhattan.
	D	All right, Engine 8-3 standby now. Engine 8-2.
	F	Engine 8-2, ... Engine 5-8's response area.
	D	Engine 8-2, make yourself available.
	F	Ten-four.
	D	Manhattan calling Field Comm, K, with an urgent. Manhattan calling Field Comm. with an urgent, K.
	F	Receive Manhattan, Field Comm.
9:42	D	All right. Male hanging from a window near the antennae in building one.
	F	Floor number?
	D	Probably be up on the top floor, K.
	F	Ten-four.
	D	09:42
	D	Manhattan to Engine 8-3.
	F	Engine 8-3.
	D	Engine 8-3 you're to respond to [coordinates?] Engine 3-5. You're going to the deployment area, K.
	F	Ten-four.
	D	All right, any other unit calling Manhattan.
	F	... 4-6 to Manhattan.
	D	Ladder 4-6.
	F	... responding to Ladder 2 for a relocation.

Time	Station	Transmission
	D	Ten-four. Ladder 4-6, make yourself available, K.
	F	...
	F	...
	D	Unit calling?
9:43	F	Ladder 6-4 switching over to Queens frequency.
	D	Ladder 6-4 you're Manhattan frequency, K.
	F	Car 4 David to Manhattan.
	D	Car 4 David.
	F	Got a report of a hanging antenna on the roof of building one?
	D	Report of a male hanging from the antenna on building No. 1, K. One person hanging from the antenna.
	F	Ten-four.
	D	9:42.41.6
	F	Squad 2- ... to Manhattan, K.
	D	Squad 2-8-8.
	F	Fire Monster[?] Squad 2-8 on the Bronx to Manhattan, K.
	D	Fire Monster Squad, go.
	F	Where's the command post, K?
	D	Command post for No. 2 World Trade Center, West Street and Liberty Street.
	F	Ten-four.
9:44	D	Other units calling Manhattan.
	F	Ladder 1-4 to Manhattan.
	D	Ladder 1-4.
	F	Ten-8 in 24's response area, K.
	D	Ten-four.
	D	Any other unit calling?
	F	Car 9 to Manhattan.
	D	Car 9, go ahead.
	F	I need the I.D. of that second alarm assignment and make sure you tell them through the Battery Tunnel.
	D	Car 9, they have been notified, K. It's in the process. Standby one minute.
	F	Thank you, Manhattan.
	F	Nine David to Car 9.
	F	Nine David, K.
	F	Ready to write these?

Time	Station	Transmission
	F	Nine David, go ahead.
	F	Are you ready to write the identity?
	F	Go ahead.
9:45	F	Engines 2-4-0, 2-0-1, 2-4-9, 2-7-8, 2-8-1, 2-2-8, 2-1-9, 2-8-0. Your four truck companies will be 1-0-2, 119, 114, 113. The chiefs 1 gave you would be the 3-2, the 4-1 and the 4-2. All coming through the Battery Tunnel. I'm not identifying any [fast?] truck. If you want a fifth truck let me know and we'll send you one.
	F	That's a negative. That last engine was 2-1-0?
	F	Negative. 2-8-1.
	F	K, thank you.
	F	Ten-four.
	F	Ladder 2-3 to Manhattan.
	D	Ladder 2-3.
	F	Ladder 2-3 is in Ladder 4's response area.
	D	Ten-four.
9:46	D	Manhattan calling Field Comm, K.
	F	Manhattan calling Field Comm. Correction. Field Comm. calling Manhattan.
	D	All right, on the 8-0 floor, northwest corner, 50 people trapped, K. That's in building one.
	F	... Manhattan, K.
	D	...
	F	Field Comm. to Manhattan.
	D	Go ahead, Field Comm.
	F	... to Field Comm. By orders of Chief Ganci, transmit an additional fifth alarm, have the additional fifth alarm units respond into West and Vesey, West and Vesey, K.
	D	Ten-four. Authority Chief Ganci, fifth alarm, West and Vesey.
	F	Ten-four.
	D	Ten-four.
9:47	F	Engine 1-4 to Manhattan.
	D	Engine 1-4.
	F	Are we assigned to the World Trade Center ...
	D	Engine 1-4, standby, K.
	D	Manhattan calling Field Comm, K. Manhattan calling Field Comm, K.
	F	Field Comm., K.

Time	Station	Transmission
	D	O.K., Field Comm., 104th floor, northwest corner, 50 people trapped, the fire's burning beneath them, K.
	F	Hundred and fourth floor, northwest corner, what building?
	D	That's building one, K.
	F	Ten-four.
	D	Manhattan to Division 3 messenger band, K. Manhattan to the Division 3 messenger band. Manhattan to Field Comm., K.
9:48	F	Field Comm., K.
	D	Field Comm., we're unable to raise the Division 3 messenger band regarding the extra handy walkie-talkies, K.
	F	Ten-four.
	D	Manhattan calling Field Comm.
	F	Field Comm., K.
	D	All right. Building two, building two, 80th floor, ... people trapped.
	F	What floor?
	D	Eight-zero, 8-0 floor in building two, 80 people trapped.
	F	Eight-zero floor, 10-4.
	F	... to Manhattan.
	D	Unit calling Manhattan.
	F	Car 5 to Manhattan.
	D	Car 5.
	F	What's the location of the staging area?
	D	Car 5, No. 2 World Trade Center is going to be West Street and Liberty Street, K.
9:49	F	Ten-four. Thank you.
	D	Another unit calling Manhattan. Time 09:48.4.12.
	F	Engine 2-2-8 to Manhattan, K.
	D	Engine 2-2-8.
	F	1 need a frequency, K, responding to box 5-0, K.
	D	Ten-four. Engine 2-2-8, you're coming through the Brooklyn-Battery Tunnel, 10-4.
	F	Negative, Brooklyn Bridge, K.
	D	That's a negative. You're being redirected. You respond through the Brooklyn-Battery Tunnel and respond to the staging area, Albany Street and West Street. Engine 2-2-8.
	F	Two-two-eight, 10-4, K.
9:50	D	Manhattan to Engine 2-4-0.
	F	Two-four-zero, K.

Time	Station	Transmission
	D	Engine 2-4-0, you're responding through the Brooklyn-Battery Tunnel?
	F	K, we were told to respond to West Street and Albany, K.
	F	Three-zero-five to Manhattan.
	D	All units standby unless urgent. Attention the following units: Engine 2-4-0, Engine 2-0-1, Engine 2-2-8 acting, Engine 2-1-9, Engine 2-8-0, Ladder 1-1-3, Ladder 1-1-4, Battalion 3-2. All companies, you are to respond through the Brooklyn-Battery Tunnel, respond to the staging area, Albany and West Street, and meet up with Chief Barbera [sp?]. Repeating, Engine 2-4-0, Engine 2-0-1, Engine 2-2-8 acting, Engine 2-1-9, Engine 2-8-0, Ladder 1-1-3, Ladder 1-1-4, Battalion 3-2. All units you are to respond through the Brooklyn- Battery Tunnel. You're to respond in to Albany and West Street. Ask for Chief Barbera. Engine 2-4-0?
9:51	F	Two-four-zero, 10-4 and 10-84.
	D	Engine 2-0-1? Engine 2-2-8?
	F	... 2-8, K.
	D	Responding through the Brooklyn Tunnel, 10-4?
	F	That's affirmative, K, 10-4.
	D	Engine 2-1-9?
	F	Two-one-nine, 10-4.
	D	Engine –
	F	One-one-four in to Manhattan, K.
	D	Engine 2-8-0? Engine 2-8-0? Ladder 1-1-4?
	F	One-one-four is in Manhattan frequency, responding in to box 5-0, K. Have any special instructions?
	D	Ten-four. You're to go through the Brooklyn-Battery Tunnel, respond to Albany and West Street. Ten- four?
	F	Ten-four. Just where is Albany and West Street in relation to the towers, K?
9:52	D	Ladder 1-1-3? Battalion 3-2? Engine 2-0-1? Time 09:52.41.6.
	D	Manhattan calling Field Comm.
	F	Field Comm., K.
	D	Building two, 100th floor, northwest conference room, people trapped.
	F	... two, 100th floor, northwest conference room, 10-4.
	D	Ten-four. 09:5 ...
	F	Engine 3-7-1 ... Engine 6 to Manhattan.
	D	Three-seven-one, go ahead.
	F	...
	D	Ten-four.

Time	Station	Transmission
9:53	F	... 7-4 to Manhattan, K.
	D	Seven-four.
	F	Coming into Manhattan, we're at Randall's Island, now picking up the ... K.
	D	Ten-four. Time 09:5 ...
	F	Ladder Company 1-7 to Manhattan.
	D	One-seven.
	F	One-seven's coming ... West Side ...
	D	Ten-four.
	D	Manhattan to Battalion 3-2. Manhattan to Battalion 3-2. Manhattan to Engine 2-0-1. Manhattan to Engine 2-0-1. Manhattan to Ladder 1-1-3. Manhattan to Ladder 1-1-3. All right, any other unit calling Manhattan.
	F	Ladder 5-9 to Manhattan.
	D	Ladder 5-9.
9:54	F	We're unable to get to 10 Truck. We're in front of 140 Park Place.
	D	All right, Ladder 5-9 standby where you are. Make yourself [A.A.?], K.
	F	Ten-four.
	F	Three-zero-five to Manhattan.
	D	Engine 3-0-5.
	F	We're on your frequency.
	D	Ten-four. Engine 3-0-5 make yourself available, K.
	D	Manhattan to Engine 2-0-1, K, Engine 2-0-1. 09:54.41.
	D	Manhattan calling Field Comm, K.
	F	Field Comm., K.
9:55	D	O.K., 86th floor, building one, room 8-6-1-7, people trapped. Also In building two, 97th floor, we have six people trapped.
	F	Field Comm., 10-4.
	F	Four-five to Manhattan.
	D	Ladder 4-5.
	F	... all the Queens units coming through the tunnel to respond to the box?
	D	Standby.
	F	Engine 2-0-1 to Manhattan.
	D	Engine 2-0-1.
	F	You got a message for us?
	D	Engine 2-0-1, you're to go through the Brooklyn-Battery Tunnel, respond to Albany and West Street. Engine 2-0-1?

Time	Station	Transmission
	F	Engine 2-0-1, 10-4.
	D	Manhattan to Car 9.
	F	Car 9, K.
	D	Car 9, be advised the third fifth alarm for box 2-0-3-3 is going to be transmitted. 1 have 13 engines so far and six trucks and three battalions responding to various staging points. Are you ready to write the identities?
9:56	F	Go ahead, Manhattan.
	D	All right. You're going to get Engines 2-5-8, 2-5-9, 3-2-5, 2-6-2, 3-1-2, 2-6-1, 2-6-0, Engines 6-8, 3-5, 5-0, 6-4, 9-4 and 8-3. 1 gave you three chiefs, the 4-5, the 4-6 and the 4-9. 1 owe you seven more engines, we're in the process.
	F	All right, Manhattan. Thank you very much.
	D	That box will be 2-0-3-3, Steve.
	F	Engine 5-0, 10-4.
	F	Engine 2-7-1, acting engine fixed to Manhattan.
	D	All units standby. Manhattan to Field Comm., urgent.
	F	Receive Manhattan, Field Comm.
	D	Tower No. 2, 19th floor, firefighter down. Tower No. 2, 19th floor, firefighter down.
9:57	F	Field Comm. received.
	D	All right, all units standby in Manhattan unless urgent.
	D	Manhattan calling Field Comm, K.
	F	Field Comm., K
	D	Building two, 93rd floor, northwest corner. Also in building one, 93rd floor, southwest corner, K.
	F	Field Comm. received.
	D	All right, I also have the 2 World Trade, 1-0-5 floor, 60 people.
	F	Ten-four.
	F	Engine 2-7-1 acting to Manhattan.
	D	...
	F	Two-seven-one acting. We're a couple blocks away. You want to give us a box ... take it in?
	D	What unit is this again?
	F	Engine 2-7-1 acting Engine 6.
	D	All right Engine 2-7-1, make yourself available at this time.
	F	Yeah, we're available, we're a couple blocks away. Do you want us to take it in?
9:58	D	Engine 2-7-1 standby.

Time	Station	Transmission
	D	Manhattan calling Field Comm., K. Manhattan calling Field Comm. Manhattan calling Field Comm.
	F	... to Manhattan, urgent.
	D	Go ahead, K.
	F	One of the buildings, the entire building has collapsed ...
	D	... urgent, identify.
	F	... major collapse in one of the towers.
	D	Which tower, K?
	F	Tower 2, Tower 2.
	F	The entire tower, major collapse.
	D	Ten-four.
9:59	D	Manhattan to Field Comm., K. Manhattan to Field Comm.
	F	Marine 6 to Manhattan.
	D	Standby. Manhattan to Field Comm. Manhattan to Field Comm.
	F	Marine 6 to Manhattan, urgent.
	D	Marine 6.
	F	Tower 2 has had a major explosion and what appears to be a complete collapse surrounding the entire area.
	D	Marine 6, 10-4. We were notified, K.
	D	Manhattan to Field Comm, K. Manhattan to Field Comm.
	F	...
	D	Attention 68 Engine, 35 Engine, 50 Engine, 64 Engine, 94 Engine, 83 Engine. Those units going to the fifth alarm box 2-0-3-3, we've been advised the West Side Highway has been opened to emergency traffic. The West Side Highway is open to emergency traffic. Take that route going to West and Vesey. Acknowledge 68.
	F	Ten-four.
	D	Thirty-five. Thirty-five engine.
	F	Ten-four, 35.
	D	Fifty.
	F	Five-zero, 10-4.
	D	Sixty-four.
	F	Six-four, 10-4.
	D	Ninety-four.
	F	Nine-four, 10-4.
	D	Eighty-three.
	F	Eight-three, 10-4.
	D	Manhattan calling Field Comm., K.

Time	Station	Transmission
	F	Engine 240 to Manhattan.
	D	Go ahead 240.
	F	There's been a major collapse to the tower. The command center ... everybody ... There was a major collapse. I'm in my ... right now.
	D	Ten-four. We've notified them that there is a major collapse in the area, K.
10:00	F	Everybody in the area had to run. I don't know if Field Comm. is available.
	F	Can anybody hear me?
	D	Go ahead.
	F	I'm a civilian. I'm trapped inside one of your fire trucks underneath ...
	D	Standby, there's ... close to you.
	F	I can't breathe much longer. Save me! I'm in the cab ...
	D	Transmitting a mayday. Where are you, K.
	F	I just told you. It's north of the World Trade Center, there's the north ... bridge. I think it collapsed when the partial building just collapsed. I was on the street ... Please, help me!
	F	... I copy that. I'm going to go look for her.
	D	Ten-four.
10:01	D	Manhattan to Field Comm, urgent, K.
	F	I can barely breath. Please, send somebody.
10:02	D	O.K., the person calling for help, listen to me, you need to calm down and relax. Standby, we do have somebody on the way. You're to maintain air – get off the air. We do have somebody on the way over to you. You're to remain calm, 10-4?
	F	It's falling on top of the truck.
	D	Ten-four. We do have people on the way over there.
	D	Manhattan to Field Comm., urgent, K.
	F	...
	D	Standby. Manhattan to Field Comm., urgent.
	F	...
	D	Manhattan to Field Comm.?
	F	Field Comm. to Manhattan, urgent.
	D	Field Comm., go.
	F	...
	D	Manhattan to Division 1-1.
	F	...
	D	Any other units calling Manhattan.

Time	Station	Transmission
	F	...
	D	Manhattan to Field Comm., K.
10:03	F	George, have them mobilize the Army. We need the Army in Manhattan.
	D	All units, standby. Everybody try to calm down. Manhattan to Field Comm., K. Manhattan to Division – Manhattan to – Manhattan to Car 9, urgent. Manhattan to Car 9, urgent. Manhattan to any unit operating at the fifth alarm, West Street and Liberty, for Tower No. 2. Any unit, K.
	F	...
	D	Any unit operating at No. 2 World Trade Center at the collapse, contact Manhattan by radio forthwith.
	F	Three-three Bravo to Manhattan, urgent.
	F	Four-fifteen to Manhattan.
10:04	D	Car 3-3 Bravo. We understand there's a major collapse. Can you give us some kind of report, K?
	F	Four-fifteen to Manhattan.
	D	Ladder 1-5, go.
	F	Four-fifteen to Manhattan.
	D	Ladder 15, go ahead.
	F	This is an E.M.S. worker. There's been a major collapse. We need additional units forthwith.
	D	Ten-four. We have multiple units on the way in. Ladder 1-5, can you ascertain if Field Comm. is part of the collapse, K?
	F	Ladder 1-5 to Manhattan. Be advised, I'm not a ..., I'm an E.M.S. ...
	D	Ladder 1-5, standby. Manhattan to any unit at No. 2 World Trade Center. Manhattan to any unit operating at No. 2 World Trade Center, urgent.
	F	E.M.S. Ladder 1-5.
	D	Ladder 1-5, Manhattan.
10:05	F	...
	D	I want you to go to the nearest chief, Fire Department chief and have him come to the radio forthwith. If you find anybody with a white hat, get him to the radio. I need a report to find out what else I can send to him.
	F	...
	D	All units standby unless urgent. Is there a staff chief or a battalion chief trying to call Manhattan?
	F	Ladder 15 to Manhattan –
	F	...
	F	– be advised –

Time	Station	Transmission
	F	... in the building, they're coming out now.
	D	All right, all units standby. Ladder 15 and Ladder 15 only, go ahead with your message. Ladder 15, you have a message? What other unit calling Manhattan? What other unit calling Manhattan?
	F	...
	D	Battalion 1, go ahead.
10:06	D	Yes, 1 want you to find a chief officer and have him come to this radio so 1 can find out what additional help 1 can send him. You have three fifth alarm assignments and a second alarm assignment either at the scene or responding. Let me know who's in command there at this moment.
	F	Two-three-one, 10-4.
	D	Do that forthwith ...
	F	Two-three-one, K.
	F	Ladder 1-2-4 to Manhattan.
	D	Ladder 1-2-4.
	F	We're at Church and West, we're at the scene of the collapse.
	D	All right Ladder 1-2-4. Are you previously assigned to one of those boxes?
	F	Negative. We picked it us as a ... we were acting Ladder 5. There are people all over the place.
	F	...
	D	All units standby, please. Please, standby. Other unit calling?
10:07	F	Car 3 to Manhattan.
	D	Two to Manhattan, go ahead.
	F	We're on 57th and West Side Highway. Let us go down West and get back to let you know what's going on.
	D	What unit is this?
	F	...3.
	D	You're breaking up. Who are you?
	F	Ladder 4-3.
	D	All right. I'm going to assign you to box 5-0 at West and Albany.
	F	...
	F	... to Manhattan.
	D	All units please standby, one unit at a time. What ladder company calling? What other unit calling?
	F	Three Charlie.
	D	Three Charlie.

Time	Station	Transmission
	F	Four Charlie, the operation is ... the command post is going to be set up on West Street, they're moving completely out to West Street.
	D	All right. The command post is being consolidated, everybody's moving out to West Street. Is that correct?
	F	That's correct. I'm in contact with Chief ... and Commissioner Feehan and that's where we're going to start moving out, moving out of a further collapse zone.
10:08	D	All right, 10-4.
	D	Manhattan to Ladder 5-6. Calling Ladder 5-6.
	F	... to Manhattan.
	D	go.
	F	...
	D	You're very low and scratchy, K, unreadable.
	F	Fire Marshall Squad 2-8 to Manhattan or citywide.
	D	Squad 2-8, go ahead.
	F	We're moving some people, be advised, moving some people to the Chase Bank on Broadway. We're setting up an ad hoc emergency ... post. We need E.M.S. personnel, K. We could use more people because the place is filling up with injured.
	D	Ten-four, we have multiple units on the way in at this time, K.
	F	Ten-four.
	D	All right, any other unit calling Manhattan.
	F	Engine 2-8-6 to Manhattan.
	D	Engine 2-8-6.
	F	Acting Engine 10, we're going to respond right to the command post, K.
	D	That's a 10-4.
	F	Engine 4-5 to Manhattan.
	D	Engine 4-5.
	F	Engine 4-5's on your frequency, relocating Engine 3-5.
	D	Engine 4-5, make yourself available, K.
	F	Four-five, 10-4.
10:09	D	All units calling Manhattan.
	F	Marine 3 to Manhattan.
10:10	D	Manhattan to Ladder 5-6, K. Ladder 5-6. Manhattan to Ladder 5-6. Manhattan to Ladder 5-6. Marine 3.
	F	Marine 3, be advised, you need personnel on Marine 1. There's nobody in south ... vessel, K.
	D	Ten-four.

Time	Station	Transmission
	F	Rudy Kelly [sp?] in Manhattan. Just tell everybody with their vessels to stand fast.
	D	Marine 3, stand fast, K.
	F	Marine 3, 10-4.
10:13	D	10:13.41.6.
	F	Marine company.
	F	Car 5 to Manhattan.
	D	Car 5.
	F	Any suggested routes from Midtown Tunnel to the command post?
	D	On the West Side, West Side Highway's open. Brooklyn-Battery Tunnel would probably be your best route at this time.
	F	I'm in Manhattan. I'll head over to the West Side Highway. Thank you.
	F	Marine Company 9 to Manhattan.
	D	Marine 9.
	F	Did you have a problem with a marine company there? Did you need us for something?
10:14	D	Marine 9, 1 don't know at this time. Standby.
	F	Engine 2-2-8 to Manhattan, K.
	D	Engine 2-2-8.
	F	Would you inform the units ... they were inspecting the Brooklyn-Battery Tunnel, the first cloud has subsided and the units can come through the tunnel now ... to proceed, K. Are there any further instructions for Engine 2-2-8 at this time?
	F	...
	D	Enqine 2-2-8, at this time respond in to the command post West Street and Albany Street. Standby for instructions over there.
	F	Engine 2-2-8, 10-4. Just put on the Manhattan frequency for the other units responding to the location that they can proceed through the tunnel, dust cloud on the Manhattan side has subsided, K.
	D	Attention all companies responding to West Street and Albany Street for the second alarm, the Brooklyn- Battery Tunnel is now open. The dust cloud has dissipated. All units can respond in to West Street and Albany Street for the second alarm for box 5-0. The dust cloud has subsided for the Brooklyn-Battery Tunnel.
10:15	D	Manhattan to Field Comm., K. 10:15.41.6.
	F	One-four to Manhattan.
	D	One-four.
	F	For responding companies, Seventh Avenue is wide open, clear.
	D	Seventh Avenue is wide open?

Time	Station	Transmission
	F	Ten-four.
	D	Ten-four. All units going in to the World Trade Center, be advised, Ladder 1-4 reports Seventh Avenue is wide open and also West Side Highway is open. All units going into the fifth alarm, West Side Highway is open and Seventh Avenue is open at this time as per Ladder 1-4. 10:15.41.6.
10:16	F	Car 5 to Manhattan.
	D	Manhattan responding.
	F	Advise the Queens unit that the bus lane heading into the Midtown Tunnel is wide open, the Port Authority has it all open for us both ways.
	D	Ten-four. Attention all companies responding into Manhattan from the Queens side, Midtown Tunnel bus lane is wide open. All units responding into Manhattan from Queens, Midtown Tunnel bus lane is wide open. 10:16.4.16.
	F	Engine 2-2-8 to Manhattan, K.
	D	Engine 2-2-8.
	F	Be advised, the tunnel is clear now ... we're trying to get to our staging area, Albany and West Streets, K, but we're encountering a lot of congestion, K.
10:17	D	Ten-four.
10:18	D	Any unit operating at No. 2 World Trade Center. Any unit operating at No. 2 World Trade Center, urgent. Any unit at No. 2 World Trade Center, urgent. Engine 2-2-8 acting. Engine 2-2-8 acting, K.
	F	Manhattan dispatcher?
	F	Can 2-2-8 10-5 your message?
	F	We have a staging area just north of the north – just south of the North Cove Marina.
	D	Ten-four. What unit is this?
	F	Three Company One.
	D	Three-One, standby. Manhattan to Engine 2-2-8.
	F	Engine 2-2-8.
	D	What's your location?
	F	We just ... Battery ...
10:19	D	All right, Engine 2-2-8 acting, is it possible you can get over to the Marriott Hotel, No. 2 World Trade Center? Firefighters trapped.
	F	I don't think we can proceed with the lead, we'll go as far as we can. Marriott World Trade Center. Where are they trapped, K?
	F	Unit calling, urgent.
	D	Reported to be in a [fell?] area. Unit calling urgent.

Time	Station	Transmission
	F	We're in that – 2 World Trade Center. We have some of the individuals in the front. We're waiting to evacuate them, K.
	D	All right, 10-4. Also be advised in the ... area at the Marriott Hotel receiving reports of firefighters trapped and down.
	F	We'll work on that.
	D	Ten-four.
	F	Mobile Command Center to Manhattan, K.
	D	Mobile Command Center, K.
	F	Manhattan, can you contact Field Comm.?
	D	Mobile Command Center, at this time we are unable to make contact, K.
	F	Thanks a lot, Manhattan. I'll get back to you.
	D	Ten-four. 10:20.41.6
10:20	F	Squad 6-1 to Manhattan.
	D	Squad 6-1.
	F	On your frequency, responding to supporting team.
	D	...
10:21	F	... 9 to Manhattan, K.
		This concludes Tape No. 1, Side B. For continuation of citywide job No. 1-44, go to Tape No. 2, Side A.
		END RESCUE TAPE 1 SIDE B
		RESPONSE TAPE 2 SIDE A, 10:22-11:10 a.m.
10:22:04	D	Mobile Command Center, K.
	F	Mobile Command, K.
10:22:15	D	Mobile Command Center, this is an urgent message: We need to set up a relay communication, K, to find out exactly what's going on. We also have numerous calls reporting people trapped. Mobile Command Center?
	F	Ten-four. Could you try and relay that to Car 9?
	D	Manhattan to Car 9, K. Manhattan to Car 9, K. Mobile Command Center?
10:22:40	F	We're direct. You're unable to raise. We'll try and work out something from -
	D	Ten-four.
10:22:50	F	Nine David to Mobile Command Vehicle. Nine David Unit to Mobile Command Vehicle.
	F	Nine David, go ahead.
	F	Yeah, as soon as you get – are you at the scene?

Time	Station	Transmission
10:23:06	F	They have us right now down opposite the Downtown Athletic Club on West Street.
	F	Get me a status report on Car 9 and all the other units that were in that area. And get them direct to me on the telephone please.
	F	Ten-four, 9 David. As soon as possible.
	F	Ten-four.
10:23:43	F	Five [nine?]-one-seven to Manhattan. [Speculating?] a second piece to Manhattan, K.
	D	Manhattan responding.
10:23:50	F	... second piece responding with seven firemen and two officers to the scene of the fire, K.
	D	Ten-four.
10:24:04	D	Manhattan to Engine 2-0-2. Manhattan to Engine 3-0-9 acting, K.
	F	Three-nine acting.
10:24:17	D	Engine 3-9 acting, report on the 22nd floor, reporting a floor collapse at that location, K.
	F	Three-zero-nine acting, 10-4. We're the one on this box, correct?
	D	At this time that's all we can send you, K.
10:24:36	D	Ladder 1-4-6 acting, receive.
	F	One-four-six, 10-5.
10:24:44	D	At this time reporting a floor collapse on the 22nd floor. Your going to have one ... response to the box at this time.
	F	One-four-six acting, 10-4.
10:24:56	D	Manhattan to Ladder 5-6, K, Ladder 5-6. Manhattan to Squad 6-1 acting, K.
	F	Six-one.
10:25:05	D	Call in to box 6-3.
	F	Ten-four.
	D	Manhattan to Ladder 3, K. Manhattan to Ladder 3.
10:25:17	F	Engine 2-3-6 acting Engine 15 to Manhattan.
	D	Two-three-six acting.
10:25:17	F	We can't get anywhere near our box 80, make it a 10-33 and we're available to go to the job.
	D	Ten-four, 2-3-6 at this time remain in service.
	F	Ten-four.
10:25:35	F	Engine 5-2-1 to Manhattan, K.
	D	Come in Engine 2-0-2, K. Come in Engine 2-0-2. Other unit calling Manhattan.
	F	Four-seven acting Ladder 15 to Manhattan.

Time	Station	Transmission
	D	Unit acting Ladder 1-5.
10:25:57	F	We've got a 10-35 code 1, we're 10-8.
	D	Ten-four. Stay in position and wait for further instructions.
	F	Ten-four.
10:26:08	D	Another unit calling Manhattan.
	F	Engine 5-2-1 to Manhattan, K.
	D	Engine 5-2-1.
10:26:14	F	Five-two-one special operations command messenger vehicle responding to Manhattan with 12 rescue firefighters.
	D	Ten-four.
10:26:26	D	Manhattan to Ladder 3, K. Three truck? [10]:26.416. Any other unit calling Manhattan.
	F	Forty Charlie to Manhattan.
	D	Four-zero Charlie.
10:26:36	F	1 don't know what you got to do, but I want all the rescue firefighters available from home to report, K.
	D	Ten-four. We have been broadcasting that, K.
10:26:48	F	We need all the help we can get.
	D	Ten-four. We have multiple units on the way in now.
	F	Ten-four.
10:27:08	D	Manhattan to Ladder 3, K. Ladder 3?
10:27:20	F	Three-three-one acting 2-1 to Manhattan, K.
	D	Three-three-one.
10:27:25	F	We're going to respond in. We have recall firefighters. Any particular place at this point?
	D	Engine 3-3-1, standby. Manhattan to Engine 3-3-1, respond over to Engine 2-1 and standby for further instructions.
	F	Ten-four.
10:27:52	D	Manhattan to Ladder 4-6 acting, K.
10:27:54	F	Mobile Command Center to Manhattan, K.
	D	Mobile Command Center.
10:28:00	F	Be advised, Mobile Command Center is set up in front of Pier A. I have Engine 2-0-9 with me. Also Dr. Prezant and Supervisor Fire Marshall Burns, K. I have no radio contact with anybody else at this time. As soon as I get something I'll let you know, K.
	D	Ten-four Mobile Command Center.
10:28:19	F	Three-three to Manhattan urgent.
	D	Three-three.
10:28:25	F	The other tower just collapsed! Major collapse, major collapse!

Time	Station	Transmission
	D	Ten-four on your urgent.
	F	...
10:28:43	F	Marine 3 to Manhattan, K.
	F	... to Manhattan.
10:28:46	F	Urgent, 2-8-9 to Manhattan, urgent. The World Trade Center collapsed. Building two has collapsed, K.
10:28:56	F	Urgent! Urgent!
	D	Unit calling urgent, K.
10:29:00	F	... we had a collapse of the second tower. Everybody's running from there. This is ...
10:29:15	D	Ten-four. Attention all units, we're receiving reports that No. 1 and No. 2 World Trade Center collapsed. All units at the scene receiving reports, No. 1 and No. 2 World Trade Center, both towers collapsed.
10:29:30	F	Engine 2-3-6 to Manhattan.
	D	Manhattan responding.
10:29:36	F	Yeah, we're jammed down in the street over here. We can't even move the car. I'm leaving ... with the rig, I'm heading over that way.
	D	Ten-four.
10:29:49	D	Any other unit calling.
10:30:11	F	Ladder 5-9 to Manhattan.
	D	Ladder 5-9.
10:30:15	F	We're going to be severely delayed to 17 Battery Place. We're in heavy, heavy traffic, K.
	D	Ladder 5-9, 10-4.
10:30:29	D	Manhattan announcing, any division or any staff chief at the scene of the World Trade Center, K? Any division chief or any staff chief at the scene of any of the World Trade Centers, K? Manhattan to Mobile Command Center, K.
10:30:51	F	Mobile Command to Manhattan, K.
	F	Engine ... acting at the command post to Manhattan, K.
10:31:04	F	Mobile Command Center to Manhattan, K.
	D	Mobile Command Center, what chief do you have at your Mobile Command Center, K.
10:31:10	F	Negative on any chief, K. Right now we're all alone. The second building came down. I can't see. So we have no contact with anybody at this time, K.
	D	Ten-four.
10:31:23	F	Division 6 acting Division 1, K.
	D	Division 6 acting, K.

Time	Station	Transmission
10:31:28	F	I'm in Division I's area. Do you want me to respond down to the scene, K?
	D	Division 6, that's a 10-4. Standby. Manhattan to Division 6.
10:31:42	F	Division 6 acting Division 1, on the West, we're heading down towards 1 and 2 World Trade Center now, K.
	D	Manhattan to Division 6 acting, K, urgent.
	F	Division 6 acting, go.
10:31:54	D	You are responding down to the World Trade Center, you are to maintain radio communication and advise Manhattan Dispatch what exactly is going on, K. We are unable to make any kind of communication.
	F	Ten-four.
10:32:05	D	10:32.41.6
10:32:15	F	Mobile Command to Manhattan, K.
10:32:20	F	This is ... 4 Alpha. We have dozens and dozens of firemen. We're at the bulkhead on the Hudson River side of the World Trade Center. We have medical emergencies. We have E.M.S. on the scene treating possible heart attacks. We're in the process of getting some kind of a roll call. We're going to try to keep the units together here, K.
	D	Ten-four. Mobile Command Center.
	F	Standby, Manhattan.
10:32:49	D	Ten-four. 10:32.41.6
10:33:05	F	Four Alpha to Manhattan, K
	D	Four Alpha.
10:33:09	F	We have a medical emergency, possible heart attack, firemen, we're on the bulkhead, west, requesting oxygen for the firemen, K. Any unit that can hear me come to the bulkhead on the Hudson River side of the World Trade Center.
	D	Ten-four.
	F	... need the oxygen.
10:33:31	D	That's at the bulkhead on the Hudson side of the World Trade Center, K. Receive?
	F	...
10:33:44	F	Engine 2-2-8 to Manhattan, K.
	D	Engine 2-2-8.
10:33:49	F	Be advised, Manhattan, we're on West Street at the Battery Tunnel ... is starting to clear up, we're starting to see ... Give us time so we can report back to you for further instructions, K.
10:34:03	D	Engine 2-2-8, 10-4.
10:34:08	D	Manhattan to Mobile Command Center, K.
10:34:18	F	Battalion 1-6 to Manhattan.

Time	Station	Transmission
10:34:21	F	Car 5 to Manhattan.
10:34:25	F	Battalion 1-6, we have ... Ladders 5 and 11 manned and ready. Have any instructions for us, K?
	D	Standby.
10:34:29	F	Car 5 to Manhattan.
	D	Car 5, go.
10:34:33	F	Did the command post establish at ... ?
	D	Ten-five, K, you're breaking up.
10:34:40	F	Did command post establish a command [cell?] ... ?
10:34:47	D	At this time we're unable, K. We're going to contact Mobile Command and see what we can do. Manhattan to Mobile Command Center. Manhattan to Mobile Command Center, K. Manhattan to Mobile Command Center.
10:35:05	F	Car 5 to Manhattan. I understand that the command post has been moved north of Vesey Street. I'm going up to Chambers and West and see if I can find out, find ... I'll talk to you when I get on the radio.
	D	Car 5, 10-4.
10:35:22	F	Division 1 acting to Manhattan.
	D	Division 1.
10:35:28	F	Everything south of the Brooklyn Bridge is in a dust cloud. There's no visibility, people all over the streets. Travel is near impossible.
10:35:38	D	Ten-four Division 1.
	F	...
10:35:51	D	Manhattan to Engine 5-1-1, K. Manhattan to Battalion 1-6.
10:36:04	F	One-six ... Manhattan. Battalion 1-6 responding.
	D	Manhattan to Battalion 1-6, Engine 511's going to respond over to Engine [quarters?] ... 6-5's
	F	Battalion 1-6, 10-4.
10:36:19	D	Unit calling Manhattan.
	F	...
	D	Battalion 4-3. Manhattan to Battalion 4-3.
10:36:32	F	Battalion 4-6 to Manhattan.
	D	Four-six, go ahead.
	F	...
10:36:42	D	Manhattan to Battalion 4-6, you're totally unreadable, K.
	F	...
10:36:51	D	Manhattan to Battalion 4-6, you're totally unreadable.
	F	...

Time	Station	Transmission
10:37:02	D	10:37.416.
	F	...4-8 ...
10:37:13	D	Division 6.
	F	Division 6, K.
	D	Disregard this message, K.
10:37:25	D	Ladder 4-6. Manhattan to Ladder 4-6, you message?
10:37:34	F	Ladder 4-8 to Manhattan.
	D	Ladder 4-8.
10:37:39	F	We're stuck in heavy traffic, still in the Bronx, and I'm on your frequency.
	D	Ten-four, Ladder 4-8.
10:37:48	D	Time 10:38.416.
10:37:55	F	Reinforcement bus to Manhattan, we're on ...
	F	Three-five-zero acting Engine 5 to Manhattan.
	D	Standby. Reinforcement unit.
10:38:07	F	Two-five-zero acting Engine 5.
	D	Engine 2-5-0 acting.
10:38:11	F	We're on the Manhattan side on the F.D.R. if you need us.
	D	Ten-four, make yourself available, K.
	F	Ten-four.
10:38:30	D	Manhattan to Engine 2-5-0 acting, K.
	F	Two-five-zero acting.
10:38:35	D	Continue in, relocation to Engine 5's quarters.
	F	Ten-four.
10:38:39	D	10:39.416.
10:39:36	D	Manhattan to Battalion 1. Manhattan to Ladder 8, K. Manhattan to Engine 2-6. Manhattan to Engine 2-6.
10:40:18	D	10:41.416.
	F	Division 1 to Manhattan.
	D	Division 1.
	F	Broadway, Vesey Street, Fulton Street, heavy debris, a huge dust cloud, people all around. We have not gotten to the scene yet, K.
10:40:49	F	Four Alpha to Manhattan.
	D	Ten-four, Division 1. Car 4 Alpha.

Time	Station	Transmission
	F	This is Battalion 4 Alpha to Manhattan. Be advised we have New York waterway boats along the Hudson River bulkhead just north of the World Trade Center, K, for evacuations to hospitals in Jersey City. I have named at least one fireman taken in already. I'm keeping a list, K.
	D	Ten-four, Car 4 Alpha.
10:41:30	F	Division ... to Manhattan.
	D	Division calling Manhattan.
	F	...
	D	Unit calling Manhattan you're totally unreadable, K.
	F	... if you can copy, command post ...
	F	... Engine 5, Park Row.
10:42:04	D	At this time all units standby unless urgent. All units standby unless urgent. The division trying to transmit, be advised you're totally unreadable. You're radio's not coming in, K.
	D	Any unit calling Manhattan.
	F	Division 1 acting to Manhattan. The command post is going to be set up at Park Row, south of City Hall at Vesey Street. It's the only place where we can, the dust cloud have relieved [possibly?].
	D	All right. This is Division 6 acting Division 1?
	F	Ten-four, Division 6 acting Division 1. The command post at this point will be Vesey Street and Park Row, south of City Hall, K. Do you copy?
	D	Division 6, that's a 10-4, K.
10:42:55	F	Have all incoming Fire Department units report to this location and stage on Park Row.
	D	Division 6 acting, that's a 10-4, K.
10:43:08	F	Division 6 acting again, the access down the F.D.R. is clear, P.D. has the F.D.R. lanes open. But have all units approach using extreme caution. Traffic is going the wrong way and numerous civilians, K.
	D	Division 6 acting, 10-4.
	F	Three-two-one acting to Manhattan.
	F	... to Manhattan.
	D	Three-two-one to Manhattan.
	F	We're in Engine 6's ... area.
	D	Engine 3-2-1, what route did you take getting into Manhattan, K?
	F	Car 5 to Manhattan.
	D	Standby. Car 5, message.
10:43:51	F	Car 5, we're trying to establish a command post at Vesey and West. Notify any department officials that's where we're trying to establish a command post.

Time	Station	Transmission
10:44:01	D	Car 5, 10-4. Car 5 be advised, as per Division 6 acting, they have set up a command post Park Row, south of City Hall by Vesey Street, and we're going to be redirecting units into Park Row ... K. Car 5, receive?
10:44:57	D	Attention all units responding in to the World Trade Center, be advised we are now receiving, we are now setting up a new command post, Park Row, south of City Hall by Vesey Street. All units are responding to the new staging area on Park Row. Repeating, all units not presently committed, respond over the staging area, Park Row, south of City Hall on Vesey Street. Be advised the F.D.R. Drive is now clear. You are to use extreme caution proceeding downtown in Manhattan. Time 10:45.416.
10:45:02	F	Squad 6-1 to Manhattan.
	F	Ladder 5-9 to Manhattan.
	F	Do you want us to proceed to 150 Broadway or to the staging area?
	D	Squad 6-1, standby. Ladder 5-9.
	F	We're 10-84 at 17 Battery Park Place.
	D	Ladder 5-9, 10-4.
	F	...
10:45:30	F	We have ... Mobile Command Post unit from Division 6. We're setting up on the corner of Ann Street and Broadway.
	D	Division 6, that was Worth Street and Broadway, Mobile Command Center?
	F	The new command post is set up there. We have a command post set up with a radio and we're going to be monitoring the frequency.
10:45:54	F	Car 5 to Manhattan.
	D	All right, Division 6 acting, 10-4.
	D	Car 5.
	F	Car 5, have we been touch with Car 3 or Car 4?
	D	Negative at this time, K.
10:46:05	F	Did you get my previous message about West Street and Vesey?
	D	Car 5, that's 10-4. Be advised Division 6 reported the new staging area will be Park Row, south of City Hall on Vesey Street. We have notified units coming in that Park Row will be the new staging area. And we also have reports that the F.D.R. is clear at this time, use caution. Also Division 6 reporting ... the command post to monitor all radio frequencies at Worth Street and Broadway. Car 5?
10:46:32	F	Car 5 is on West and Vesey. We trying to establish a command post up here. I've got E.M.S. and everybody at Vesey and West Street ... and we've got plenty of help with the E.M.S. people.
	D	Car 5, that's going to be Vesey Street and West Street, K?
	F	Vesey and West. If you'll get Division 6 up here I'd love you.
	D	Manhattan to Division 6 acting, K.

Time	Station	Transmission
	F	Two-four to Manhattan.
	D	Engine 2-4 go.
10:47:04	F	Two-four ... members out of the building. I've got two members trapped. I can't tell the command post. Two members trapped in the promenade between the two towers.
	D	Ten-four.
	D	Manhattan to Mobile Command Center.
	F	Mobile Command Center, K.
	D	Receive that report Engine 2-4 has firefighters trapped in the promenade?
10:47:21	F	We'll try to relay that message. Right now we're at the intersection of Battery and West.
	F	...
	D	Attention all units, standby. Manhattan to Division 6, K.
	F	Division 6 acting Division 1, go ahead.
	F	...
10:47:45	D	Division 6 acting Division 1, be advised we have a mayday transported by, transmitted by Engine 2- ... All units in the Borough of Manhattan, standby unless urgent. Division 6 acting, Engine 2-4 transmitted a mayday, in the promenade they have firefighters trapped. That's No. 1. No. 2, Car 5 is establishing a command post, West Street and Vesey Street. He would appreciate it if you could respond over to that location and coordinate the efforts with him, K.
	F	Division 6, 10-4. We have a command post set up at Vesey and Park Row on the corner. Vesey Street and Park Row.
	D	Ten-four. We do have units coming into that staging area on Park Row, K. See if you can contact Car 5, K.
	F	Ten-four.
	D	Any other unit calling Manhattan.
	F	Two-zero-nine to Manhattan.
	D	Engine 209.
	F	Yeah, Manhattan. We got over here. Where is our new staging area, K?
10:48:41	D	Engine 209, as per Division 6 – standby Engine 209.
	F	Engine 33 to Manhattan, urgent.
	D	Engine 209, go to Vesey and West Street, K.
	F	Verify that Manhattan.
10:49:02	D	You're going over to Vesey Street and West Street.
	F	Ten-four, Manhattan. Thank you.
	D	Engine 33 urgent, go.

Time	Station	Transmission
10:49:24	F	Engine 33 is being manned by an off-duty member from Rescue 1. Be advised it appears that we have lost water pressure down in lower Manhattan. Can you have Marine 1 or any other available fire boat respond to Vesey Street on the West Side? We're going to need water supply into the area, K.
	D	Manhattan to Car 4-0 Charlie, K.
	F	Marine Company 4, we're responding to Vesey Street.
	D	Marine 4, 10-4.
	F	Did you get that Manhattan?
	D	Marine 4, 10-4. Engine 3-3, 10-4. We have Marine 4 responding over there.
	F	O.K. thanks. I'm going to ...[wait?] for Marine. That's what we got for now.
	D	Manhattan calling Car 5. Manhattan to Car 5. Manhattan to Division 6 acting for Division 1.
10:50:09	F	Division 6, go ahead Manhattan.
	D	Did you copy that message about the water pressure and request for marine units to establish a water supply.
	F	I received that message. Be advised, our command post is set up on Broadway and Park Row where Vesey Street is. You got that?
	D	Ten-four. Are you going to take care of that message regarding the water supply?
	F	We're right on Park Row, we're not down on Vesey Street.
10:50:46	F	Mobile Command to Manhattan.
	D	Mobile Command if you can get in touch with Car 5 or any other staff people at the scene, advise them of the report of poor water pressure in lower Manhattan and the request for units to set up water supply using marine companies and/or satellite. And get back to us forthwith, please.
10:51:03	F	Mobile Command, 10-4, we will attempt to do so.
	D	Ten-four.
	F	Marine 6 Alpha to Manhattan, K.
	D	Marine 6 Alpha, go ahead.
	F	You're requesting water relay, over?
	D	Marine 6 Alpha, are you located down at the Battery?
	F	We're in the Brooklyn Navy Yard, over.
	D	According to units at the scene, Marine 6 Alpha, they want to augment the water supply using marine companies. That's going to have to be coordinated through the staff chief at the scene.
10:51:31	F	Where is he located, over?
	D	The staff chief is located at West at Vesey Street we believe.
	F	... Division, urgent.

Time	Station	Transmission
	D	Unit with an urgent, go ahead.
	F	We've got numerous people trapped here from the previous collapse. We need a hand to get them out, K.
	D	Where are you?
10:51:52	F	We're about four feet under. 1 really don't know.
	D	Where were you operating?
	F	North Tower, K.
	D	Tower No. 1 or Tower 2?
10:52:03	F	No. 1.
	D	Ten-four.
	D	Calling the Mobile Command Vehicle. Calling the Mobile Command Vehicle, K.
	F	Mobile Command, K.
	D	1 have an urgent message from ... we have contact with units that are trapped in the vicinity of the west side of Tower No. 1. They're requesting urgent help.
10:52:26	F	Ten-four, on the west side Tower 1. That's contact Car 5, K?
	D	... Car 5 tell them that we have reported members who are trapped under debris.
	F	Ten-four.
	F	Battalion 1 to Manhattan, K.
	D	Battalion 1, go ahead.
	F	The recalls have just come in. Listen, 1 have about 15 people down in 415 right now. Call them on the voice alarm, send them over to where you want them on that side. Also if you can release 14 Engine, have them take a chauffeur and go up and pick up the spare apparatus. That was in our original plan, K.
	D	We're working on that.
10:52:53	F	We do have about 15 firefighters right now in the quarters of 415, K.
	F	... Battalion.
	D	Manhattan.
10:53:03	F	Marine 6 to Manhattan, K.
	D	Marine 6.
10:53:31	F	Be advised, the – as far as the marine resources go we have the two big fire boats, Marine 1 and Marine 9, on the West Side of Manhattan. Have them rendezvous for the water supply. We have Marine 6 and Marine 6 Alpha on the East Side. We're going to stay on this side of the smoke plume and see what we can handle on this side. If you have any further ... transport or other.
	D	Ten-four.

Time	Station	Transmission
	D	Manhattan to Marine 1, K. Manhattan to Marine 1. Manhattan to Marine 9, K.
	F	Marine Six Alpha to Manhattan, K.
	F	Nine to Manhattan.
10:53:50	D	Marine 9, you go over to Vesey Street on the West Side. Establish a water relay, K.
	F	Ten-four. Do you have a box assignment on this, box number? Because we at some point are directed to the Staten Island side so we're going to be heading over there now. Do we have a box number on this?
10:54:08	D	Marine 9 responding into box 8-0-8-7, fifth alarm.
	F	Marine ... Manhattan, we're on our way.
	D	Marine 9, 10-4.
	D	Manhattan to Marine 1, K.
	F	One, K.
	D	Marine 1, you're to respond over to Vesey Street on the West Side, establish a water relay. Marine 1.
	F	We're 10-4. Be advised we have numerous injured people on board, babies and hundreds of people. So we might have to ... off our boat with another boat or something, K.
	D	All right, Marine 1 that's a 10-4 ... assistance over there.
10:54:45	F?	We're right below the North Cove Marina about 100 yards. I'm not sure what street we're on, K.
	D	All right, standby.
	D	Unit with urgent, go.
	F	Yeah, this is ... 6, I'm on the West Side Highway, I'm pinned. I can't seem to get out, K.
	D	This is a firefighter from Marine 6?
10:55:04	F	An officer from Marine Division, K.
	D	You're on the West Side Highway or the west side of the building?
	F	West Side Highway.
	D	You're on the West Side Highway? Are you pinned in a piece of apparatus?
	F	Ten-four.
	D	All right, we're going to get some members over there to assist you.
	D	Calling the Mobile Command Vehicle.
	F	Marine 6 to Manhattan.
	D	Go ahead.
10:55:33	F	The member you just spoke to is Captain Fuentes [sp?]. He is the Marine Division.

Time	Station	Transmission
	D	I'm trying to get him some help.
	D	Calling the Mobile Command Vehicle.
	F	Engine 2-8 to Central.
	D	Two-eight Engine.
	F	... members trapped.
	D	... 2-8 Engine.
10:55:33	F	We're on the West Side Highway opposite the World Trade Center. We have Captain Fuentes trapped in a vehicle.
	D	Ten-four.
	F	Marine 6 Alpha to Manhattan, K
	D	Six Alpha.
	F	Where do you want us?
	D	Six Alpha, where are you right now?
	F	Brooklyn Navy Yard.
	D	Sign out for lower Manhattan opposite the World Trade Center.
	F	Six Alpha, 10-4, K.
10:56:13	D	Calling Captain Fuentes.
	F	Ladder 1-7 acting 1-5 to Manhattan.
	D	One-seven acting 1-5.
	F	We are ... as a unit in the quarters of Ladder 1-5 ...
	D	Standby, one minute. 1 may have a run for you.
	D	Calling Captain Fuentes.
10:56:33	F	Conway [?] calling Manhattan, K.
	D	... Manhattan.
	F	This is Dennis [?] Conway [?]. At least ... engines down on ... We've got car fires that need ...
	D	Unit transmitting, you're totally unreadable. Everybody standby unless they have an urgent message. If there's an urgent message, go ahead.
	F	...
	D	Unit, you're breaking up and tying up the frequency. Go to another radio.
10:57:08	F	Ladder 101 recall to Manhattan, K.
	D	Standby 101.
	D	Calling Car 4 Charlie, 4 Charlie. Calling the Mobile Command Vehicle.
	F	...

Time	Station	Transmission
10:57:19	D	Standby. Calling the Mobile Command Vehicle. Calling the Mobile Command Vehicle. Calling Division 6 acting 1. Division 1, K, 6 acting 1. Calling the Mobile Command Vehicle.
10:57:57	D	Units, you're cutting each other off. I'm not reading you. Calling the Mobile Command Vehicle. Calling Division 6. Calling Car 5. Calling the Mobile Command Vehicle. Calling the Mobile Command Vehicle. Calling Car 5 or Division 6.
	D	Calling Car 4 Charlie.
10:59:22	D	Unit you're breaking up.
	D	Go ahead.
	F	I'm going to sleep [?].
	D	Mobile Command Center.
10:59:38	F	Yeah listen, we going to need all hands, we've got numerous trapped on the West Side. Rescue 1 Squad.
	D	Hello? Unit you're breaking up. Repeat your message.
	F	People trapped on the West Side, lower Manhattan, K.
	D	What unit is this?
10:59:53	F	Marine Battalion 8.
	D	All right, Marine Battalion, we have help coming in. If you tell me exactly where you are I'll get you some help. Where are you?
11:00:02	F	I can't read it. Building's on top of me.
	D	Calling the Mobile Command Vehicle. Calling any unit at the scene of the World Trade Center.
	F	Mobile Command Center to Manhattan, K.
11:00:32	D	Mobile Command Center, we have firefighters from 4 Engine responding to the location, off-duty members. You have members trapped on the West Side of Tower No. 1. We believe it's Captain Fuentes. He's unable to give us his exact location. Reported to be several members trapped. Do you have that message and copy it?
	F	Ten-four, Manhattan. I got it. I relayed it to Chief Blakees [?]. He was on his way up with several members, K.
	D	Ten-four.
	F	Engine 7 calling from Ladder 1-2-4.
	D	Calling the Mobile Command Vehicle.
	F	Go ahead, Manhattan.
11:00:49	D	Be advised. 1 have a third alarm assignment sitting in Brooklyn waiting to come over. Find out from the staff chief where he wants them.
	F	All right, 10-4.
	D	All right, 10-4. All right, who's acting 112?
	F	Engine 7 to Manhattan, K.

Time	Station	Transmission
	D	Go ahead 7 Engine.
11:01:05	F	Could you give me the location of Chief Blakees please?
	D	We believe they're at the west side of building No. 1, on the west side of building No. 1.
	F	Engine 7, 10-4. Be advised we're several units, we're transmitting out of Ladder 1-2-4. We don't have a rig or anything.
	D	All right, we believe there are numerous members trapped in the vicinity of the west side of that building in the collapse zone.
	F	... side of building one.
	D	That's the best I can do for you. I'm getting that from a member who is trapped and unable to tell me where he is.
11:01:33	F	Ten-four. He's in a vehicle?
	D	I don't know that.
	D	Calling Captain Fuentes.
	F	Command Post to dispatcher.
	D	Go ahead Command Post.
11:01:49	F	... Car 3 and Car 5, let them know that we're setting up a command post at Broadway and Vesey Street, K.
	D	Mobile Command Vehicle. Mobile Command Vehicle.
	F	...
11:02:03	D	Is this the Mobile Command Vehicle? Calling the Mobile Command Vehicle.
	F	Go ahead, Manhattan.
	D	All right, Broadway and Vesey is the new command post, Broadway and Vesey. If you can find Car 3 or Car 5 or any staff chief, let them know that.
	F	Repeat your message. You cut out, Manhattan.
	D	Broadway and Vesey reported to be the new command post, Broadway and Vesey. Give that information to Car 3 or Car 5.
11:02:32	F	Be advised I have Chief Nigro [?] in the vehicle at this time, K.
	D	All right, 10-4. Advise Chief Nigro ...
	F	...
	D	Other unit calling Manhattan.
	F K	
	D	What unit?
	F	Yeah, we need some relief here. We are the collapse unit [?]. This is Captain Fuentes and a couple other members, K.
11:02:51	D	Are you trapped, Captain?
	F	...
	D	Captain Fuentes, are you trapped?

Time	Station	Transmission
	F	Ten-four.
11:03:01	F	Mobile Command to Manhattan, K.
	D	Go ahead Mobile Command.
	F	What units do you have at Broadway and Vesey at this time?
	D	Unknown, K. We're not sure. You're going to have to send somebody over there. Also be advised that we're in radio contact with Captain Fuentes and his people. They are trapped. He's trying to give me a location but he's unable to.
11:03:32	F	All right, 10-4. Like 1 said, Chief Blakees is on his way up with members. He's trying to get in to them now. As soon as Mobile Command Center can we're going to head out to Broadway and Vesey, K.
	D	Ten-four.
	D	Calling Captain Fuentes.
	F	...
	D	All units standby. Calling Captain Fuentes.
	F	... Manhattan.
	D	Is this Captain Fuentes?
	F	Ten-four.
11:03:51	D	All right. We have help on the way to you Cap, we believe that you're in the west side of the No. 1 World Trade Center, out in front in the collapse zone. Is that correct?
	F	In the collapse zone, 10-4.
	D	All right. We're sending you some help.
11:04:03	F	Engine 7 and Ladder 1 members have received that message. Let them know.
	D	All right. Seven Engine and 1 Truck's members are on the way and the staff chief is aware of your location, Cap. Just standby, we'll be there in a little while.
	D	Another unit calling. Any other unit calling Manhattan?
	F	Division 6, we have a command post set up on Broadway and Vesey Street, K.
	D	All right. Division 6, be advised there's a full third alarm assignment sitting in Brooklyn. Do you want them to report to Broadway and Vesey?
	F	...6.
	D	All right. They're actually on the Manhattan side of the Brooklyn Bridge. If you need them let us know.
11:04:42	F	Division 6 to Manhattan, absolutely. Send them to Broadway and Vesey right all Park Row.
	D	All right, 10-4.

Time	Station	Transmission
	D	All units who are responding to the staging area at the Brooklyn Bridge are to report in to Broadway and Vesey Streets, Broadway and Vesey Streets.
	F	Four-two Battalion to Manhattan.
	D	Four-two Battalion.
11:05:06	F	Four-two Battalion has the third alarm assignment right now on Chambers between Church and the bridge. You're redirecting us?
	D	Four-two Battalion, 1 want you to take that whole third alarm to Broadway and Vesey, hook up with Division 6 acting Division 1. He will give you further instructions.
	F	Four-two, 10-4.
	D	All right.
	F	Ladder 4-7 acting Ladder 6 to Manhattan.
	F	This is Command Post.
	F	Four-two Battalion to Manhattan.
11:05:32	D	Go ahead Battalion 4-2.
	F	You want us to walk into that spot or bring rigs?
	D	Get as close to that location as you can without being in the collapse zone and you get the members – they're looking for manpower.
	F	Ten-four.
	D	Four-two, they're looking for manpower and tools. You have members trapped in the street in collapse zones all over the World Trade Center.
	F	Ten-four.
	F	Safety to Command Post.
	D	Safety, go ahead.
	F	... we got about 10 units that reported in from the Brooklyn to the Battery.
	D	What unit is this?
11:06:06	F	This is Safety Command. We're on West and Albany. We've got about 10 units.
	D	Unit, standby. Go ahead 4 Adam.
	F	Safety to Rescue.
	D	Calling Battalion 4-2.
	F	Four-one for the 4-2, go ahead.
	D	Car 4 Adam has redirected you. Go into West and Chambers Street with your assignment, West and Chambers and meet Car 4 Adam.
11:06:38	F	Four-one, 10-4. Can you announce that over the radio please for all these units?

Time	Station	Transmission
	D	All Brooklyn units that were responding in to the fire in Manhattan at the World Trade Center, go to West and – Broadway and Vesey Street, Broadway and Vesey Street for all the first units coming into the scene of the World Trade Center. Four-one and 4-2 Battalions, you got that?
	F	Four-one, 10-4.
11:07:05	D	All right, calling Division 6 acting 1.
	F	Division 6 acting Division 1, have all officers report in when they park on Park Row to Chief Brandies [sp?]. You got that Manhattan, K?
	F	... to Rescue Battalion.
	D	Everybody standby unless urgent.
	F	Urgent.
	D	Go ahead urgent.
11:07:21	F	I'm trapped here from the previous collapse. I need to make it out, K.
		This concludes Tape No. 2, Side A. Turn tape over to Side B for continuation of citywide job No. 1-44.
		END RESPONSE TAPE 2 SIDE A

Appendix K: Additional Resources

This document serves as an index of additional resources for researchers, policymakers, and interested parties studying the September 11, 2001, World Trade Center disaster and its long-term effects on first responders and operational protocols. Organized by category, the table below offers a curated set of resources – ranging from official government inquiry reports and longitudinal health studies to technical engineering analyses and firsthand oral histories – along with specific examples and linked sources to facilitate further investigation.

Resource Category	Description	Key Examples & Sources (with Links)
Official Inquiry Reports	Comprehensive post-incident evaluations and statutory investigations into the collapse and response.	9/11 Commission Report, NIST WTC Investigation Reports, McKinsey FDNY Report (2002)
Health & Medical Longitudinal Studies	Scientific research and clinical data tracking the long-term physical and mental health of responders.	WTC Health Program Data, Peer-reviewed studies on "WTC Cough" and cancer via *The Lancet*
Command & Operational Manuals	Updated tactical protocols and Incident Command System (ICS) frameworks developed post-2001.	FDNY Strategic Plans, NIMS Integration Guides (FEMA), High-rise communication protocols
Oral Histories & Firsthand Accounts	Recorded testimonies and interview transcripts from firefighters, EMS personnel, and dispatchers.	Library of Congress 9/11 Oral Histories, 9/11 Memorial & Museum Oral Histories
Legislative & Policy Documents	Records of funding, advocacy, and legal changes affecting first responder benefits.	James Zadroga 9/11 Health Act (Full Text), Congressional legislation to provide and fund medical treatment for responders and survivors.
Technical & Engineering Analyses	Detailed studies on structural failure, fire behavior in high-rises, and equipment performance.	NIST NCSTAR 1: Federal Investigation of WTC Disaster, National Institutes of Standards and Technology reports
Multimedia & Documentary Films	Significant visual documentation, including the "accidental" recording of the first strike and the harbor evacuation.	*9/11* (2002) by Jules & Gédéon Naudet, *BOATLIFT: An Untold Tale of 9/11 Resilience* (Narrated by Tom Hanks)

Resource Category	Description	Key Examples & Sources (with Links)
Non-Fiction Books & Monographs	Narrative and investigative literature documenting the department's history and internal culture.	*WTC In Their Own Words* (Harvey Eisner), *Report from Ground Zero* (Dennis Smith), *So Others Might Live* (Terry Golway) *Fire Department City of New York, The Bravest* (Hashagen, Kimmerly)
Dramatic Plays & Performance	Theatrical works based on verbatim testimonies or fictionalized accounts of FDNY responders.	*The Guys* (Anne Nelson), *110 Stories* (Sarah Tuft)
Music	An emotional, album-length reflection on the 9/11 attacks and their aftermath. The title track and songs like "Into the Fire" specifically honor the courage of firefighters ascending the towers and the spiritual weight of their sacrifice.	*The Rising* (Bruce Springsteen)

Endnotes

1 For additional information on the interview protocol, recording procedures, and participant rights, see Appendix B: Interview Protocol - Subsection 4: The Interview Protocol, page 379.

2 For additional information on how the project developed and the selection of participants, see Appendix B: Interview Protocol - Subsection 1: Project Overview and Evolution, page 377.

3 For additional information on the authors, see About the Authors, page 479.

4 *New York Times,* February 16, 1910. Public rebuttal.

5 FDNY Press Office Video, September 10, 2001.

6 For additional information on the individuals quoted throughout this book, see Appendix A: Interviewee Biographies, page 371.

7 FDNY Press Office Video, September 10, 2001.

8 CNN Network broadcast "*Parts Unknown,*" Season 2 Episode 1.

9 Opinion, *New York Post,* 24 January 2005, Col Allan Editor-in-Chief; Bob McManus Editorial Page Editor.

10 For additional information on the full command hierarchy as it stood on September 11, 2001, see Appendix D: FDNY Command Structure, September 11, 2001, page 388.

11 For additional information on the layout and geography of the World Trade Center complex, see Appendix F: World Trade Center Map, page 390.

12 The Order of Friars Minor, to which Judge belongs, is defined by the vow of poverty. Poverty that is not merely economic; it is the state of living without anything of one's own. St. Francis of Assisi commanded his brothers to be "pilgrims and strangers" in this world, possessing no fixed abode and claiming no rights over their time or their ministry.

13 FDNY Press Office Video, September 10, 2001.

14 For additional information on FDNY-specific terminology, equipment designations, and radio codes used throughout this book, see Appendix C: The Responders Lexicon, page 382.

15 For additional information on the geographic positioning of command posts, staging areas, and unit assignments across the WTC complex, see Appendix F: World Trade Center Map, page 390.

16 For additional information on FDNY radio codes, signal designations, and operational terminology, see Appendix C: The Responders Lexicon, page 382.

17 James, Erica H. and Lynn Perry Wooten. *The Prepared Leader: Emerge from Any Crisis More Resilient Than Before*. Philadelphia: Wharton School Press, 2022.

18 Murphy, Emmett C. and Mark A Murphy. *Leading on the Edge of Chaos: The 10 Critical Elements for Success in Volatile Times*. Paramus, NJ: Prentice Hall Press, 2002.

19 Snowden, David J. and Mary E. Boone. "A Leader's Framework for Decision Making." *Harvard Business Review* 85, no. 11 (November 2007): 68–76.

20 Kahneman, Daniel, *Thinking, Fast and Slow*. New York: Farrar, Straus and Giroux, 2011.

21 James, Erica H. and Lynn Perry Wooten. *The Prepared Leader: Emerge from Any Crisis More Resilient Than Before*. Philadelphia: Wharton School Press, 2022.

22 Snowden, David J. and Mary E. Boone. "A Leader's Framework for Decision Making." *Harvard Business Review* 85, no. 11 (November 2007): 68–76.

23 For additional information on the FDNY command structure and rank designations referenced throughout this chapter, see Appendix D: FDNY Command Structure, September 11, 2001, page 388.

24 "New York City Fire Department Dispatches for September 11." *New York Times* online release. August 12, 2005.

25 "New York City Fire Department Dispatches for September 11." *New York Times* online release. August 12, 2005.

26 Trist, Eric. "The Environment and System-Response Capability." *Futures*, April, 1980, pp. 113–127.

27 Ibid.

28 Snowden, David J. and Mary E. Boone. "A Leader's Framework for Decision Making." *Harvard Business Review* 85, no. 11 (November 2007): 68–76.

29 Trist, Eric. "The Environment and System-Response Capability." *Futures*, April, 1980, pp. 113–127.

30 Ibid.

31 Ibid.

32 Ibid.

33 Ibid.

34 Response mode entails all-out effort in the initial stages to save lives during a fire or emergency. More and greater risks are taken; risk much to save much [life].

35 Snowden, David J. and Mary E. Boone. "A Leader's Framework for Decision Making." *Harvard Business Review* 85, no. 11 (November 2007): 68–76.

36 Ibid.

37 Ibid.

38 Ibid.

39 Heifetz, Ronald and Laurie, Donald, "The Work of Leadership." *Harvard Business Review*, 1997, 75, no. 1 (January/February 1997): 124–134.

40 USAR; Urban Search and Rescue, are teams of specialized, technical rescue experts. Their primary mission is locating and extricating victims trapped in collapsed structures or confined spaces due to disasters like earthquakes or explosions. Staffed by multiple agencies, they are deployed as a federal resource.

41 For additional information on the structure, personnel, and sector assignments of the FDNY WTC Task Force as constituted on September 15, 2001, see Appendix E: FDNY WTC Task Force 0700 September 15, 2001, page 389.

42 Fleishman, E. A. (1953). "The Description of Supervisory Behavior." *Journal of Applied Psychology*, 37(1), 1–6.

43 For additional information on the content and format of the Incident Action Plans used at the World Trade Center site, see Appendix G: WTC IAP September 27–28, page 391.

44 Schein, Edgar H., *Helping: How to Offer, Give, and Receive Help*. Berrett-Koehler Publishers, Inc., 2009.

45 Shea, G., Brown, P., and Kotzé, A. (2022). "FDNY, Twin Towers and Organizational Change," *Firehouse*, https://www.firehouse.com/leadership/article/21264922/fdny-twin-towers-and-organizational-change, April 21.

46 Tedeschi, R. G., & Calhoun, L. G. (1996). The Posttraumatic Growth Inventory: Measuring the Positive Legacy of Trauma. *Journal of Traumatic Stress*, 9, 455–471.

47 Van der Kolk, Bessel A. *The Body Keeps the Score: Brain, Mind and Body in the Healing of Trauma*. Viking, 2014.

48 For additional information on resources related to FDNY mental health support, responder wellness, and 9/11 legacy organizations, see Appendix J: Additional Resources, page 419.

49 For additional information on the FDNY's subsequent activations of its Incident Management Team and the expansion of its national role, see Appendix I: FDNY IMT Activation Log, page 414.

50 Irvine, William B. *The Stoic Challenge: A Philosopher's Guide to Becoming Tough, Calmer, and More Resilient*. New York: W. W. Norton & Company, 2021.

51 Shea, Gregory P., and Robert Gunther. *Your Job Survival Guide: A Manual for Thriving in Change*. Upper Saddle River, NJ: Pearson Education, 2009.

52 Frankl, Viktor E. *Man's Search for Meaning*. Boston: Beacon Press, 2006.

53 Ibid.

About the Authors

Gregory P. Shea, Ph.D., is Senior Fellow at the Wharton Center for Leadership and Change Management, Senior Fellow at the University of Pennsylvania's Institute for Implementation Science (PISCE), and Adjunct Senior Fellow of the Leonard Davis Institute of Health Economics at the Wharton School of the University of Pennsylvania. He is lead author of *Leading Successful Change: 8 Keys to Making Change Work* (Wharton School Press, 2020), and *Your Job Survival Guide: A Manual for Thriving in Change* (FT Press, 2008). His writing has appeared in the *Harvard Business Review, Sloan Management Review, California Management Review, World Economic Review, Directors & Boards,* and many other publications.

As an educator, Greg currently teaches Wharton Executive Education classes and programs to more than 200 leaders a year, including in *Becoming a Leader of Leaders and Leading Organizational Change*. His teaching of executives includes sessions based on the research and insights from *Rising from Ground Zero*. His work in the classroom has been recognized with honors including Wharton's Excellence in Teaching Award. Greg also consults with nearly a dozen organizations annually and coaches numerous senior executives. He also serves on several advisory boards.

He holds an A.B. from Harvard (magna cum laude and Phi Beta Kappa), an M.Sc. in Management Studies from the London School of Economics, and a Ph.D. in Administrative Science from Yale.

Paul Brown is a retired New York City Fire Captain and educator. A third-generation firefighter, Paul spent over 30 years as a first responder. While a member of the FDNY Incident Management Team, he deployed numerous times to natural disasters and wildfires throughout the nation. He speaks regularly on managing crises, high stakes decision making and organizational change. Outside his role with the FDNY, Paul has been involved in experiential and executive leadership education for over 20 years, sharing his experiences involving high-stakes decision-making, resilience, and change leadership.

Rising from Ground Zero began with Paul's desire to memorialize the experience of 9/11 first responders, including his own experience on that day and the days that followed. Following the 10th anniversary of the September 11 attacks on the World Trade Center, Paul realized that there was "no learning being derived from the experiences of those in the FDNY. The McKinsey & Company Report (2002) was the only feedback that most firefighters had seen. This report was particularly critical of some of the principles which firefighters feel make the FDNY great, including the involvement of off-duty firefighters to ease the burden of their on-duty brothers and sisters and the fact that senior leaders 'lead from the front.'"

Noting that little had been written about the recovery and transformation of the FDNY, particularly regarding training, incident management, and mental health, Paul sought to bring to light the "real triumph of the FDNY. It is not that it recovered and rebuilt. The triumph is the monumental change within the department and its culture – how the department learned to look outward and to partner with others. The lessons lie in how the FDNY matured from an effective-yet-dated firefighting force into a modern emergency management agency."

André Kotzé is the CEO of AirtimeBA and an executive at Teamworks Training and Development. An organizational development specialist and executive coach with over three decades of experience, André works globally with institutions ranging from the World Economic Forum to the Wharton School of Business. He is a pioneer in the digitization of Behavior Analysis, having founded AirtimeBA to transform human interaction into visible, data-driven insights that help teams improve decision-making and collaboration.

André's expertise in crisis leadership and the "ethical use of power" is grounded in his formative years in South Africa during the volatile transition from Apartheid. A veteran of the South African Defence Force, he managed logistics in refugee camps during the Mozambican Civil War, served for 15 years on a mountain rescue team and is a responder to the 1993 St. James Church massacre. These experiences in conflict zones and emergency work shaped his conviction that leadership, relationship, and a strong sense of purpose are a necessity for resilience rather than a theoretical luxury.

For *Rising from Ground Zero,* André applies his experience to the team's longitudinal research and writing. He views the FDNY's evolution not merely as a recovery, but as a timeless example of "re-creation" – using the energy of a crisis to metabolize trauma and build a fundamentally new, more adaptive organization.

• • • • • • •

Lauren Starkey is a writer and editor of more than 25 books, specializing in business and higher education. She collaborates with academics, executives, and founders to develop research- and experience-based ideas for a range of publications including *Forbes, Harvard Business Review, Knowledge@Wharton,* and *TheStreet.com.*

Lauren has been a contributor to the *Wharton@Work* newsletter since 2007, writing regularly on leadership, finance, and strategy. Her work for Wharton Executive Education also includes the development of Wharton Nano Tools, which translate faculty research and practitioner insight into practical resources for leaders.

In addition to her bylined work, Lauren serves as a collaborative writer and ghostwriter on books and long-form projects focused on leadership, entrepreneurship, and institutional transformation, including serving as an editor on *Rising from Ground Zero* and contributing to the project's development.

www.ingramcontent.com/pod-product-compliance
Lightning Source LLC
LaVergne TN
LVHW020052110826
845155LV00022B/73

* 9 7 8 3 1 1 2 2 4 7 2 0 4 *